Zealous Reformers, Deadly Laws

Dear Debbie,
I hope this will mark the beginning of an enduring friendship with Manushi.
Madhu Kishwar
19 Nov 2009.

Zealous Reformers, Deadly Laws

Battling Stereotypes

Madhu Purnima Kishwar

SAGE Los Angeles • London • New Delhi • Singapore
www.sagepublications.com

First published in 2008 by

SAGE Publications India Pvt Ltd
B1/I-1 Mohan Cooperative Industrial Area
Mathura Road, New Delhi 110 044, India
www.sagepub.in

SAGE Publications Inc
2455 Teller Road
Thousand Oaks, California 91320, USA

SAGE Publications Ltd
1 Oliver's Yard
55 City Road
London EC1Y 1SP, United Kingdom

SAGE Publications Asia-Pacific Pte Ltd
33 Pekin Street
#02-01 Far East Square
Singapore 048763

Published by Vivek Mehra for SAGE Publications India Pvt Ltd, typeset in 10/12 pt Goudy Oldstyle BT by Star Compugraphics Private Limited, Delhi and printed at Chaman Enterprises, New Delhi.

Library of Congress Cataloging-in-Publication Data

Kishwar, Madhu Purnima.

Zealous reformers, deadly laws: battling stereotypes/Madhu Purnima Kishwar.

p. cm.

1. Women's rights–India. 2. Sex role–India. 3. Women–India–Law and legislation. I. Title.

HQ1236.5.I4K57 305.420954–dc22 2008 2008009154

ISBN: 978-0-7619-3637-4 (PB) 978-81-7829-802-3 (India-PB)

The SAGE Team: Rekha Natarajan, Samprati Pani, Amrita Saha and Trinankur Banerjee

Cover illustration by Rustam Vania, courtesy *Manushi.*
All chapter illustrations (except chapters 2, 3 and 4) by Rustam Vania, courtesy *Manushi.*

Dedicated to the memory of my mother
who I miss every moment of my life,
whose nurturing and unconditional love,
like that of Mother Earth,
has been the most precious gift of my life,
and to Mohini *masi*, my first love in life.

Contents

Part III. Inheritance Rights

Part IV. Challenges of Politics and Organization

Acknowledgements

None of this writing would have been possible without the enduring and loving support of *Manushi* readers who have played a vital part in keeping the journal alive as a platform for out-of-the-box thinking on various issues which have a vital bearing on the well-being of women in India.

I am also thankful to members of *Manushi*'s Editorial Board, many of whom play an active role in shaping *Manushi* and hone my own thinking on various issues.

I also wish to express my sincere thanks to my colleagues at CSDS—Ashis Nandy, Dhirubhai Sheth, the late Giri Deshingkar and founder Director Rajni Kothari—for creating an institution which provides a rare kind of freedom and space for intellectual quests. I deeply appreciate the support they have provided me so that I have been able to make my work at CSDS and *Manushi* complement and enhance each other.

Last but not least, I acknowledge my deep gratitude to my numerous women friends, associates, neighbours, relatives—especially the many women I came in contact with during my travels, research and other work, who have time and again forced me to rethink my own ideas by showing me through their own lived example which measures of legal reform actually work and which do not work to empower women.

Introduction

Right from its inception in 1978, *Manushi* was conceived as a platform that would provide a space for investigations on important issues, informed intellectual debates on vital matters of national importance, as well as activist interventions. One of our consistent endeavours has been to bridge the divide between research and activism. Much of my own writing is a product of that fusion.

Research on social issues becomes sterile if it does not have a vibrant connection with people's lives and concerns. Likewise, informed activism is possible only when one is constantly learning from one's own mistakes and experiences, as well as keeping oneself open to new ideas and approaches based on the experiences of others, staying abreast of their new research and writings; there are obvious limits to what one can learn firsthand.

The articles selected for this book were written at different points of time in the last 25 years. They continue to be in demand. That SAGE considers them worth publishing is an indication that the issues they deal with are as alive today as they were when these articles were initially written in response to earlier debates and challenges. The continuing relevance of these articles also indicates, unfortunately, that as a society we have failed to solve the problems addressed through these articles, even though since then several new and far-reaching legal enactments have been introduced, which have created a new wave of problems. I have refrained the great temptation to revise and rewrite these to provide readers a glimpse of how my own thinking has changed and evolved over time, even while in some ways my basic approach to social reform issues remains consistent insofar as it draws sustenance from Gandhi's worldview, which mistrusts statist and authoritarian means as the primary instruments of social reform.

Several of these articles offer critiques of various laws proposed or enacted with much fanfare in the last two and a half decades, ostensibly for the purpose of strengthening women's rights. Another set of articles deal with common stereotypes regarding women's role and status in Indian society, as well as the social and cultural norms that many believe are responsible for the supposedly uniformly low and vulnerable position of women in our country. These over-simplistic conclusions have come to acquire so much salience that the complex reality of women's lives, as well as those aspects of our culture that serve as a source of strength to women, are undermined. One of the main purposes of several of these articles is to try and demonstrate the harmful outcomes that inevitably flow from political interventions based on such simplistic stereotypes.

Most of these articles deal with the position of women in the family, with a section on women in politics. Thus, several important aspects of women's lives are not included here, such as their roles as workers and professionals. This is not because I consider these aspects of women's lives less important but simply because, for this book, I have chosen mainly my articles on those issues, which have provoked a great deal of public debate and discussions among women's organizations in the last two and a half decades. Moreover, there is a limit to the number of articles that could be fit into a book of this size.

My critique of various laws enacted in recent years at the behest of some women's organizations has by and large been vindicated. Each one of them has either proved a dismal failure or produced results contrary to those intended. At the time, when the laws were under consideration, my warnings were received with either puzzlement or hostility. Many feminists found it hard to understand why I was opposing laws that claimed to be 'pro-women'. However, after witnessing the actual operation of those laws, many feminists have revised their positions and are more open to dialogue.

A recurring theme in most of these articles, as well as in a good deal of my other writing, is that we must 'learn to listen to people carefully', view their problems through their eyes rather than assume we know what is good for them. This restraint needs to be observed even more vigorously when we are dealing with communities, groups and individuals who are poor and vulnerable. Those attempting to impose social reform measures through coercive means, such as police action, arrest, imprisonment and lengthy legal proceedings, can even with the best intentions end up causing a great deal of harm. Attempts to change social practices by imposing new laws without the active involvement of the people concerned can often backfire—pitting reformers against the very society they wish to reform.

The following pages provide a few glimpses of how I learnt this the hard way—by making and correcting mistakes in the course of our own interventions, by recognizing errors of strategy through constant review of our own campaigns, by showing a willingness to change our methods and approach to suit the requirements of those on whose behalf we claimed to wage those battles.

The Dangerous Gap between Laws and Social Practice

One of the great challenges faced by social reform movements in India is the big and growing gap between legislation on various issues and the actual practices prevalent in our society. Many people interpret this discrepancy as a sign of the 'continuing hold of traditional values and customs' and expect that as people get 'modern education', and as women become aware of their rights, they will inevitably move towards following 'modern laws' enacted for their benefit. However, there is overwhelming evidence that even among the avant-garde elite groups in India, social legislation does not determine social behaviour.

What is even more ironic is that the biggest violators of these laws are those in high positions in the government. For example, ever since dowry was made illegal in 1961 through the Dowry Prohibition Act of 1961, the practice has flourished in an unprecedented manner among all strata of people. It has spread to regions, castes and communities that did not have any such tradition. Wedding expenditures and dowry demands have become more and more elaborate. Reformers, assuming that this was because the law was not strict enough, got several new amendments added to the Dowry Prohibition Act and the Indian Penal Code during the 1980s, making dowry giving and taking a cognizable offence, inviting prison terms and fines (see Chapter 12). And yet, the practice continues to spread, and the amount demanded continues to escalate. The biggest dowry transactions take place among the families of educated elites, especially those in high positions in the government, with the elite administrative services like the IAS, IPS and IRS topping the list. Sons of ministers and judges are offered exorbitant dowries. Likewise, no family of any status and social standing would marry off its daughters without a hefty dowry.

Similarly, despite the Child Marriage Restraint Act, passed way back in 1929, a large proportion of the population has continued to marry off their daughters before the permissible age. It is the same story with the law banning the use of sex determination tests (SDTs). It is a fairly draconian piece of legislation—both for those who request SDTs, as well as for the doctors who provide this service. In Delhi, performing an SDT for the purpose of determining a child's gender pre-natally invites jail terms up to five years and a fine of up to Rs 1,00,000. And yet, the use of sex selective abortions has grown even as the law has been made increasingly stringent over the years. This is obvious from the continuing sharp decline in the sex ratio and the drop in the birth rate of female babies, especially among the well-off sections of the population. It is noteworthy that the imperial enclaves of New Delhi, which house senior bureaucrats and ministers, as well as the elite areas of south Delhi have recorded among the lowest sex ratios in the country at 791 and 797, respectively. Doctors in the know tell you that the most persistent and desperate demand for these tests comes from senior government officers, including those in the police. Several nursing homes in posh localities have bizarrely skewed sex ratios among their deliveries. For example, seven girls were born in one such nursing home as compared to 67 boys.

Defiant doctors carry out SDTs brazenly; some even conduct the test from their automobiles, carrying ultrasound equipment with them to provide service at the family's doorstep. Law-abiding doctors who decline to perform SDT tests even though they use ultrasound for other diagnoses are up in arms against the Act, complaining that the inspectors use the law to harass and fleece them under bogus pretexts. Some have even gone to court challenging its legality.

Given such a state of affairs, it is legitimate to ask the question: What is the purpose of passing laws, which are routinely violated? Why have laws that are not even followed by the parliamentarians who make them, let alone by the police officers and judges who are supposed to implement them? These laws are not implemented even among the family members of those who campaign to get these laws enacted. I am certain that no more than a handful of the militant anti-dowry campaigners can claim with honesty that in their own family circles they have successfully 'abolished' the practice of dowry. Likewise, I doubt that any among those who worked hard to get stringent provisions added to the law banning SDTs can say with confidence that, in their own community, families are not taking recourse to sex selective abortions.

A common reaction in India is to attribute this gap between the law and actual behaviour either to hypocrisy or to the absence of effective enforcement and punishment for non-compliance. This bolsters the position of those who argue that the problem lies with the implementation machinery—a corrupt and inefficient police, and a cumbersome and dysfunctional legal system. These criticisms are undoubtedly true. But they are only partly responsible for the widening rift between what different groups and communities consider acceptable norms and what governmental laws define as 'legal' or 'illegal' behaviour.

Even the best policing and the most efficient law courts can only succeed in their mandate to uphold the laws if their violations are exceptions rather than the norm. If 99 per cent of the people in a region consider dowry giving and receiving the right thing to do, how can any law enforcement agency arrest the bulk of that region's population? Likewise, if an overwhelming majority among certain communities, numbering several million people, consider teenage marriages a desirable norm, how can any state machinery make space for so many millions to be locked up in jails, even if it manages to conduct their requisite court trials? Who will even come to give evidence in such cases?

This is not to say that I support the present system of dowry, sex selective abortions or child marriages but simply to underscore the need for a more self-critical and socially sensitive approach to legal reform. There are two ways of responding to social practices running contrary to government-enacted laws:

1. Assume that people are either too foolish and backward or too set in their own ways to heed to laws that are ostensibly meant for their benefit

and welfare. Therefore, act under the belief that such people need to be forced out of their 'backwardness':

(*a*) through police action, threat of imprisonment and other punitive measures, or

(*b*) by subjecting them to moral and political sermons and legal literacy campaigns.

2. Those interested in changing social practices in more effective ways and making community and family norms more democratic ask of themselves: 'What is lacking in our measures for social reform, in the laws we enact, that people for whose benefit they are meant are unwilling to adopt them?' They are likely to get one or both of the following answers:

   (*a*) There is something wrong in the way we are delivering our message. Therefore, we have failed to convince people of the worth of the legal reform. This would lead us to recognize the need to fine-tune our communication strategies.

   (*b*) There is something lacking in our understanding of the problem and its possible solutions. That is why no one is willing to heed our prescriptions for cure. Therefore, we need to make a more serious effort to view the issue through the eyes of those supposedly afflicted by it.

This latter approach would lead to a thorough review of the basic features of the social legislation as well as the hurdles to be overcome in implementing it. There should also be an attempt to create appropriate instruments within the state machinery that have the capacity and the will power to implement social legislation with dignity and honesty. If the implementation of certain laws causes more problems than it solves, then we should be open to undertaking an honest review of its value, necessity and strategy.

Just as a doctor is expected to review her/his diagnosis rather than blame or terrorize the patient if s/he gets sicker upon being administered medical treatment, so also those involved in the work of healing social wounds or righting the wrongs of vulnerable groups and individuals ought to be constantly reviewing and questioning their own strategies when they fail in their campaigns, rather than merely blame society for rejecting their social prescriptions. However, what we witness in India is usually the very opposite. When a law fails, instead of undertaking a cool-headed, honest review, the tendency is to blame its failure on the laxity of the implementation machinery and on the lack of stringent provisions for punishment. That is why all the failed laws are bolstered with more and more draconian provisions, usually leading to many new messy consequences while the original problem remains unsolved. Let me illustrate this by the example of what has happened to the attempt to enforce laws to curb child marriages.

Sometime back, a new Bill was introduced in Parliament titled 'Prevention of Child Marriages Bill, 2004' to replace the Child Marriage Restraint Act of 1929. As per the Census of 2001, 6.4 million Indians under the age of 18 are already married, although the legal marriageable age is 18 for females and 21 for males. Counting those already widowed or divorced, the total number of underage men and women who have been married at least once before reaching the legal age for marriage, is about 12.1 million. The 1901 Census indicated that underage marriages were more or less confined to a few upper castes in some regions of India. Now it is more prevalent among groups lower down in the social hierarchy.

Instead of trying to understand what compels certain communities to arrange early marriages of their children, activists have tended to adopt the following strategies:

1. Encourage police action and litigation against offending families, thereby unleashing a virulent backlash from communities who feel outsiders have no right to interfere in their internal affairs.
2. Demand that the child marriage law be made more and more stringent, to frighten people into obedience.

It is noteworthy that, in recent decades, despite such early marriages being illegal, communities in different parts of rural India have taken to organizing mass marriage ceremonies that openly defy the legal ban on child marriages. Powerful politicians and Members of Parliament (MPs) come to bless the couples and lend legitimacy to the occasion. For instance, on 22 March 2005, responding to a Public Interest Litigation (PIL) by a social organization seeking stringent action against officials who failed to prevent child marriages, the Supreme Court directed district collectors and superintendents of police across the country to take steps to prevent child marriages, especially mass marriages organized on special auspicious days such as the Teej festival.

The non-governmental organization (NGO) that filed the PIL demanded stronger punitive provisions against offenders and the plugging of loopholes inherent in Section 3 of the new Bill. This Section provides that a child marriage would be rendered void only if the affected children file legal proceedings requesting its annulment. This provision was obviously inserted to avoid upsetting the legitimacy of the marriages where both parties have accepted the arrangement, while allowing an exit route mainly for those persons who are unhappy enough to want to walk out of a bond imposed by their families.

The 1929 Child Marriage Restraint Act had provided for a minimal interventionist role. It rendered all child marriages 'illegal' but not 'void'. In a country where less than a miniscule percentage seek legal recognition for a marriage by registering their nuptials in a court of law, where almost all marriages draw their legitimacy from the social sanction provided by their *jati biradari*, it would be foolish and often harmful to the women and children of such marriages to enact a law that declares all these marriages 'void' after they have received community sanction. That power would make sense only when people require or demand such a legal sanction. However, the NGO which filed the PIL reflects the opinion of many zealous reformers in India who would like the state to play an aggressive role in tearing asunder by force millions of well-established marriages where the groom and bride are below the permissible age. Attempts at stopping such marriages in which whole villages were involved have led to terrible backlashes. The famous Bhanwari Devi case is a good example.

Even the best of laws will have only limited use without a sound prescription for dealing with the social compulsions underlying the illegal choice. Merely attacking a social problem without understanding the reasons for the problem can never eradicate social ills. To attribute the phenomenon of child marriage merely to the hold of 'patriarchal norms' is to have a very limited and short-sighted view of the situation.

Let me illustrate this by the dramatic changes I witnessed in the lives of a community of 'low caste' Tamil migrants in Delhi, among whom there was no tradition of child marriage till a generation ago. My friend Jaya began working as a part-time domestic help in half a dozen middle class houses in south Delhi when her impoverished landless poor family migrated from a village in Tamil Nadu to Delhi in the early 1980s. As is commonly the case, her family set up a small 'illegal' *jhuggi* on railway land along with nearly 300 other families of the region from which Jaya hailed. While the women all took to working as domestic help and got regular work, most of the men got only intermittent daily wage labour or menial jobs such as rickshaw pulling. Since the entire *basti* was illegal, a section of the men had to learn to cultivate the police and other government agencies whose officials made them conduits for collecting monthly bribes on their behalf. With enforced idleness for many young men, along with contacts with criminal elements in the police came many anti-social activities such as peddling drugs, manufacturing illicit liquor, prostitution and petty crime.

The increasing hold of anti-social elements in the *basti* meant greater insecurity for women and girls. Consequently, while many of the little boys were sent to school, almost all the girls were kept at home. Their mothers felt they were safer under their vigilant eye all day. The only way domestic workers could watch over their daughters was to take them along from house to house. Therefore, these little girls then began helping their mothers with cleaning utensils and mopping floors in the houses of their employers—not primarily because their labour was needed but just because, unlike boys, girls could not be left alone in *jhuggis*.

The anxiety about female safety is so high that, even in the boiling hot summer months, women and girls sleep inside ill ventilated *jhuggis* with the doors firmly shut while men sleep out in the open—all because there had been cases of some young girls and women being abducted or attacked at night when they slept out. The police did not even register a proper case when the bodies of two such females were found in a badly mutilated condition. The popular perception is that the local police was behind the crime. As a consequence of living under conditions of such insecurity, one witnessed a dramatic fall in the age of marriage within this community. For example, Jaya herself was married when she was past 18 in her village and her mother at about the same age. However, her daughter Laxmi was married off between 15 to 16 years of age, not long after she reached puberty, which was celebrated through a beautiful public ritual characteristic of many south Indian communities.

When I protested with Jaya that she was being unfair to her daughter, this is how she explained her decision.

> In our *basti,* infested as it is with criminals and touts who carry influence with the local police, my daughter is not safe and can't be left alone for a minute. What if she is seduced by someone and ends up pregnant? Where will I go then? Or what if she is raped at night? How will I get her married off then?

'But can't these mishaps happen even after marriage?' I asked. 'Sure they can,' she replied, 'but then the responsibility for protecting her falls on her husband. Moreover, a mishap of that kind leading to pregnancy can be easily covered up if the girl is married. But for an unmarried girl even a small slip will ruin her forever.'

Therefore, when Lakshmi got married, I undoubtedly felt sorry for her but I had no urge to report the marriage to the police and get it stopped by getting Jaya and her husband arrested for the crime of child marriage, given their experience of the police who in their eyes are more dangerous than ordinary criminals. In all likelihood, the police would have locked them up for a few days, then released them on bail after taking a hefty bribe. Jaya's family would have then spent years and all their savings on bribes and lawyer's fees, fighting the slow moving legal case against them.

These are telling examples of how increasing violence and insecurity are making the lives of women more vulnerable and, therefore, making families feel that bringing up daughters is a high-risk job. This is in large part due to the increasing lawlessness of the police and other arms of the government, as well as the large-scale criminalization of politics.

Remote villages where the police rarely, if ever, makes its presence felt have much lower crime rates. But the closer a village is to a police station and other institutions of government as, for example, a zilla parishad office or a district court, the higher the level of insecurity and crime. Just as it is often difficult for Jaya's family and community to exercise restraint over anti-social elements because of the criminals' frequent connections with and patronage of the police, so also in villages, families with one or more sons in politics or government jobs, especially in the police, come to acquire tyrannical hold over the lives of others. This power is often reflected in increased sexual assaults against women.

What are the other factors rural communities cite for marrying their children young?

1. Since the village economy does not provide year-round subsistence for those working in the farm sector, a good proportion of young men have to leave the village to find work outside at a very early age. If they are sent out without marriage, there is no saying who they will end up living with and marrying within the city. If such a marriage is not within *jati* and *biradari*, there is far less chance of sons taking care of their parents in old age.
2. As boys get more educated, their chances of getting better paying jobs increases. Such grooms command heavy dowries because they are scarce. Therefore, it is better to catch them young with smaller dowries.
3. In most villages, educational opportunities for girls are far more limited beyond primary classes while more boys continue with education even if the school is far away. Sending girls to distant schools is risky. Employment opportunities for girls are even more limited. Therefore, there is very little for them to do except wait for marriage. The sooner she reaches her ultimate destination in her husband's family the better.
4. It is almost impossible to enforce youth's abstinence from sexual encounters once they attain puberty. Sexual activity before marriage is even more risky for women as it may result in pregnancy. If the man who got her pregnant disowns responsibility, she will it find much harder to gain acceptance in another family.

5. There is a difference between a betrothal ceremony and a consummated marriage. In what are called child marriages whereby small children are married off, all that takes place is an engagement type ceremony. The girl child thereafter usually returns to her parental home. She is sent to her husband's house in most communities only when she is around 15 in a ceremony called *gauna*.

   Thus, the strategy for putting an end to child marriage has to be different from that dealing with marriages of girls between 14 to 18 years. Unfortunately, campaigners against child marriage seldom distinguish between the two age groups, or between betrothal and marriage.

In India, marriage age has risen dramatically in communities that have easy access to educational opportunities, and in those who can provide secure homes, a relatively safe social and educational environment, and have access to skills that lead to well paying jobs for their daughters. People in such communities choose to have their children marry late, without the imposition of punitive laws. Moreover, today, mainly those vulnerable rural communities who live in poverty, practise child marriages. The moment a section of this *jati* rises in terms of income earned and educational level, and acquires a middle class status and the social security that goes with it, the anxiety level about the safety of girls is not so acute. That is when child marriages cease to take place without sermonizing and without recourse to coercive measures.

The speed with which the marriage age rose among families in my own community indicates how greater security is the primary instrument for achieving this end. Before the Partition, my mother's family lived in Peshawar, which is a frontier zone in the turbulent North Western Provinces of what is now Pakistan. So unsafe was the atmosphere at that time that city gates used to be shut in the evening and even men rarely ventured out at night. The *tonga* in which my mother went to school used to be covered with a thick sheet so that no one could see the girls inside. This despite the fact that my grandparents were very liberal and believed in women's freedom. Had they stayed in Peshawar, my mother and aunts would have lived very restricted lives and married relatively early. The Partition undoubtedly brought about great dangers, economic hardship and the trauma associated with violent uprootment. After reaching Delhi as refugees, they were at first allotted a refugee accommodation in a conservative Muslim dominated area of old Delhi. Despite this, the lives of all the women changed within months. My aunts began going to school and college on bicycles. They would go for shopping sprees and evening film shows without any male escort. The thick *chador* like *dupatta* gave way to fashionable and lacy *chunris*. All of them got an education and married in their mid or late 20s and one of them in her 30s. All this because the Delhi of those days was a much safer city.

We would also do well to realize that the notion of a marriage below the age of 18 being wrong and illegal is a fairly new one in the history of humanity. The world over, young people being married off in their teens was fairly common. While we do not hesitate to let the police crack its whip on families that marry off their teenage daughters, we would be amazed at any aggressive intervention by the police to control pre-marital teenage sex in America or Europe where early marriages may not be common but pre-marital, teenage sex is. From the point of view of many in India, if teenage sex is okay, why not teenage marriage?

For many Indians, marriage at 16 is far more preferable to pre-marital sex at 16, just as for most Americans or Europeans, pre-marital teenage sex has today become a normal expectation but marriage at 16 is seen as a sign of 'cultural backwardness', especially if it happens in a Third World country. We think nothing of passing a law giving the police the right to arrest those who marry their daughter off at 16 but would never dare suggest that police lock up all those parents whose teenage daughters indulge in sex.

Personally, I am strongly opposed to child or early marriages even if it could be shown that a large number of them result in happy conjugality. The reason is simple. Such arrangements rob all agencies from the persons concerned and foreclose all options for the future. We would also do well to remember that child and early marriages do not just go against the interests of females. They also affect the lives of men adversely because by getting chained to domestic burdens and responsibilities at such an early age, they too lose out on many opportunities and freedoms. No doubt the impact on women's lives is far more severe. But if we do not also take account of their negative impact on men's lives we turn it into a simple case of gender conflict. More is actually at stake. Healthy societies are those that provide ever-expanding horizons of freedom to both men and women. The point of viewing child marriage through the eyes of the community that practises it is not to offer a justification for early marriages but to underscore the need to view with empathy the problems and dilemmas of those whose social mores and customs we wish to 'reform', so that we can make them partners in finding effective solutions and viable alternatives.

Authoritarian measures and draconian laws produce results far more different from those intended and create new and bizarre problems if people are not convinced of their intrinsic worth. China's one-child policy is a good example of that. Unlike the Indian state, the Chinese state means business when it enacts laws. Therefore, it enforces them with an iron hand. The strict and brutal enforcement of the one-child norm in a culture where son-preference is deep-rooted led to large-scale female infanticide and consequently an even more skewed sex ratio.

Our Own Learning Graph

As mentioned at the outset, this book is not merely about critiquing failed laws and the misconceived interventions of others. It is as much about describing the process by which we at *Manushi* learnt through our own interventions, our failures and successes, about how we began to avoid being cast in the role of hostile and unwanted outsiders and instead tried to work in a spirit of partnership with communities and families that seemed to us to be following self-harming practices. Our experience has taught us that one gets much better results when social, economic and political reform measures aim at creating positive incentives rather than rely solely on punitive measures for reworking power relations in favour of disadvantaged groups. This is not to undermine the importance of using state laws to bring about desired social changes but to point to the necessity of a prudent and imaginative use of law to create a new social consensus and popular resolve in favour of desired changes.

Manushi's founding in 1978 coincided with an unprecedented rise in press reports about young married women dying due to burn injuries. It was very common in those days for newspapers to routinely publish terse eight to ten line news items on the city news page describing the burning to death of women as kitchen accidents or suicides based on police reports. Investigations by *Manushi* as well as two older Delhi organizations, Mahila Dakshata and Nari Raksha Samiti, demonstrated that many were actually cases of murder but were passed off as suicides or accidents with the active collaboration of the police, provided the police were suitably bribed. Even when they actually were suicides, they pointed to a history of violence and abuse in the marital home. Burning oneself to death is one of the most painful ways of ending one's life. By choosing such an agonizing form of death, these women seemed to be making a statement that death by burning themselves alive seemed preferable to daily torments and torture inflicted on them in their husbands' homes. When our investigations indicated clear evidence of foul play and we saw that aggrieved families were not getting justice, we felt we could not just stop at reporting such cases of marital abuse, but also needed to help the victimized women and their families get redress.

However, with a criminalized police establishment often refusing to even register an honest First Information Report (FIR), while actively destroying evidence of crime for a bribe, getting justice through the slow, inefficient and often corrupt judicial institutions seemed a remote prospect. Therefore, our engagement spontaneously took the form of holding protest demonstrations outside the house of the deceased woman, calling for a social boycott of the family, which had tortured the woman to death or driven her to suicide. Each such demonstration would then move on to the local police station, either protesting against their complicity or demanding that they take appropriate and swift action in booking the culprits. The first such demonstration in Delhi come to be organized on 1 June 1979 outside the marital home of 24-year-old Tarvinder Kaur at F 3/7, Model Town. She had died of burns on 17 May. In her dying statement, Tarvinder had stated that while she was watching TV on the evening of 17 May, her mother-in-law poured kerosene on her clothes and her sister-in-law set her afire. A dying declaration is treated as a strong piece of evidence in our law. Yet, the Model Town police registered a case of suicide, rather than murder.

Manushi, along with a small group of concerned women and some civil liberties activists, created a broad platform called Stree Sangharsh to protest not just against the murder of Tarvinder Kaur, but also to oppose the role of the corrupt police.[1] Being close to Delhi University, Model Town has a large number of college and university teachers living in that colony. We went from house to house talking personally to hundreds of families in the days preceding the planned demonstration. Consequently, over a thousand people joined the protest demonstration on 1 June, endorsing our call for the social boycott of Tarvinder Kaur's marital family. Thereafter, the protestors walked down to protest against the *malafide* action of the police in converting what was a *prima facie* case of murder into one of suicide. As news of this demonstration was widely publicized in the media, it came to be adopted as a prototype for demonstrations in cases of bride burning across the country, especially if the violence had resulted in the gruesome death of the women. It is significant that this protest demonstration was not just a women's affair. A large proportion of men of the neighbourhood as well as from the university community made common cause with us.

Many of our demonstrations could be well considered subversion of due process of law as well as disturbing the peace of a neighbourhood with noisy protests, if one went by the criteria set by 'modern laws'. However, women, in particular, and society, in general, respond with great passion to such modes of protest on behalf of victims of domestic violence. Our demonstrations rarely faced hostility, even when we invaded neighbourhoods without prior notice

---

[1] Even though Stree Sangharsh was envisaged as a broad-based joint platform of women's activists and organizations, due to internal conflicts it soon transformed itself into a separate organization, with many of the original participants forming their own independent organizations.

or warning. In most cases, men and women of the neighbourhood joined us spontaneously to endorse our call for social boycott. Even the police watched quietly, instead of trying to prevent us from holding demonstrations outside homes that had witnessed murders or even outside police stations. I personally remember only one case in Patel Nagar where we faced aggressive and hostile neighbours who threatened to beat up *Manushi* volunteers who had gone to merely investigate the suspected murder of a young wife, not even to hold a demonstration. In all other cases, a good number of neighbours cooperated in giving us information. Some even expressed open support by joining the protestors, while others remained quiet in an effort to maintain amicable relations with their neighbours.

During these years, most of us were led to believe that the murders or suicides of young wives were primarily due to dowry demands. Therefore, our campaign was mainly directed against the giving and taking of dowry. Since then, the issue of dowry has become the defining symbol of the vulnerable plight of Indian women, both within India and internationally.

Most women's organizations interpreted these murders as a sign of the anti-dowry law being 'weak'. Therefore, they pushed for further amendments to the anti-dowry law and demanded that it be made stringent and draconian. This marked a parting of ways between *Manushi* and all those organizations that demanded more and more stringent laws without ensuring that the existing laws were adhered to—at least by those who claimed to be anti-dowry. This difference in approach came to be the hallmark of many subsequent conflicts over strategy and goals.

For example, the anti-dowry campaigners overlooked the fact that even feminist activists were guilty of the flagrant violation of the law. Many of those who vociferously shouted slogans outside other people's homes and in public fora calling for a social boycott of all those who gave or accepted dowry, did nothing whatsoever to ensure that dowry is not given or taken in their own families. We felt that if we did not lead by example, we had no moral right to condemn others. That let to our issuing a call through *Manushi*, appealing to women activists and organizations to boycott all marriages in which dowries were either given or taken to build up pressure among our own families for dowryless weddings. This resolve to try and practise what we preach became one of the most useful self-correcting mechanisms in *Manushi's* approach and interventions.

The first humbling jolt came when I found that, except for my own immediate family and half a dozen *Manushi* volunteers, hardly anyone else heeded our boycott call (See 'Beginning with Our Own Lives', *Manushi*, No. 7, 1979). The marriages of my brothers in 1990 and 1991 were strictly dowryless out of love and respect for me. But other than that, the boycott call did not evoke much of a response, even among women's organizations and activists.

I was then too young to understand the reasons for our campaign failing and attributed it merely to double-speak and hypocrisy. As a result, I became even more zealous in observing the boycott in my own life. In the process, I ended up causing needless estrangement and hurt to some of my dear friends and relatives.

A dowryless wedding, in my view, meant the bride going to her marital home with only her existing clothes and items of daily use. There was no place even for new clothes and jewellery for the bride. This rigid definition was in response to what I saw as the convenient escape route adopted by all those who claimed to be anti-dowry but routinely provided or accepted the customary gifts for marriages in their own families. I then believed that if we applied a very rigorous definition, we could then not only uphold our conviction but also make the law more effective, considering most parents justify lavish expenditure on the wedding trousseaus and expensive household goods, saying these are 'voluntary gifts' for their daughter rather than call it dowry. The net result of my stringent definition was that for 13 long years no weddings qualified for my presence. Several women argued with me vehemently saying that my stand was absurd. Their logic was as follows:

- Since in most cases only sons inherit parental property and family businesses, it was only in the form of *dahej* that daughters got a share—albeit an unequal one—in parental property. After marriage, even the parental home comes to be their brothers' and *bhabhis*' home. A dowryless wedding would not work in their interest because that did not bring any benefit to the daughters. It only meant their brothers would end up with an even bigger share of family resources.[2]
- When a young woman enters a new family, she feels diffident to ask for basic things she needs for her daily use. If she goes to her marital home without anything to call her own, her dependence on her in-laws and husband increases, unless she has a reasonable income of her own—which most women cannot bring because the proportion of women in paid jobs is very low in India. Therefore, all the household requirements and clothes parents provide their daughters help them feel they have something to call their own in their new home.

[2] For a detailed analysis, see 'Dowry Calculations', *Manushi*, No. 78, 1993. This theme is also dealt with in my documentary film, *Dahej: Zaroorat ya Majboori?*, available on www.manushi-india.org.

- Since daughters in most cases are disinherited by their parents after marriage, their main security lies in strengthening their economic rights in their husband's family. However, if they go 'empty-handed' to their husband's home, how can they expect to be treated as equal partners? The dowry is, therefore, in part an 'investment' made by parents to secure a share for their daughter in their husband's family property.
- When women go as new brides, their in-laws are also expected to provide them with expensive new clothes and jewellery. How can gift giving be one-way? Why should women's parents not give gifts to their husband's relatives as a goodwill gesture when the bride is going to become claimant in the husband's income and property?

When I raised the issue of marital violence and abuse due to dowry demands they responded with this question: Are you suggesting that women get beaten and abused only in India, and that too only among communities that give dowry? Don't women in America, Europe, Australia, the Philippines and Africa also get beaten and killed, even though in these countries dowry giving is not an issue?

That forced me to think: Who am I helping by my stand? If women themselves do not perceive their interest in dowryless weddings, who am I to decide what is good for them? In fact, seen from this viewpoint, one could even say Indian men who beat up their wives demanding higher dowries and larger offerings from in-laws are at least rational—they beat up their wives for economic gain. But perhaps all those men the world over who beat up their spouses and even girl friends without any hope of gain ought to be treated as the truly deranged—they gain nothing tangible by their brutality. The article 'Rethinking Dowry Boycott' was an attempt to share with our readers why our anti-dowry campaign was destined to be a failure if we did not work hard to ensure inheritance rights for women in parental property (see *Manushi,* No. 7, 1980).

This also explained why the anti-dowry campaign seldom went beyond protesting outside the homes of those families who were alleged to have either murdered or driven their daughters-in-law to suicide. As long as its ire was confined to 'dowry murders' or 'dowry suicides', it could draw upon a large sympathetic response. However, as soon as anyone crossed that line to protest against dowry per se, most people, including anti-dowry campaigners, felt upset or threatened, as I discovered at great personal cost.

However, it is noteworthy that, even among those who practise the giving and taking of dowry, almost all are strongly in favour of deterrent action against those families where women are tortured for bringing inadequate dowry, or those who blackmailed the bride's parents after marriage into giving more and more gifts and cash by using the threat of violence or divorce. The social consensus on the issue is clear: voluntary giving is fine, but extortion through subtle or blatant coercive means is wrong and ought to be severely punished. In such a situation, it makes far more sense to de-emphasize the anti-dowry laws and have those sections of the Indian Penal Code that deal with extortion and blackmail enforced with vigour in cases where a woman is being tortured with a view to blackmailing her parents to 'gift' more money or goods to the groom's family. A law against giving dowry, which no one obeys, would be completely redundant.

The article 'Dowry: To Ensure Her Happiness or to Disinherit Her' was written during a period when my boycott was still intact but I was beginning to see the weaknesses of our anti-dowry campaign, which attributed the prevalence of this practice to people's greed. By 1984, I was convinced that the entire thrust of the anti-dowry campaign was misplaced and we needed to rework our strategy.

People's Protests and Vigilante Justice

However, apart from the need to correct our understanding of the basic issues, time and again we have also had to rethink and reconstruct our strategies for combating violence against women. For example, in most cases of unnatural deaths of young brides, the pattern was pretty much the same—even when there was clear evidence that the concerned woman had been murdered, the police would invariably register a case of suicide or accident. Women's organizations had to fight long drawn out battles to simply get a proper FIR lodged. And yet, at the end of it all, the man was often let free for 'want of evidence'. In cases of wife murder, the legal outcome is very uncertain and the judicial processes are so lengthy, cumbersome and soul destroying that even if, after 10 to15 years of effort, you managed to get half a dozen men convicted for murder or abetment to suicide—a very unlikely outcome—it will not help all those still trapped in brutal marriages. Seeing how frustrating this whole exercise was turning out to be, we decided to focus mainly on cases where the woman, though caught in a violent marriage, was still alive. If we could save such women from being further brutalized, help them rebuild their lives afresh, they might inspire by personal example hundreds of other similarly placed women to recognize that they have workable alternatives to submitting to domestic violence. They might also see by example that even without continuing a marriage, women can live dignified lives.

The article '*Ab Main Jalkar Nahin Maroongi*' in *Manushi*, No. 13, 1992, describes the conscious shift in focus. By holding a surprise protest demonstration outside the house of a man who was refusing to give divorce to his wife and was hell bent on destroying her life and harassing her family, we were able to bring adequate pressure on him to agree to divorce by mutual consent. However, such demonstrations also created many unexpected problems. For example, during the course of that demonstration, the man came out of the house with his grown-up sons from his first wife and they showered filthy abuses on us. Some of our demonstrators got so agitated that they went and blackened his face with the paint meant for writing slogans calling for social boycott of the family. This so enraged the family that they started throwing stones at us. Some of the men present in our demonstration retaliated by throwing stones back at their house, leading to an ugly fracas. Luckily, no one was seriously hurt and I was able to bring the situation under control fast.

However, even though we got very positive press coverage for this demonstration, some of us were very upset and ashamed at the ugly turn it had taken and vowed never to undertake any public protests without taking sufficient precautions that they do not degenerate into crowd violence and undignified scenes. We had investigated the case thoroughly. I had checked the facts through reliable sources and personally met the concerned man prior to the demonstration to persuade him to agree to a dignified divorce by mutual consent or at least stop stalking and attacking her, and stop creating violent scenes in the house of her sister where she had taken shelter to escape his violence and abuse. It is only after he reacted abusively to my intervention that we decided to put social pressure on him through a demonstration. However, some other organizations, notably those with a political axe to grind, did not take even such basic precautions.

When I look back on those days, I marvel at how we could get away with taking endless liberties with laws and law enforcers without facing any negative consequences because we were seen as sincere defenders of the women who were being abused. For example, apart from demonstrations outside police stations, we also took our protests right inside the court compound to protest against judgements we perceived unjust without taking prior permission from the police, which is a mandatory requirement even for ordinary demonstrations (see 'Is It Normal For Women To Commit Suicide?—A Manushi Protest Demonstration', *Manushi*, No. 27, for a report of one such action). On one occasion, when a busload of us with banners and loudspeakers landed at Tees Hazari Courts, the policemen on duty did try to stop us from entering the court compound in a procession, shouting slogans on a loudspeaker and with banners denouncing two judgements of the court. But we brushed aside their objections and they meekly let us proceed. We held an hour-long protest with numerous lawyers joining us in support. A few lawyers did try to argue that our action was improper but the police stood and watched the whole drama spellbound rather than drive us out, while we amplified our speeches with a loudspeaker.

Other examples of legal and political indiscretions included publishing in *Manushi* first person accounts of victims of domestic violence verbatim without crosschecking facts or allowing the accused persons to give their versions. A couple of such families sued us for defamation but nothing really came out of those lawsuits since both the petitioners died of a heart attack soon thereafter. However, I soon realized the irresponsibility inherent in this approach when we published verbatim the account of a woman from Bombay levelling serious charges against her husband, who is among the more respected film directors of Bollywood, a creator of serious cinema. We did not take the trouble to get the husband's version, assuming everything she told us was 100 per cent correct. In later years, when she began running a similar campaign against her own mother, we realized that the story was more complex than what we had presented. And yet this story proved such a hit that several papers and magazines reprinted it in full. A woman's glossy magazine named *Savvy* carried it as a cover story and thereafter started a regular feature titled 'I Believe' that published similar accounts by women of high society. We were told the film director was planning to sue *Manushi* for defamation. For reasons unknown to us, he decided against it. Therefore, it was not the fear of legal suits that stopped us, but rather an inner realization that in my role as an editor I was duty-bound to verify such allegations. Even if they were found to be true, I owed it to *Manushi's* credibility as a journal to give the accused a fair chance of rebuttal. We also wanted to shift the focus away from personalities to issues.[3]

The positive press coverage given to investigative reports and protest actions by women's organizations created many unanticipated problems. The articles 'Women's Organizations I: Vengeance Squads, Firefighters or Counsellors?' and 'Women's Organizations II: The Pressure of Unrealistic Expectations' describe the kind of unreasonable pressures people had come to impose on women's organizations due to their frustration with the legal machinery. Many parents of a married daughter would seek our help in 'fixing' the husband by getting him and his family arrested and punished through the law courts for the harassment and violence they had inflicted on their daughter. Demonstrations and *dharnas* outside the house of the husband and in-laws who had allegedly

[3] However, the failure of the law courts in dealing fairly with such situations is evident in the way we were prevented from publishing anything at all on many notorious legal cases. For example, when a 45-year-old woman came to seek our help in suing a leading gynaecologist of south Delhi who she reported had removed her ovaries and uterus without her permission and under the pretence of carrying out a routine test which she botched up, the court gave a patently illegal stay order in favour of the doctor, forbidding *Manushi* from publishing anything whatsoever on the subject. All this because when we sent an account of the charges to the concerned doctor asking her to clarify her position, she instead went to court to get an injunction against *Manushi* publishing anything about the case whatsoever. Thus courts do not always help you when you follow rules and laws with sincerity.

tortured or thrown out a young bride, for example, mistakenly came to be seen as a means of swift and sure redressal. It took some work to convince all those who expected us to be forever ready for street action that no matter how hard social organizations like ours worked to get them redressal by creating social embarrassment for the groom's family, that alone would not help rebuild their daughter's shattered life.

Moreover, it quickly became evident that this kind of 'instant justice' was a double-edged sword and could easily lead to miscarriage of justice and lawless elements using it to settle personal scores. The turning point came when, in our own neighbourhood, hoodlums associated with a political party not only stoned the house of a family where a young bride was allegedly burnt to death but also burnt their car and tried to set fire to the house. From then on we decided that we would use this method of redressal far more judiciously than we had done thus far. Also, we decided not to help families that were merely interested in seeking revenge and did not want to take responsibility for providing the required protection and support to the battered woman (see article Women's Organizations I: Vengeance Squads, Firefighters or Counsellors?).

The idea of protesting outside the residence of the accused family was borne out of the realization that getting justice through the police and law courts was a remote possibility, given the high level of corruption and inefficiency endemic in these institutions. In India, the verdict of one's neighbours, relatives and other close associates continue to matter much more for most people than the verdict of government appointed law courts. The notion of *izzat* or honour is a powerful determinant of social behaviour, often more so than the laws enacted by the Parliament, because the colonial structure of our government machinery and the tyrannical behaviour of its functionaries do not enable state agencies to command respect from citizens. Government laws often run contrary to popular opinion and social consensus on various issues. Therefore, in India, people's protests in both rural and urban areas often take the form of protests outside the house of the family accused of wrongdoing. There are any number of instances of village drunkards and wife-beaters being paraded round the village lanes after their faces have been blackened by the women of the area to bring shame on them.

Positive Potential of Family's Role

If some parents wanted help in taking 'revenge', at the other end of the spectrum were parents who came with the expectation that we would help their daughter by pressurizing their abusive husbands and in-laws into a compromise and take the woman back. Often parents narrated bizarre stories of how they went on suggesting 'adjustment' formulas to their daughters in the face of untold humiliations and brutal torture, how time and again daughters were sent back to their marital home even while they were being subjected to sadistic tortures. This was said not with regret or shame but with pious self-righteousness at having done their social duty. Even at the cost of their daughter's life they did not want to 'break up her marriage'—as if they would be committing a sin by bringing the abused woman back from her marital home.

In many cases, the husband's legal defence rests on justifying his actions or claiming innocence by accusing his parents-in-law of destabilizing the marriage by 'unnecessary interference', by giving shelter and support to their daughter every time she fled from her husband's home. We often heard lawyers advise the woman's parents never to admit in court that they supported their daughter's decision to live away from her husband, no matter how cruelly he had been treating her. There is a genuine fear among those with legal experience that many judges tend to be prejudiced against the wife's case if they suspect that she left her marital home of her own volition. She is treated sympathetically only if she can prove that she was literally thrown out by her husband and her parents offered her shelter only because they had no other choice.

In the early years, we used to respond with impatience at the number of relatives—parents, brothers, sisters in-law, uncles, aunts—who came and spoke on behalf of the woman. We assumed that these relatives would dominate her thinking and not let her make up her mind as to what she wanted to make of her life. Therefore, we would encourage victims of domestic violence to come by themselves. We soon realized that this made most women very uneasy and suspicious. They wondered why we were driving a wedge between them and their family, whose care and concern is vital for their survival. It took a while for us to understand that the presence of so many concerned relatives was, more often than not, a definite asset for the affected woman, rather than a liability.

In societies that believe that the individual is responsible for and accountable to only himself or herself, apart from having to obey state rules and regulations, a victim of marital violence or child abuse does not feel she has the right to call upon her neighbours or kin for protection. Even if she did so, she would most likely be advised to call the police and lodge a case against her husband, or go to a state welfare agency. Even while there is increasing pressure in social democratic societies to make laws more egalitarian and state enforcement agencies more efficient, relatives, neighbours and other community members have pretty much shed their responsibility for protecting vulnerable individuals in the community and sharing each other's joys and sorrows. That is why even with an efficient police and relatively efficient courts in such societies, women continue to be victims of violence and often have to fight lonely battles to get redress because most of them lack supportive neighbours and relatives who consider it their prime responsibility to assist them in times of crisis. By contrast, most women in India are able to count on their relatives to come to their aid. This often works better than the help of police or distantly placed women's organizations.

Therefore, we began to pay far greater attention to making these relatives understand that their love and concern should not be confined to putting all their efforts into saving her marriage, if it meant jeopardizing her life and well-being. In the few cases when a woman came alone, it was no indication that she was more independent minded. Most women who lack parental support tend to be emotionally fragile and less able to take bold decisions because they feel they have no safety net. If we fill them with strong notions of their own rights, and they find no supportive echoes in their own environment, they feel doubly demoralized. Often they come back and tell us our ideas are too 'airy-fairy' and go back to their own coping mechanisms. Instead of putting the entire burden of struggle on their already tired shoulders, we began to put more effort into and convincing their parents, siblings and other relatives that they owe it to their daughters, sisters, etc., to take them back without making them feel like a burden. The simplest way of saving a battered woman from abuse and violence is to remove her from the scene of abuse and reassure her that she has a right to her parental home and support, just like her brothers. Police help and legal battles cannot by themselves help a woman live a life of dignity. Far more important is unconditional love, support and a sense of rightful due, which she should receive in her parental home, rather than being viewed as an object of charity.

Our message to her family is simple: 'You have to give priority to saving the life of your daughter and helping her rebuild a new life. Getting the offending husband and in-laws humiliated through demonstrations or punished through the courts ought not to be the main focus of your efforts.' I still remember how jolted some parents felt at our approach when we refused to yield to their pressure that we help them in getting the police and courts to 'teach the man a lesson', while they let the daughter stay in the marital home where she was being tortured, by their own account. I would tell them bluntly:

> Was your daughter born in a police station that you want to put the entire burden on that agency to solve her problems? Would you let a son continue living under such dangerous circumstances? If you are not willing to bring her back and make her feel welcome in your home, make her feel that she has a right to be there, you will be as guilty of her murder as her in-laws.

My impression is that in 90 per cent of the cases, the message went home. In all those cases where a woman received whole-hearted parental support, she recovered quickly from the trauma and was helped in rebuilding her life. However, in all cases where the family concentrated on legal action, they got relatively little gain from it. Hence, *Manushi*'s pragmatic emphasis is on the need to work towards a new social, family consensus on women's rights rather than focus obsessively on legal rights with nothing but an inefficient, corrupt and venal state machinery as their ally.

For example, in a typical case, a young woman named Sithalakshmi came in a rather distraught condition because her abusive and violent husband had thrown her and her 5-year-old son out of the house without allowing her to take even her clothes or the child's books. She had a modest job but years of brutal treatment had shattered her self-confidence. When we found that her parents were ready to give her a respectful place in their home, we went with her one afternoon and helped her bring back all the household belongings in a truck, while the husband was away at work. This gave a major boost to her morale while her husband was left shell-shocked at this commando type operation. He tried filing a case against his wife for theft but under the law a wife cannot be accused of theft from her marital home. Thereafter, it was his turn to beg and plead to get a portion of the household goods back from her. An interview with Seethalakshmi published in *Manushi*, No. 18, Oct–Nov 1983, shows how quickly she regained her confidence and built a new life for herself.

Thus, we found, our counselling and moral support worked well when we worked in collaboration with a woman's own family. But in cases where a woman was also battling with her own natal family, our help and support could only play a relatively limited role. A woman who can count on her own family support, especially that of her father and brothers, can easily battle forces of discrimination in the outside world and deal with marital problems from a position of strength. She needs only marginal support from the legal system. Working with men of the family and mobilizing them to take an active role in strengthening women's rights is no less important than encouraging women to take charge of their lives rather than live a life of hapless dependence. Fortunately, in India, one does not have to work too hard or make any demeaning compromises in order to get many men to play an active role in championing a woman's cause and sensitizing other men to act responsibly towards women. Indian men's involvement with women's issues runs very deep because family and kinship ties are held very sacred. Irresponsibility towards family is looked down upon and those men who stay emotionally rooted in these bonds and put them above their own self-interest are held up as worthy role models. Most of them respond to emotional appeals. They are also relatively easy to guilt-trip into action. Unconditional obedience towards mothers is considered a desirable norm. Even grown men who reverentially accept their mother's commands are seen as praiseworthy role models rather than held up for ridicule, as they would be in western societies that believe in the absolute supremacy of the individual and would consider such deference by a grown man to his mother as a sign of infantilism or personality disorder. Men are expected to treat aunts, grandmothers and other senior female relatives with deference. In addition, the brother–sister bond is extremely strong. Elder sisters have the right to demand deference and young sisters expect to be pampered. Special festivals and rituals such as *raksha bandhan* and *bhaiyya dooj* reinforce the notion of brothers' lifelong responsibility towards sisters. Indian family life is replete with stories of brothers making big sacrifices for the well-being of their sisters, spending a good part of their hard-earned income or savings on providing dowries for their sisters or helping them tide over a crisis. Therefore, when a woman is being maltreated in her marital home, it is not uncommon for of the family's men—brothers, uncles, cousins and sons—to get deeply involved in solving her problem.

Men are present in large numbers in virtually all demonstrations organized by women's organizations, whether they are against wife beaters, drunkards or rapists. Women's organizations all over India continue to get all manner of support from men in India. There have been hardly any instances of open attack on women's organizations by men, including those women's groups that define themselves as radical.

Viewing family as a source of support is anathema to many feminists. Many of them view the Indian family as a particular site of oppression, tyranny and subjugation of women. It is seen as an instrument of patriarchal control over women's lives, bodies, sexuality and social relationships. While there is no denying that in most parts of the world, family is the primary instrument for socializing women into accepting a subordinate role in society, it is also the most important source of support, protection and fulfilment for most women. Many of those who rant and rave against it in their treatises and campaign literature, themselves try to stay firmly rooted in their own respective families. The best government laws cannot do for women what a supportive family can. Emotional sustenance, a sense of belonging and being cared for is as vital to a person's well-being as a secure livelihood and a safe and comfortable shelter. Especially for those women who wish to have children, a stable family life is crucial.

The structure of the Indian family makes it possible for a woman to draw support from a very large and diverse range of people. This is particularly helpful in raising children because those who are able to get emotional nurturing from diverse sources grow up to be far more healthy and resilient than kids whose emotional nurturing comes from a small nuclear family and not a very stable one at that.

Conversely, if one's family and kinship group, or the dominant males within it, turn against a woman, her life becomes truly endangered.

Rights become meaningful only when they are respected, honoured, even celebrated, when they are considered your due. However, they become a painful cross to carry, if every time you assert them you get a slap on your face or a kick in your belly or people simply jeer at you for claiming them. If rights are continually asserted and rejected in a hostile environment it seriously damages a woman's sense of selfhood. If she is encouraged by outsiders to assert her rights aggressively in a family or village where no one else understands or empathizes with her ideas she is likely to end up a nervous wreck or have it lead to a breakdown of her family life, thereby ending up worse off than before. We learnt this the hard way when we challenged the denial of land rights to women among certain peasant communities of India without preparing adequate ground for it among men.

Wealth of Aliens, Herself Poor

The major source of vulnerability for women in most parts of India arises not so much because their natal families do not care for them but because, in most communities, they are viewed as *paraya dhan* (the wealth of aliens), as temporary members of their parental families whose real place lies in their marital home. The main reason why so many women feel compelled to put up with violence and humiliation is that they feel they have nowhere else to go, since after marriage they are not expected to treat their parental home as their own. Most women describe their parental home as *bhabhion ka ghar* (the home of their sisters-in-law) where they would be treated as unwelcome, unwanted burdens after marriage rather than an integral and welcome part of the family. It is as if after marriage they sign away all their rights to their parental home. Even when a woman's parents are supportive, they hesitate to ask her to walk out of a bad marriage, fearing that her brothers and sisters-in-law would treat her and her children very shabbily, especially after the parents' death.

Therefore, from very early on *Manushi* shifted the main focus of our campaign from dowry to inheritance rights in parental property, especially the right to shelter in her natal home, in the belief that if daughters got equal share in the property of their parents, that would signify that they are not *paraya dhan*, and that the culture of dowry giving would automatically get eroded. The various articles I wrote on the subject, both in *Manushi* as well as in newspapers, magazines and journals, essentially argued that giving of wealth per se is not in itself evil; it is the form of giving which often makes it a liability for a daughter. The message was also carried through a street play, *Roshni*, that was written and enacted by *Manushi* volunteers in the streets of Delhi. It tells the story of a young girl who battles against parental discrimination and wants to become self-reliant. Since most parents consider it inauspicious to send their daughters 'empty handed' and feel strongly that they want to give a portion of their wealth to their daughters in their own lifetime to avoid the possibility of their brothers short-changing them, we tried to get the message across that 'giving' would have more meaning for their daughters if it takes the form of income-generating forms of property rather than spending vast amounts of money on consumer goods, most of which depreciate in value, leaving nothing substantial in the hands of the daughter in case her marriage fails or turns abusive.[4]

How did the culture of disinheriting women come to acquire such power despite the claims made by Jawaharlal Nehru's government that a revolutionary new law for giving equal inheritance rights to daughters was passed in the form of the Hindu Succession Act (HSA) in 1956? My archival research clearly showed that a big hoax had been played on women. In the guise of providing equal rights to wives, a totally alien concept to traditional Hindu law, 'the right to make a will', was introduced in order to facilitate the growing concentration of property in male hands (see 'The Hindu Code Bill: Myth vs Reality', *Economic and Political Weekly*, 13 August 1994). A more deadly blow was inflicted on women's rights during the course of land reform legislation in various states that placed a ceiling on the amount of land a family could own. This was ostensibly for the purpose of abolishing absentee landlordism and attacking the concentration of land in a few hands. However, while fixing the ceiling on the amount of land a family could legally own, the government provided only for sons to be included as claimants of shares. Daughters were left off the list of legitimate claimants to land titles. Consequently, even among those communities that had a tradition of giving land to daughters, government laws forced families to eliminate the practice of women's ownership rights in land.

Therefore, the focus of *Manushi*'s campaign came to centre on the demand that any testament or will which disinherits daughters should be treated as an illegal document. It has been found that, after the enactment of the HSA in 1956, most fathers make wills with the sole purpose of disinheriting daughters. Many responded to our demand by saying that forbidding wills militates against

[4] This is also the theme of two of my documentary films in Hindi: *Dahej: Zaroorat ya Majboori* and *Aurat: Na Ghar ki Na Ghaat ki*, available at www.manushi-india.org.

the idea of individual freedom, thereby conveniently forgetting that under the current Hindu law, sons cannot be disinherited by fathers from joint family property. But nobody sees that as an infringement on individual freedom. It is only when you extend the same limitation on a will to fathers and daughters that people see it as an infringement of individual rights.[5]

One-dimensional Concern

While it is easy to build a consensus in India in favour of women's property rights as wives, there is much greater resistance to giving them their due right to property as a daughter. This is also reflected in the one-sided focus of some women's organizations. They focus almost obsessively on women's rights as wives, while neglecting their rights as mothers, sisters and daughters. Therefore, when enacting matrimonial laws or legislation against domestic violence and abuse, we assume the violation of rights is a one-sided affair and that in-laws, especially mothers and sisters-in-law, are carrying out a unidirectional torture spree against young wives, who are assumed to be always right, and always the victim.

We have paid scant regard to the abuse and neglect of old mothers at the hands of daughters-in-law or denying daughters the right to the parental home. We overlook the fact that daughters-in-law resent their husband's sisters being given the right to a share in parental property. Even when legislating on inheritance rights, we have ensured a better deal for women as widows but undermined their interests as wives, daughters, sisters and mothers.

This came out poignantly after the Kargil war in 1999 when a few cases of alleged murder by the in-laws of widows of soldiers were reported due to tussles over sharing the compensation money received from the Army. There were many more cases of young widows walking out on aged in-laws, and reports of sharp conflicts and break-ups occurring in families where the daughter-in-law alone got the entire compensation amount, ranging between Rs 20–28 lakh. In response to such reports, there was a proposal to split the compensation amount equally between the parents and the widow. However, the Army ruled

[5] The Hindu Succession Act was amended in 2005 to give co-parcenary rights to daughters as well. However, since land ceiling laws are a state subject, this amendment is not likely to bring the benefit of land rights to women in rural areas. Even in urban areas, there are few women demanding and getting their share of parental property. Since the provision allowing heads of family to make a will that excludes daughters is still intact, the tendency to disinherit daughters by making them sign away their share in favour of their brothers will take much longer to be reversed.

out any change in its rules in favour of giving parents a share of compensation money. The demand was dismissed with the advice: 'Treat your daughter-in-law like your daughter and she will never even think of leaving you.... When a tragedy of such magnitude befalls her, she [the widow] needs special attention and care. It is for the in-laws to provide it to her.'

Nobody denies the legitimate claim of the widow to the love and care of her in-laws. It is also true that too many widows, far from getting love and protection from their in-laws, get treated shabbily, sometimes even sent back to their parents or left to fend for themselves under adverse circumstances. However, we cannot remain indifferent to the needs of the parents and younger siblings.

When I suggested in an article in *The Indian Express* that the Army should work out a more balanced formula for splitting the compensation amount between the wife and parents or institute two separate lifelong pensions for the two, ensuring that an adequate portion actually remains in the control of the widow in a way that neither her own brothers nor her in-laws can force her to part with her share, this too was interpreted by many feminists as a sign that *Manushi* had abandoned its commitment to women's rights. Their assumption is that women are hapless only in one *avatar*–that of wives–and that in their roles as mothers and sisters they only play a negative part. Therefore, they lose their claim to consideration as women.

An important reason for the increase in domestic conflicts, rising dowry demands and the transformation of dowry from *stridhan* to groom price is that our legal enactments, administrative interventions and state policies are forcing the nuclearization of families without due attention to the fact that the only or main old age security for the vast majority of people in India are their children, especially their sons. Parents invest all they can in their son's education and career building in the hope and expectation that sons will get jobs or other forms of earning opportunities bringing about upward mobility for the family, contribute to the education and marriage costs of other siblings as well as the resources to take care of parents in their old age. In a country where there is a near total absence of any other form of social security, this is an understandable expectation.

However, too many parents find this expectation belied after their sons get married, especially if their sons take up well paying jobs or succeed in an independent enterprise separate from the joint family economy. Not just in metropolitan cities, but even in the small towns and villages of India, young wives are increasingly prone to insist on moving away from the joint family and set up their own independent establishment, even when the in-laws may be reasonable. A man continuing to financially support his parents or younger siblings even after nuclearization of the family often finds stiff resistance from his wife. Many even give up. Sometimes parents themselves withdraw from receiving such support in order to prevent friction in the marital life of their sons. Without doubt, in some cases, daughters-in-law willingly endorse their husbands' efforts to support their natal families. But the overall trend is more in the direction of moving away from taking responsibility for the in-laws.

This increasing insecurity and uncertainty is at the heart of family tussles between the bride, her natal family and her in-laws. While some gracefully resign themselves to this fate and even encourage sons to set up a separate house after marriage, many fight a grim battle to keep their sons under their influence, which often means using even vicious methods to prevent the couple from enjoying a close conjugal relationship. The young bride has a formidable weapon in her armoury—her youth and sex. The old parents have very little in their favour except the emotional appeal of blood bonds. This bond is easier to sever where the parents are dependent on the sons for support. The few who are wealthy may succeed in using their property as a glue to keep their married sons close to them.

This anxiety and uncertainty about their fate vis-à-vis their sons is partly responsible for strengthening the culture of 'dowry demands'. In recent years, I have heard any number of parents tell me that marriage no more means *kanya daan* (gift of a daughter) but *putra samarpan* (handing over of son to the daughter-in-law). They have to be prepared that even occasional visits to the son's house may be resented and blocked by his wife, if she succeeds in winning him over to his side. That is why one finds parents trying to marry off their daughter before they arrange their sons' marriages because of the fear that their sons may not be allowed to contribute to the expenses after they get married. This is also the reason why dowry is taking the form of 'groom price', with parents expecting that a certain sum of money be given to them almost as 'compensation' for their handing over the income and assets of their son to the woman who becomes his wife.

If we want domestic and inter-generational harmony, it is necessary to work out new and more egalitarian norms, with every family member feeling assured that his or her rights are well protected, well respected and inalienable. This was one positive feature of traditional Hindu law. Each member had the right to benefit from the common resources of the family, with the head of the family acting as a manager and trustee rather than as sole owner of family property. We have already seen and suffered the ill-effects of concentrating all of the family's resources in the hands of men during the last century and a half. This resulted in wives leading a life of dependence and vulnerability because elderly males commanded disproportionate power over resources. Negating altogether the rights of other members of the family and making the old depend on the charity of the young cannot correct that imbalance.

The fierce battles between daughters-in-law and parents-in-law are in large part due to the fact that women in most communities are conditioned to believe that their rights lie henceforth in their husband's families. Therefore, they feel extremely insecure and resentful about the claims of other members of their husband's families. The answer, therefore, lies in giving women inalienable rights in their parental property so that they enter their marital homes with a sense of self confidence in the knowledge that they do not have to keep the marriage going 'at all costs' and do not have to carve out a niche for themselves by curbing the rights of their in-laws.

One is not likely to get an accurate or reliable perception of family politics and familial power relations if one views the situation solely through the eyes of the daughter-in-law, as many of us are prone to do. The fact that it is usually a daughter-in-law who comes to complain against her husband and in-laws does not necessarily mean that she is the only victim of the imbalances in our family system. Members of the groom's family, including the much-reviled mother-in-law, are unlikely to take their complaints against their sons and daughters-in-law to the police or even to NGOs. Despite the stereotype of the *Sati-Savitri*, long-suffering Indian wife, many more women in their role as wives complain and seek outside intervention to solve their marital problems than do mothers or sisters when the latter are abused by their son's or brother's wives because of blood ties and sense of family loyalty. They have a greater compulsion to keep things within the family and feel humiliated complaining to outsiders against their own sons and brothers, especially if it involves legal interventions. If one goes by the records of women's organizations, police stations or court cases, one gets the impression that the only underdog/wronged person in the Indian family is the *bahu*, especially in a joint family. However, it is naive to form an opinion about marriage and family life in India on the sole basis of the bad marriages that women's organizations are asked to deal with. We need to look at the entire range of tolerable/insufferable, good/bad and abusive/loving marriages in order to have a more realistic view of the diversity in the family situations within different communities in India.

A Major Turning Point

The study report 'Toiling without Rights: Ho Women of Singhbum' describes how the fragile and uncertain rights of women in their parental property make them easy targets of violence. Even within communities where women are the economic mainstay of the family and run farm operations and the village economy without much help from men, women find it difficult to hold on to landed property if they have no men in the family—sons, brothers or husband—to bolster their claim.

In 1981, *Manushi* filed a petition in the Supreme Court on behalf of Maki Bui and her daughter, Sonamuni, Ho tribal women of Lonjo Village in Singhbum District, Bihar, whereby we challenged the denial of equal inheritance rights to women of the Ho tribe. Though this petition focused on the plight of Ho women, the conditions that contribute to women's vulnerability are as true for tribal women in most other parts of India as well as peasant women in many other caste Hindu communities.

I was introduced to Maki Bui and the plight of women like her through a social worker and missionary named Pilar. This happened while I was travelling through Singhbum, gathering information on police atrocities against tribal women. When I first met her, Maki Bui was in her early fifties. She had recently been widowed. Her husband had been a retired police constable who had served for many years. Like most rural women with a husband who worked outside the village, Maki Bui stayed in the village, working on the land through most of the period he was employed elsewhere. The couple had no sons, just one daughter named Sonamuni. According to customary practice in her area, Maki Bui was entitled to occupy her husband's share of the family land during her lifetime. After his death, the land would revert to one of her husband's agnates rather than her already married daughter, Sonamuni, who would have been allowed limited usufructuary rights in her natal family land only if she had remained unmarried.

Maki Bui wanted to pass on the land to her daughter, Sonamuni, who had been married into a poor family. At first she tried to get her daughter and son-in-law to come and live in Lonjo so that they would have some customary claim to her land after her death. Customary law does have provisions for adopting a son-in-law for inheritance purposes. The strategy was resented by Maki Bui's husband's family, who began to threaten her with violence. When Maki Bui sought my help, I suggested we challenge the constitutional validity of the discriminatory tribal law. It appeared to me that it would be simple to get the Supreme Court to rule that those aspects of tribal customary law that discriminate against a woman's inheritance rights were unconstitutional.

Following Maki Bui's petition, which was published in *Manushi*, No. 13 (in 'Challenging the Denial of Land Rights to Women'), many other individuals and activists wrote to us saying that the situation was similar among several other communities and, therefore, they wished to join us in challenging these laws that discriminate against women in matters of inheritance. One of *Manushi*'s subscribers, Mary Roy, who belongs to the Syrian Christian community, wrote to say she had filed a petition along the lines of the *Manushi* petition, challenging similar discrimination against Syrian Christian women.

From Maharashtra's Dhulia district, Sharad Patil, a prominent political activist working among tribals, also filed an intervention petition because many tribal communities in that area practised a similar denial of land rights to women. From within Bihar some activists working with the Jharkhand movement brought more intervention petitions involving other tribal communities. In Mumbai, activists of Nivara Hakk Samiti, who were fighting for the housing rights of pavement dwellers, wrote to say that they had decided to demand house *pattas* in the name of the women in these families. Even in far off Nepal, activists who were in touch with *Manushi* such as Hsila Yami, who later became a prominent Maoist leader, responded to this issue with great enthusiasm and made it part of their own campaigns in villages of Nepal. Maki Bui's case seemed to have a large ripple effect. Within a short time, we had succeeded in getting the issue of women's land rights debated and discussed among a whole range of social and political organizations.

However, in Singhbhum, influential leaders all opposed our intervention. Some prominent church leaders in the Chhotanagpur area came out against it on the specious ground that giving women inalienable land rights would destroy the 'tribal culture and way of life'. Tribal politicians of all mainstream parties also joined the chorus of opposition, dubbing it a conspiracy to facilitate the takeover of tribal lands by scheming outsiders. They argued that it was impractical to give land rights to women because they go away to their marital homes and claim land rights there.

At the other end, the lawyers arguing the case as well as judges hearing the case seemed so removed from the ground level reality that I decided to bring the situation of women in the village society and economy to life by writing a detailed report from Singhbhum District. Pilar—my host, informant and translator—knew the lives of most of these women closely. Most women trusted her even with intimate information since she had worked as a primary healthcare provider for many years. In addition, I travelled to numerous other villages, with local activists assisting me in collecting information. Spread over four visits, the study was an eye opening experience for me in more ways than one. 'Toiling without Rights' attempts to answer the various objections raised by local leaders against giving land rights to women. It is interesting that the points they raised are not very different from those offered as justifications by caste Hindus for denying women a share in family inheritance, even though the stereotype notion is that tribal culture is far more pro-women than caste Hindu culture and practices. The similarities are evident in the article 'Inheritance Rights for Women: A Response to Some Commonly Expressed Fears'. This piece was addressed mainly to urban middle class audiences who prefer to spend large amounts of money on providing daughters exorbitant dowries but do not consider them worthy of independent property rights.

Several urban, educated, left-oriented activists leading various tribal rights movements in the region actively assisted *Manushi* in mobilizing opinion in favour of our petition. Veer Bharat Talwar, a respected intellectual activist, travelled through Jharkhand with me to hold discussions with important politicians and activists; Josna, Alosius Raj and Xavier published a Hindi version of our petition and held several meetings in the area on this issue. Rose Kerketta of Ranchi University intervened in the Court on behalf of her own Munda tribe requesting to be impleaded in the case since similar discrimination was practised among her tribe as well. And yet, women of this region who stood to gain most from our intervention, could not get organized and put up a united front in the same way that men did to safeguard their collective interests. In fact, Maki Bui's own female relatives turned very hostile since her land was expected to revert to their families after her death. Since in most instances women's identification with men of their own families is much stronger than their sense of solidarity with other women, we could not unite them on gender lines. Had a few mainstream male leaders championed the women's cause, that might have brought a much larger number of women together to stand up for their rights. We have seen it time and again: if all men gang up against a move to empower women as a group, a good proportion of women themselves often join men in attacking and undermining an initiative for women's rights.

At the other end, the Supreme Court proved very ineffective in dealing with the case. Getting the case admitted into the Supreme Court was no problem. Getting the case heard was a far more difficult matter. The years that followed were full of unending petty harassment, slipshod court procedures and interminable delays. After the case was admitted on 20 August 1981, the Supreme Court ordered the Bihar government to ensure that during the period that the case remained before the court and until final orders were passed, they were to see to it that Maki Bui continued to enjoy her customary rights as a widow without fear or hindrance.

But that was not to be. After the court ordered an enquiry into her allegations through the Block Development Officer (BDO), her-in-laws' family began to harass and intimidate her even more for having dared to take them to court. We did all we could to get her case expedited. However, the Bihar government kept requesting postponement after postponement under one pretext or the other. In the meantime, Maki Bui was getting desperate as her in-laws made concerted efforts to drive her out of the village. Finally, she had to leave her village, Lonjo, and go far away to live in her daughter's village. Maki Bui had started off by asking our help to enable her to pass on her piece of land to her daughter. Instead of assisting her to get more than the discriminatory customary law allowed, her coming to the Supreme Court had actually endangered her life even further and she could not even continue living in her village. The local police as well as the BDO and other officials actively supported those who were endangering Maki Bui's life, both in the village as well as by submitting false affidavits in the Supreme Court.

We filed a petition alleging contempt of court against the Bihar government for violation of the court's interim orders that Maki Bui be offered protection. Even though by now our expectations of the Supreme Court had been scaled down considerably, we were still not prepared for what happened. Justice Mishra, who heard the case at that stage, said openly in a packed court:

> We can pass a contempt order if you insist. But what good will it do for the petitioner? The Bihar government or its police are not going to heed it any more than they did our original order. Better that you advise that old woman to continue staying with her daughter so at least she is more safe than in her own village. Or else bring her to Delhi and keep her with you so she is safe.

The Bihar government showed no inclination to propose a solution and the Supreme Court insisted on forever waiting for the Bihar government's proposal for finding a satisfactory formula on this issue.

We had approached the Supreme Court in the hope that its judgement would help millions of women, not just Ho women but other peasant women as well. Now the Supreme Court was itself admitting that it could not even provide this one woman with elementary protection, leave alone strengthen her economic rights.

What was the point of fighting this case for so many years if the highest court of the land was admitting that its orders carried no weight whatsoever with the government of Bihar, that even a BDO does not have to pay any heed to it? What good would any final judgement be in such a situation? Maki Bui and her daughter both died under mysterious circumstances years before the Supreme Court pronounced its judgement. Their deaths left me so traumatized with guilt and remorse that I was physically sick for months. When the court judgement was finally delivered I did not even bother to read it for several years. Maki Bui's fate came to be a permanent symbol and reminder of the dangers of political intervention without preparing adequate support within the community. Since then I have tried hard to stick to my resolve that never again would we endanger the life of an already vulnerable person by taking their battle to a level which was beyond their strength and our control. Even if risks had to be taken, they would be of such a nature that the brunt is borne by those of us leading the initiative. It also taught me, yet again, the importance of avoiding situations in which our interventions appeared like an attack from 'outsiders'. This caution becomes doubly necessary when you are dealing with groups and communities who are much poorer and in a weaker position than those of us who take up their causes. Men of such communities are already victims of exploitation, discrimination and contemptuous treatment meted out to them by powerful outsiders. The low self-esteem and frustration of men of such downtrodden communities finds an easy outlet in oppressing women in their own community because that is the only way they can feel 'manly' since in the outside world their manhood is constantly crushed by powerful aliens. In such a situation, when an outside agency or individual descends in their midst to attack their treatment of their own women, their response is inevitably one of aggression and hostility.

When instead, you appeal to people's sense of honour and justice and work *with* them to find a solution to their problems rather than present them in a humiliating light to the outside world, it produces far better results. But if you rely on shame as a weapon of behavioural transformation, it leads to greater resistance to changing power equations. By contrast, we saw much better and swifter results when we appealed to the conscience of fathers and brothers to take responsibility to save their daughters and sisters facing violence or abuse.

Therefore, we began to emphasize the need to work towards creating a new social consensus in society and in the family to strengthen the notion of what is a woman's rightful due. We endeavour to help her secure it with honour rather than focus obsessively on securing legal rights that would leave her at the mercy of an inefficient, corrupt and venal state machinery, while everyone else disowns responsibility for her well-being.

Freeing of Enslaved Goddesses

My reading of Indian history as well as our experience with victims of domestic violence in Delhi convinced me that it was possible to make men active participants in movements for strengthening women's rights, provided you knew how to appeal to their sense of honour and fair play.

Fortunately, we got a chance to test this approach out on a large scale through *Manushi*'s association with Shetkari Sangathana–one of the largest mass based movement of farmers founded in Maharashtra in 1980 by Sharad Joshi. In 1986, Joshi invited *Manushi* to come and participate in their newly formed women's front–Shetkari Mahila Aghadi–and evolve a programme of action aimed specifically at empowering women of farm households who had till then been mobilized mainly on economic issues affecting the farm sector.

Since the Sangathana is committed to non-violent agitational methods, and their meetings and rallies are exceptionally disciplined without any policing methods, women have always felt very safe and comfortable in this movement. Therefore, all their agitations have included massive participation of women, many of whom come with a do-or-die spirit. For many years they participated only on general issues affecting the farm sector as a whole, without raising gender specific issues, till Joshi decided to set up a separate wing for women.

My contribution was to convince Joshi and his colleagues that, just as, for the farm sector as a whole, their emphasis was on farmers getting their due price for their labour, with economic freedom being the core issue rather than a demand for subsidies or protection from the government, so also it should be their strategy for women of farm families. The organization ought to ensure that women too did not have to live a life of hapless dependence with all economic resources concentrated in the hands of the men of the family. I was able to convince Joshi that for strengthening women's rights in the family, they need not wait till the government agreed to change this or that law. It was far more important that the Sangathana be able to persuade its followers to willingly give women of their family their due share; the best of laws can be rendered useless if people are not convinced of their worth. I wanted to see whether the success we had in convincing individual families in Delhi to avoid begging for help from the police and law courts and instead ensure that women got justice within the family itself could be replicated on a large scale. The product of this collaboration between *Manushi* and Shetkari Mahila Aghadi was a unique campaign called Lakshmi Mukti Karyakram.

Sharad Joshi announced that any village which performed the following three acts for women's empowerment would be honoured as a *Jyotiba Gram* named after Jyotiba Phule, one of the most revered late nineteenth century social reformers of Maharashtra:

1. Ensure by consensus the victory of an all women panel in panchayat elections.
2. Close the village liquor shop by mobilizing the whole village in order to curb drunkenness and wife beating.
3. Voluntarily transfer a piece of land from husband to wife by a hundred or more families in the village. Such a village would be honoured as a Lakshmi Mukti Gaon (a village which had liberated its hitherto enslaved Lakshmis) through a public function at which Sharad Joshi would personally distribute certificates of honour to each such family.

A small remote village named Vitner in Jalgaon district made history by performing all the three tasks within a month and received the Jyotiba Phule award from the then prime minister of India. My very positive report on the amazing change in village culture as a result of these achievements enthused Joshi to launch a movement for the implementation of Lakshmi Mukti in all the districts where the Sangathana had a stronghold. The only incentive offered was that Sharad Joshi himself would go and bestow certificates of honour to each such village. Given the respect and affection enjoyed by Joshi among Maharashtrian farmers at the time, this in itself gave the movement great legitimacy and the aura of a sacred mission.

The nomenclature and symbolism of this unique campaign is itself fascinating. The Indian goddess of wealth is named Lakshmi. However, a wife is also traditionally referred to as *griha* Lakshmi, that is, Lakshmi of the household. Likewise the birth of a daughter or arrival of a daughter-in-law is also meant to be celebrated as the coming of Lakshmi in the family, even though many communities have come to see females as a burden rather than a blessing. Thus, the message of the Lakshmi Mukti Karyakram was that by enslaving their household Lakshmis, the farmers had incurred the curse of poverty. Therefore, in order to free themselves from economic bondage, they had to liberate their own Lakshmis and earn her blessings. My own campaign speeches were more focused on the advantages Lakshmi Mukti would bring to farm families but Joshi's speeches dexterously used economics, mythology, and a sense of sacred and dharmic responsibility to get his point across. Joshi would introduce the Lakshmi Mukti campaign by saying that so far the Sangathana had worked tirelessly to get various exploiters off the farmers' backs and ensure that farmers got fair and remunerative prices for their produce. Now it was time for the Sangathana to ensure that men associated with the movement also were just to the women of the household.

Joshi linked the whole endeavour to an earlier Karzmukti Andolan (movement for freedom from debts), whereby he had built a case through careful economic calculations that the farm community needed to be liberated from the stress of indebtedness to government banks by writing off of their loans, since the government robbed the farm sector of Rs 72,000 crore every year by artificially depressing prices of farm produce through numerous authoritarian, statist controls. He would then give them a similar lesson in household economics to explain the debt they owed their wives. Joshi told me some of these ideas took shape in his mind after reading certain articles in *Manushi*, notably a report of a Punjab village study by Bernard Horowitz published in *Manushi*, No. 11 (see 'Family Life—The Unequal Deal'), as well as my study of the Hindu Code Bill ('Codified Hindu Law: Myth and Reality', *Economic and Political Weekly* Vol. XXIX, No. 33, 13 August 1994). I have rarely seen academic studies put to better creative use in a campaign speech.

In village after village I would see men reduced to tears listening to Joshi's appeal. Within two years, husbands in hundreds of villages carried out the Lakshmi Mukti programme of land transfer to wives, celebrating the occasion as though it were a sacred festival. The entire village would be spruced up and decorated with men dancing to the beat of drums. We would be received with much fanfare, with women performing a *arti* and singing songs as they received Joshi to preside over the certificate giving ceremony. Men seemed even more elated than women. Much of the initiative for preparing villages for Lakshmi Mukti was taken by young male cadres of the Sangathana. Some of the men I interviewed described the whole campaign as a *mahayagna* (a sacred *dharmic* ritual).

The occasion would attract many people from neighbouring villages. After each public meeting, men from surrounding villages would come up and volunteer to effect similar transfers of land in their own village, provided Joshi joined them likewise for the celebration. Thus far from creating a backlash among men, the approach of appealing primarily to the sense of fair play and justice among men created a supportive atmosphere for women to exercise their rights. Domestic violence went down dramatically in all such households where the beginnings of a new equation between men and women were being established.

I attribute the success of this campaign to the following factors:

1. The high-level credibility of Sharad Joshi in those days among the farmers of Maharashtra. His track record of self-sacrifice, of being non-corrupt, played a vital role in influencing opinion in favour of Lakshmi Mukti.
2. Joshi had a long enough track record of demonstrating to the farmers that his ideas and methods of struggle yielded beneficial results for them. Therefore, when he told them Lakshmi Mukti is good for the well-being of their family and for their own self-respect, they trusted his word. Their slogan '*Bheekh nako hawe ghamache daam*' (we do not want charity, we want the due price for our labour) could easily be used for lending legitimacy to women's right to land because women in most farm families are the primary workers on the land.
3. The Gandhian paradigm within which Joshi operated put great emphasis on self-respect and justice. While many other contemporary movements of farmers were more oriented towards appealing for concessions and subsidies and government supports of farm prices, Joshi's movement chose economic freedom and justice rather than concessions.
4. Once men become self-respecting by giving up grovelling before their own tyrants (in this case various government agencies), they are more easily able to extend the same respect to women. Men who themselves

live under authoritarian regimes and controls become less self- assured and, therefore, more tyrannical towards women.

5. Key men of the Sangathana led by personal example. They not only transferred land to their wives' names but also encouraged them to take a part in Sangathana work. Their domestic conjugal lives showed visible improvements rather than becoming more stressful. Therefore, people could see for themselves that strengthening the rights of women need not lead to breakdown of the family or greater conflicts between husband and wife. Rather it could lead to happier relations. Men did not feel attacked; rather they felt elevated when being called upon to do justice and being honoured for it.

This campaign led to far-reaching changes in the area, including creating greater space for women in the political and public life of Maharashtra and curbing domestic violence. While the entire might of the Supreme Court and agencies of the Indian State failed to protect one Maki Bui, the enthusiastic response to the message of a respected leader could move thousands of families into changing repressive norms towards women.

Unfortunately, the campaign could not be sustained in a consistent manner beyond the first three to four years because Lakshmi Mukti Karyakram was pursued or abandoned depending on the urgency and priority it received in comparison to the other Sangathana campaigns. Over the years, the Sangathana got more and more embroiled in electoral politics, which curtailed its appeal and made it appear as yet another politically partisan group. Moreover, while it was relatively easier to build a consensus in favour of a share in land for wives, most families were not willing to concede that daughters too should get a share. Since women depended too much on the family's men to carry forward this task, they could not keep the momentum going when men's interest declined. Even though many women emerged in leadership roles through the Shetkari Mahila Aghadi, very few commanded the kind of respect and reverence given to Joshi. Therefore, when Joshi's attention shifted to other issues, Lakshmi Mukti took a back seat. Joshi repeatedly pressed me to take charge of the campaign and keep it going in a consistent manner. However, my work with *Manushi* and my teaching job in Delhi made me reluctant to shift base to Maharashtra. Thus, though people did not lose their enthusiasm, the leaders could not sustain their commitment for a long enough period. However, an important fallout of this movement was that the government of Maharashtra yielded to the demand of Shetkari Sangathana and passed a Government Order on 15 September 1992 that government officials would not raise needless objections or put needless hurdles in the way of husbands applying for ownership of their farmland.

Despite several limitations, the movement clearly showed that building a campaign based on compassion and trust in the inherent goodness of human beings, making them active agents of redressing wrongs, works far better than attempts to make them passive and supine recipients of authoritarian measures of reform carried out through threats of punishment to ensure compliance.

Men's Contribution Vital

The modern upsurge and concern for strengthening women's rights in India that began in the mid nineteenth century emanated largely from men. Numerous male reformers bore the brunt of social hostility while confronting their respective communities with the injustices meted out to women, challenging various oppressive norms that prevailed in their respective communities and regions with regard to women's role in the family and society. Many of them, like Mahatma Phule in Maharashtra, Pandit Vidyasagar in Bengal, Lala Devraj in Punjab and Veerasalingam in Andhra Pradesh, devoted their lives to setting up institutions for women's education, homes for widows and fighting for their right to equal opportunity, including equipping women to earn an independent livelihood. These men also helped women enter the professions as teachers and doctors and worked hard to create a dignified space for them in social and public life as partners in movements for social reform. As a result of this active involvement and the leading role played by men in combating the then prevailing social prejudices in India, women did not have to bear the entire brunt of social criticism for exploring new social options and roles; men often acted as buffers between them and forces of social resistance against women's empowerment.

This trend was further strengthened during the twentieth century freedom movement after Mahatma Gandhi assumed leadership of the anti-colonial struggle. He openly admitted that his choice of non-violent *satyagraha* as a weapon of struggle was imbibed from the example of women, including his own mother. He was determined to see women play a leading role in the freedom movement in particular and public affairs in general. The importance he gave to feminizing politics in order to make it woman-friendly is also evident from the fact that most of Gandhi's symbols of struggle were also culled out from the feminine domain. For example, the *charkha* (spinning wheel) has primarily been a feminine activity. Similarly, his famous salt *satyagraha* linked the civil disobedience movement to the everyday domain of every woman in the household because salt is one of the most essential ingredients in everyday food, which is almost always cooked by women. His vision of an ideal society was one in which the feminine genius played a dominant role. He expected men to feminize themselves by learning the art of non-violent *satyagraha* and practising feminine activities like spinning every day rather than expecting women to masculinize themselves in order to gain equality.

Gandhi consistently emphasized that the struggle for women's equality had to be an integral part of the struggle for India's freedom and devoted a considerable part of his energy trying to redress the power imbalance between men and women. It is noteworthy that Gandhi and most other major social reformers were against using coercive laws to bring about the reforms they were working towards.

Even in contemporary India, some of the most important mobilizations of women in the struggle for their rights have emerged out of movements among farmers, landless poor and other oppressed groups that were led by men. Chandi Prasad Bhatt and Sunderlal Bahuguna of the Chipko movement, Awadhesh Kaushal of Uttarakhand, trade unionist Shankar Guha Niyogi of Chhatisgarh Mukti Morcha, Rajendra Singh of Tarun Bharat Sangh and numerous other men have each in their own ways in their respective regions contributed to mobilizing women to claim their rights, both within the family as well as in the social and political domains. Even in the field of women's studies, it is men like J.P. Naik and B.N. Ganguly who acted as mentors, setting up women's study institutions and giving legitimacy and impetus to women's studies in India.

This active involvement of men has had both positive and negative dimensions. The biggest advantage is that the struggle for women's empowerment in India did not assume the form of gender war. When male reformers lead the struggle for women's rights by personal example, including even building new partnerships with their own daughters, wives, mothers and sisters, other men feel less threatened. They can see the basis for healthier, stronger male–female bonding. They do not think it will lead to a breakdown of the family. Women too feel more confident that engaging with women's rights issues will not estrange them from their families. Thus, women's rights issues get greater legitimacy and become shared social concerns, rather than remain only women's concerns. As a result many significant measures for the empowerment of women in India came gracefully, without women having to battle aggressively for them. For example, women in all western countries had to wage long drawn out battles to win the right to vote and to participate in political life. They were ridiculed and some were even attacked viciously for decades before they could get their society to make progress on women's rights. However, women in India were granted constitutional equality and the right to equal participation in politics without even a token fight and that too much before these became established principles in most western democracies. That is why most women politicians of the freedom movement rejected the idea of special women's quotas in legislatures when affirmative action was being introduced for Scheduled Castes and Scheduled Tribes. Similarly, the right to equality of opportunity in employment and education came to be won with men playing a leading role, rather than women having to fight for them on their own. The All India National Congress elected Annie Besant and Sarojini Naidu as presidents of the Party in 1919 and 1925, respectively, at a time when elsewhere in the world, it was considered outrageous for women even to demand the right to vote, let alone hold political office.

However, this has also caused women some difficulties. It has meant that women in India got into the habit of expecting men to fight major battles for them, to feel beholden to men for promoting their cause in the public domain. When men come to determine the agendas of action on women's issues, women seldom acquire enough independent strength to carry forward their own agenda according to their own requirements. This has meant that men could draw the limits of the movement as and when they thought fit. During the freedom movement Mahatma Gandhi's special efforts to make a respectful space for women in public life as valued colleagues in movements for political and social reform became the inspiration for many of his followers. At that time, the work involved making personal sacrifices. Therefore, there were fewer reasons for conflict and men saw that social movements gained by the participation of women. However, in post-Independence India, when politics quickly became synonymous with acquiring a measure of control over the levers of state power and licence to use those for self-aggrandizement, we have witnessed a steady process of women's marginalization in politics. With men dominating the seats of power, most women find it convenient to attach themselves to or seek the patronage of powerful men rather than work to build gender solidarity. How this tendency affects the fortunes of contemporary women politicians is discussed in the article 'Lack of Gender Solidarity: Systematic Degrading of Women Politicians'. The few women who make it to position of power mostly on account of their connections with powerful male patrons, tend to sideline rather than promote other women because they tend to see them as rivals for patronage rather than potential allies.

While dependence on men in major ways has stayed intact, the rhetoric of contemporary women's movements has changed considerably. While women of the freedom movement usually went overboard paying homage and tribute to men who helped them come forward or lent support to their battles, most contemporary feminists are loathe to acknowledge the contribution and help provided by men to women's struggles in India.

Misplaced Critiques

Even while First World feminism has become more and more nuanced and sophisticated in its approaches to women's issues, as well as in dealing with the internal politics of their respective countries, influential sections among feminists in India thrive by presenting an over simplistic stereotypical portrayal of Indian women and society. Some characteristic features of such feminist portrayals are as follows:

1. Project the entire 5,000 years old history of Indian civilization as proof of the evil genius of Indian males, whose main aim in life was supposedly to find newer and newer ways of oppressing women and manipulating them into accepting servility as an essential characteristic of being an Indian female.
2. Create a distorted picture of India's past by relying on a small sample of writings in English of colonial administrators and missionaries, and on a select few portions of traditional Indian texts, which tend to bolster the case that women were kept forever oppressed and downtrodden. For example, they emphasize a few lines from the *Ramayana* dealing with the *agnipariksha* of Sita, a few lines from *Manusmriti* which hold the view that women need to live under the protection of men, an episode or two from Buddha's life where he restricts the entry of women into monasteries, a few incidents from the *Mahabharata* where Draupadi or other women characters are locked in conflict with men. These are considered the sum total of ancient opinion on women's status, enough to damn a whole civilization. They tend to ignore all those other texts and traditions, which present a favourable picture of women's status.
3. Impose contemporary notions of equality and individual rights on all phases of history without regard for the fact that every age has to be first judged by the ideals and standards of morality it chose for itself and how far it lived up to its chosen standards before we judge it by our standards of political and social morality. For example, if a person wrote a historical treatise evaluating King Ram of the epic *Ramayana* not by the *dharmic* code of kingship prevalent in the age and time when that epic was composed but rather by standards of contemporary democratic politics in the USA or England, that person would not be taken seriously by academics. However, many movement authors display no qualms in judging characters out of ancient epics and *Dharmashastras* by the yardstick chosen by contemporary western feminism.

4. See the entire history of India through the prism of gender, caste and class struggle. They romanticize those characters, episodes and phases in Indian history where they see or imagine signs of struggle against gender, caste and class oppression. This has led to serious distortions in the writing of Indian history. The so called upper castes, especially Brahmins, are projected as being quintessentially evil manipulators whose only contribution to Indian history has been to build a self-serving ideological edifice to justify their dominance and make all others accept a sub-human status. In left-feminist literature, the term upper caste or Brahmin is almost always used as a social pejorative and the term 'upper caste norms' is used almost as a shorthand for anti-women, anti-human social values and behaviour patterns. Upper caste Hindu women are accepted into the feminist fold when they heap scorn on upper caste men, when they rebel on fashionable issues against their own family and community. Men acquire respectability mainly if they are from 'lower' castes and raise their voices against the power and privilege claimed by upper castes, notably Brahmins.
5. Men of the 'upper' castes, even when they devote their entire lives to fighting for the rights of women or other disadvantaged groups, are projected as devious characters who attempted to invent newer and newer ways to enslave women. So also the entire gamut of nineteenth and twentieth century social reformers who devoted their entire lives to the cause of women's education and their right to freer lives, and worked hard to make space for women in public life, are dismissed as being motivated by the desire to recast women into being servile in newer ways (see, for instance, *Recasting Women* by Sudesh Vaid and Kumkum Sangari published by Kali for Women). Going by this definition, nothing good happened for women in the 5,000 years of Indian history, except when a bunch of valiant feminists came along.
6. The word 'tradition' itself is more often than not used as a pejorative. All negative values are attributed to Indian tradition and all that is positive is supposed to be gained from modern feminism.
7. Another common feature of 'progressive-feminist' historiography is to treat various traditional texts as though they pronounce God's own commandments and legislate social norms for all times, for all classes, for all people. Thus, many feminists have come to believe that all the supposed 'ills and evils' of Indian society are because *Manusmriti* includes a few lines advocating that women live under the protection of fathers when they are young, be cared for by husbands after marriage and be provided protection by sons in their old age. This is produced as adequate evidence that women in Indian civilization were kept under the total control of male patriarchs.

8. Female deities in their militant *avatars*, in their Kali, Durga, Chandi *roop* are acceptable, but are treated with disdain in their benign and loving *avatars* as Parvati or Radha. The article, 'Allies or Adversaries? The Continuing Hold of Traditional Female Moral Exemplars in India', argues that there is a strong tendency among feminists to misunderstand and misrepresent the meaning of traditional religious female divinities as role models and argues that we need to celebrate the diverse manifestations of the feminine rather than only the militant and aggressive manifestations.

The image that is communicated to the world outside India is of an inevitable doom. If a female somehow escapes being aborted as a fetus following an SDT, she will inevitably be undernourished and neglected in comparison to the male child. Thereafter, every woman is bound to be tortured for dowry and suffer untold indignities at the hands of her in-laws and husband. Any and every woman who has the misfortune to live longer than her husband is bound to live a life of indignity and humiliation as a widow, that too if she providentially escapes being burnt on the funeral pyre as a *sati*. In this narrative, there is no place for daughters with secure, loving parents and happy childhoods, for whose education, health and well being her parents gladly make sacrifices. Men only appear in these stereotypes as authoritarian patriarchs denying daughters their full humanity. Brothers are mostly painted as villainous characters out to grab hold of family property and rob their sisters of their share. There is no place in Indian feminist literature for brothers who dote on sisters and who happily come to their sisters' aid in times of emergencies at great personal cost. There is also no place for couples that have built a life of happy conjugality for themselves, or in-laws who are loving and caring towards their daughters-in-law. The Indian family is always viewed as a site of oppression, and nothing more. The joint family system is portrayed as a device to keep women oppressed and ghettoized, never mind if in actual life some of the most successful women professionals of India attribute their ability to balance the tough requirements of their demanding, high status professions with a happy domestic life to the support they get from the joint family which frees them from a good part of the responsibilities of child care and house-keeping.

So powerful is the hold of oppressive stereotypes of Indian women's lives in the media, that most of us are treated as exotic survivors of a vicious and murderous civilization. The following snippets from a real-life conversation over a lunch meeting with a feminist MP from a European country is fairly typical of how the lives of Indian women have come to be viewed internationally.

Q. *Were you tortured for dowry?*

A. I chose not to be married, so there was no question of dowry or torture.

Q. *Oh, how lucky! How did you manage to survive? Must have been very tough escaping the pressure for an arranged marriage!*

A. Not really, my parents never pushed me to get married. And if I ever wanted to get married they would as easily have accepted my own choice of a partner as they would accept the responsibility of finding a suitable partner for me, if I asked for their involvement in the matter.

Q. *You must be very unusual, a typical modern woman! Was your mother tortured for dowry?*

A. No, my mother's parents-in-law didn't even bother to see what came in her dowry. However, one of my aunts had a very nasty mother-in law who took away her entire trousseau and treated her very shabbily.

Q. *Isn't that more normal?*

A. It is as 'normal' or abnormal as wife abuse cases in your country. Just as all women in Europe are not battered wives, so also in India, all women don't get tortured or abused in marriage. Happy wives don't hit newspaper headlines, only some of those who are battered to death get noticed by the media.

Q. *But you can't compare the situation of women in Europe with those in India. Western women would simply not put up with the treatment that women in India tolerate.*

She then swiftly changed the topic to another favourite theme.

Q. *How many women have committed* sati *in your family?*

A. Not one in all the generations I know of. The community I belong has no such tradition. In any case, you don't 'commit *sati*. The word *sati* is an adjective to describe a woman who has extraordinary power of *sat* or truth force, a woman who is steadfast in her resolves.

Q. *But how many widows in your family were burnt on their husband's funeral pyre?*

A. I repeat. Not one that I know of. The practice of women burning on their husband's pyre is not a routine event. In the last 50 years, no more than 50 to 60 cases have been reported from all over India, amounting to no more than one per year. That should give you an idea of how typical it is.

By this time, she was so enraged at my responses that she cut short the conversation and started a similar dialogue with a couple sitting on the other side of the table. They too could not oblige her by providing answers that would fit in with her carefully nurtured view of the brutality and oppressiveness of the Indian family life. As far as I can remember, the husband was a senior professor and his wife a corporate executive earning far more than the husband. When they described their family life as a happy one with the woman's mother-in-law supporting her demanding career choice by freeing her from household responsibilities and child care, our European interlocutor had had enough. She just clamped down in anger and frustration assuming that we were giving her a false, rosy picture of our society simply because we were too embarrassed to admit the truth.

It is not as if either I or the couple are unaware of the many injustices suffered by many women in India, or that we hesitate to acknowledge it. We were only providing through our personal circumstances examples of the vast variations that exist in the life situation of women in India, with a good number even living privileged lives and many others able to carve out advantageous positions for themselves in the family.

It is not as if only uninformed foreigners carry this simplistic negative view of Indian society and family. Several leading Indian feminists in India get even more upset at the mere mention of families in which women hold the key to power or families in which women are not brutally oppressed. For example, in a TV discussion over the fate of widows in India, Mrs Mohini Giri, former Chairperson of the Women's Commission, waxed eloquent on the inhuman treatment meted out to all widows in India, pointing to the widows living on charity in Vrindavan. She attributed it all to the influence of *Manusmriti*. She got very upset when I intervened with a corrective saying:

> All widows are not brutally oppressed and discarded by families like those living on charity in the temples of Vrindavan. In many families, they continue holding the keys to power as revered matriarchs for whose happiness their sons will move heaven and earth. My own two grandmothers both outlived their husbands and both of them retained their autonomy and power in the family till the end.

I ended by saying, 'Why do you have the impression that *Manusmirti* was treated as God's own commandments? It carries as much or as little weight as *Madhusmriti*, that is, my writings in *Manushi*'. That comment became the occasion for Mrs Giri and some others to dub me a defender of *sati* as well oppressive patriarchy and *manuvadi sanskriti*. Some others thought I was being facetious in the face of a serious issue such as the fate of widows in India. The article 'From *Manusmriti* to *Madhusmriti*: Flagellating a Mythical Enemy' was written to explain why the obsession with *Manusmriti* amounted to fighting an imaginary foe. That led to an even more vigorous campaign to dub me a 'Hindu fundamentalist', and an apologist for anti-women traditions. I have faced similar absurd attacks for daring to say that the anti-*sati* law is both draconian and ill conceived because it fails to distinguish between suicide and murder, between a woman jumping on to her husband's pyre out of their own desperation and a woman dragged forcibly or by fraud by her in-laws to burn along with her dead husband. The article entitled 'Zealous Reformers, Deadly Laws: The Conflicting Interpretations and Politics of *Sati*', analyzing responses of some feminists to the controversial death by burning of Charan Shah, was written in response to a hasty and callous campaign demanding the arrest and trial under the ferocious anti-*sati* law of a very poor low caste family and community of Satpura village in Uttar Pradesh even though there was no evidence of Charan Shah's family having any knowledge of her sudden decision to fling herself on her husband's pyre. This article came to be used as yet another proof of my turning 'pro-*sati*' just as my critique of the easy-to-abuse provisions in the 1986 anti-dowry law amendments provided ammunition to brand me as a pro-dowry defender of the patriarchal status quo. An example of this intolerance of dissent can be viewed through a fiery debate on this issue carried out through the pages of *The Hindu* in December 1999 with Subhashini Ali and Jayanti Natarajan accusing me of justifying and condoning the burning of women on their husband's pyre. I leave the readers of this volume to judge for themselves whether those allegations hold true.

The article 'Using Women as a Pretext for Censorship: The Indecent Representation of Women (Prohibition) Bill' criticizes a poorly thought out campaign leading to a hastily drafted law whose supporters dismiss all suggestions for careful consideration of the appropriate strategy to deal with a sensitive and complex problem with far-reaching repercussions for press freedom and civil rights. In most advanced democracies, where people take laws seriously, such measures have been extensively researched, discussed and debated, with the best minds—both male and female—providing their intellectual inputs to dealing with such challenges. In India, even the pretence of debate and discussion is seen as an unnecessary distraction.

The origin of this campaign is itself revealing. The United Nations declared 1986 as the 'Year of the Media'. Suddenly, certain internationally networked NGOs were flush with grants from UN agencies and other international aid organizations to work on this topic. Since, in this one year, they had to claim and spend a lot of money for the cause of 'Women and Media', what better way to justify their existence and prove their influence than by enacting a banning law for one billion people? A meeting or two is all it took to have a certain number of activists and organizations back a campaign by these NGOs. I remember trying to raise questions about the wisdom of certain provisions in the proposed Bill. They were rudely dismissed as an attempt to sabotage a holy crusade. Sure enough, the government of the day happily obliged by enacting yet another easy-to-abuse, ill-defined, harmful law as a token offering to women's organizations.

It is now over 20 years since that noxious law came into effect. Apart from benefiting the police and licensing inspectorate who make a regular killing by taking bribes after invoking this law in the name of curbing obscenity in the media, there is no sign that the mass media have become more responsible in portraying women. However, since the Year of Media is long over, this issue is now being described as a retrogressive obsession of the Hindutva brigade simply because in recent years the same laws are being invoked by women of the BJP and RSS.

The feminist fundamentalists in India create an atmosphere of such rigid polarization on every issue that you are only allowed two choices—either be willing to blindly follow the positions they hold or be dubbed as anti-women, anti-progress, anti-freedom. If you are not 'for' them, you are assumed to be 'against' women, never mind that the vast majority of women in India do not endorse the positions taken by this sort of feminists. It is this culture of intolerance that is largely responsible for an ugly stalemate over an important legislation—the Women's Reservation Bill—that has met with stiff opposition within every political party, including those that had made public commitments in its favour. In characteristic style, most feminists dubbed the opposition as proof of the patriarchal bias and anti-women attitude of our legislators. They steadfastly refused to heed suggestions to take stock of the serious flaws inherent in the Bill. As with the anti-dowry campaign, *Manushi*'s detailed critique of the flaws in the Bill caused a major rift within the women's movement.

However, unlike with the anti-dowry and other campaigns, women's organizations have failed to get a law of their choice bulldozed through the Parliament this time. The reason is simple: social legislation directed against dowry, *sati* or sex determination tests, no matter how ill conceived and draconian, do not touch the lives of parliamentarians who pass those laws. They know that merely paying lip service to those laws is enough, since they will be among the millions who do not need to heed them in real life. However, women's reservation in the legislatures affects every politician and every party. Therefore, they would not let any odd Bill get passed as law without thoroughly scrutinizing its implications for them.

To start with, *Manushi* was alone in voicing a critique of the Bill and calling for improvements, both through articles in *Manushi* as well as in the mainstream media. The article 'The Logic of Quotas: Women's Movement Splits on the Reservation Bill describes the hostility and intolerance with which suggestions for improvement were received. The proponents of the Bill did their best to polarize the issue on gender lines, hoping thereby to shame resistant politically powerful men into yielding ground on this issue. The hysterical campaign deliberately overlooked the fact that it was male politicians like Nazir Sahib, Ramakrishna Hegde of Karnataka and former Prime Minister Rajiv Gandhi who had mooted the idea of women's reservations starting from the panchayat level, while movement leaders like Sharad Joshi and Chandi Prasad Bhatt among others began to create the conditions for women to participate in political institutions. They also ignored results of various surveys and elections, which showed that most voters in India, including males, favour rather than discriminate against women politicians in India.

When numerous pleas for reconsideration of the Women's Reservation Bill fell on deaf ears, *Manushi* decided to go into campaign mode. Since in India there are hardly any experts among women on electoral reform issues, we made common cause with those men and organizations with solid expertise in the subject, as well as a known track record of being gender sensitive. With our Alternative Women's Reservation Bill in hand, we launched a signature campaign through *Manushi*. We found ourselves engaged in a very unequal battle, since we were pitched against the combined might of numerous powerful organizations that had been mobilized into supporting the flawed Bill by well-funded, internationally well-connected women activists and organizations. Together they had spent crores of rupees for this campaign, including resources from the National Commission of Women, as well as various state level commissions; *Manushi*, by contrast, had hardly any money available for such a campaign. With great difficulty, we earmarked about Rs 40,000, which included the cost of publishing the document as well as covering postage and miscellaneous expenses. Since we did not have the money necessary to organize all-India or regional conferences to present our Alternative Bill, we used an effective low cost strategy. I let it be known that I was available to lecture on this issue in any town or city of India, provided my travel cost was paid. Within no time, several invitations arrived. The numerous meetings I addressed resulted in a marked shift in opinion in favour of our Bill.

The experience was eye opening in more ways than one. In meeting after meeting of activists and academicians, I would start my presentation by asking how many of those present support the existing Reservation Bill. About 90 per cent of the hands would go up. I would then ask: 'How many of you have read the provisions of the Bill?' In most cases, not one person raised their hand. This was clear evidence that the all-India solidarity of women's organizations in favour of the Reservation Bill was built on emotive slogans. Therefore, it was easy to win over substantial numbers of activists and organizations in favour of our Alternative Bill by explaining the harmful implications of the provisions of the proposed legislation, as well as put forth better ways to achieve enhanced representation of women. Even the then Election Commissioner retracted his support from the original Bill and adopted ours as the basis for the Election Commission's proposal. Several leading politicians cutting across party lines also expressed their preference for our Bill.

Unfortunately, for at least some in the women's movement, blocking free and open-minded discussion and debate on other options has become a matter of prestige. This has lead to a continuing stalemate on the issue. It is a matter of great regret that organizations that aspire to represent the interests of millions of women have not developed the required wisdom and skills to conceptualize and frame laws that have the potential to benefit and mobilize their own claimed constituency.

Moreover, political corruption and the crying need for electoral reforms have been the key issues on the national agenda for nearly a decade now. It is one of the most hotly debated issues in our public life. It speaks volumes about the marginalization of women's movements from the political mainstream in India that none of the proponents of the official Women's Reservation Bill are actively involved in the struggle over these issues. No meaningful suggestions for cleaning up the malpractices have come from the major women's organizations in the ongoing public debate on electoral reforms.

Their campaign for nothing more than cornering a quota for women at a time when our polity is facing grave threats from the criminalization of politics and malgovernance is a tragic indicator of short-sightedness. The *zenana dabba* mentality cannot take women too far. The ghettoizing of women's concerns to narrowly defined issues will keep them forever marginalized. Why should the task of thinking through meaningful, overall electoral reforms be left to men while women confine their attention to securing a share of the political pie without examining whether the pie is worth eating at all? Are we then not accepting that men will inevitably set the rules of the game, that women are destined to be bit players—that too in the 'reserved' category?

Interestingly, some feminists have reacted with impatient disdain with regard to the demand that there be a quota within a quota for women of Backward Castes, lest the reserved seats all be cornered by upper caste women. This again shows lack of adequate preparation to build a united front of women among all castes and communities to push for reservations for women qua women. They tend to ignore that their lack of influence in politics is not just due to opposition from some men but is also a consequence of the fact that most women prefer patronage by powerful men rather than support each other, as discussed in the article 'Lack of Gender Solidarity'. Even those who never tire of shouting slogans in favour of women's empowerment are found spending a good deal of their energy undermining other women within their own party rather than join hands to promote more women in their organization. This is an important reason why women politicians end up playing a marginal role or are used as token representatives. Their failure in organizing women as an electoral force and their tendency to confine their concerns to a narrowly defined agenda of women's issues are important reasons for their lack of clout in national politics.

A lack of adequate expertise on issues of political and economic reforms, a tendency to substitute emotive slogans for practical wisdom, combined with a high level of intolerance towards thoughtful debate has thwarted healthy consideration of issues and kept the women's movement from becoming an effective agent of social change. The atmosphere of intolerance is also creating a serious backlash in our society against feminist groups in India. This often gets translated into a backlash against women's rights in general. This is new for our country. As discussed earlier, so far there has been a healthy tradition of a good number of powerful men taking an active part in promoting women's causes and an equally well entrenched tradition of almost all male politicians avoiding attacking or opposing measures for women's empowerment openly in public, even though in practice they may be rank chauvinists.

Working with Women rather than against Women

If the women's movement is to emerge as a powerful force capable of influencing and determining the political agenda in the country, we would do well to realize that by treating our own people and communities as passive objects of reform through coercive and ill conceived laws, we have damaged our social fabric as well as our effectiveness. The increasing gap between social legislation and actual practice within communities ought to be cause for serious concern.

The tendency to pass heavy-handed laws without comprehending the societal forces behind those practices, and without preparing the ground politically for the reforms to be acceptable, did not work even under the British, who could use coercive measures with ease because theirs was an authoritarian colonial regime. For example, their attempt to outlaw female infanticide through strong measures such as imposition of collective fines on villages did not lead to a more balanced sex ratio. All that happened is that outright murder gave way to slow killing of baby girls through deliberate neglect in feeding and healthcare. This strategy spread and gained salience even in regions where such practices did not exist before, while the use of violence for causing the death of baby girls did not stop altogether. Consequently, the twentieth century witnessed a further decline in the ratio of baby girls to that of boys in the overall population.

Whenever law has been used as the main or only instrument of social reform in India, it has produced very limited and often even negative results. Despite serious erosion of traditional institutions, for most people in India, community norms still carry more weight than parliamentary legislation. Prior to British rule, India had no centralized authority, either religious or secular, that could claim the right to impose its will in these matters on all the communities of India. This is what accounts for the wide diversity of customs and practices among various communities. The authority of traditional community leaders who preside over enforcement of customary practices operates mainly on the basis of commanding consensual acquiescence and respect. In well-knit communities, everyone within the community knows of their rights and obligations and the mechanisms available for redressal of wrongs. Matters are decided in close proximity and those adjudicating disputes know the facts of the case from close knowledge (unlike judges in our modern courts, who are far removed from the situation and whose information sources are third hand and mostly unreliable). Decisions are swift and enforced by the adjudicators without exorbitant cost to the parties to the dispute. The system in its fully functional form has many advantages and some disadvantages in comparison to modern law courts. That is why even today people cling to whatever is left of community managed dispute resolution mechanisms even though both their authority and competence have been considerably eroded, because in recent times many of these institutions have come to be dominated by people whose sole authority derives from political clout and muscle power. However, there are numerous cases where *biradari* panchayats have been led by people commanding genuine respect out of regard for their fair mindedness and care for the community. Such panchayats have made significant contributions in curbing anti-women practices such as foeticide and taking a firm stand against extortionist dowry demands. Whether the modernists like it or not, *biradari* managed institutions and conflict resolution mechanisms continue to have some relevance because people feel these institutions give them a sense of belonging and security that the modern legal system does not yet provide to most citizens in India.

Unfortunately, our national media, which cater mainly to the urban elite, tend to notice these institutions only when their actions involve a grave miscarriage of justice. At such points, we witness hysterical indignation by elite groups, demanding that the government must use its power to put an end to the power and influence of such institutions. We pay little heed to the positive contributions and potential of these civil society institutions, even while it has become fashionable to pay lip service to empowering civil society organizations—a nomenclature being increasingly appropriated for themselves by NGOs. This in effect often means denigrating genuine civil society organizations to create space for a new social segment, which owes its origins primarily to the international development organizations.

The notion that the state can make laws to govern the internal affairs of families and communities has not found full acceptance among our people. This is mainly due to the fact that the track record of the colonial institutions of governance and their inheritors did not inspire much confidence. Since most laws are still enacted in the same way, without involving citizens, most people do not even know what the provisions of those laws are and how to get them to deliver justice. Since laws are observed mostly in their violation, no one, including the parliamentarians who enact them, really takes such legislation seriously. Nor do law makers know what will actually produce the desired results because they have never implemented them seriously. The Lok Sabha is usually empty when important Bills concerning women's rights are passed. Very few MPs even bother to read the text of laws they are supporting or opposing. Government agencies whose job is to enforce laws lack the will and determination to do their job because those in positions of power think they, and those they personally protect, are above the laws. Consequently, most legislation in India, including laws that are ostensibly enacted for protecting or strengthening women's rights, tend to be either subverted by law makers themselves or ignored by our people, who continue to follow what is considered right in their own specific community, rather than what the latest *sarkari* law demands. In addition, we witness large-scale misuse and abuse of laws by the police, lawyers and unscrupulous citizens.

We would do well to recognize that:

1. Laws work best when they represent a strong social consensus in their favour. Even the best of laws become infructuous if they go against popularly held beliefs about what is right and what is wrong.
2. Laws can only be effective when directed at those who are seen as deviants from popularly respected social norms. If laws target entire populations who view the efforts of reformers as an unwanted intrusion in their internal affairs, you create a powerful wave of hostility, which obstructs, rather than assist, efforts at social reform.
3. Laws make sense only when used like small doses of antibiotics to help the body kill disease germs. Making them the sole instrument of social reform is like giving a patient with a nutritional ailment large doses of vitamins without adjusting his/her diet. Such a person would eventually react against and be harmed by the overdose of artificial nutrients.

It is only under the more pervasive, efficient and brutal totalitarian and militaristic regimes that unpopular laws can at times be rammed down people's throats. Reform through terror or authoritarian measures may work temporarily but it usually eventually produces a ferocious backlash. For example, the Shah of Iran's forced 'modernization' gave way to the Ayattolah's Islamic fundamentalist regime, which came to power initially through popular support.

Individual Rights vs Community Rights

The last few centuries have seen the growth of the notion of individual rights as separate from and often in opposition to the family and community, which are seen as institutions and forces that curb individual freedom and initiatives.

This has happened more in the West than elsewhere, though the ideology is catching on even in many non-western societies. Nevertheless, the uneasiness and sense of loss that many people have felt due to making individual freedom the single key indicator of modern civilization, have resulted in various counter reactions. These have ranged from a healthy assertion of the collective self-worth of a community by connecting and drawing from the deep civilizational core of the subjugated people, as was witnessed during the Mahatma Gandhi led freedom movement, to aggressive and violent retaliation by engineering an imagined history which legitimizes attempts to subordinate and submerge individual rights to authoritarian leaders who are supposedly the embodiment of the will of the community. Jinnah's politics is a good example of this. Some of these reactions have moved in the direction of making race, blood, religion or language the defining features of 'the community'. Such ideologies try to convince their people that unconditional acceptance of the authority and dictates of an overarching, glorified entity called the 'state' is the most effective strategy for winning respect and power in the world. This kind of social engineering, creating mainly fictional homogeneous ethnic blocks, have actually weakened the bonds within real communities based on family and kinship ties, shared culture and common neighbourhood.

Alternatively, there have been several successful examples of attempts to combine individual initiative and rights with a sense of belonging to and being embedded in some sort of a community. These attempts have, by and large, remained confined to relatively small groups. At the same time, the twentieth century witnessed the creation and growth of many state-run institutions that claim to protect individual human rights. In these states, especially in some social democratic western democracies, government agencies are viewed as the primary ally and protector of individual freedom and rights. While the development of such institutions and the welfare state offered a measure of protection to individuals against economic insecurity and certain abuses, it is now being increasingly acknowledged that these institutions also tend to weaken civil society and often resulted in people abdicating responsibility for the well-being of their fellow human beings—including those living in close proximity. Such atomized societies are often not conducive to emotional well-being because, among other things, even family ties become fragile and feeble, leaving people very insecure and lonely, even when their material needs are well protected.

The big challenge before us in India is to figure out ways to strengthen and reinvigorate civil society's own organizations, especially the family and kinship ties, in ways that ensure that individual rights remain inviolable, and that these institutions are also capable of protecting vulnerable individuals through communitarian efforts and vigilance. Our endeavour has to be to persuade people to respect the rights of others—not simply out of fear of being locked up in jail, but because they do not feel it is right to damage the interests of others. We must learn to make laws that are respected by people for their genuine capacity to protect the legitimate rights and claims of women. This is a deep civilizational quest, as is evident from the fact that almost all our popular Bollywood films grapple with this challenge, in however *filmi* and melodramatic a style. The future of democracy in India is in large part dependent on whether we can evolve a legal framework that creates egalitarian and workable rights for men and women in the family, rights that commands respect for their ability to maintain a healthy balance between allowing a good deal of autonomy to communities to manage their internal affairs and effective countervailing forces to restrain them from violating the fundamental rights of individuals within each community and in society at large.

Today, the biggest threat to women's lives and well-being comes from the utter lawlessness of government agencies. This is an important reason why the colonial-minded Indian State lacks the credibility to act as an effective instrument of social reform. Most government offices, including the police and the legal profession, function primarily as extortionists. Government functionaries patronise an army of touts and anti-social elements to assist them in their operations. This adds to the vulnerability of those families who do not have connections with power wielders in the government. Their rights can be violated with impunity because the police rarely come to the rescue of victims who cannot pull strings. The slow, inefficient and corrupt legal process consumes so much time, energy and money that mainly those with money power and clout come out winners. The colonial system of administration institutionalized by the British has grown progressively more tyrannical; its outreach as well as greed has grown manifold since Independence. Leave alone women, whose security is being daily jeopardised by the brutal mafias that have come to dominate political, economic and social life in every village, town and city, men also feel powerless before the combined might of *sarkari* and allied non-*sarkari* parasites. This is an important reason why people seek protection by clinging to their *jati* and *biradari* ties. Thanks to the trappings of electoral democracy, being part of a cohesive vote bank gives you a measure of leverage with the system. That is why, when people of poor communities have to lodge a police complaint, they go with a large contingent of their village or *biradari* elders and tend to seek the intervention of some kinsman or community member in a position of influence with the government to get the police to register a case.

This lawlessness of the state, more than any other factor, certainly far more than the hold of patriarchal norms, has tilted the scales of power against women as a group and in favour of anti-social elements among men. Status and power in post-British and post-Independence India is primarily determined not so much by your caste or the amount of land or property you may own, but by the amount of control you can exercise over various arms of the government machinery and how far you can make the institutions of government subservient to personal aggrandizement. Folk sayings that are still current such as '*jitne ladke utne latth, jitne latth utna kabza*' (the number of sons a family has determines its power to inflict violence, which is in direct proportion to the amount of land a family can hold) are an apt commentary on the actual source of power and prestige in large parts of India and in most sectors of the economy. In such a scenario, the birth of a daughter appears a burden and sons become valued assets. A widow without sons or other powerful male relatives to support her is the most endangered species, especially in rural India, not so much because of the stigma attached to widowhood but because whatever land or property she owns makes her an easy target of unscrupulous property grabbers. For example, it is very common for village land record keepers to surreptitiously transfer the land of single women or widows without grown-up sons to others for a consideration at the time of Land Settlement Operations. Agencies of the state are unable to provide redress against such wrongs. Therefore, most such cases get settled on the strength of brute power. Similarly, very few women dare start their own businesses, whether as street vendors or as manufacturers and entrepreneurs, because government officials who have the power create numerous hurdles and cause endless harassment unless they are placated through outrageous bribes or kept at bay through political patronage. Women, especially if they are from poorer backgrounds, are often forced to offer sexual bribes in addition to monetary bribes. Given this situation, producing sons appears a necessary survival strategy and daughters appear as liabilities.

The Way Forward: An Agenda for Action

Since the lawlessness of the government machinery is the prime reason for the increasing hold of crime and violence in our society, leading to the powerlessness and marginalization of women as a group, even while a tiny minority among women from elite families are able to scale unprecedented heights, reforming the machinery of governance ought to be the highest priority for society in general and for women in particular. Making the police an honest, accountable and non-partisan instrument of law enforcement ought to be the first step in this process. This should be accompanied by matching judicial reforms so that our law courts are capable of delivering speedy justice at affordable cost to the ordinary citizen.

Alongside putting such systems in place, we can start the process of figuring out how to enact laws that can be implemented with integrity. The following rules of thumb may provide a few reliable guidelines for assessing the worth of social reform measures.

To begin with, each reform measure should be divided into two components:

1. Role of opinion mobilizers and social movements.
2. Role of state interventions.

Responsibility of opinion mobilizers: Before a group or set of organizations demand a law to outlaw any prevalent custom or social practice, they ought to demonstrate the viability of the legal reform they propose. One way to show that they have prepared the ground for it is to try it out within their own community, neighbourhood or city. For example, those who insist that dowry giving be made a punishable crime might be required to submit at least 500 statements on oath by their own relatives, friends and neighbours that they would comply with the anti-dowry law, as well as laws against domestic violence in their own community, by reporting each violation to the police irrespective of whether the victim complains or not. Since this commitment would be made voluntarily, rather than through a legal mandate, social reformers would have to dialogue and discuss the matter with the concerned people in their own community to try to get them to sign such an oath in a public manner. In the process, each reformer will get firsthand feedback including suggestions for improvement in the proposed measure.

If our ideas of reform are first attempted in our own community and neighbourhood through moral persuasion, we will soon find out the strengths and weaknesses of those measures. If we avoid relying solely on legislative coercion or other forms of force and violence as a first step, we will be allowing people the freedom to reject those measures they consider unsuitable or inappropriate; our efforts at reform are then more likely to succeed and yield more practical laws because they would be attuned to people's own requirements.

Role of state interventions: The next step involving state intervention, including legislation, should also go through a similar test. If the government of the day is convinced that a particular law is worth enacting, it should try out its feasibility through yet another pilot project involving civil servants. Before, making it a law for the entire population, the government might introduce an Ordinance requiring all Class I Officers in the police, judiciary, various administrative services, as well as MPs, to sign statements on oath promising compliance. Anyone accused of violating that Ordinance should be suspended from service for a period of three months within which a full and final enquiry should be held into the violation of the law. If found guilty, the person would be dismissed from service. Once a proposed law has been tried and tested in this fashion, the government will have acquired the moral authority as well as the know-how to implement it at the state or national level. An additional, enduring effort should be to figure out strategies and the creation of new opportunities that would have the effect of enhancing the value of girls and women in the eyes of their families and communities.

Those who think these are impractical way of going about things overlook the fact that the existing manner of imposing legislation has failed miserably and calls for corrective measurers of a radical kind.

Madhu Purnima Kishwar

Part I
Battling Stereotypes

1

From *Manusmriti* to *Madhusmriti*

*Flagellating a Mythical Enemy**

On 25 March 2000, copies of *Manusmriti* were burnt by reformers protesting against the ill-conceived installation of the statue of Manu in the precincts of the Rajasthan High Court. The protestors believed that the text is the defining document of Brahmanical Hinduism, and also the key source of gender and caste oppression in India. In the ensuing controversy, defenders of *Manusmriti* projected it as a pivotal canonical source of religious law for Hindus.

In a somewhat similar fashion, Deepa Mehta's film *Water* revived an ongoing controversy about whether those who exploit and degrade women are following *shastric* injunctions. In the course of trying to explain why this debate amounts to a misunderstanding of the role of the *shastras* in Hindu

*This article appeared in *Manushi*, No. 117, March–April 2000.

religious life, I commented in a recent TV interview that *Manusmriti* (and other *shastric* texts) has as much or as little authority for Hindus as *Madhusmriti* (my writings)—or for that matter the pages of *Manushi*.

This perfectly serious statement was dismissed as 'facetious' by many feminists.[1] Others, claiming to speak on behalf of the Hindu culture, took my comment as an insult to the great *shastrakar* himself. These diverse responses indicate that there is a serious misconception among the modern educated elite about the actual status and role of the *shastras* in our religious life and cultural traditions.

The confusion is not theirs alone; these common misrepresentations are an unfortunate byproduct of our colonial education to which we slavishly cling, even though it has been more than five decades since we declared our Independence. We keep defending or attacking the same hackneyed quotations from the *shastras* and the epics which, incidentally, colonizers used for the purpose of creating a new discourse about these writings. Their inaccurate and biased interpretations have continued to inspire major misreadings of our religious tenets.[2]

The Search for Non-existent 'Hindu Fundamentals'

The Englishmen who came as traders in the seventeenth century were befuddled at the vast diversity and complexity of the Indian society. Having come from a culture where many aspects of family and community affairs came under the jurisdiction of canonical law, they looked for similar sources of authority in India. They assumed, for example, that just as European marriage laws were based in part on systematic constructions derived from church interpretations of Biblical tenets, so must the personal laws of various Indian communities similarly draw their legitimacy from some priestly interpretations of fundamental religious texts.

In the late eighteenth century, the British began to study the ancient *shastras* to develop a set of legal principles that would assist them in adjudicating disputes within Indian civil society. In fact, they found there was no single

[1] See, for example, *Images of Widowhood* in the *Hindustan Times* of 19 February 2000 by Urvashi Butalia and Uma Chakravarti.

[2] For a more detailed analysis see Dr P.V. Kane, *History of Dharmasastra*; Duncan Derret, *Religion, Law and State in India*. The Free Press, New York, 1968. Also see 'Codified Hindu Law: Myth and Reality' by Madhu Kishwar, *Economic and Political Weekly*, Vol. XXIX, No. 33, August 13, 1994.

body of canonical law, no Hindu Pope to legitimize a uniform legal code for all the diverse communities of India, no Shankaracharya whose writ reigned all over the country. Even religious interpretations of popular epics like the *Ramayana* failed to fit the bill because every community and every age exercised the freedom to recite and write its own version. We have inherited hundreds of recognized and respected versions of this text, and many are still being created. The flourishing of such variation and diversity, however, did not prevent the British from searching for a definitive canon of Hindu law.

Perhaps more egregiously, in their search, the British took no steps to understand local or *jati*-based customary law or the way in which every community—no matter how wealthy or poor—regulated its own internal affairs through *jati* or *biradari* panchayats, without seeking permission or validation from any higher authority. The power to introduce a new custom, or change existing practices, rested in large part within each community. Any individual or group respected within that *biradari* could initiate reforms. This tradition of self-governance is what accounts for the vast diversity of cultural practices within the subcontinent. For example, some communities observe strict *purdah* for women, whereas others have inherited matrilineal family structures in which women exercise a great deal of freedom and social clout. Some disapprove of widow remarriage, while others attach no stigma to widowhood and allow women recourse to easy divorce and remarriage.

The multiplicity of codes was a major reason for the wide divergence in judgements, interpretations and reports provided by the pundits appointed to assist British judges presiding over the newly established colonial courts. Often, the same pundits even gave different opinions on seemingly similar matters, confounding the judges of the East India Company. The British began to mistrust the pundits and became impatient with having to deal with such a range of customs that had no apparent *shastric* authority to back them, since that made it difficult for them to pose as genuine adjudicators of Hindu law. The British were even more nonplussed because they had a history of using the common law system based on precedent. However, given the myriad opinions of the Indian pundits, they could not depend on uniform precedents to make their own judgements.

An Anglo-brahamanical Hybrid

In order to arrive at a definitive version of the Indian legal system that would mainly be useful for them, the East India Company began to recruit and train pundits for its own service. In 1772, Warren Hastings hired a group of 11 pundits to cooperate with the Company in the creation of a new digest of

Hindu law that would govern civil disputes in the British courts. The Sanskrit pundits hired to translate and sanction this new interpretation of customary laws created a curious Anglo-brahmanical hybrid. The resulting document, printed in London under the title *A Code of Gentoo Laws, or, Ordinations of the Pandits*, was a made-to-order text, in which the pundits dutifully followed the demands made by their paymasters. Though it was the first serious attempt at codification of Hindu law, the text was far from accurate in its references to the original sources, or to their varied traditional interpretations.

The very idea of 'Hindu' law, in fact, was as much a novelty as the idea of a pan-Indian Hindu community. In the pre-British era, people of this subcontinent used a whole range of markers based on region, *jati*, language and sect to claim and define their identities. Hardly anybody identified themselves as 'Hindu'—a term first introduced by foreigners to refer to people living across the Indus River. The British lent new zeal in bringing actual substance to the new identity markers imposed by Europeans on the diverse non-Muslim inhabitants of the subcontinent. The codification of their so-called 'personal laws' became an important instrument in that endeavour.

Maha Pundit William Jones

This codification still could not put an end to the conflicts of opinion. The British mistrust of the pundits increased, along with their frustration at the way they thought they were misleading the court, primarily by favouring the interests of their own caste, and dealing with a spectrum of customs that were not certified by any apparent *shastric* source.

The resulting confusions and reports of corruption led William Jones, the then judge of the Supreme Court of judicature at Calcutta, to work on a more 'definitive' code of Hindu law as a reference work for Europeans in India. Jones's statement says it all: 'I can no longer bear to be at the mercy of our pandits who deal out Hindu law as they please, and make it at reasonable rates, when they cannot find it ready made' (Derret 1968, p. 244).

He was determined that the British should administer to the Indian people the best *shastric* law that could be discovered. Jones went on to translate *Manusmriti*. It became one of the most favoured texts of the British. A policy decision was taken at the highest levels in the India Office to keep this particular document in circulation and project it as the fountainhead of Hindu jurisprudence for the purpose of perpetuating the illusion that the British were merely enforcing the *shastric* injunctions by which Hindus were governed anyway, and that they had inherited the authority to administer this law.

Thus *Manusmriti* came to influence Oriental studies in the West far more profoundly than it had ever influenced the practices of any actual living communities in pre-British India. After Jones, Colebrook tried his hand at a similar compilation. In a few years time, Colebrook's translations of the *Mitakshara* and the *Dayabhaga* became the two most frequently referenced sources in court judgements. At the same time, several Sanskrit scholars were also writing legal treatises, but the work of European authors on *shastric* law was held in higher authority than even the genuine Sanskrit *shastric* works.

The British consistently promoted the myth that Hindus were governed by their codified versions of *shastric* injunctions. The modern educated elite in India, whose knowledge of India came mainly from English language sources, were thenceforth systematically brainwashed into believing that the British were actually administering Hindu personal laws through the medium of the English courts. This was part of a larger myth-building exercise whereby the people of the subcontinent were taught that theirs was a stagnant civilization. The ignorant assumptions of our colonial rulers that social stability in India was due to the supposed proclivity of its people to follow the same old traditions, customs and laws that had allegedly remained moribund for centuries, slowly came to acquire the force of self-evident truth over a period of time, both for those supporting as well as those opposing British rule.

Custom vs Anglo-*shastric* Law

Since then, the dynamism of customary law has been in constant conflict with the frozen and artificial Anglo-*shastric* law. *Dharmashastras*, for instance, were not strictly religious treatises. *Dharma* itself means the aggregate of duties and obligations—religious, moral, social and legal—delineated for every individual and collective performing a specific role in society. For example, the obligations and duties of a person in his role as a king (*raj-dharma*) are different from his obligations as a husband or son (*pati-dharma* or *putra-dharma*). Similarly, *guru-dharma* demands specific responsibilities from a teacher, just as *shishya-dharma* binds students to their own set of obligations. Even war demanded a very rigorous code, *yuddha-dharma*. The list is endless and refers mostly to secular duties.

Similarly, the *smritis* are collections of precepts written by the *rishis*, the sages of antiquity. *Smritis* are presumed to be the compositions of human authors, not gods; these authors make it clear that they are merely anthologizing traditions handed down to them over generations. They did not hesitate to propose changes and reforms in their writings. For instance, Apastamba, whose work embodies the customs of certain regions of southern India, and who authored one of the most respected *Sutras*, takes care, at the end of his work, to impress upon his pupils the idea that: 'Some declare that the remaining duties (which have not been taught here) must be learnt from women and men of all castes'. He adds, 'the knowledge which...women possess is the completion of all study' (Mulla, 1986, p. 15).

Neither *shastras* nor *smritis* suggest that there exists an immutable, universal moral doctrine. Rather, they emphasize that codes of morality must be specific to time, person and place, and evolve according to changing requirements. For example, Narada states, 'Custom is powerful and overrides the sacred law.' *Manusmriti* itself stresses that the business of the ruler is not to impose laws from above but that:

> A king...must inquire into the law of castes (*jati*), of districts (*Ganapada*), of guilds (*Shreni*), and of families (*kula*), and settle the peculiar law of each. Thus have the holy sages, well knowing that law is grounded on immemorial custom, embraced as the root of all piety good usages long established (Mulla 1986, p. 23).

The authority to change or create new customs rests with not just the *biradari* but also the *kula* or family. Our *smritikars* repeatedly stress the primacy of custom and practice over textual axioms.

People as Law Makers

Since different *smritikars* documented the customs of different communities, there were substantial differences in their approaches, perspectives and precepts. But characteristically, none of the *smritikars* denied the authority of other *smritikars* or attempted to prove that theirs was the supreme, most authoritative version of a code of conduct. They acknowledged that the authority of the king and the law was derived from the people. Most of the leading *smritikars* made explicit statements to this effect. The *smriti* of Yajnavalkya, for instance, lists 20 sages as law givers. The *Mitakshara* explains that the enumeration is only illustrative and *Dharmasutras* of others are not excluded. Nor is the authority of any *shastrakar* assigned hierarchical importance.

The *smritikars* were not rulers. Nor did they owe their authority to any sovereign political or military power. The authority of the codes they enjoined was not enforced by punitive measures. Their influence depended solely on the voluntary internalization of such value systems by the groups they addressed themselves to, and people's respect for their judgement. Actual enforcement was left in the hands of the local communities. An oft-repeated maxim was that reason and justice are to be accorded more regard than mere texts. Most important of all, a *dharmic* code, in the *rishis*' view, was one that was 'agreeable to good conscience'.

Gandhi is one of the few modern social reformers to have understood this principle underlying the *shastras*. Therefore, he could unhesitatingly declare: 'My belief in the Hindu scriptures does not require me to accept every word and every verse as divinely inspired.... I decline to be bound by any interpretation, however learned it may be, if it is repugnant to reason or moral sense' (Gandhi, Vol. XXI, p. 246). He goes on to add:

1. I believe in varnashrama of the Vedas which in my opinion is based on absolute equality of status, notwithstanding passages to the contrary in the *smritis* and elsewhere.
2. Every word of the printed works passing muster as 'shastras' is not, in my opinion, a revelation.
3. The interpretation of accepted texts has undergone evolution and is capable of indefinite evolution, even as the human intellect and heart are.
4. Nothing in the shastras which is manifestly contrary to universal truths and morals can stand.
5. Nothing in the shastras which is capable of being reasoned can stand if it is in conflict with reason (Gandhi, Vol. LX11, p. 121).

Gandhi could present himself as a modern-day sage, calling upon people to overthrow beliefs and practices that did not conform to principles of equality and justice–or went against 'good conscience'–because he had inherited a tradition whereby the power to change its own customary law rested with each community.

People in India have demonstrated time and again that they are willing to accept changes in their customs, provided those who propose change take the trouble to win the confidence of the community, rather than attack or humiliate the community as hostile outsiders. The success of the nineteenth century social reformers is testimony to this inherent flexibility of Hindu com-munities. In recent decades, the Radhasoamis and Satnamis in northern India and many other reform movements have carried forward the same tradition.

Practice of Self-governance

Thus, the practice of self-governance continues to be a dynamic tradition in India. Each caste, sub-caste and occupational grouping continues to assert its right to regulate the internal affairs of its own community and does not pay much attention to either ancient textual authorities or to modern Parliament-enacted laws. When an individual or a group in India seeks to defend a particular practice, the common statement one hears across the country is '*Hamari biradari mein to yeh hi chalta hai*' (This is how we do things in our community), rather than quotations from the *shastras*.

Those who insist on attributing our social ills to the *shastras* repeat the mistake of our colonial rulers. Just as a doctor can kill a patient through incorrect diagnosis and treatment—no matter how benign the intention—in the same manner, social reformers can wreak havoc on the people if their understanding of social ills is flawed.

Discrimination against women or Dalits is neither inherently 'Hindu' nor is it scripturally mandated. This is not to suggest that such practices do not exist. Sadly enough, the disgraceful treatment of Dalits and vulnerable rights of women are among the most shameful aspects of contemporary Indian society. But they will not disappear by burning ancient texts because none of the 'Hindu' scriptures have projected themselves as commandment-giving authorities, demanding unconditional obedience from all those claiming to be Hindus.

For example, oppressive widowhood was and is practised only in certain castes and communities in some regions among the Hindus. According to the 1901 Census, the ban on widow remarriage applied to only 10 per cent of all the communities in India. And yet, in colonial critiques, this ban came to be projected as the universal situation of all widows in India.

If we look closely, we will find that many of the older widows have ended up in exploitative institutions of Varanasi and Vrindavan not because of Manu's commands, or any other religious stipulations, or even the dictates of some contemporary patriarch. They are there primarily because of the failure of their community to provide secure rights for women in the family and many are there even because of ill-treatment by their daughters-in-law. It is also important to remember that of all the millions of widows, only a few thousand end up in places like Vrindavan and Varanasi. True, many may live oppressed lives within their own homes. But it is also true that many others live respected lives as honoured matriarchs. If all Indian women are so subordinate, as suggested by a certain kind of feminist literature, we would not so frequently encounter the phenomenon of the dominating mothers-in-law who, in many homes, have the power to make or break their sons' marriages. Nor would we witness innumerable older women putting up with humiliation and neglect because their daughters-in-law have come to acquire such a powerful hold over their husbands that they can make them abuse their own mothers. Those who find this description of the situation far-fetched should do a survey of their own families. They are likely to find both these extremes co-existing within their own family circles, along with instances of fairly balanced and reasonably happy equations.

We are free to rid ourselves of any text that debases women or certain castes. Let us not imagine that Manu or any other *shastrakar* is obstructing our efforts to improve the lot of women or other oppressed groups. Despite some of the very negative and offensive things he might have said from our point of view (which many scholars hold to be later day interpolations), Manu did have the wisdom to pronounce that good *karma* was more important than biological lineage. He also emphasized that families and societies which demean women and make them lead miserable lives inevitably move towards destruction. He noted that truly prosperous families are only those in which women are honoured and happy.

I believe that Manu would fully endorse my writing a *Madhusmriti*, no matter how much I differ with him. He would probably rejoice in the fact that many people of today prefer *Madhusmriti* to *Manusmriti* because Manu, like all other *smritikars*, emphasized that codes of morality are not fixed by some divine authority, but must evolve with respect to the changing requirements of generations and communities.

References

Derret, J. Duncan M. 1968. *Religion, Law and State in India*. New York: The Free Press.

Gandhi, M.K. *The Collected Works of Mahatma Gandhi*, Vol. XXI.

——. *The Collected Works of Mahatma Gandhi*, Vol. LXII.

Mulla, D. 1986. *Principles of Hindu Laws*, 15th ed. Bombay: N.M. Tripathi Pvt.

2

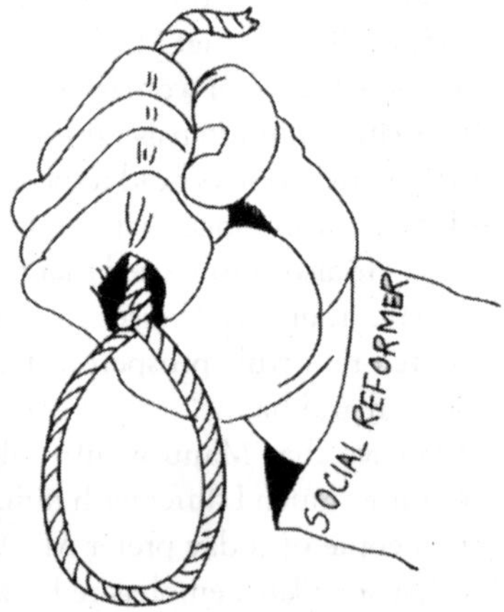

Zealous Reformers, Deadly Laws

The Conflicting Interpretations and Politics of Sati*

Quotable Quotes on Charan Shah's Immolation

- 'Nothing short of a national shame. It is embarrassing in the extreme that the native religiosity of rural people continues to be exploited by the heartless custodians of the orthodoxy.... Sati is illegal. It is dangerous in a secular democracy to allow religious obscurantism to keep the law of the land in suspend animation. The law must apply to all those who aided and abetted this tragic development. Any laxity in this regard on the part of the State amounts to a gross dereliction of duty' (Swami Agnivesh in *The Times of India*, 21 November 1999).

---

*This article appeared in *Manushi*, No. 115, November–December 1999.

- 'Medieval Madness: An act of desperation by a distraught widow in the backward Bundelkhand regon becomes a cause for a grand religious celebration by the people' (*India Today*, 29 November 1999).
- 'The police chief of Mahoba ... said the woman had jumped onto the pyre in a fit of madness' (*The Times of India*, 11 November 1999).
- 'Above all, Charan Shah's self-immolation shows how entrenched medieval social practices are in India and how superficial is penetration of modernity in vast social sector' (*The Statesman*, Calcutta).
- 'While illiterate women will be led to such actions by their beliefs, the authorities have their own duties to perform. If any action is illegal, the prime duty of the police and the administration is to prevent it if possible, or at least to take punitive action against the perpetrators of the crime or those in the family who did nothing to prevent it' (*The Sentinel*, Guwahati).

In large parts of the world, people are busy making preparations to celebrate the end of the second millennium and the beginning of the third. This millennium has not been a particularly happy one for India. Throughout the past thousand years, this subcontinent witnessed a series of invasions with certain regions experiencing repeated plunder and political subjugation by the rule of conquerors. In some instances, however, instead of returning to their homelands after collecting enough loot, the invaders settled down in India giving impetus to a new cultural mix and thereby creating a need for building bridges of communication between the conflicting groups. But nothing disrupted and damaged this country as much as British colonization, which lasted nearly two centuries.

Unlike earlier conquerors, the British did not just stop at pillage and appropriation of wealth. They attempted to destroy almost all indigenous institutions, knowledge, notion of ethics and, most importantly, the sense of self-worth among the people of South Asia. The modern education system they imposed on us created an elite trained to look at its own society through colonial eyes, and to treat its own people as colonial subjects–especially if they happened to be poor and uneducated.

Our erstwhile colonial rulers, who needed the pretence of being on a civilizing mission here to justify their brutal reign, had a vested interest in identifying select criminal acts and projecting them as Indian traditions in need of reform. They began this cultural invasion by deliberately targeting a few cases of young widows in Bengal who were forcibly burnt on their husband's pyres, calling those murders *sati* and banning it by law, so they could appear as agents of a superior civilization rescuing victims from a savage culture. They even called their mission the 'white man's burden'! Thereafter, the supposedly miserable plight of a newly invented creature called the Indian woman became emblematic of the inferior civilization and culture of the Indian people.

There is absolutely no evidence that any of our vast array of religious texts sanctified such murders as *sati*. The word '*sati*' derives from the word '*sat*' which means 'truth'. So *sati* means a woman who is true—not a woman who spontaneously combusts. In this context, it is noteworthy that none of the mythological heroines revered as *mahasatis*—Sati (Shiva's wife), Draupadi, Mandodari, Tara, Ahalya and Sita—burned on their husband's pyre. Though some references to women committing voluntary self-immolation along with their dead husbands can be found in the *Mahabharata* and *Puranas*, the practice never received much sanctity or popularity. It is only in nineteenth century British discourse that forced immolation of women on the husband's pyre came to be regarded as *sati*.

It is understandable that the British should resort to such distortion and defamation as part of the imperial game of convincing Indians that they were 'uncivilized' and hence unfit for self-governance. When reformers in post-Independence India operate with the same colonial mindset while dealing with the customs of their own people, it only goes to prove that the brown sahibs of India have learnt to treat the people of this country with the same contempt as did our colonial masters.

The recent debate on *sati*, following Charan Shah's self-immolation on 11 November 1999 in Satpura village, located in Uttar Pradesh's Mahoba district, illustrates this attitude very well.

Misinformed Verdict

Without as much as conducting a preliminary investigation into the circumstances under which the immolation took place, several activists passed a verdict solely on the basis of some sensational and misleading media reports that Charan Shah's in-laws and other relatives were guilty of abetting her suicide.[1] They, along with some powerful voices in the media, demanded that the family along with other villagers should be arrested and charged under the

[1] Investigative reports by women's organizations came several days later. All India Democratic Women's Association (AIDWA) released its reports on 16 November 1999, followed by another one by National Commission for Women. Since AIDWA's findings went contrary to the demand for stringent action by several women activists, yet another multi-organization team went and made its own enquiry. Two of these reports were published in *Manushi*, No. 115, 1999. As is evident, there are substantial differences in their 'factual narration' as also in their interpretation of events.

Sati Prevention Act. This was even before they checked to find out if her in-laws were indeed alive and/or living in that village. As it turned out, Charan Shah lived with her grown-up son and was surrounded by her own natal family at the time of her husband's death. Some had decided in advance that there must have been a property angle to it, without finding out whether this poor Dalit family had any land worth its name.

Among others, Charan Shah's own sister, brother and son have repeatedly stated that they had no idea she was contemplating such an act. She quietly walked out of the house and rushed to the burning pyre, while other women attended to post-cremation ceremonies and the men had left for the ritual bath. By the time people realized what had happened, Charan Shah was already in flames. Despite such repeated clarifications, some zealots are still insisting that the draconian provisions of the Sati Prevention Act must be invoked against the people of Satpura. Thanks to this concerted pressure, the police felt compelled to save their skin by arresting Charan Shah's son and maternal uncle. These two were kept in police custody for two days and pressured into stating that Charan Shah was mentally deranged.

One section of reformers is also demanding that all those who witnessed the event ought to be arrested and punished. In addition, they demand action against all those who interpret her immolation as a case of *sati*, under the Sati Prevention Act. It is shocking that several responsible and respected people and even some human rights organizations should respond in such a high-handed manner to the death of 55-year-old Charan Shah.

Forced into Stereotypes

No one actually knows whether Charan Shah killed herself on the spur of the moment, or if it was a premeditated act. One thing is certain: there was no ceremony, no ritual preparation, no ideological statement made before she flung herself on the pyre. Yet, it is assumed that Charan Shah acted out of an obscurantist belief that her life as a widow was useless and that she would gain religious merit by following her husband in death.

Why is she considered incapable of other motives or sentiments? Could she not have acted out of love? After all, by all accounts, she nursed her husband, a tuberculosis patient, for 30 long years with total dedication. Maybe, they had a tender loving relationship. Some villagers were reported to have remarked: 'She has been a *sati* for thirty years. This was only the culminating act.' Or may be she became so worn out from her life of poverty that she thought there would be no purpose in living on any further. Could it be that she killed herself in a mood of quiet rage and protest because her son reportedly turned down her request for carrying Man Shah's dead body in a decorated *doli*, and cremating him with ceremonial *band-baaja*? Could it be that Charan Shah felt hurt at this refusal and burnt herself on her husband's pyre, as though to say, 'I save you the expense of my funeral as well?'

I am not suggesting that my speculations are correct. This is only to point out that no one really knows what transpired in Charan Shah's mind, what motivated her to take her own life in such a dramatic way. Yet, the social reformers both in the media and in some non-governmental organizations (NGOs) have chosen to dub her act 'medieval madness', a symptom of her cultural backwardness. Why? Because she was a poor, illiterate, rural Indian woman who is only permitted to live up to the stereotypes the so-called culturally advanced people have of her.

An Attack on the Defenceless

There is something macabre about the fact that the torchbearers of modern civilization who wish to cure Satpura villagers of their 'cultural backwardness', 'superstitious beliefs' and 'obscurantism' are paying little attention to the fact that people of this region live in abject poverty. Situated in a chronically drought-afflicted, neglected region of Uttar Pradesh, this particular village is located 7–8 km from the main road, accessible only through a dirt track. Satpura lacks even a primary health centre. One located in a nearby village exists only in name and does not provide even minimal services, as is the case with most primary health centres in villages of north India.

Charan Shah's own family has a small plot of unirrigated land, which does not provide year-round subsistence for them. Therefore, they work as labourers on other people's fields as well. Even land-owning families in this drought-stricken region are pathetically poor. Thus, wage rates are also abysmally low. The family is so poor that they could not afford medical treatment for either Charan Shah's tuberculosis-infected husband or her elder son, who died earlier from the same disease. That people are succumbing in the prime of their lives to a curable disease like TB speaks volumes about the failure of our healthcare system.

What is the wonderful gesture of concern our reformers have to offer to all these people living such impoverished lives? Vigorous demands that the police should be sent to arrest them and criminal cases should be instituted for 'murdering' Charan Shah, or at least 'abetting' her suicide, since they did not or could not prevent her death. Thus, they are to be taught their mandatory lessons in modern cultural values through the agency of our notoriously corrupt and tyrannical police.

Despite the fact that no one has been able to provide any evidence of coercion in this case, Charan Shah's family and community are still considered liable for action because they effectively did nothing to prevent her from killing herself. The facts, as given in several reports, suggest otherwise. A shepherd boy did raise an alarm as soon he saw her moving towards the pyre. Women did come running after her as soon as they realized she had left for the cremation ground. Men who had left to bathe also rushed to the scene upon hearing this. But they all say she was already burning by then. At this point they are held guilty for failing to pull her out of the fire. I find this expectation unreasonable. First, pulling someone out of a raging pyre amounts to running the risk of getting burnt yourself—the kind of courage even those recommending such action for Satpura villagers are not likely to have.

More important, who in their sane mind would want to pull out a half-burnt person in a village which lacks treatment facilities even for ordinary diseases, leave alone for life-threatening injuries? If this family could not access TB treatment, could they possibly handle a case of severe burns without proper medical help? Charan Shah would have died a far more painful and slower death. In the process of saving her, people could have endangered their own lives as well.

Conflicting Versions

Much is being made of the supposedly conflicting versions coming from villagers now. In the article 'Countering Earlier Reports: Charan Shah's Immolation', the versions of some neighbouring villagers in Imaliya are counterpoised against those of Satpura's inhabitants to build a case that the latter's story cannot be trusted even with regard to the timing of Man Shah's death. By turning the village into a police camp and starting an aggressive campaign against a whole community through the national and international press to label them as criminals, are we not creating conditions for them to protect themselves by doctoring their story according to police requirements? However, even in these circumstances, the Satpura villagers have, by and large, given one consistent story. Narratives of nearby villagers are bound to vary with ones from Satpura because those people are likely to depend on hearsay rather than firsthand eyewitness accounts. Charan Shah's son's plea says it all: 'I will call it whatever you want me to. If you want to call it a suicide then so be it. Equally, if you say it was a *sati*, then I will follow suit.'

In this context, it is noteworthy that Satpura does not seem to have a very repressive code for widows. Several reports have told us that when Charan Shah's eldest son died, his widow was remarried to the younger brother, with whom she has raised a family. If a young widow in that family was not treated as an inauspicious pariah or forced to immolate herself, it is far-fetched to believe that Charan Shah's sons would have pushed their 55-year-old mother to commit such an extreme act—especially when she was an earner, an authority figure and an effective head of the family, rather than a hapless dependent.

Moreover, as the All India Democratic Women's Association (AIDWA) report points out, members of this family are followers of a progressive sect, the Charan Data Panth. Charan Shah's son let it be known in all the interviews that among their community, they did not encourage practices such as *sati*. Had the family any intention of building a *sati* cult and temple around her, they would not have chosen the common cremation ground of the village for the last rites because according to traditional beliefs a temple cannot be built on such a site. They would have chosen a special spot as happened in Roop Kanwar's case. But once Charan Shah committed the act, it was not within their control to stop others from treating it with awe and reverence. Dramatic acts of self-sacrifice in any society evoke such sentiments.

Even after it was grudgingly acknowledged after more careful investigations that Charan Shah was not impelled to burn at her husband's pyre, many social justice advocates are convinced that the Sati Prevention Act must be invoked against the people of Mahoba, the UP district where Satpura village is located. They are upset at 'the local people who refuse to regard the incident as a crime'. Their reasoning: irrespective of whether she died voluntarily or whether she was pressured into the act, the very fact of her deification by villagers, and evidence indicating the existence of a whole *sati* cult centring around her, consolidates and propagates injurious traditions against women. The reformers insist that anyone from a neighbouring village who comes to pay respects at Charan Shah's cremation site should also be arrested and tried for the crime of glorifying *sati*.

Commercializing *Sati*

An additional concern voiced by our reformers is that the villagers of Satpura have started propagating a mystique about Charan Shah 'in order to translate the alleged *sati* into a money-spinning enterprise'. It has also been said that villagers are keen on converting that immolation site into a pilgrimage spot, since they expect many visitors after the interest generated by the event. This in turn may lead to some increased income for the community.

First, most of this is in the realm of speculation. Both the National Commission for Women and AIDWA reports have emphasized that media reports about 'devotees' thronging to the cremation site are highly exaggerated and irresponsible. Pressmen took photographs of a couple of family members of Charan Shah performing the usual post funeral rituals to build a case that they were promoting a *sati* cult.

Even if it were true that by romanticizing the death of one Charan Shah, this horribly neglected and poverty stricken village hopes to receive a little cash flow, I find it a more understandable venture than other more modern and socially approved forms of commercialization. Today, thanks to generous grants available from international aid organizations, a whole slew of educated, 'enlightened' people are making a living from writing about atrocities on Indian women, organizing seminars on the theme and filming the subject. There will not be any dearth of people likely to want to make documentaries on the Satpura *sati*; any number of research grants will be proposed to discuss the misery and cultural backwardness of this region where a few *sati* temples already exist. Myriad careers will be enhanced as people suddenly become experts on the culture of *sati*. Even those who would never subject themselves to the inconvenience of making a trip to Satpura village and spending a couple of days there, will organize glamorous conferences in foreign universities, write glamorous treatises on the subject, and construct and deconstruct Charan Shah's life until it becomes unrecognizable to even her own children. These will be important additions to various resumes, but there is not a faint chance that even one rupee from all the thousands of dollars or lakhs of rupees thus earned would reach those miserable creatures whose lives we castigate and pontificate upon.

What if Satpura villagers were to demand the enactment of a law which stipulates that anyone making money by writing about or filming a *sati* case should be declared a criminal? How about laying down a law which states that getting hefty grants to produce 'research' for foreign universities and international aid agencies will invite life imprisonment? Or those making films on the real or imagined miseries of Indian women will be subjected to punitive fines if they make any money from it?

Today, these activities documenting the event fetch far more money, name and fame than running a *sati* temple in India. Those who disapprove of commercializing Roop Kanwar or Charan Shah's *sati* cults by people of their respective communities, ought to be willing to have similar curbs put on the commercialization of social concern, whereby a whole tribe of people have made hi-fi, jet-set careers out of peddling the poverty and misery of Indian women in the international arena—of making a lucrative profession of defaming and condemning people with whom they have no relationship. More often than not, these commentators do not even embrace the ethical responsibility which calls for accuracy in their facts and credibility in their interpretations. Information is disseminated to the world on BBC, CNN and ABC—not to those people whose lives are to be critiqued and presumably reformed. If a money-making scheme in the name of various Charan Shahs and Roop Kanwars is a condemnable practice when done by their own communities, how does it become a respectable moral intervention when taken up by total strangers?

Need to Repeal Anti-*sati* Law

The Sati Prevention Act of 1987 was added to the statute book under pressure from women's organizations and other progressive activists, following Roop Kanwar's *sati* in Deorala village. Even at that time, *Manushi* had protested against this ill-conceived and draconian piece of legislation (see *Manushi* Issue No. 42–43). Unfortunately our voice went unheeded by obsessed reformers who campaigned for a stringent law to deal with *sati*. Recently, when the debate was revived following Charan Shah's immolation, we were surprised to find that not many people who vigorously demand its implementation are aware of its actual provisions, which are not only draconian but also just plain stupid.

To begin with, the Act states that if any person commits *sati*, all those accused of abetting *sati*, directly or indirectly, 'shall be punishable with death, or imprisonment for life and shall also be liable to a fine'. Those accused of abetting any *attempt* to commit *sati* 'shall be punishable with imprisonment for life and also be liable to fine'. A woman accused of attempting *sati* is also liable to a prison term of up to six months plus a fine, the same as for attempted suicide.

How does the Act define 'abetment'? Apart from inducing or encouraging a widow 'directly or indirectly' to commit *sati*, abetment includes 'being present at the place where sati is committed as an active participant to such commission or to any ceremony connected with it'. In addition, whoever performs any act for the 'glorification' of *sati* is also punishable with a fine and jail term not less than one year, but extendable to seven years.

Most important of all, when the state accuses any person of 'abetting' *sati*, the burden of proving that he/she has not committed the offence shall be on the accused. That is, you are assumed guilty until you can prove, to the court's satisfaction, that you are innocent.

What would this mean in actual practice? That the police can arrest, as it did in Deorala, any number of people in an area where a woman, either voluntarily or through family pressure, ends up immolating herself. They can all be accused of 'abetting' *sati* by having witnessed the act. Those accused will have to corroborate they were nowhere at the scene of crime. It is not enough for them to establish that they did not encourage the woman to die along with her husband. The accused have to convince the authorities that they tried to actively prevent her from committing suicide in order to certify innocence.

Here, it is necessary to point out that no such onus falls on those who may perchance witness a murder. They are not expected to offer proof of their innocence by demonstrating they tried to save the murdered person. Thus, the anti-*sati* law is very similar to anti-terrorist laws like the Terrorism and Disruptive Activities (Prevention) Act (TADA), where the burden of proof also rests with the accused. It is noteworthy that numerous civil liberties groups all over the country worked hard to have TADA repealed, dubbing it a 'black act' because its draconian provisions allow for gross misuse. Many innocents have been implicated under TADA, and consequently are kept rotting in jail without trial. If a person is falsely charged by the police, it is as difficult for him/her to prove that he/she did not 'actively' assist in disruptive or terrorist activities, as it is to prove that he/she was not present at an immolation site or that he/she did not 'actively participate' in the event. Granting the state agencies the right to execute any number of people who are accused of 'witnessing' one woman's immolation and thereby being declared guilty of abetting *sati* can by no stretch of imagination be called an exercise in dispensing justice, or an exemplary instance of judicious law making.

It is absurd to have a law which threatens to punish people with a death sentence, if they admit to having witnessed the voluntary or coerced immolation of a woman, because their presence at the site makes them guilty of having participated in *sati*. Would anyone in their right mind want to give evidence in court in such a case? Does the law not force people into lying out of sheer self-defence? Is a death sentence the appropriate response to such an event?

Given the ways of our police, it can well be imagined how opportunities for abuse are built into the anti-*sati* law, which gives the authorities arbitrary powers to arrest and implicate anyone they choose to target?

This is exactly what happened in Deorala. Is it any surprise, then, that all the witnesses turned 'hostile', that is, denied having any knowledge of circumstances under which Roop Kanwar died? Consequently, all of the accused were acquitted by the lower courts and even today we do not know whether Roop Kanwar killed herself voluntarily, or if she was forced into the act. For a change, the police have not shown much interest in arresting all and sundry in the Charan Shah matter, as they did previously in Deorala. One reason could be that there are some exceptionally decent officials overseeing this case. But a more likely (or at least additional) reason could be that seeing the community's abject poverty, they do not see any possibility of being able to extort money by arresting and harassing the villagers of Satpura and neighbouring regions. Deorala, by contrast, has many well-off families because a large number of men from the village are in government jobs, notably the police.

Yet leading civil rights activists and other reformers want to see such a vicious law invoked on the villagers of Satpura. It is worth noting that these organizations have earlier valiantly fought for the democratic rights of even known terrorists because their treatment under TADA violated the whole idea of due process and fair trial. But when it comes to poor illiterate villagers of India, our fervour for social engineering makes us overlook the illegal and undemocratic nature of the enactments meant for the apparent reform of those we have unilaterally and presumptuously dubbed 'backward'.

All those who have campaigned for the right to a fair trial of those accused of terrorism have not cared to raise similar objections against the inherently abusive provisions of the Sati Prevention Act. The fear of being 'politically incorrect' has silenced the most courageous human rights campaigners, allowing extremely punitive provisions to receive enshrinement as pro-women laws in our statute books.

Only Approved Modes of Worship Allowed!

It has been a long-standing demand of feminist reformers that ancient *sati* temples must be declared illegal and shut down because they glorify the *sati* cult, thus beckoning women to follow suit.

First, for all the so-called glorification of *sati* in certain regions, we have not witnessed anything resembling a *sati* epidemic. For all the *sati* temples in Rajasthan, not many women offer themselves for immolation, including those who might bow in reverence before a *sati* shrine. After Roop Kanwar's immolation in 1987, there have been no more than three cases of attempted self-immolations by widows in India. Each of these was easily averted by timely intervention. Even before the anti-*sati* act was passed, a very small number of women killed themselves on their husband's pyres within the last several decades.

Trying to close *sati* temples by force has the potential of setting into motion a very dangerous dynamic. Taking an authoritarian route to social reform is mostly counterproductive. Today, one group demands the closure of *sati* temples because they violate the values of one community. Tomorrow, another group might demand the closure of all Kali temples because they might see her worship as idealizing vengeful aspects of femininity. Some others might want Krishna temples declared illegal because he was a known philanderer and polygamist. Still others might want Ram temples banned because he subjected his wife to a cruel *agnipariksha*. Then there will be some group of 'rationalists' who might want all churches closed down because Jesus Christ claimed to be the son of God without offering any 'scientific' evidence for the same. There is indeed no end to this game of any self-declared group of social reformers seeking to discipline others into 'approved' behaviour and making them worship only certain 'approved' deities.

One of the great strengths of our civilization is that people are free to choose their own deities (*devis* and *devatas*), and their own modes of worship. New icons are constantly invented without need for sanction from any hierarchical authority. Each village has its own preferred pantheon of gods and goddesses, with varied sets of qualities for which they are deified. For instance, Ram is valued because he was supposedly perfection incarnate. Likewise, Krishna is revered despite the fact that he deceived and played tricks on everyone, including his mother, lovers, wives, friends and enemies as part of an elaborate *leela*. There are goddesses like Parvati who are looked upon as benign mothers, symbols of happy conjugality and wifely devotion. However, worshipping Sita or Parvati does not come in the way of the same people celebrating Radha's 'illicit' extramarital love for Krishna. In Mahoba itself, a Radha–Krishna temple and a *sati mandir* exist in the same complex. Then, there are ferocious Chandi–Durga type of goddesses who strike fear in the hearts of devotees because any man who tried taming or desecrating them invited death in the most brutal manner.

Even the Mahoba district has very recently created such an icon. To quote Smeeta Mishra Pandey:

> It was in March last year that I had visited Mahoba chasing yet another tale: The story of Ram Shree, the village woman who along with her brother and father killed her relatives. Shree was the first woman to have been given a death sentence after Independence.... It was no different last year [in Shree's Tingra gaon in Mahoba district]. Villagers then spent their evening narrating tales about Ram Shree. They often debated whether Ram Shree did the right thing. Shree had apparently killed her relatives because they had tortured her and beaten her up mercilessly. Women wondered...why the court had anything to do with happenings in their village. In no time, Ram Shree became a living legend. When the Supreme Court swapped her death sentence for life imprisonment, taking pity on her one-and-half-year-old daughter, the villagers believed the Goddess had come to her rescue (*The Indian Express*, 16 November 1999).

The coexistence of Ram Shree's legend along with Charan Shah's shows that the culture of this region allows for diverse ideals and icons to be celebrated simultaneously. The people who worship Sita or Charan Shah as symbols of wifely devotion are also capable of valourizing Durga-like behaviour by ordinary village women.

Moreover, there is no sharp divide between the divine and human in the Hindu tradition. On the one hand, gods come to earth in varied human *avatars* to share the trials and tribulations of ordinary human beings. On the other, human beings can easily achieve divine status by living extraordinary lives and displaying inspiring qualities. Numerous village gods and goddesses in India are creations of this latter process. What is best is that deification is not confined to the human form of creation. We sanctify various living and non-living beings—cows, trees, elephants, snakes, mice, monkeys and even rivers, stones, mountains, earth, sun, moon and winds. At the same time in some states like Tamil Nadu there are temples where popular film stars are enshrined as deities.

Those who have tried to cure us of polytheism and become subservient to the dictates of monotheistic faiths have inflicted a great deal of violence on our people throughout this millennium. Let us not become willing agents for carrying that legacy forward.

As long as *sati* shrines coexist with Durga and Yogini temples, as long as Parvati is not forced to repress her Kali *roop*, as long as none of our gods claim perfection and demand the banishment of others, we will continue to value tolerance, dissent, diversity, respect for different ways of doing and living, and maintain regard for the diverse species that inhabit this earth and life forces that coexist in this universe. As long as our people feel free and empowered to choose their own gods and goddesses, they will respect the choices of others as well.

Those who wish to arrogate to themselves the right to subject other people's modes of worship to an arbitrarily determined qualifying criteria—no matter how well intended—can easily veer towards Stalinist forms of repression or trigger off counter-demands for more censorship. If I demand a ban on *sati* worship through coercive means, others can very well demand a ban on *Manushi* because it advocates easy and stigma-free divorce. To safeguard my own freedom, I have to respect that of others.

However, as emphasized earlier, the call for state intervention is valid when there is evidence of force being used to make someone adopt a pernicious tradition, or when violence is committed in the name of religion and social custom. Invoking laws to deal with crime is perfectly legitimate, but using the *danda* of the police, and threatening imprisonment to force a change in cultural values, inevitably leads to backlash.

Real reform lies in creating viable options which are easily accessible and help women move out of dependence. We have to have faith that the vast majority of people tend to act in self-affirming ways when circumstances do not constrict their choices. But nihilistic acts come easily to defeated people whose life is a long, arduous struggle without hope.

Zeal without Compassion

The truth is, despite a highly draconian law, that provides for the death penalty for anyone accused of participating in *sati* and life-imprisonment for anyone glorifying *sati*, several million people in this country refuse to be 'modernized' into believing that voluntary self-immolation is a crime. Just as most people do not believe that suicide is a crime though many modern states in the world (even India) have declared it to be so. The question is, how do we wish to deal with people who hold different values? How many millions do we want to imprison for life and put to death for subscribing to cultural norms which somehow do not meet the approval of 'modernists' like us?

I personally abhor the practice of *sati* and would do everything in my power to persuade or prevent a woman from killing herself in such a gruesome fashion. Similarly, I abhor killings in the name of national wars and do all I can to build opinion against warmongering. However, I would not suggest 'ruthless action' against those who refuse to heed me.

Responsible societies lay down certain limits of conduct even during war, such as the principle of not attacking unarmed populations. The fervour of self-appointed reformers knows no limits. They are not bothered with mundane details like confirming if even one family in that entire village has the means and money to secure bail, or to hire lawyers for fighting the prolonged litigation that would follow such a case. In all likelihood, the accused would rot in jail till death releases them from the benevolent concern of our social activists. The Charan Shah episode only underscores how reforming zeal without respect for facts, empathic understanding and compassion can easily degenerate into colonial-minded interventions by the educated elite who have donned the mantle of self-appointed reformers.

Why does no one demand the arrest and conviction of health ministry officials of the Uttar Pradesh government for criminal negligence and dereliction of duty, since they failed to provide a decent health centre in Satpura? Or that public works department officials face trial for failing to provide basic public transport in five decades of Independence, so that it would have been easier for Charan Shah to take her spouse to a city hospital? If both her eldest son and her husband did not have easily avoidable premature deaths, she may not have felt the need to end her own life in such a way.

An Unfashionable Death

Let us face the question squarely: what is it about her death that bothers us? That she did not want to outlive her husband? Or that she chose a politically incorrect form of death? Is it conceivable that Charan Shah's death would have evoked similar outrage if she had popped a few dozen sleeping pills along with a few pegs of liquor in Marilyn Monroe style, and let it be known through a poetic suicide note that she was ending her life because she felt jilted by a lover? Then she might have qualified as a subject for many a bestseller, as well as a Hollywood romance. Monroe continues to be one of the most celebrated icons of femininity in the western world. But Charan Shah was foolish enough to be born poor in a country which is the favourite object of contempt and flagellation for twentieth century modernists, and so she becomes a symbol of Indian primitivism. Would we be as outraged if, out of grief, she stopped eating and slowly starved herself to death?

The sad truth is that the educated elite expresses horror mostly about those things which the West looks down upon. People who cremate their dead instead of giving them a decent Christian burial are already somewhat uncivilized in the eyes of many westerners. Therefore, a Charan Shah who jumps onto her husband's pyre instead of swallowing sleeping pills becomes ten times more uncivilized. When women demean themselves in ways currently approved by the West, nobody is particularly upset.

There is some validity in the argument that by idealizing such sacrificial acts, women are conditioned into believing that their lives are essentially worthless after their husband's death. But is it fair that people whose value system meets our disapproval, or whose deities we do not judge worthy of respect, should be treated as criminals simply because we have the privilege and power to implement any kind of legislation against them? Do the reformers give others similar rights to impose restrictions on their practices, values and objects of worship?

Some others taking a more benign approach argue that the poor villagers of Satpura take to extolling *sati* because they have been denied the benefits of modern, liberal education. Hence they retain 'primitive' cultural practices. Reformers are convinced it is 'a lethal combination of superstition and prejudice that accounts for the veneration elicited by Charan Shah'. They tell us that 'apart from stern official measures, it will take years of educational effort with a pronounced bias in favour of the cultivation of a rational and scientific temper', and 'a genuine campaign for the empowerment of women through a sustained liberal education' to combat the culture which valourizes anti-women traditions like *sati*.

Icons of 'Modern' Times

However, the beneficiaries of liberal and rational education often worship and deify far more harmful varieties of icons on a much grander scale—and that too proudly—without granting others the right to protest or condemn.

A good example of a lavish glorification cult constructed around a negative role model is that of Princess Diana, a woman who led a very self-destructive existence. She began her public life by willingly offering a virginity test to prove herself worthy of marrying a known philanderer—all because he belonged to a rich and royal family. Despite that, she failed to win either his respect or love. Diana herself admitted to constant humiliation and neglect by her husband, while he had a merry time with his mistress. Yet, she desperately kept trying to be sexually attractive for him. In the process, she developed severe eating disorders, starved herself until she became a mental, emotional and physical wreck—all so that she could stay fashionably trim and beautiful for her uncaring prince. She spent a good part of her life shopping, buying designer clothes and jewellery in order to mesmerize people with her glamour and charm. When all those tactics failed with her prince, she got into a series of exploitative clandestine relationships, including one with her riding instructor, who literally auctioned their love story for millions of pounds. Finally, she died a perfectly unheroic death with yet another clandestine lover.

Diana had everything going for her, a rich family; good, modern, 'liberal' education; beauty; health; social status and powerful connections. Yet, what a sorry mess she made of her life. She lent a bit of glamour to a few good causes by occasional forays into social work, but the bulk of her energy seems to have been channelled into looking pretty, engaging in unsatisfactory romantic alliances and coping with the resultant emotional melodramas.

Not just the royalty-stricken Brits, but millions all over Europe, America, Australia and other parts of the world have remained star-struck, obsessively following the shenanigans of this foolish woman. When Diana died, thousands of people—all beneficiaries of modern, liberal education—queued up to offer tributes to her. Even today they buy tickets to have a *darshan* of her grave, which is crowded with mounds of flowers, trinkets, love epistles and much more. Dresses worn by her are auctioned at astronomical prices. A whole industry has emerged around the myth and legend of Lady Diana. Even the saintly Mother Teresa's demise was overshadowed by the mass mourning and hysteria evoked by Diana's death, which occurred under melodramatic circumstances.

Now, many of us do find this whole drama and glorification not just silly but also damaging. Diana's life holds up a very negative role model for women. It teaches women to be self-pitying, hungry and desperate for male attention, and to give in to feelings of worthlessness if men do not respond as desired. Yet, would one have the right to propose that the crowds thronging to Diana's grave should be declared criminals, lathi-charged by police (as was done at Charan Shah's immolation site), arrested on charges of idealizing this woman and then sentenced to life imprisonment or death?

Since I do not believe in authoritarian, statist measures for reforming or curing people out of their mental kinks or personal values, 1 would not actually suggest death sentences or prison terms for the crazies who went into mass madness over Diana. But I would certainly want to recommend psychiatric treatment for all such people, including some in our country who stayed glued to television for days on end, wallowing in Diana's tragic saga, and those who wasted huge amounts of newspaper space to give us detailed glimpses of a life spent chasing one demeaning relationship after another.

Needless to say, we would not be allowed the right to rectify the worldviews of Diana devotees. But the rest of the world thinks it has the right to 'educate', to 'civilize', to 'modernize' those who consider Charan Shah praiseworthy.

Secular Icons More Sacred?

Some 'rationalists' might well argue that the exaltation of Diana or Marilyn Monroe is secular whereas Charan Shah has become a religious icon. There are serious flaws in this line of argument. Are we concerned about potentially harmful icons and role models or about whether they come with religious or secular connotations? Why should only religious icons be banned and not secular ones? What is so sacred about the secular domain?

All this, however, is not in support of a culture that encourages women to devalue their own being and adjudge their own worth only as *suhagins*. There is an urgent need to actively combat all those received notions which condition women to act in self-destructive ways. To do that effectively, we need to learn to distinguish between crime and culture. For example, if honest and judicious investigations reveal that Charan had been goaded into killing herself, then the act can be legitimately classified as murder, in which case the Indian Penal Code can be justifiably invoked. Even calling it '*sati* murder', as some reformers have done, is absurd because the two words are mutually contradictory. Even supporters of *sati* cults would be able to make common cause in preventing such acts because according to the logic of their own value system, they cannot possibly apotheosize a murdered woman as a *sati*. However, if Charan Shah's devotion to her spouse and unwillingness to live without him leads to a whole heroic cult emerging around her, this falls in the realm of culture, not crime.

In such situations, there is need for not only a dialogue, for understanding the mainsprings of such ideologies, but also for channelling the idealism that sustains them into more creative expressions. We have to approach people as caring insiders rather than as attacking outsiders if we want their cooperation in building a new, life-affirming culture of respect for women. By refusing to draw a distinction between coerced immolation and a voluntary act of Charan Shah's, we are needlessly lending respectability to criminal acts of violence against women.

3

Naive Outpourings of a Self-hating Indian

Deepa Mehta's Fire*

Now that the heat generated by *Fire* has cooled down and the Shiv Sena's antics have backfired on them, it is time to take stock of the film. Had I said one critical word about it while the controversy was raging, I might have been damned forever as a Hindu fundamentalist. Now that I have passed my *agnipariksha* by defending, in public, the right of Deepa Mehta to screen such a film in India without threat of violence from the lunatic guardians of Hindu morality, I want to take the debate beyond the issue of censorship.

If I had seen Deepa Mehta's *Fire* without first being subjected to the whole barrage of propaganda hype surrounding it, I would have simply dismissed it as a naive and boring film about two unhappy housewives compelled to seek emotional and sexual satisfaction from each other because their husbands

---

*This article appeared in *Manushi*, No. 109, November-December 1998.

provide none. The film depicts the growing friendship and eventual sexual intimacy between Radha and Sita, married to two brothers who are living in a joint family. The laboured attempt to exploit the lesbian aspects of the Radha–Sita relationship tó the neglect of other aspects of their lives is both immature and schematic, indicating that the director lacks an understanding of family life and emotional bonds in India.

Most amazing of all, even the sex scenes between the two women were dull and insipid. It was almost like watching two Egyptian mummies presented in a series of tableaus. It does indeed require special genius to transform love-making into such a lifeless act and yet sell the film as a hot, sensuous and radical statement on women's sexuality. One of my aunts made a rather perceptive comment after having yawned all the way through it: 'Normally film directors add sex for titillation. In this film, the sex scenes are amazingly boring. Perhaps that's why the director had to add controversial scenes from the *Ramayana* in order to provoke the audience into taking notice of her film.' Many of those who have seen the film shared my sentiments about *Fire*. Yet most were not willing to say a word of criticism even before the Shiv Sainiks polarized the debate. We had been brainwashed into thinking that it was a smash hit at international film festivals, that it had won applause in Toronto, London and elsewhere. When Gloria Steinem herself had called it a landmark film, how dare feminists and other cultural czars of India do anything but applaud it?

I am sure Gloria Steinem would not be so generous in judging films made in the US on this theme. Third World feminists are to be given grace marks because they belong to the underdeveloped category, in the same way that we set lower qualifying criteria for Scheduled Caste/Scheduled Tribe candidates in education and jobs.

Politics of Fire

The film would have been less irksome to view if the director had at least given her theme a creative cinematic treatment. From the way she went about promoting *Fire* from the very start, it seems Ms Mehta did not want her film to be judged on aesthetic merit. From the time of its first screening at the Toronto film festival in 1996, she began insisting in carefully planted interviews that *Fire* was not merely a movie to be judged on how well it showed the lives of the characters portrayed. Instead, she introduced the film as a political statement, intended to combat the maltreatment of women inherent in Indian culture. Mehta repeatedly emphasized that her film was meant to throw a challenge to what she considers as oppressive norms for women among Hindu traditionalists. I give a few quotes where Ms Mehta describes her intent:

> For me *Fire* is about...fighting tradition when oppressed. My favorite dialogue in the film is when Sita tells her sister-in-law Radha that 'the concept of duty is over-rated'.
>
> —*The Hindu*, 4 December 1998

> The film is about desire and control and the choices we make in life. And it's about India. That is why I have used colours of the Indian flag throughout the movie.
>
> —*The Sunday Review* of the *Times of India*, 15 September 1996

On other occasions, she let it be known that she deliberately highlighted the colour saffron throughout the film because of its association with Hindu culture. Similarly, she claimed that she named her two heroines after the cultural icons Radha and Sita because they are 'the two wronged women of Indian mythology'. Also, that the idea of 'two goddess in bed together' was bound to provoke a certain set of people (*Outlook*, 2 October 1996)

Repressed wives rejecting their respective spouses and becoming lesbian lovers was intended to have shock value. In the publicity blitz that was organized around this film, Deepa Mehta kept announcing that the film was bound to have trouble with Indian views and the Indian Censor Board because the film shows how oppressive India's religious and cultural traditions are, and how miserable Indian family life is.

As if that were not enough, the title *Fire* is given the subtitle *Trial by Fire* in a laboured attempt to link the domestic melodrama in her film to Sita's *agnipariksha* in the epic *Ramayana*. To hammer into our heads that the film is about the harmful, even murderous, effect of the continuing hold of Indian traditions, the film ends with the crudely contrived *agnipariksha* of Radha to prove the heroine worthy of her new-found lesbian love.

To make sure we do not miss the point, there is the repeated visual replay of mythical Sita's *agnipariksha* scene from Ramanand Sagar's TV serial *Ramayan*, as well as repeated enactments of Deepa Mehta's scripted pseudo-folk *Ramlila* spiced with lots of cheap melodrama. To quote her: '[the *agnipariksha*] happens three times in the film, to make sure that...it wasn't just me indulging in the *agnipariksha* for Radha and Sita, but that [the film is set] in the whole context of tradition, and the stereotyping of Indian women, that we, I, the actors understood where they were coming from' (*Trikone*, October 1997).

Crude Caricature

If we take her version of the *Ramayana* seriously, we would be led to believe that there are only two purposes behind the writing of this popular Hindu epic:

(*a*) to condition women into accepting servility and even death by torture without protest; and
(*b*) to encourage men to be crude and insensitive in their relationships with women, to feel righteous about inflicting insults and cruelties on them and to have no compunction about burning them to death because, after all, they are supposedly following the glorious tradition set by Lord Ram.

Deepa Mehta also let it be known that her ire is not just confined to icons from the epics, but that she also aims to show up poor Mahatma Gandhi as a sexual-moral hypocrite. Gandhi is brought under her critical scrutiny through the character of Radha's husband Ashok. After Radha fails to bear children, Ashok takes a vow of celibacy under the influence of his guru in his pursuit of *moksha*. This becomes a take-off point for a crude, lifeless and superficial caricature of Mahatma Gandhi's experiment with sexual abstinence. It also offers her an opportunity to ridicule some of the philosophical tenets of Hinduism, for example, the quest for *moksha*.

However, the film labours hard and unconvincingly to be politically correct. Mundu, the servant, has hardly any redeeming qualities. Yet he must be shown in a sympathetic light because a 'progressive' film-maker knows she better not take liberties with leftist sensibilities. After all, Mundu is not a mere male, but a representative of the poor working class. Therefore, even when he is acting as a low level blackmailer, words of sympathy must ooze out for him in Deepa Mehta's script: he is overworked, has no job security and no avenues for entertainment except masturbation and sexual fantasies. Therefore, even Radha turns sympathetic to his plight when she gets this brilliant insight as to why he masturbated in plain view of the old woman and watched blue films while pretending it was the *Ramayana*. She voices her sympathy in the following words 'Is it really so bad what he was doing? He was being selfish and caring only about his own desires—just like us.'

You do not have to be a Shiv Sainik to feel offended and hurt by the gratuitous insults aimed at Indian culture in this crude caricature. Yet an overwhelming majority of those who saw the film or heard about its contents chose not to be manipulated. I wanted to ignore it as an exercise in self-flagellation by a self-hating Hindu and a self-despising Indian—a very common type among the

English-educated elite in India. While a few people mistakenly celebrated this film as path-breaking, by and large, I found that most people I discussed it with found it unexciting and pretentious. The media reviews, however, were virtually all favourable, even gushy, and on the whole defensive and politically correct. The Censor Board gave it clearance without any tampering or cuts.

One would have thought this would be interpreted as a sign of the cultural maturity of the Indian public. It was, after all, not too long ago that people in western Europe and north America faced hostility, social ostracism and even threats to life and limb when suspected to have homosexual inclinations. Long after writers like Oscar Wilde were jailed and hounded as criminals for their sexual orientation, this harassment continued. It has not yet fully ended. It took many decades for homosexuals to organize themselves as a political force and an articulate vote bank to counter this social hostility, before western societies began to yield a limited space for assertion of a homosexual identity or open discussion on this subject.

Homosexuality in India

By contrast, our society has no comparable history of persecuting homosexuals. In every culture and society throughout history, there are people who attempt every anatomically possible form of sexual stimulation and gratification. The difference in patterns of sexual expression among societies derives from their history, culture, present circumstances and power relations. These factors also determine whether their actual patterns of sexual behaviour are open or hidden.

In India, homosexuality has usually been treated as one of the many expressions of human sexuality. For example, our celebrated poet Firaq Gorakhpuri was known to be a homosexual, yet no one made much fuss about it. Nor was he attacked or humiliated for it. And he lived in a supposedly conservative small town in Uttar Pradesh.

Jayalalitha, the former chief minister of Tamil Nadu and president of the All India Anna Dravida Munnetra Kazhagam (AIADMK) is known to have a long-standing intimate relationship with her friend Sasikala. But that has not come in the way of her being deified by cadres who are forever falling at her feet. Despite being reputed to be authoritarian and corrupt, even her opponents have not made Jayalalitha's sexual life the target of attack, either in the media or on other public platforms. The following comment of an auto-rickshaw puller in Chennai pretty much sums up the popular attitude on the subject: 'We don't care who she rolls in bed with, as long as it is not a bed of gold made with money stolen or looted from the public.'

Deepa Mehta herself acknowledges that her inspiration for this film came largely from a story called *Lihaf* written in 1941 by one of the India's foremost women writers, Ismat Chugtai. A small section of conservative Muslims did attack Chugtai and even made her the target of obscene mail. Some even filed a case demanding a ban on her book on the charge of obscenity, using the British enacted penal code, which had declared homosexuality to be a criminal offence. But those who took her to court could not build a worthwhile case and the ban had to be lifted. Progressive writers like Manto stood firmly in her defence. But most important of all, far from facing social persecution, right from the start Ismat Chugtai became an admired cultural heroine for the bold themes of her stories, her uninhibited linguistic style, her iconoclasm, her subversive sense of humour as also her unconventional lifestyle and beliefs. To quote Chugtai:

> In spite of all this criticism, my stories were very popular and widely read. They were hardly ever rejected for publication. In 1935, Premchand founded the Progressive Writers' Association in Lucknow. I joined it, but no association could dictate to me what I should or should not write.
>
> In 1941, three months before my marriage, I wrote a story called *Lihaf*. In 1944, I was charged with obscenity by the Lahore government. A summons arrived: 'George the Sixth versus Ismat Chugtai'. I had a good laugh at the idea that the king had read my story. So we went to Lahore to fight the case. Lots of my supporters who knew me through my writing came to me. We had a nice time, buying the famous Lahore shoes. When anyone asked how the case went, I would calmly say: 'I bought lots of shoes'.The obscenity law prohibited the use of four-letter words. *Lihaf* does not contain any such words. In those days the word 'lesbianism' was not in use. I did not know exactly what it was. The story is a child's description of something which she cannot fully understand. I knew no more at that time than the child knew. My lawyer argued that the story could be understood only by those who already had some knowledge. I won the case.

Whenever we have published a poem or story on this theme in *Manushi* (see for example, Rajasthani short story 'Naya Gharvas' by Vijaydan Detha, translated into English in issue no. 86 of *Manushi*), we faced no hostile criticism nor upset readers. In fact, we received letters of appreciation from both male and female readers. Before *Manushi* got it translated into English, it had already been published in Rajasthani and in Hindi, and even enacted on stage in Delhi by one of our leading directors. It played to packed houses and received rave reviews.

India, despite more than two centuries of western influence and indoctrination, has still not become homophobic. While there is pressure on all to get married, this has not resulted in the extinction of sexual engagement with persons of the same gender. A space for bisexuality usually remains. There is relatively less of a demand here that people acquire a unidimensional frozen sexual identity.

I personally know several gay men and women, many of them in high profile professions. Not one has been fired from his or her job or made the butt of public ridicule. Male homosexuals do get fleeced by the police who use the Victorian anti-gay laws to extort bribes from gay men found cruising in public places. But to the best of my knowledge, there have been no public attacks on gays after they have begun openly organizing themselves around their sexual identity. Some years back, when two policewomen from a small town in Madhya Pradesh got married to each other in a public ceremony with the full support of their respective families, the entire national press rallied around their right to sexual–marital choice after it was found their police bosses had suspended them.

Likewise, most of those who saw *Fire* expressed no shock or horror at the open portrayal of a lesbian relationship. A handful of Shiv Sainiks in Bombay and an even smaller number in Delhi instantly became big national and international news. The vast majority of viewers in India, including influential public figures, resolutely defended the film's right to be screened, including those like me who had disliked the film. Yet that defence did not get as much notice as the antics of a few thugs. Why? Because liberal, tolerant behaviour does not conform to the studiously cultivated stereotype about India held by westernized Indians like Deepa Mehta.

Tradition vs Modernity?

The two opening cameos of *Fire* introduce the two heroines of the film. Radha is a depressed, over-worked and exploited middle-aged housewife, and Sita is a lively new bride with a sour faced and disinterested husband. Sita's husband neglects her cruelly even during their honeymoon. It is fairly obvious from the outset that the younger woman is to be the agent for promoting rebellion in this supposedly conservative tradition-bound middle class society. Deepa Mehta introduces her campaign for 'liberating' Indian women within moments of Sita's entry into her new marital home. Annoyed at her husband's callous neglect of her, she takes off her *saree*, wears her husband's oversized pants, pulls out a cigarette from his table-drawer, bares her shoulder, and takes a few mimed puffs from his cigarette, all in the style of a clothes model, and breaks into a disco dance to the tune of a silly, noisy Indi-pop number.

Most thinking women in the West have already rejected the fantasy that women can achieve equality or freedom by emulating men not just by learning to wear pants, but also by copying their self-destructive habits such as smoking. But in this film, such a style of juvenile rebellion is supposed to act as a catalyst for a revolution against moribund, tradition-bound Indian society. Just as in the field of science and education, we tend to import outmoded, even discarded technologies and obsolete intellectual fashions from the West, so with ideologies and feminist role models.

Deepa Mehta's Sita in her cross-dressing role-play establishes her persona as a modern (meaning westernized) woman. However, Radha needs to be coaxed and seduced into liberating herself from her traditional mould. Sita proves herself worthy of the male pants she had donned in an earlier scene by taking the lead in awakening suppressed sensual desire in Radha in the most unconvincing manner. Thereafter, the road is clear. Once sexually awakened, Radha acquires the courage to say 'No' to her husband's demands. She refuses to be his drudge and slave, and refuses to participate in his attempts to attain *moksha* by extinguishing sexual desire—and what's more, she learns to enjoy her rebellion. Sita has been able to convince her that 'the concept of duty is highly overrated', that it makes women into mindless slaves like the Sita of the *Ramayana*. Ms Mehta's disdain for Indians, except those who are supposedly sabotaging 'tradition' by seeking sexual fulfillment in defiance of social norms (like Mundu's obsessive masturbation before an old, crippled woman), oozes out of virtually every dialogue in the film. For example, when Radha declares: 'We are bound by customs and rituals, that someone has just to press the button called "tradition" and I start responding like a trained monkey.' All Indians are thus reduced to nothing better than servile, mindless apes.

Poor Indian Culture!

Thus, for Mehta, liberation can only come by overthrowing the stranglehold of Indian tradition. For example, Sita declares, after a love-making session with her sister-in-law Radha, 'There is no word in our language to say what we are to each other.' In other words, because Ms Mehta could not find the verbal counterparts to the English word 'lesbian' in any of the Indian languages, she treats it as proof that the Indian languages are supposedly incapable of expressing modern sensibilities and desires, therefore Indian culture is incapable of coping with something so supposedly 'new' and 'radical' such as two women caressing, fondling and obtaining sexual satisfaction from each other. Hence the need and compulsion to write this 'script of rebellion' in English. Deepa Mehta says in her various interviews that she attempted to get Hindi translations of the script but was satisfied with none. She cites two sentences as examples of the profundities in the script that were untranslatable: 'The concept of duty is overrated', and 'The Swamiji's testicles have grown too big for his loin cloth' (*Trikone,* October 1997).

By this time the viewer is puzzled into asking: what is Deepa Mehta's version of Indian tradition? Is it true that Sita's unfair banishment and *agnipariksha* is the most dominant aspect of Indian gender traditions? Are not Shiv and Parvati in Indian tradition the most popular archetypes of happy, blissful conjugality, including euphoric joy in sexual union, the most celebrated couple of Indian mythology? After all, the supposedly traditional Indian woman keeps fasts on Monday to pray to be blessed with a Shiv-like husband—not for an incarnation of Ram. I have rarely, if ever, heard a woman wish for a Ram-like husband.

Similarly, if voluntary celibacy has been glorified as an aid to a spiritual quest in one part of Indian tradition, there is a parallel tradition of spiritual quest via sexual union at a level of sophistication rare in most other cultures. Not too long ago, the West saw such Indian expression of sexuality as evidence of decadence and immorality. Today, the western-educated elite want to liberate 'sexually repressed' Indians by importing for us their recently discovered fashionable western versions of sexual freedom.

Stereotyping of India

According to Deepa Mehta's worldview, women in the Indian tradition are allowed only one role, that of long-suffering Sitas. What about Indian women and goddesses who appear as Durga, Chandi, Kali and in a host of other fierce and benevolent forms? When they are indignant, they make the most powerful men tremble with fear. They vanquish their enemies with their earth-shaking ferocity. Such women and goddesses are not only an integral part of village lore but a role model for women of all ages throughout India. Remember how many in India saw and responded to Indira Gandhi as Durga incarnate? Even ordinary women, like our first woman police officer, Kiran Bedi, are often referred to as Durga and are held up as role models for young girls. Her appeal cuts across urban/rural, caste, class, regional and religious divides. Popular TV serials and Bollywood films have projected her as a role model. It is common to hear parents not just in elite circles but also in villages and slums in India express the desire that their daughters become like her. However, what sells in the international media market is the unidimensional stereotype of India as solely a land of beggars and oppressors, a country where brides are commonly burnt to death for money and consumer goods.

Apart from the unremitting attack on the *Ramayana*, the Indian family system is also condemned as stifling human happiness because we are still foolish enough to believe that the old should be taken care of by their children rather than consigned to old age homes or left to fend for themselves. Jatin's Chinese girlfriend, who wants to live in Hong Kong, refuses to marry him because she would feel suffocated in a 'joint family'. Deepa Mehta, an innovative radical, introduces this Chinese girlfriend as a symbol of a free life in a worldwide modern urban society. She asserts her choices and individuality by refusing to be a baby-making machine in an Indian joint family. He ends up spurned by her, not because she does not enjoy having sex with him but because he is an Indian. The Chinese girlfriend's father seems to give vent to deep hatred for Indians, which sounds more like Ms Mehta's own disdain for fellow-Indians. He endorses his daughter's rejection of Jatin by launching a diatribe of insults against Indians.

The Chinese father feels sorry for himself that while forward-looking Chinese went away to Australia and Canada after the cultural revolution in China, his own working class parents chose miserable India for migration. Among the things he cannot stand about 'stupid, bloody Indians' is that 'they shit sitting on a hole in the ground'. He declares with imperial arrogance, 'When I want to shit, I want to shit comfortably, reading *Kowloon News*'.

Ms Mehta invents an ingenious reason for his hatred and contempt for India. His son is teasingly called Chinki by his schoolmates. That is reason enough for him to conclude that 'there is no place for minorities here' since 'these bloody Indians have fooled themselves into believing that they can transform themselves from a developing country to a developed one'.

And what is the 'rebellious' Jatin's response to these insults? A sheepish 'You are right sir, we Indians are a very complex people'.

True enough, Ms Mehta. Some of us even enjoy pouring shit on the heads of our fellow Indians because it has become a lucrative proposition in the western market.

Revolt Against Tradition

Jatin's revolt against tradition is peculiar indeed. While aspiring to assert his independence from the mumbo-jumbo of India, he is willing to quietly accept the worst of racist abuse hurled at him by the man whose daughter he wishes to wed! Is this Deepa Mehta's idea of modernity? His romance with a Chinese hairdresser made up to resemble a call-girl is presented in so crude and unrealistic a manner that only someone unable to control her hatred for India would use it as a device to portray a quest for individual freedom from the tyranny of Indian values. This is Ms Mehta's way of assuring us that even men are victims of the horrible Indian way of life and value system. The stifling of his rebellion and yearning for modernity take him to literally licking the feet and legs of a westernized Chinese girlfriend who is dying to migrate to Hong Kong and hook some rich American there so she can escape living in India.

If Deepa Mehta knew the basics of Indian family life, she would know that Indian men grow up expecting to be pampered and honoured like little gods by their prospective in-laws. Their inverted racism may manifest itself in accepting insults from a western woman but they certainly do not take such shit from an ethnic Chinese woman or father-in-law. Deepa Mehta's lack of understanding and mean-spirited caricature of middle class family life among urban Hindus is amazing considering she claims to belong to such a family and says Radha could be her own mother or aunt. An unrealistic element in her depiction is that the *Fire* family seems to live in complete isolation. This *Fire* family strangely enough never gets a visitor, even at the ritually important moment when the young couple returns from their honeymoon. The post-marriage period is usually filled with guests and neighbours in Indian families. In this case, the couple is merely greeted by a depressed-looking Radha who welcomes them with an *aarti*. The total isolation of this family is not only unrealistic but also claustrophobic. The air of depression is all pervasive–there is no laughter and no enjoyment. As a long-time resident of Lajpat Nagar, where the film was supposed to have been shot, I can say with confidence that such a family is not likely to exist among the community she portrays. One of the hallmarks of Indian family life, especially in a Punjabi neighbourhood like Lajpat Nagar, is that there is constant interaction with neighbours and relatives. But Deepa Mehta has cooked up a new variety of Indian family to conform to her schematic picture of all-round oppression. To quote her: '...in the Indian context, nobody sits down and has family chats. That is such a western concept. Nobody says: we can talk it out... Women talk during weddings, when they are hanging around. Men talk at weddings, get-togethers...or when someone's died. They get together around rituals and then there's gossip... But nobody as a whole, as a family unit, sits and chats' (*Trikone*, October 1997). As a result, she claims that 'the incredible loneliness of being [is] often the lot of women of India' (*Outlook*, 30 November 1998).

I have heard of artistic licence, but this is a curious case of sociological licence! The West has not only the onerous task of teaching us how to be liberated from our culture, but also how to learn to talk and chat with our own families.

No less unrealistic is the portrayal of Radha and Sita as cooks in the family-owned take-away. Not even mildly traditional middle class men in such a neighbourhood would be comfortable with their wives working as *bawarchis*, along with low-paid male servants, in their self-owned restaurant. The really hardcore traditional middle class male would consider such an arrangement a matter of great shame. For a woman of such a middle class traditional family to perform menial tasks in a public restaurant would be highly unlikely, even though she might take on a managerial role, a fairly common arrangement among this class. However, in the interest of making them the stereotypical victims of exploitation at the hands of males, Ms Mehta shows the two men merely acting as managers and cash collectors, while the two women sweat it out all day in the kitchen with the servant.

It is noteworthy that all the scenes associated with Hindu spaces and symbols are sites of oppression. Their one and only happy outing as a family is also in a garden built around a Muslim monument. The major moment of freedom and liberation from Hindu middle-class tyranny comes during the first happy outing of Radha and Sita at Nizamuddin *dargah*. It is also the place of their final union when Radha asks Sita to leave home and wait for her there at a pre-arranged spot. They don't choose a hotel as would any sane couple who needed a place to stay the night, or a gurudwara which provides both *langar* and shelter to anyone in need. They chose this *dargah* as their symbol of freedom.

Ms Mehta has mesmerized herself into believing that by making these two women walk out of bad marriages, she is doing something altogether alien and path-breaking, as though so far such a 'radical' option had never been exercised by Indian women. To quote her: 'When you look at it, what are they going to do? I have no idea. It's going to be tough, but will they deserve to.... But I know that they will not end up as prostitutes on the street, and in that way their relationship has liberated them from the stamp, which is what women who have left their houses usually end up being in Hira Mandi in Lahore or GB Road in Delhi or in the cages in Bombay' (*Trikone*, October 1997).

In other words, Ms Mehta wants to convince us that before she showed the way, any Indian woman daring to walk out of a bad marriage would end up as a prostitute. Amazing arrogance combined with gross ignorance of the society she wishes to reform.

Boring and Grim Sex

The film is obsessive in its focus on grim depictions of sexual desires. All the male characters are brought in as stereotypes of some or the other sexual kink. Ashok is experimenting with celibacy, subjecting his wife to the indignity of having to play the role of a rejected, mistrusted object of the lust, a lure he has chosen to conquer. Mundu, the obsequious live-in servant, specializes in masturbating while watching blue films in full view of the paralysed mute old mother of the brothers, while he is supposedly caring for her. His fantasies of a sexual union with the elder daughter-in-law of the house find open outlet in his teasing her with the lewd singing of the film lyric *Bol Radha bol Sangam hoga ki nahin* (Speak Radha, will we be united or not). Jatin gets a sexual high only when a woman treats him with contempt and disdain. As long as his wife is nice and affectionate to him, he neglects, her, treats her crudely and prefers to be at the feet of his Chinese girlfriend who not only spurns his marriage offers with casual contempt but also allows her father to insult him. However, as soon as his wife turns disdainful towards him and starts to repel his sexual advances, he begins to find her attractive and declares with new-found interest: 'I like my women to be fiery and spirited'. Even schoolboys are introduced in one scene asking Jatin for the most titillating blue film at the family-owned video parlour. They are given nothing less than a hardcore pornographic film which makes *Basic Instinct* seem like child's play. Sex enters into Mehta's reference to Ashok's *guru*, who is described as needing expensive surgery because his 'testicles have become too big for his loin-cloth'.

Deepa Mehta wants to be celebrated for taking on a bold theme depicting the growth of lesbian love between two women. I found its portrayal rather callow. To begin with, the film suggests that same-sex relationships among women are most likely to arise only when they are treated badly by men. Second, the sexual part of the relationship is too laboured and lacking in subtlety. Even something as common between women as a hair-massage is melodramatically portrayed as foreplay.

From the start, the film's marketing has insisted that the lesbian affair is a liberating breakaway from bad heterosexual relationships. However, close emotional bonding accompanied by displays of a good deal of physical affection are commonplace household occurrences among women in many Indian families. Deepa admits in some of her interviews that her own mother experienced a very nurturing relation with her sister-in-law in the early years of her marriage.

The truth is that in most Indian families, even when sexual overtones develop in the relationship of two women situated as are Radha and Sita, no one generally gets upset about it, provided people do not go around flaunting their sexual engagement with each other. I have known of any number of such relations in very ordinary, traditional families. Given that in a gender-segregated society like ours, women spend a lot more time with each other than they do with men, such close bonding is fairly routine. Indians, by and large, are not horrified at witnessing physical affection between two people of the same gender. Two women friends or female relatives sleeping together in the same bed, hugging, massaging each other's hair or bodies is seen as a normal occurrence and even encouraged in preference to similar signs of physical affection between men and women. Such physical affection between women is not ordinarily interpreted as a sure sign or proof of lesbian love.

An Agit-prop Film

By crudely pushing the Radha–Sita relationship into the lesbian mould, Ms Mehta has done a big disservice to the cause of women. She could have portrayed their relationship to be as ambiguous as was her own mother's relationship to her sisters-in-law, who apparently were the main source of emotional sustenance in the early years of her mother's marriage (*Outlook*, 2 October 1996).

But an agit-prop film cannot afford to leave anything to the audience's imagination. I suspect that the net result of this political tract of a film, determined to create programmed individuals, will be to make many women in India far more self-conscious than earlier in their relationships with other women. There is a danger that many of those exposed to this controversy will learn to view all such signs of affection through the prism of homosexuality. As a consequence, many will feel inhibited in expressing physical fondness for other women for fear of being permanently branded as lesbians.

Ms Mehta provides us with yet another insight into what went into the making of this film. Many of her interviews bring in her personal experience of a bad marriage to explain the inspiration for *Fire*:

> Every film of mine has an autobiographical element. That time I was going through a bad marriage and was not able to make a decision for divorce and suffered for two years. Traditional values were firmly ingrained in me, which made it difficult for me to go ahead with my decision, I was preparing myself to go against the traditional system and make my choice. This phase gave me a lot of time to contemplate on such things and it gave me the food for a film like *Fire* (*The Asian Age*, 29 November 1998).

> *Fire* is a result of bitter personal experience of a bad marriage for 11 years and it took me two years to get out of it. The reason I could not get out of it was my subconscious upbringing that said marriages should last forever... The hold of traditional values set me thinking of what tradition

> means and how tenuous it can be... that his how *Fire* started, between doing something for your personal desires and the pull of tradition (*Hindustan Times*, 9 August 1997).

Macaulay's Children

Strange words indeed! Here is a woman who has all along received western education, even while living in India. She tells us she even thinks in English (*Trikone*, October 1997). Very early in life, she migrates to England and then to Canada, becomes a Canadian citizen, marries a Canadian man of her choice and this non-traditional, very modern marriage turns sour. She takes two years to make up her mind about whether or not to walk out of that marriage—and the product of that uncertainty is a film about India demeaning to Indian culture and its people.

Macaulay, who claimed that through English education he hoped to create a class of Indians English in tastes and morals, though brown in skin colour, would be proud of his achievement if he saw Mehta's *Fire* or heard her pontificate on Indians and India.

I know several very modern western women who took a great deal of physical and emotional abuse for years before they dared walk out of an unhappy marriage. I also know many western women who did not even gather the strength to leave such marriages. Instead, their husbands usually walk out on them. When directors in the West make films about unhappy marriages, they do not feel obliged to caricature the Bible and use it as a peg on which to hang all women's troubles. This is true even though the Biblical commandments often make it difficult for men and women in strongly Christian communities to walk out of bad marriages. In any case, the pervasiveness of divorce is not an obvious symbol of women's freedom and modernity. In fact, the tendency of a certain variety of western-educated women to see divorce as a statement of self-assertion by women, a move towards greater freedom, often makes the life of both women and children more vulnerable. Lesbianism may well be a lifestyle option for some women but cannot be viewed as a universal antidote to bad marriage, as this film would have us believe.

Marketing 'Poor Hindu Women'

If Ms Mehta had described this film as one more domestic melodrama dealing with marital incompatibility due to the insensitivity of some husbands, I would have confined this review to assessing how well the film deals with this well-worn theme. Anywhere else in the world, a film about unhappy marriages would be treated as just that. But when a film about domestic relations is made with Indian characters, it becomes a film about Indian family life—a peculiarly Hindu phenomenon, a product of Indian tradition. It is only because she labours hard to call the marriages of Radha and Sita Hindu marriages and attributes their failures and crudities to the Hindu worldview, that one begins to view Deepa as one more among a growing tribe of Indian women who have understood that there is a lot of money to be made by portraying the real and imagined miseries of much-pitied Indian women in the western market.

Hitherto, the most common way to do that was to float a non-governmental organization to do research on the status of Indian women, to write tracts and make tear-jerking documentaries proposing half-baked, amateurish solutions to alleviate the sufferings of this hapless species by 'empowering' her with slogans approved by donor agencies. But now the Hindu/Indian woman has become a marketable commodity in the global entertainment world as well.

Smashing Myths?

It is not a coincidence that this film about Hindus was originally made in English and was first released in the West. It was made primarily for a western audience, something Mehta herself acknowledges: 'The international audience is exposed to a very stereotyped picture about India. I want to break this myth about our society' (*Femina,* 1 February 1997).

And what is the myth she wants to smash before the international audience? Who are the myth-makers she disapproves of? Mehta cites Satyajit Ray as an example of someone who fed westerners with an unrealistic picture of India. One can understand her discomfort with Ray because he portrayed both, the rich and the poor, the educated, the illiterate, Indians endowed with a unique dignity even in difficult circumstances. He projected their dilemmas and conflicts with insightful empathy. Mehta considers such cinema as having misled western audiences. To quote from yet another of her interviews from Toronto: 'It's amazing how ignorant people are about India over here (meaning north America). The audience here is fed on a diet of Satyajit Ray on the one hand and the Raj on the other.' Ms Mehta instead decided to focus on the 'throbbing middle class of India' that was supposedly not portrayed by Ray and others, and of whose existence the West is not even supposedly aware. This middle class was chosen because it 'carries the burden of tradition more than anyone else'. She, therefore, wants to show up the hypocrisy and cruelty inherent in its connection with Indian tradition and 'how the Radhas of this world catch fire' (*The Asian Age*, 9 February 1997).

Neo-colonial Reformers

This device of professing sympathy for 'oppressed' Indian women in order to condemn the traditions and culture of all Indians has a more than two-century-long history. After the establishment of *Pax Brittanica* in India, and the emergence of a new class of natives who began to challenge the legitimacy of the British Raj, oppressed Indian women became a favourite prop of our colonial rulers and missionaries. Customs like *purdah*, child marriage and the ban on widow remarriage prevalent among a minority of castes and communities became the universal symbols of the uncivilized nature of Indian society.

In their reforming zeal, the British conveniently forgot that some of these customs were confined to a segment of upper caste Hindus in certain regions of India. For example, even their own census in 1901 had recorded that the custom of child marriage and the ban on widow remarriage affected no more than 10 per cent of British India's castes and communities. The rest have uncomplicated, traditional ways of divorce and easy acceptance of remarriage for women. Nothing the Indians did escaped condemnation. If, among certain patrilineal communities, they kept women in seclusion, they were considered backward. If, among matrilineal communities, they allowed sexual freedom and economic and social clout, they were condemned as being immoral. Either way, Indians needed to be reformed, that is, learn to adopt and copy whatever sexual mores the British considered 'moral' at that point of British history.

For example, the British delighted in expressing their outrage at north Indian Brahmins and certain upper castes because of their oppressive sexual norms for women. At the same time, they were outraged for completely opposite reasons with tribal communities which followed much freer sexual norms than their own. The women of matrilineal communities of the south were condemned as immoral and promiscuous because they exercized the right to change spouses at their discretion, without much ceremony or permission from any religious authority.

Among many of the animist communities of India (derogatorily termed tribals by the British), the fact that most women wore blouseless *sarees* had a different concept of illegitimacy and that they enjoyed a great deal more sexual freedom than was common in England caused them to become targets of attack and reform. Christian missionaries worked zealously to introduce European concepts of sexual chastity and monogamy among such communities. The British mesmerized themselves as well as educated Indians into believing that the British were here on a civilizing mission to reform Indians and make them fit for the modern world. Nothing was spared. We were declared uncivilized because we worshipped false gods and exercised the freedom to invent new gods. We were condemned for seeing divinity in rivers, trees, air, water, sun, moon and even stones, rocks and mountains, monkeys and snakes.

Rediscovering Tradition?

Deepa Mehta inherits this tradition of using outrage over the plight of Indian women as a means to attack not only contemporary Indian culture but also a way to demean and caricature Hindu family life. Even more disappointing than her film was the way Ms Mehta reacted when attacked by a small bunch of Shiv Sainiks. It is understandable that she wanted to play martyr to Hindu zealots because that would go down well with western liberals and radicals. While her early posture was that of a first-time radical introducing a subversive ideal like lesbian love in tradition-bound Indian society, when Shiv Sainiks took the bait and expressed outrage at her self-confessed attack on Hindu culture, she suddenly discovered that lesbianism was indeed a part of Indian heritage (*Pioneer*, 8 December 1998). Her supporters too began emphasizing the versatile celebration of myriad forms of sexuality in the temple sculptures of Khajuraho, as well as the open depiction of homosexual love in a whole array of Indian paintings and other art forms. Her new discoveries were meant to bolster her case that she had done nothing outrageous, nor had she injected western ideas into traditional Indian minds.

Worst of all, she quietly changed the name of her rebellious heroine from Sita to Nita for the Indian version of the film and began pretending there never was a Sita in her film. I would have respected her much more had she shown the courage to say her Sita could indeed be lesbian. In India, we have a well-respected tradition that any individual or group can interpret or rewrite any scripture or sacred text in whichever way they like. Not just Tulsidas, but a host of literary writers have used the Valmiki *Ramayana* as a take-off point for their own versions of the epic.

There are *Ramayanas* which portray Ravan as the real hero, just as in some other versions Sita actually falls in love with Ravan. There are folk versions in which Sita kills Ravan while Ram swoons with fear. In the Jain *Ramayana*, Sita is portrayed as Ravan's daughter. In many, Ram is subjected to very harsh critical scrutiny rather than being portrayed as *maryada purushottam*. If ordinary village women in India have felt free to exercise the right to rewrite the Ram–Sita script in many radical ways, why did Deepa Mehta chicken out so easily and dare not proclaim with pride that *her* Sita is indeed a westernized lesbian?

All this only goes to show that those who wish to engage in creative reform of our traditions must be people who understand our traditions, who are deeply involved in and concerned about the well-being of the society they wish to reform, rather than those who descend on us as attacking outsiders. Such efforts can only aggravate the sense of inferiority among our people, who have had to bear centuries of brutal attack by foreign invaders. We need to heal those wounds, not inflict new ones that hold up our own people to undeserved caricature and ridicule.

When people are constantly subjected to humiliation and unmerited attack, they lose their sense of self-respect and often even start transforming their behaviour into that of the stereotyped image projected of them. This may be what happened to some Blacks in America. The behaviour of our Shiv Sainiks, Bajrang Dalis and other members of the Sangh Parivar shows that a similar loss of self-respect is coming to afflict a large number of Indians as well. We would do well to remember that a people without self-respect do become dangerous, both to themselves and to others. In that sense, the likes of Deepa Mehta are indeed playing with fire, in a way not very different from the Shiv Sena's fireworks. The politics of both is based on cashing in on or stoking the sense of inferiority among the Hindus.

I wish we could learn to ignore their antics. However, the way this film was marketed to gain attention by becoming the focus of a major national controversy, with virtually every newspaper, magazine and TV channel giving it prominent headline space for weeks on end, shows how easily we are manipulated into engaging in empty debates around phoney issues that tend to waste so much time and energy and take attention away from more important and meaningful public issues.

4

THE MANY FACES OF TRADITION IN INDIA

Allies or Adversaries?

*The Continuing Hold of Traditional Female Moral Exemplars in India**

I am one of those who grew up oblivious of and somewhat indifferent to matters religious. Therefore, during my childhood years, secular figures like Gandhi and Nehru were more important as symbols of inspiration than our vast array of gods and goddesses. However, our *devis* and *devatas* do not presume to punish us or even get angry with us if we choose to ignore them. The Hindu deities actually make no moral demands on us. No matter what one does, they do not retaliate by rejecting or threatening to excommunicate us if we work out our code of conduct rather than follow their precepts. And yet they have clever ways of quietly intruding into our lives and knocking at the doors of our consciousness. It is very common, for example, for a dutiful son to be praised as Ram incarnate, or a talented daughter to be commended as a virtual Saraswati. I have often heard a happy and satisfied mother-in-law refer to her son's wife as the 'coming of Lakshmi incarnate' into her home. One

*This article appeared in *Manushi*, No. 136, 2006.

constantly meets living incarnations of the divine in everyday life. Frequently, their worldly behave-alikes are genuinely lovable and even inspiring in the way they live up to their commitments.

Thus, Hindu *devis* and *devatas* are not distant heavenly figures, but are a living presence in most people's lives. They exercise a powerful sway as moral exemplars, who are believed to have standards of morality that even ordinary people can aspire to emulate, in whatever doses they think appropriate. But the codes of morality they live by are not prescriptive. They are simply there to provide valuable insights that people use in their own lives in an extremely flexible way, keeping the contemporary situation in mind. Hindus usually do not fall into the trap of replicating the behaviour of the deities they revere, for that would produce absurd or tragic results.

A special feature of Hindu *sanatan dharma* is that there is no sharp divide between the divine and the human. Various gods and goddesses take *avatars* and descend on earth to appear before us like ordinary mortals in intimate familial relationships. They are willing to be judged by the same rules and yardsticks that one would use for any fellow human being. Devotees and non-devotees alike have the right to judge them by how well they perform or fail to perform those roles. They neither claim perfection nor do they command us to unquestioningly approve of all they do. They allow us the freedom to pass judgements on them, to condemn those of their actions that we might consider immoral or unfair, or to praise those actions we find honourable or benevolent.

For instance, Vishnu *avatar* Ram is revered as *maryada purushottam*, thereby acknowledging the fact that Ram—the hero of the epic, *Ramayana*—becomes worthy of our reverence by proving himself to be the best of men in diverse roles. He is an ideal son not only to his doting father, but even to his spiteful stepmother. As an elder brother, his actions command love and devotion. As a king, the wishes and interests of his subjects are far more important than his own. But where he fails, as he does in his treatment of his wife Sita after her release from Ravan's captivity, he has to accept condemnation like an average human being.

In fact, one is even allowed to punish the gods for their misbehaviour or their failure to keep a pact. For example, Krishna as the son of Yashoda has to take many a beating like any ordinary child or adolescent for playing naughty pranks on his mother and other women. The right to punish the gods is exercised not just in legends, but by ordinary people in real life as well.

For example, in drought-prone villages of India, when the rains are delayed, it is not uncommon to find villagers keeping the *shivalinga* (or the icon of whichever deity they worship) submerged in water as punishment to the god till the rains actually materialize.

To give yet another example of 'punishing' the gods: even today, the people of Mithila, 'the region to which Sita belonged', refuse to marry their daughters into families living in and around Avadh, because King Ram belonged to Avadh. The people of Mithila repeatedly recite Sita's name in wedding songs, but Ram's name is omitted, as they still hold a grudge that Sita, the daughter of their town, was made to undergo needless suffering by Ram to supposedly please his subjects.

Thus, while the celestial figures do not claim special privileges on account of their divinity, human beings are allowed to be elevated to the status of the divine, overriding the gods and goddesses in matters ranging from valour to morality. A powerful route to divinity is also through *bhakti* or devotion—not just to some god or goddess, but also to some human being or even animal. For example, Hanuman became worthy of worship on account of his total devotion to Ram. Others have achieved divinity by being devoted sons or brothers. It is, for instance, common to hear grown men proudly declare: 'My mother is more important to me than any god' or 'In our family we worship "so-and-so"' who could be an uncle, an elder sister or a grandmother.

The Hindu deities thus enter into an intimate kinship type of relationship with their devotees. The deities do accept gifts and devotion, but in return are expected to grant wishes and give boons. The human–god relationship is collaborative in kinship, where there is a regular exchange of gifts. Even affection and loyalty are expected to be mutual. The *ishta devata* or *devi* ('preferred' or 'beloved' divinity) is expected to come to the rescue of the devotee in times of need, just as relatives are expected to do all they can to lend a helping hand in times of distress.

Thus, every village in India has its *gram devi* or *devata*. The *gram devatas* are usually connected with extreme piety, but myths of *gram devis* all tell us of ordinary women who rose in rage because they were cheated or were sought to be ravished by some evil male. Out of such desecration, they rise in terrible fury and thereby grow in stature so that they are able to span both heaven and earth. Their power of destruction, born out of righteous indignation, terrorizes everybody into submission. But once their rage has achieved its purpose and when the devotees are ready to propitiate them, they can be relied upon for protection as well as healing and showering bounties. Theirs are myths of ascent from human to divine forms, rather than of descent from the divine to the human.

Any woman who manifests extraordinary strength and who is believed to be her own mistress, totally unafraid of men, begins to be treated with special awe and reverence and often commands unconditional obedience in her male colleagues who are mortally afraid of her and rarely dare challenge her commands. Indira Gandhi, who was celebrated as a virtual Durga, began to lose her hold on power only after she let it be publicly known that she had become dependent on her younger son, Sanjay, who was beginning to call the shots in politics and governance. Women of even humbler origins have this choice. For example, India's first woman police officer, Kiran Bedi, is an all-India cult figure and is often referred to as a Durga because she too projects the image of a woman who can outperform men in every way and who is fearless even in dealing with criminals.

One comes across such mini-Durgas all over the country. Every other village and urban neighbourhood would have some such women who command respect and deference, at least within their kinship group, if not in the public domain.

I remember, as a child whenever I got into one of my righteous rages, my mother would warn the others, saying: 'Don't provoke her into manifesting her Durga–Chandi *roop*.' Thus, very early on, my relatives understood that it was best to be careful about stepping on my toes. Even without being a Durga devotee, I unconsciously began to successfully 'play Durga' in dealing with a whole range of situations from sexual harassment to intervening between two groups of riotous men to bringing under control neighbourhood drunkards and wife beaters.

One essential tenet of Hinduism—pre-Vedic, Vedic and post-Vedic—is that *Shakti*, the feminine energy, is believed to represent the primeval creative principle underlying the cosmos. She is the energizing force of all divinity, of every being and every thing. Different forms and manifestations of this Universal Creative Energy are personified as a vast array of goddesses. *Shakti* is known by the generic name *Devi*, derived from the Sanskrit '*div*', meaning 'to shine'. She is worshipped under different names, in different places and in different appearances, both as a creator and destroyer.

Epic and *Pauranic* literature gives a whole new array of names and attributes to the universal feminine power and the various goddesses take on distinct iconographic forms. For example, Sri Lakshmi is celebrated as the goddess of wealth and prosperity; Saraswati, as the presiding deity of the arts and learning; and Usha, the goddess of dawn, is the dispeller of ignorance. Durga is the vanquisher of evil. Earth itself is worshipped as the goddess Prithvi. The knowledge aspect of the *Devi* is represented by a *Shakti* cluster of ten goddesses known as *Dasa Mahavidyas*, the Ten Great or Transcendental Wisdoms, who encompass the entire universe of knowledge. The consort gods are placed much lower in status and power. The energy of god is feminine, and almost every god is static, even dead, without his *shakti*. But *Shakti* is complete in herself because her existence does not depend on extraneous force. The male gods are incomplete, even powerless, without a consort, barring rare exceptions like

Dattatray, who also remained single. But the goddesses become even more powerful in their non-consort *avatars*. When the energies of the male gods prove inadequate, they have to turn to the female for protection.

For example, the great goddess Durga, who was born from the energies of divinities when the gods became impotent in the long-drawn-out battle with the *asuras*, is believed to be the vanquisher of evil. Her battle represents a universal war between knowledge and ignorance, truth and falsehood, the oppressor and the oppressed. But she also promises that as Shakambhari she would nourish the world in times of need with the vegetation grown from her own body and that in her terrible form she would deliver her worshippers from their enemies. She needs no male to legitimize her power, nor is she dependent on the need to conciliate any male divinity. In her Mahakali *roop*, she is awesome, ruthless and completely uncontrollable.

Thus, the manifestations of the *Devi* are in response to different requirements and different times. The all-powerful feminine force assumes diverse forms, taking on different *avatars* to fulfil diverse purposes at different times. Sometimes she is frightening and even vengeful, like Chandi; often she is the unconditionally nurturing mother, like Parvati; an ideal daughter, wife, daughter-in-law and a compassionate, forgiving mother figure, like Sita; a dominating and demanding wife, like Draupadi; or a besotted lover, like Radha.

Even though goddess worship is a living and growing tradition in India starting as early as the Harappan culture of 3000 BC (if not earlier), there have been many fluctuations in the fortunes of various goddesses. Some ancient goddesses have continued to hold sway, while others have lost some of their preeminence. While some reappear in newer versions, there are also instances of brand new goddesses taking *avatar*. Two examples of such new births: Bharat Mata invented in the late nineteenth century during the freedom movement to represent the enslaved Mother India calling out to her sons to free her from colonial bondage, and Santoshi Ma, a hitherto unknown goddess who gained popular currency thanks to a Bollywood film released in the early 1970s called *Jai Santoshi Ma*.

Santoshi Ma combines some of the qualities of the non-consort goddesses with those of the consort goddesses. The *Shakti* form of goddesses comes to the aid of human beings and gods in periods of cosmic darkness by killing the demons who threaten the cosmic order. But Santoshi Ma, being a modern goddess, does not establish herself by annihilating any particular demon. Instead, her miraculous powers come to the rescue of her devotees, who are being harassed and tyrannized by fellow human beings. She is particularly popular among women, who observe fasts on Fridays as symbolic penance in order to achieve their desired goals in this life and to bring about general contentment. I often say it jokingly—but the statement itself is serious—that we could solve all the financial problems of *Manushi* by building a shrine to Manushi devi, a new goddess who would combine the qualities of Saraswati, Durga, Joan of Arc and more.

The range of moral exemplars available to Indian women is indeed spectacular. Apart from goddesses who work hard to win respect as wives, at the other end of the spectrum are those who consider it an affront that any male should dare consider them sexually accessible or the assumption that they would condescend to be mere consorts. Radha's complete abandon in her extramarital love affair for Krishna is no less deified than Sita's devotion to her husband. Yet another category of women exemplars are those who spurn the bond of matrimony, either by refusing to get married at all despite social expectations, or by disowning the marital relationship after being forced into it for a while. Almost all the women saint-poets around whom religious cults have emerged chose to either walk out on their husbands or to never get married. Meerabai, the sixteenth-century saint-poet of Rajasthan and Lal Ded of Kashmir gave free vent to their protest against the suffocation and tyranny that they experienced in their respective marriages and choose to break out of the constraints of this institution. They became roving mendicants and rose above all social constraints imposed on women in the name of family honour. Women like Mahadevi Akka, the sixth-century saint-poet of south India, never married at all; she, too, like Lal Ded, shed all her clothes. Their nudity was an assertion of their refusal to abide by social conventions and norms with regard to a woman's role in society.

I remember when as a child I read the stories about Meerabai, I was not quite able to grasp the meaning and power of *bhakti*. I was, however, much inspired and influenced by what appeared to me a clever ploy on her part in getting herself married to a stone image of Krishna and then using him as a shield against the demands of her real-life husband. A stone image cannot order you around, dictating the do's and the don'ts, in the way a human husband can. In the name of devotion to Krishna, she acquired the right to go where she pleased, when she pleased, intermixing freely with people of all castes and classes. She sang, she danced and she declared herself to be beyond the restrictive norms expected of a Rajput queen. My interpretation of Meerabai's life is not too farfetched, given that I saw the living example of one of my grand-aunts who, in her own way, did many of the things Meerabai had done. She was a fashionable socialite in her youth, but was married to an unsocial, scholarly man. Marriage to him was too dull an affair for her. So she adopted the white robes of a *sanyasin* and took to singing devotional music. Her *bhakti* songs brought her numerous invitations from near and far, from the wealthy and the poor. That gave her ample opportunities to travel on her own, build friendships, enjoy the hospitality of a vast range of people who invited her for singing *bhajans*, all this without invoking any stigma. The whole family understood that her *bhakti* was in response to an oppressive marriage but she did not suffer the censure she would have, had she followed the same free and roving lifestyle without adopting a Meerabai-like persona.

Meerabai, thus, became a symbol of feminine freedom in my own life. Even though devotion to a deity of the Meera variety is not the route I could choose with any honesty for my personal freedom, I interpreted her life to mean devotion to any idea which is larger than one's own self-interest, including devotion to a social or political cause. Gandhi, for instance, interpreted Ram *bhakti* to mean working for the freedom of his motherland and to bring about an exploitation-free life for farmers, for the oppressed and marginalized, and for women. In my experience, once people in India are convinced of one's commitment to a higher cause and one's strength to live by it, be it religious, social or political, one can break out of all the restrictions meant for ordinary mortals with impunity and yet be respected for it.

The lives of non-consort goddesses and women saint-poets creates a unique kind of social space in our otherwise marriage-obsessed culture for women who wish to opt out of matrimony altogether. This has also made voluntary celibacy a very respected choice for women. In many modern cultures, especially those influenced by Freudian theories, sexual abstinence is seen as an unhealthy aberration that is supposed to lead to all kinds of neuroses and a disoriented personality. In India, however, we are still heavily inclined towards the opposite tradition that holds that voluntary sexual abstinence bestows extraordinary powers on human beings. Not just men, but many of the most revered women in Indian religious history opted out of sexual relations altogether. They have been treated as virtual goddesses, so much so that the gods come to fear them and are compelled to do their bidding. During the nineteenth century reform movements, and even more so during the freedom movement led by Gandhi in the twentieth century, many of the male leaders exhorted women to follow the example of Meerabai and follow the call of their conscience rather than tread the well-beaten track of matrimony. A large number of women who became active in these movements were thus encouraged and chose to stay single. In the tradition of non-consort goddesses, many came to be treated as symbols of feminine power in their respective regions because a woman like Durga, who becomes sexually inaccessible, consort of none, nor in search of a consort, tends to command tremendous awe and reverence.

Hindu Goddesses are not Competitive

While Hindu deities are not permitted to be jealous gods demanding exclusive loyalty from their devotees, the latter do occasionally come into conflict with each other, as, for example, the historic clashes between Shaivites and Vaishnavites. But there are no comparable ego clashes between the various goddesses or their devotees. They do occasionally get into competing with each other over who is more virtuous or whose husband is more powerful. But these stories invariably end with their reconciliation and acceptance of each other's worth. Our goddesses believe in peaceful co-living, in graceful acceptance of each other's worth rather than claiming or establishing superiority over each other. For example, a martial goddess like Durga does not consider herself superior to a quiet sufferer like Sita. Nor is Radha treated with disdain for being lost in Krishna's love despite his polygamous dalliances. It is accepted that they represent many aspects of feminine behaviour and diverse responses to similar and varied situations. Even if one has an *ishta devi* or *devata*, it does not imply hostility or disregard for other *devis* and *devatas*.

Our goddesses, like our gods, allow their devotees and non-devotees a great many liberties, including the freedom to demand responsible and improved behaviour of them as well as the right to rewrite and redefine their roles for them. That is how there came to be hundreds of known versions of the *Ramayana*, the *Mahabharata* and other such texts. Even the numerous *shastras* repeatedly emphasize that codes of morality have to be given time and place and even be person-specific, so that they must evolve in response to the changing requirements of human beings. Hence, there is great variation between different *shastras* and *smritis* written in different regions at different times. Keeping this in view, our gods allow us to rework our responses according to the changing demands of the times. They have successfully lent themselves to numerous social causes, have become powerful allies even in contemporary movements for social justice and are accepted with ease in these new roles even by their traditional devotees, provided the devotees are convinced of the sincerity of the effort and the good faith of the alliance-seeker. There are also various examples of our gods being used for partisan purposes as did the Bharatiya Janata Party (BJP) with the Ram Mandir issue in the 1990s.

But I would like to illustrate my point by describing some very positive movements for women's rights that have made very creative and progressive use of traditional religious symbols. I deliberately pick on the use of the Sita symbol because most of those who consider themselves modern/progressive and feminists consider Sita to be a very negative role model, as the hallmark of wifely slavery. Needless to say, this projection is altogether contrary to the popular perception of Sita, which is why her charisma can be put to such positive use.

The *Ramayana* is the story of a whole spectrum of voluntary sacrifices and hardships endured by most of the main characters in their resolve to adhere to their *dharmic* codes of conduct. Dashrath, for instance, sends his beloved son into exile for 14 years rather than break a promise to his misguided wife Kaikeyi. Ram's mother Kaushalya lets a co-wife condemn her only son to be banished to the forest like a hermit. Lakshman, Ram's younger brother, voluntarily follows Ram into exile, solely in order to help Ram honour his *dharma* of parental worship. Many different versions of the *Ramayana* rework the characters and their responses as well. For example, Rabindranath Tagore and Maithali Sharan Gupt's renderings of the *Ramayana* revolve around the pain and sacrifice of Lakhsman's wife Urmila. Yet Sita's sacrifices and the raw deal meted out to her loom large in the Indian consciousness, compared to all the other sacrifices made by a whole range of the main and subsidiary characters. Sita emerges as the final moral touchstone of the epic. Her pain and sorrow hang heavily on the collective consciousness of the Indian people like that of no other character, divine or mortal.

Sita makes her first mark by insisting on sharing Ram's exile despite the advice of her husband and other family members, who suggest that she stay back in the palace and live in comfort. This reaffirms her credentials as a devoted partner with a strong mind of her own. However, this is not the reason for her being enshrined in the Indian psyche, since there is no dearth of devoted, dutiful wives in the Hindu *Puranas* and myths. Till then, Ram is an appropriate match for her. If she is an ideal wife, he too is an ideal husband and lover, so it is not particularly noteworthy that she chooses his company, albeit in a forest, over living without him in a palace.

The popular obsession with Sita's predicament is rooted in the three episodes after her liberation from Ravan's captivity. The first is the *agnipariksha* (ordeal by fire) which she must undergo to prove her purity and publicly ascertain her worthiness in order to be taken back as Ram's queen. The second is the way she handles her banishment by Ram in deference to public doubts about her chastity. The third is the manner in which she rejects Ram's demand that she undergo a second fire ordeal and appeals to her mother Prithvi (the Earth) to receive her back into her womb.

These episodes, as depicted in Valmiki's *Ramayana*, have disturbed devotees and non-devotees alike through the centuries—so much so that numerous attempts have been made to reinterpret, rewrite and re-examine the three events. Hardly anyone has tried to create a new Dashrath, who refused to make himself and so many others suffer to satisfy the whims of a jealous queen; or to recreate Ram, who believed he could challenge the dictates of his misguided stepmother, dictates which actually cost his father's life. But Ram's treatment of Sita, in the latter parts of the *Ramayana*, demanding the two *agnipariksha*s and abandoning her in a forest, remains immensely controversial and has provoked innumerable attempts by successive generations to critique and rework their relationship. Unlike many other gods like Krishna and Shiva, who are allowed to retain their imperfections, Ram has been compelled to undergo countless improvements. Even at the popular level, there is great uneasiness at Ram's behaviour. One common feature of many of the reworked *Ramayanas*, including the most famous of them all, Tulsi's *Ramayana*, is an attempt to reform Ram's behaviour to prove himself a more worthy husband for Sita and thereby mitigate or undo the injustice he inflicted upon her.

This obsession with reforming Ram has to do with the popular perception of Sita as perfection incarnate, so much so that even *Maryada Purushottam* Ram does not measure up to her. Sita is seen as flawless, despite the fact that she brings about trouble for everyone by crossing the *Lakshman Rekha*. In this projection, people have voluntarily glossed over those few occasions when Sita behaves unreasonably as when she castigates Lakshman, accusing him of lustful intentions towards her at the time he refuses to follow her dictates and go to rescue Ram in the forest. She is not just the daughter of Earth, but is a symbolic extension of Mother Earth herself: loving, nurturing, compassionate, forgiving and inviolable in her dignity. She is someone who is considered so much more superior to Ram that her name precedes his in all invocations, as in the greeting 'Jai Siya Ram'. Her absence is a stigma for Ram, who has to have an image of Sita by his side when performing any important ritual, as an acknowledgement that he is incomplete without her, whereas Sita was able to bring up her children without even informing them of their father's identity. 'As an *avatar* of Shree, Sita is one with Ram and yet in her shakti *roop* she is altogether different from and even considered superior to Ram (Sachidanand, Vatsayan [ed.]. 1986. *Jan Janak Janaki* [Hindi]. Delhi: Prabhat Prakashan).

Ila Dalmia sums up the popular sentiment in this regard very well:

> Sita's heart has no anger against Ram, she loves him, she understands him. She realizes his predicament as a king. Thus in her power of tolerance, ability to understand and forgive, she becomes greater than Ram. Even in a situation of grievous hurt and misery, there is no *dainya* (loss of dignity) in her. Janaki (Sita) is like the Mother Earth, the epitome of compassion, tolerance, forgiveness (see 'Sita Samaropit...' in *Jan Janak Janaki*, edited by Sachidanand Vatsayan, pp. 28–33).

Sita may have forgiven Ram, but most people in India have not really made peace with him on account of her being made to undergo needless suffering. I quote from a couple of typical interviews with people from fairly traditional families to illustrate how strong the sentiment of censuring Ram's behaviour is, even by those who are otherwise deeply pious.

Surubhi comes from a Brahmin family of Ram devotees, but is unsparing about this one aspect of Ram's behaviour:

> Ram sounds like a raving lunatic when he subjects Sita to that nasty harangue about her not being pure enough for him on account of her being in Ravan's captivity. He loses both his reason and his dignity in the process. How dare he have even suggested the first *agnipariksha*? He is supposed to be *antaryami* (all-knowing). Then how come he doesn't know and understand that Sita is above suspicion?

Interestingly, I find no real gender divide on this issue in India. Most Hindu men relate to Sita as a long-suffering but awe-inspiring mother whose hurt they have to alleviate, in much the same way that Lakshman and Luv–Kush were willing to battle on her behalf with their father. A peon in my office described Ram as 'suspicious, unreasonable and '*kaan ka kaccha*' (someone who is easily swayed by any floating rumour or talk). 'A man who needs other people to give his wife a good character certificate is no man at all', is how he summed up Ram's character, adding that he did not deserve Sita as a wife in any case, whatever else he may have deserved. A neighbour of mine, a BJP enthusiast and an ardent Ram devotee, described Ram as being a totally unworthy husband and father who showed how cruel men can be to women.

It is not just women who disapprove of Ram's attitude towards Sita and who see Sita as an ideal. Even the most devout of Ram devotees among men feel embarrassed and uneasy about Ram's sudden change in behaviour towards Sita in the latter half of the *Ramayana*. The Hindi writer Pandit Buddhinath Mishra describes Sita Marhi, the birthplace of Sita, as the most important *teertha* (pilgrimage centre) on this earth because *Adyashakti* appeared in this land as the daughter of Earth and went back to Mother Earth after scornfully rejecting all of the luxuries and riches of 'Raja Ram' (Sachinanand, 1986). However, while for most women Sita represents an ideal wife, men mostly think of her Sita Mata. She is not just the daughter of Earth, but she is Jagat Janani (Mother Earth) herself, who inspires awe and veneration rather than one who evokes images of a desirable spouse. 'Sita is like a mother to whom you go for blessings. You can't think of her as a wife because you never feel anywhere near equal to her' is a commonly heard sentiment among men. She seems too formidable in her role as a wife. But when placed on the pedestal of maternal love she becomes nurturing and compassionate.

Ram's desertion of Sita, far from being a stigma against her character, enhances her status far above Ram's; he shrinks in stature, while she is further elevated. Sage Valmiki, in fact wrote the entire *Ramkatha* in order to vindicate her.

Feminists are prone to interpret Sita's offer to undergo the *agnipariksha* as an act of servile surrender to the whims of an unreasonable husband. But in the popular perception, it is seen as an act of defiance that challenges her husband's aspersions against her character. It shows him to be so flawed in his judgement that the gods themselves have to admonish Ram for his imprudence. Sita emerges as a woman whom even Agni (the fire god)—who has the power to destroy everything he touches—does not dare touch nor harm.

Sita, in fact, is often used as a symbol of Indian womanhood and is, as such, the most common reference point both in literary writings as also in the writings of social reformers used to drive home the point that even the best of men—the *maryada purushottams*—find it hard to do justice to the best of women like Sita. In this way, she has been kept alive as a powerful reminder that men need to be seriously reformed in order to become worthy of Sitas.

As mentioned earlier, this uneasiness has found expression in numerous reworkings of the *Ramayana* by male authors where they try to do one of the following:

- Show a genuinely reformed Ram who does not maltreat Sita. For example, Kalidasa's Ram remains a trusting and loving husband. He does not entertain the slightest doubt with regard to his beloved and breaks down at the news of the slanderous talk about Sita among his subjects. And yet, when he is compelled to abandon her, Kalidasa's Sita makes a powerful indictment of Ram in her own dignified way. Her way of disowning Ram is to bring up her children without disclosing to them the identity of their father, while she resumes her own identity as Vaidehi, daughter of King Videha, rather than as the wife of Ram.
- Ram is re-imagined as making amends for all the wrongs done to Sita. For example, Bhavabhuti's Ram is first and foremost a lover. His duties and obligations as a king do not come in the way of his commitment to Sita. And yet, when he has to abandon Sita, Bhavabhuti creates a whole new set of characters to counter the impression left by Valmiki's *Ramayana* that Ram's action was necessitated by his regard for the opinion of his subjects. His own mother Kaushalya is so upset at Ram's cruelty to her beloved daughter-in-law that she vows never to see the face of her son again, or even live in Ayodhya, till Sita is brought back with due honour. Finally, Mother Earth, Arundathi, convinces Ram of the injustice of this action and tells him that he is unfit to perform any *yagna* (religious ritual) till he restores Sita to her rightful place. Thus, family and public pressure make him realize that his notion of duty towards his subjects is in itself faulty, and he cannot be a *keertimaan* (renowned/meritorious) king if he fails to be a responsible lover and an honourable husband.

> Many other male authors, including several contemporary writers like Bharat Bhushan Agarwal, have used Lakshman, his devoted brother, to challenge Ram's behaviour towards Sita. In some other versions, Ram's own subjects and soldiers are shown as disapproving of his behaviour.

Texts such as the *Adhyatam Ramayana*, a canonical book of the Vaishnaavas, use a clever ruse to let the world know that their Ram is an altogether improved version. Tulsi borrows from this image to create his ideal Ram who does not demean himself by subjecting Sita to any *agnipariksha*. The popular serial of Ramanand Sagar also pegs itself onto this version because the producer realized that most of his viewers were not willing to accept a repetition of Ram's disgraceful treatment of Sita. This sanitized version of Ram is shown entering into a pact with Sita so that all her travails would be borne by a shadow Sita, while the real Sita would stay in the safe custody of the fire god Agni for a certain period of time during which Ram is expected to kill Ravan and the other demons to restore righteousness on earth. Sagar's Ram is not allowed to entertain even a moment of doubt about Sita's purity.

These literary reworkings of the *Ramayana* as part of the Ram Reform campaign have found their counterpart in the efforts of numerous social reformers in India who, at different points of time, have played leading and pioneering roles in seeking to strengthen women's rights, enhance their status in society and demand a change of attitude from contemporary Rams.

It is noteworthy that a majority of women's rights struggles and movements in modern India have often been initiated, led and sustained by men. On the one hand, the traditional culture trains men to accept the multi-dimensional power and manifestations of the feminine principle. Men are taught and conditioned to be reverential towards women, at least towards women in motherly roles. On the other hand, traditional literature, including the great epics, makes them aware of, and guilty about, the many ways in which they have wronged women; the numerous *Pauranic* tales of women' strength, loyalty and *dharmic* steadfastness are constant reminders that men need to make amends.

People in India find it difficult to justify or reconcile themselves to the fact that in a culture that worships Saraswati as the goddess of learning, so many girls are deprived of even primary education; in the culture that worships Lakshmi as the goddess of wealth, so many modern-day Lakshmis live a slavish life of economic dependence; in a culture where male gods have had to appeal for protection to the feminine Shakti, women among many communities are not allowed to venture out of the domestic confines without male protection.

This bewilderment and guilt has compelled numerous men to pick up cudgels on behalf of women, throwing up important social movements, especially since the nineteenth century, considered by many as the period that saw severe erosion of women's rights among many communities of India. Men like Vidyasagar in Bengal, Ranade and Phule in Maharashtra, Veerasalingam in Andhra, Lala Devraj in Punjab and a host of others committed their entire lives to the cause of women. In the writings of those social reformers, cutting across regional and caste boundaries, women as the wronged *matri shakti* (mother power) is a recurring metaphor. A good part of their efforts went into convincing other men that Indian men could not progress as long as their partners stayed oppressed, that the country's freedom could not be won as long as women were denied their rightful due in the family and in society. To the women, their message was to recognize their own feminine *shakti* and become modern-day Durgas, without, of course, losing the qualities of Sita, the perennial favourite.

For example, Mahatma Gandhi used the Sita symbol to advocate the idea of women's strength, autonomy and ability to protect themselves rather than depend on men for safety. His Sita was a 'lioness in spirit' before whom Ravan became 'as helpless as a goat'. To protect her virtue even when in Ravan's custody, she did not 'need the assistance of Ram'. Her own purity was her sole shield. Ravan dared not touch her against her will. Gandhi's Sita was 'no slave to Ram'. She could say 'No' even to her husband if he approached her carnally against her will. His message that women had the right to define and follow their own *dharma* rather than be constricted to wifehood brought hundreds of thousands of women out of their domestic confines into the political arena. He wanted to create a whole army of new Sitas who were not brought up to think that a woman 'was well off only with her husband or on the funeral pyre'. Gandhi's Sita also became a symbol of the swadeshi movement which aimed at the decolonization of the Indian economy. He asked the women of India to follow Sita's example, wear Indian homespun and boycott foreign finery because Sita would never have worn imported fabric. The rules of social conduct had to be framed by 'mutual cooperation and consultation rather than unilaterally imposed on women by men'. Gandhi often admitted that he learnt that his first lesson in *satyagraha* (non-violent truth force) from women like his mother and wife, both of whom were indeed Sita-like in their steadfastness and commitment. The essence of *satyagraha* lay in securing a moral victory over one's opponent by winning over his heart rather than vanquishing or humiliating him, as well as gaining the sympathy and support of all those who witness the conflict. For a detailed analysis, see my paper 'Gandhi and Women', *Economic and Political Weekly*, Nos 40–41, 1985. Gandhi worked to ensure that he got sympathy from all in his battle of right against might. That is exactly how his favourite heroine, Sita, managed to get one up on Ram.

Even those who are put off by Gandhi's use of Hindu religious symbols for political mobilization and who have problems with many of his views on women and sexuality do not deny that more than other modern leader, male or female, he helped create a favourable atmosphere for women's large-scale and respectful entry into public life. Gandhi legitimized the right of women to hold political office without them having to wage long-drawn-out battles as the suffragists in the West did to win simple things like the right to vote and the right to equal political participation. His Sitas were encouraged to break the shackles of domesticity, to come out of *purdah*, to lead political movements and to teach the art of peaceful coexistence to this warring world.

In recent years, the Shetkari Sangathana leader, Sharad Joshi, has also used the Sita symbol to drive home a radical message of gender justice among the farmers of Maharashtra. It was in 1986 that I was first invited to come and work out a programme of action for the Shetkari Sangathana's women's front, the Shetkari Mahila Aghadi. In the early years of my involvement, my main contribution lay in persuading the Sangathana leadership to:

- give emphasis to women's economic rights, especially land rights, given that we were mobilizing women from farmer families; and
- not depend on statist interventions for empowering women, but to work instead towards building a new culture and forge a new social consensus for strengthening women's rights in the family and community.

An important outcome of my input and interactions with the Shetkari Mahila Aghadi was the Lakshmi Mukti campaign. The Sangathana announced in 1989 that any village in which a hundred or more families each transferred, of their own accord, a piece of land to the wife's name would be honoured as a Lakshmi Mukti Gaon, a village which had liberated its hitherto enslaved Lakshmis. (Sita is believed to be the incarnation of Lakshmi, and wives are also referred to as Lakshmis of the house, *griha* Lakshmi.) This would be done at a public function in which certificates of honour would be awarded both to the village as well as to each such family.

The Lakshmi Mukti campaign revolved around the idea that the peasantry could not get a fair deal for itself and would remain exploited by urban interests as long as the curse of Mother Sita stayed on them, as long as they kept their wives or *griha* Lakshmis enslaved by keeping them economically dependent and powerless in the family. This campaign was the real turning point in my understanding of the powerful emotional hold of certain traditional symbols on the psyches of men of all ages and communities in India. During the campaign tours, while I would use images and examples from contemporary life, Sharad Joshi's speeches revolved around the Sita story, which seems to have played a crucial role in striking a deep emotional chord among the Sangathana followers. I quote from Joshi's very evocative speech, which first establishes a link between the daily privations, drudgery and acts of loyalty of the wives of ordinary, poor farmers and the privations suffered by the *Ramayana*'s Sita:

> During our struggle for remunerative prices I taught you to calculate the cost of production of farm produce and asked you to get into the habit of noting down each and every item of work and the cost involved. I would now suggest another exercise: on an off day, just sit down in a quiet corner of your house and start noting down on a long sheet of paper the various tasks your Lakshmi performs from as early as five in the morning to late at night: feeding the cattle, followed by all the chores required for the upkeep of the house and its surroundings, cooking, fetching water and the care of children. All these by themselves represent a full day's work. But she goes on non-stop. After completing the housework, she goes to the fields and, at the end of a back-breaking day of work, on her way back home, she tries to scrounge around and collect anything that can be used as firewood for the evening meal. She comes home to cook, look after little children, feed the animals and tend to the needs of other family members, including the old and the sick. From the time she wakes up to feed the cattle to the time she lies down to sleep, she probably put in no less than 15 hours of work. How do you put in rupee terms the love, care and affection that she puts into all these tasks? How do you put a money value on the services of a person who saves the honour of the family by going and stealthily borrowing milk and sugar from the neighbours so she can provide tea for your guests who come at an unexpected hour at a time when the house does not have those provisions? Let us put the value of all these acts of loyalty and love at zero. But shouldn't she get at least as much money as a person working for the Employment Guarantee Scheme gets for simply moving earth from one place to another? Let us figure this out on the basis of a minimum wage of Rs 12 per day. She works 365 days a year. Let us say she has been married to you for 20 years. Given that she has worked 365 days a year for 20 years, the amount comes to more than Rs 1,60,000. She has never tried to demand this amount you owe her, not sent a notice, or a jeepload of people to come, seize and take away your household utensils as the banks do when you owe them much smaller amounts. On the contrary, to save you from other creditors, remember how often she even took off the little bit of jewellery she was wearing? If we calculate along with the interest on the minimum amount you owe her, it comes to a minimum of Rs 4 lakhs. What have you given her in return? Two *sarees* for a whole year and that too forgotten if there is a drought. No guarantee of even adequate food. If there is not enough food in the house, the husband's share is

not reduced. And a mother will hardly snatch food away from her own children's mouths. She makes do with whatever is left over, a half or a quarter *chapati*, and fills the rest of her stomach by drinking water. This has been her fate so far.

Having thus established the credentials of their wives as no less self-effacing that Sita Mata herself, Joshi goes on to show the farmers that they are emulating a very negative role model and being as ungrateful and uncaring as was Ram:

> That this situation is not new is certain. But how and when did it start? Ram is considered a *purushottam*. But think of how he treated Sita Mata who joyfully embraced exile in a forest for 14 years to be with him. As soon as Ram was appointed king, he decided to cast her off. It is not necessary for us to get into a debate on whether it was right or not for Ram to give up Sita. But was it not necessary for him to at least take the trouble of explaining to Sita why, as a king, he was compelled to abandon her? He could have assured her that she need not lack anything after his parting company with her, that she could continue living respectably in Ayodhya. Better still, Ram should have told his subjects that if she is not good enough for you as queen, I will go along with her. After all, that is what she had done when Ram was banished by Kaikeyi, who had told Sita she could continue living in the palace. But Sita had said '*Jithe* Ram, *tithe* Sita' (wherever goes Ram, there goes Sita). Even if Ram was not ready to leave his kingship for her, surely there were less cruel ways to deal with the situation. Sita was pregnant at that time. If Ram had provided her a small straw hut till the time of delivery, he would not have lost any of his greatness by doing so.

Joshi then links Sita's story to another moving relic which stands as testimony to the injustice done to Sita in the popular imagination:

> There is a Sita temple at Raveri village in Maharashtra. The villagers in that area tell you that Sita Mata delivered her two sons on that very spot. She was in such a destitute condition that she went begging for a handful of grain. The people of the village Raveri spurned her and refused to give her any. Sita Mata cursed them in her grief. Such was the power of the curse that not a grain of wheat would grow in that village for centuries (until the arrival of the hybrid variety) even though the neighbouring villages produced plentiful harvests of wheat. In other words, the message driven home is that the poverty of Indian farmers will not go away unless they repay their debt to their Lakshmis and free themselves their curses. After all, the husband of a slave cannot be a free man.

Sharad Joshi would conclude his speech by saying that the purpose of the Lakshmi Mukti programme was to see that no modern-day Sita would ever have to suffer the fate of Ram's Sita because she had nothing to call her own, no house or property of her own. By transferring a portion of land to their wives, they were paying off 'a long due debt' to Sita Mata: 'Through this gesture, you, my farmer brothers, will be vanquishing that monster of male tyranny which even Prabhu Ram could not vanquish though he slayed a great warrior like Ravan with ease.'

In village after village, I saw men reduced to tears listening to the story of Sita. Within a couple of years, hundreds of villages had already been honoured as Lakshmi Mukti villages and hundreds more had volunteered to carry out Lakshmi Mukti. Most of the villages that carried out Lakshmi Mukti celebrated it as though it were a big festival. The entire village would be spruced up and decorated, with men dancing to the beat of drums and women performing *aarti* and singing songs. Men seemed even more elated than women, and much of the initiative for preparing villages for Lakshmi Mukti was taken by young male cadres of the Sangathana. Some of the men I interviewed described the whole campaign as a *mahayagna*.

The occasion would attract many people from the neighbouring villages. After each public meeting, men from the surrounding villages would come up and volunteer to effect similar transfers of land in their own village, provided Joshi joined them likewise for the celebration. The Sangathana campaign became such a wave that the organization found it hard to cope with the growing number of villages clamouring for Joshi's visit. Thus, the leadership could not match the groundswell it had created and other pressing priorities of the organization began to take precedence.

Needless to say, this campaign for women's economic rights could take off in rural Maharashtra mainly due to Joshi's charisma and credibility as a leader who had sacrificed his own family life and given up a lucrative personal career to devote his life to fight for the rights of the exploited and debt-ridden peasantry. But I am also convinced that this unique campaign was able to draw such a powerful response from men also due to the evocative symbolism employed by Joshi. Mother Sita has the power to guilt-trip even the most hard-hearted Hindu men to respond to appeals for justice.

There is a long history of men like Joshi playing a very leading role in movements for women's rights in India. Because of this active male involvement, it is not surprising that women's rights struggles have rarely acquired the dimensions of a gender war in our country.

However, this also produced two negative fallouts.

First, the over-dependence of even modern-day Sitas on men to right their wrongs. When they feel such help is not forthcoming, they do not always fight strongly on their own steam and strength. Even in the case of the Shetkari Sangathana, when the male leaders went back to work on other political priorities, the women activists of the Mahila Aghadi also let go of the Lakshmi Mukti campaign.

Second, men and even women tend to expect women to be really Sita-like in order for them to pick up cudgels on their behalf. All those women who betray ordinary human failings are less likely to find such strong support among men.

Those Who Want Sitas Reformed

So far I have described Ram reform efforts but, as mentioned earlier, the continuing hold of Sita on the popular imagination is interpreted by many Indian feminists and other modernists as proof of Indians not having broken the hold of crippling traditions. Sita is seen as a harmful role model, one who culturally enslaves women and conditions them into accepting subordination and maltreatment at the hands of men without having the courage to protest or retaliate. She has been condemned by them for her passivity and subservience. Her suffering is seen as a product of her masochism, lack of selfhood and supine surrender to patriarchy.

Therefore, she is an adversary whose influence among people is to be countered. The feminists object not only to the fact that Sita bore a great deal of injustice without a tit-for-tat battle but also because she emerges as the all-compassionate, all-forgiving mother. The association of the feminine with the nurturing mother-figure is seen as a patriarchal conspiracy to confine women in restrictive and self-effacing roles. Most feminists identify with aggressive, militant goddesses such as Durga and Kali. Goddesses who are content with marriage are looked upon with disapproval even if they are honoured as wives, as was Parvati and even Sita for most of her life. Some even empathize with Sita and want her to reform and change herself, learn to retaliate and prove her selfhood by being more aggressive. The broad thrust of feminist politics has been to goad modern-day women to revolt against social norms that encourage them grow into the Sita mould. In other words, as opposed to the mainstream society's efforts to reform Ram and make him worthy of Sita, the feminist project has been to reform Sita and to make her forget Ram. Supporters of this thought would have liked to see Sita emulate Ibsen's Nora and defiantly walk out on her husband to build a new life for herself or, better still, a sexually 'liberated' woman like Erica Jong. If she has to stay within the traditional social boundaries, she becomes acceptable only in a Kali-Durga *roop*.

A good example of the Reform Sita campaign is Deepa Mehta's film *Fire,* in which a modern-day Sita is made to use a radically different shock therapy—she walks out not just on Ram, but also gives up the traditional role of a wife. She is one-up on Ibsen's Nora by choosing lesbian love as a mode of self-assertion and in defiance of social norms. In contrast, the feminist writer Snehlata Reddy's Sita provides a milder shock by actually building a close emotional bond with Ravan and declaring that he would have made a much better partner than Ram.

The traditional Sita is not a slave but a loved and loving spouse. Mehta's Sita makes it clear that she continues living with her husband only because she has no viable option. As soon as an alternative appears, off she runs. The film *Fire* rejects not just the bad part of Ram's behaviour, but also all the social norms and ideals represented by the worldview of the *Ramayana* and the value system that Sita lives by.

My assessment is that while no one in India feels offended if Ram is asked to improve, reform and change some of his anti-women notions, people unencumbered by 'isms' do not take kindly to Sita being subjected to similar 'improvements' and reforms that make her behave altogether out of character. Not surprisingly, despite all the high-profile hype accompanying the release of *Fire*, the accolades it won abroad and the media buzz generated around the bedroom scenes, the film was a box office flop in India. Compare that to what happened during the telecast of Sagar's series *Ramayan.* The traditional Sita jolts Ram and all others into recognizing their own faults and compels them to make amends. The Sitas of the Deepa Mehta variety may cause a momentary shock and elicit some sympathy but they command little admiration and therefore tend to become socially marginalized. They may become symbols of individual protest and assertion but they are not able to force people around them to rethink their own attitudes. In contrast, the traditional Sita shakes the very moral core of her society.

This is not at all to suggest that I object to the modernizing of Sita or that I share the objections of the *Hindutvavadis* to Mehta making her Radha and Sita turn to lesbian love.

Since in the Hindu tradition no one dare assume the final authority in defining our gods and goddesses, each one of us has the freedom to make them behave in ways we find necessary or inspiring. However, when the *Hindutvavadis* create a Durga brigade whose members enthusiastically lead riotous mobs against Muslims, it becomes a gross distortion of the very quintessence of Durga as the destroyer of evil. She simply cannot be cast as a murderer of innocents. So also politically motivated attempts to make Sita loose the very qualities that make her Sita are resented or simply dismissed by those who have some roots in their culture and tradition.

In any case, why force Sita to act like Ibsen's Nora or insist that all Sitas and Radhas turn themselves into Durgas and Kalis, especially since the choice of invoking new goddesses as new moral exemplars is available to all of us, if the existing array fails to satisfy us? Such monotheistic, unidimensional, standardized behaviour is neither good for ordinary women, nor for goddesses, nor, for that matter, is it good for men or gods.

If we want people to gracefully yield space for our new goddesses, we have to learn to be tolerant and respectful of those worshipped by others. There is no need to treat them as adversaries simply because they do not conform to our newly acquired ideologies, especially considering that they are willing to come a long way to support our causes. At the heart of this controversy between the two opposing approaches to social and religious reform is the key question: How can we relate to our cultural heritage and define our relationship to our own people and the values they cherish?

Do you disown tradition and position yourself outside it, or do you accept it as your own in the way that you accept your inherited genes? Accepting it as your own gene stock does not mean that you do not try to cure the physical diseases you may have inherited.

This kind of distinction is even more necessary for cultural inheritance. Owning up to it does not imply subscribing to every one of its pathological norms, nor does it mean endorsing harmful practices. It simply means learning to distinguish between inherently unjust practices and those that you do not like because you have adopted a different framework of values. Social reformers can be effective only when people see them as having compassion and empathy for their predicament and are willing to stand by them in their various trials and tribulations (as shown by the success of the Sangathana campaign). But if you descend as attacking outsiders, focussing solely on select practices disapproved by self-appointed reformers, you do not make much of a dent in popular attitudes. Only by creating a shared sense of right and wrong with the people whose lives we wish to change for the better can we create a new social consensus for a more just and humane society within our respective communities.

5

Learning to Take People Seriously*

In 1998, I was invited to read a paper on the theme of 'The Subjectivity of the Researcher versus the Subjectivity of the Researched' organized by the Department of Sociology, Delhi School of Economics. I was asked to describe and discuss my experience as an activist doing investigative work for Manushi. *I used the occasion to make explicit some of the rules of thumb I had evolved over the years, learnt through exposure to a wide variety of often puzzling and difficult situations. This is a revised version of that paper. I am not a professional sociologist. This article may appear simplistic to those who have been formally trained in methods of research and investigation, which are reputedly more sophisticated. However, my main purpose in publishing it in* Manushi *was to initiate a dialogue with other activists who are also involved in trying to figure out how to make useful interventions for social reform.*

One of the most important things I have learnt is that even the most well-meaning efforts to help improve people's lives can end up in disaster if you do not take people's own lives and perceptions sufficiently seriously or fail to

*This article appeared in *Manushi*, No. 56, January–February 1990.

understand the effects of any particular effort at change on other parts of a complex situation and society. Contributing to social change involves deliberate attempts at mobilizing opinion in a particular direction. However, if the conclusions are predetermined by the activist's own predilections and ideas, without taking into account the situation, perceptions, wishes and aspirations of those on whose behalf we seek to help bring about change, we can easily end up either being irrelevant, pompous impostors or authoritarian manipulators. For example, an important reason for the failure of the anti-dowry campaign is that it was a well-intentioned effort at social change based on an inadequate understanding of social reality.

Before we can effectively intervene to help bring about the desired social changes, we need to understand why things are as they are and not as some group or theory tells us they are. Only a more accurate understanding of what is really going on can enable us to help concerned activists create a relevant and meaningful agenda for improving the lives of women and other oppressed groups. The task, though not easy, requires us to maintain a degree of scepticism regarding predetermined explanations and political formulae. Reality rarely matches up well with available preconceived notions, whatever their origin.

We need to be sensitive to unexpected information and to what may appear to be puzzling contradictions. If the people who could provide firsthand information of the situation are unwilling to talk to the researcher, this must be seen as a sign that greater care and effort is required to make sense of the situation. The researcher has to be alert not only to explicit cues but also to implicit ones regarding people's experience and conclusions they have drawn from their experience.

Many Sided Truth

A common dilemma relates to how much one should tell one's informants in advance about what one is trying to do. By withholding from them one's assumptions, is one acting under false pretences? The first time I had to deal with this problem was when I was assisting a colleague with a Punjab-based village study documenting the lives of women of peasant and landless poor households. One important aim of our study was to try to explore the reasons for the unnaturally low sex ratio in Punjab and how this was connected to women's status in the village (see 'The Unequal Deal', *Manushi* No. 11, 1981).

The investigators found that the villagers were extremely cooperative and helpful. This was chiefly because a revered local leader had introduced the investigating team to them. The team gathered detailed information that included the daily caloric intake of male and female members of a small sample of households and surveyed a larger sample about facts such as the hours of work put in by women, the nature of women's labour contribution, marriage practices, dowry, decision making in the household, domestic violence and women's mobility. Apart from an overall census and detailed interviews with a sample of women, the investigators spent a substantial part of their time in the village recording and discussing women's situation with knowledgeable villagers not included in the formal sample.

However, when we came to interpreting the information, we faced serious dilemmas to the point of almost abandoning the report. The overall picture that emerged portrayed the village as abounding in wife-beaters, drunken husbands and opium addicts. Daughters appeared somewhat less likely to survive than sons. Very few positive features emerged in our description of women's status. Clearly, this was not the whole truth about the community, although the team had been fairly careful in gathering the information.

We had relied principally on information from discussions with women, without men ordinarily being present, on male–female relations within the family. This was necessary since we feared we would fail to get much of the information we sought if men provided or monitored the answers. Objective information such as the exact caloric intake of males and females, the body weights and measurements of men and women belonging to different strata of the society was collected by actual observation and measurement. Yet, we could not escape the feeling that in a few important areas our results read like an oversimplified version of a complex reality.

We were left with many unresolved questions. Did the women view their relations with men of their families as merely exploitative? Would they recognize our picture of women's place in the village? If not, what would be the reasons for any divergence between their version and our interpretation? Also, if they did not agree with our description of reality, they were less likely to agree with our prescriptions for change.

Further, could the men's version be totally dismissed? Were there not fathers who took on large debts to raise dowries for their daughters and did they and their daughters not genuinely believe that this was done out of love? Could we dismiss altogether the image of a fair number of these Punjabi farmers as industrious, good-natured, warm-hearted, supportive and family-minded men? Did not the generosity, hospitality and openness that we observed and benefited from, in itself shed light on an aspect of reality and of interpersonal relations that had not emerged in our study? That depended to a great extent on structured questions addressed to the women alone. No doubt, an out-of-the-way effort to obtain women's version of reality helped us get important glimpses of village and family life which are often overlooked. But a more authentic version would be far more complex and derive from many additional sources of information.

Which Women, When?

While in some ways women's lived experience may be said to be different from that of men as a group, it took me a long time to realize how women's perceptions are also diverse. A woman's version of social reality varies substantially depending on where she is placed. I am referring not just to differences in caste and class, which do matter a great deal, but also to the differences that separate women within the same family. For instance, when gathering information about women's labour contribution, one has clearly to assess who is talking about whom. A woman's version of her own workday and workload is often very different from what the other women of the same family might perceive it as being.

So also, a woman is likely to give one sort of description of how much dowry was given at her daughter's marriage and another of how much dowry her daughter-in-law brought. This is not at all to suggest anything as simplistic as that her account will be more accurate for her own dowry, exaggerated for her daughter's dowry and underestimated for her daughter-in-law's. The description one gets in any one of these three situations is likely to be influenced by a complex set of criteria related to family politics, status considerations and numerous other factors.

Woman to Woman

For years, as an activist, I had simplistically assumed that women's experiences would be more accessible to me because I am a woman who professes to be somewhat sensitive to women's predicaments. I continue to believe that, as a woman, I have certain advantages in gaining access to a woman's world. However, these advantages can be offset by several limitations.

In a society like ours, where women's subordination and exclusion often assume fairly extreme forms, women are frequently not allowed to share their experiences, perceptions and opinions with other women, particularly those who are seen as outsiders to the family. Such sharing is seen as a kind of defiance and therefore a threat to family honour. Women are required to funnel their opinions and experiences to outsiders through the men of the family.

For instance, when conducting a survey of marriage practices in a Madhya Pradesh village, I found that women very often answered my questions regarding the amounts and items given and taken at their children's marriages with the remark: 'I don't really know. Ask the men, they arrange it all. They know.' This could easily be interpreted as duplicity, since I know they were not really so ignorant. It could also be seen as their ignorance, springing from their isolated housebound role, which prevented them from acquiring basic information regarding their own lives. This perception was doubtless part of their own self-view too, linked somewhere to the sentiment that respectable women do not engage in economic deals pertaining to the public arena, that being men's domain.

One reaction to these problems in investigations might be to stop asking women, and ask only men, since men tend to be more forthcoming. This, however, does not mean they are necessarily more accurate in their descriptions. One could also see the woman's response as meaningless stupidity and hence neglect to report it at all in one's writing.

It took me a while to figure out that even in not divulging information, the women were in fact divulging an important aspect of their situation within marriage and the family. This aspect was that of their lack of authority to decide on their own whether I, a stranger, should be told anything at all about complex internal interrelationships and economic matters. Even if it were all right to say something, it might be even harder for them to take responsibility for how much I should be told and in what ways. Men took these decisions without consulting women and gave me a version that was carefully tailored in different ways. But women did not feel certain that they could undertake to do this tailoring without the men's approval. Hence they felt it safer to refer me to the men even though most often they did have the details themselves.

It is significant that the only woman who was forthcoming in the Madhya Pradesh study was the one who was in open confrontation with the men of her marital family. She had been able to do so because she had the backing of the men of her natal family who were powerful and wealthy and lived in a nearby village.

Men may not be physically present but the fear of their power often acts as an effective censor in women's minds. My initial access to women's lives is almost always in some important ways determined by how far men of the community decide to cooperate. There is rarely any way I can reach women by bypassing men. This is especially the case in rural areas.

The Question of Timing

The hold that men have over women's minds and over women's perceptions of their subjective experience tends to get weakened under certain circumstances. It has often been observed that women's participation in political movements tends to get a fillip during phases of political repression and violent attacks because that is when men feel compelled to bring the women out. In their own interest, they often loosen the traditional bonds, so as to better combat outside forces such as the repressive arms of the state.

Similarly, men are compelled to loosen their control over what women will say and how they will describe their experiences to each other and to outsiders, during phases of extreme crisis. I have noticed this during different investigations of massacres, whether unleashed by the state or by other forces.

After the November 1984 anti-Sikh pogrom in Delhi, I began to interview members of the Sikh community. This was within three or four days of the events. The entire community, including the men, was in a state of trauma. Therefore, I did not once face a situation of the men of a family saying: 'Why ask women? We'll tell you better.' Women poured out their experiences of personal humiliation, sexual assault, gang-rape, even in the presence of men.

However, whenever I have investigated such atrocities a couple of weeks or a month after the event, women's voices are always more subdued. Men take over literally as well as in women's minds. The male-defined censorship norms of the community get to be imposed again once the men have regained some of their lost composure. Women's experience gets to be pruned and edited automatically without any formal decisions necessarily having been taken in this regard.

In Meerut, which in 1987 witnessed a large-scale massacre, our team, which arrived a couple of weeks after the violence, did not come across any women narrating their experiences. Women would tell how male relatives had been killed or arrested and tortured, or at most how the police had beaten, shot or killed a particular woman.

Does one assume that women were not sexually assaulted because they did not talk about it? I think that assumption would not be justified. The one woman who described to us the sexual brutality she had suffered was lying wounded in hospital. She had lost all the members of her family. Her vagina had been ripped with a knife up to her stomach and her intestines had spilled out. I recalled the very telling comment of Gurdeep Kaur, a woman victim of the November 1984 violence in Delhi: 'Why should I hesitate to tell? I have no one left.' She meant that all the men of her family were dead and there was now no one for the sake of whose 'honour' she should censor details. The female members of her family had all survived.

On another occasion, in 1980, when investigating cases of police atrocities in a tribal area, we were baffled by the fact that the political activists at district level who had invited us to the area to conduct an investigation were full of stories of police and Bihar Military Police (BMP) gang-rapes of women. Yet in the villages hardly any women or families stated that they had been victims of such assault. They would always evade the question by saying it happened in other neighbouring villages. Based on that response, some of the members of our team concluded that all the stories about police rape and atrocities were politically motivated and, therefore, needed to be discounted. I was also puzzled and felt that the silence on the subject of rape needed to be further investigated, especially since all of the other allegations of police atrocities had been corroborated by the victims without any hesitation.

On further perseverance, one episode shed some light on the situation. At one of the villages on the Gua-Manoharpur road, we interviewed a group of women who all denied that they had suffered any personal indignity but told us in detail about the beating up and arrest of the men and the looting indulged in by the BMP. At the next village, the account was the same. We expressed our confusion and inability to write the report we had come prepared to write, since no woman was forthcoming about what had happened to women. As we were leaving, a young man quietly came up and said he would take us to meet his sister. He brought us back to the village we had left and introduced us to one of the same women who had denied having been molested. He was at least 10 years younger than this sister of his. But when he told her to tell all, she did so, not just about herself but also about other women.

The reason she had withheld this information earlier was that she feared that her husband, who had been arrested and for whose release she had sold her jewellery and her family's animals, would ask her to leave his house if he got to know she had admitted to being raped by BMP men. Yet, even the support of a younger brother was sufficient for her to risk talking about her experience to us.

In this area, only two other women were also willing to describe their experience. They did so because a revered trade union leader of the village persuaded the men of the family that the women should be allowed to speak of this to our team.

My woman-to-woman communication thus has limited possibilities, because it is almost always the men of a community who directly or indirectly decide how much of a woman's experience is allowed to be expressed. This is primarily because the collective and individual power of men comes to determine what the consequences of that talking will be for women.

Interpretation vs Distortion

All writing is inherently selective and interpretive. However, interpretation is different from distortion. One needs to be careful that prior to offering an interpretation one does not distort facts, for instance by leaving some out, in order to reach a conclusion that suits one's own political predilections.

I am not arguing in favour of becoming apolitical, because the supposedly apolitical also have their unstated political prejudices. I am suggesting that (*a*) as far as possible we should make our political assumptions explicit; (*b*) we should search out and have the courage to face those facts that go contrary to our predilections and then root our conclusions in the facts; and (*c*) we should review any investigation, which neatly confirms our original premises without offering any surprises, sceptically.

One way of combating the tendency to impose one's preconceptions on the facts is to make a special effort to elicit as many versions or interpretations as possible of a situation from the different persons involved in it as participants or observers. The realization that there are usually a variety of versions that may be relevant, some easily available and others that require more probing, will determine how carefully we weigh, sift, crosscheck and give meaning to what we hear and see. It is true that no matter how careful we try to be, it is still likely that a lot will be missed. Nevertheless, in general, the more sources we are able to query on the same issue or set of known events, the more likely we are to get a more accurate view of the situation.

Let me give an example of the limitations of hearing only one version, even when it is that of a quite knowledgeable local observer. In the course of a village study on women's land rights, the woman social worker who was helping me gather data informed me with great enthusiasm that for the first time in the 12 years she had lived in the village as a social and political activist, she had witnessed a spontaneous case of 'class struggle'. She was referring to the case of a tribal man who, along with his sister, niece and other relatives, had beaten up a tribal woman of the same village who had worked as the recruiting agent for a contractor who supplies tribal labour to brick kilns around Kolkata. The reason for the outburst was that the niece of this man had returned pregnant from one of her migration trips to Kolkata and the recruiting agent who took her from their village had not helped or protected this young woman. The political activist who informed me of the case interpreted his beating up of the agent as a case of revolt against capitalist exploitation. She saw the village-based recruiting agent as a symbol of the system–the last and lowest link in the chain of exploiters.

When I talked to the wife of the man who had given the agent a beating, she saw the matter very differently. She had always complained that her husband was a good-for-nothing who beat her up often and snatched away the little she earned. While she toiled and starved, he drank rice beer and had fun at the weekly market. Others confirmed her description. Now that he had got into a fight, a police complaint had been made against him and he had to pay a bribe of Rs 1,000 or else go to jail. Much against his wife's wishes, he had mortgaged a part of their agricultural land in order to pay the bribe. His wife said she would rather he went to jail for a few months than that the family land be mortgaged. How would they survive if they lost part of the little land they had? She saw the beating as another example of her husband's irresponsible behaviour.

The woman who was beaten up and her mother were angry and bitter at being thus assaulted. Part of their anger arose from their perception that this man would only dare beat them up because they had no adult males in their household—they were three sisters living with their widowed mother. Like most such female-headed households, they had hardly any land. The mother had been widowed when her daughters were quite young, therefore she had not been able to retain her share of the family land, which was grabbed by her husband's male kin.

The other villagers saw the affair as a family matter springing from the outrage felt against the woman contractor who, although she belonged to the same *killi* or clan as the young woman, had not adequately protected her. But they were not as perturbed by the pregnancy or the beating in themselves. They were much more perturbed that the beating had led the woman to go and lodge a police complaint. The villagers panicked lest the police descend on the village. Police entry into the village signified for them indiscriminate extortion of bribes from all and sundry. Therefore, the elders got together and prevailed upon the accused man to go to the police station and voluntarily surrender before the police came to the village.

The man who did the beating did it because he felt his family honour was involved. He had expected a member of their *killi* to take special care of his niece while she was working away from home. It was not as if he had any grouse against the contracting system. Far from leading any 'class struggle' against the system, in all likelihood, he would not have been averse to acting as a recruiting agent himself.

Thus, the imposition of a formula, in this case that of class struggle, acts as a distorting rather than an illuminating factor and can lead one to adopt inappropriate strategies.

Keeping Prejudices in Check

All of us have certain culturally inherited prejudices that we may not be able to overcome entirely. Prejudices of this kind among higher status groups often take the form of considering lower status groups as irrational, unaware of their own interests, culturally backward or otherwise deficient and inferior. Europeans and Americans tend to have such prejudices against Africans and Asians, upper castes against lower castes, Hindus against Muslims, the rich against the poor, and vice versa. These prejudices may not always be stated. They could take the form of patronizing condescension towards those perceived as backward. One may see oneself individually as being above prejudice, but if one belongs to the hegemonic community, which has a strong antipathy against the other community, one has to be particularly vigilant. It is not sufficient merely to accumulate the accounts of more and more individuals when an entire community has begun to parrot a received version. In a situation where the two communities do not normally socialize, one's access to the other community in day-to-day life is in any case limited, no matter how liberal or radical one considers oneself. Having a few friends from the other community does not materially alter the fact of one's essential distance from its felt life. Therefore, whenever violent conflict occurs, it is important to get the versions of ordinary members of the other community, as well as to have sufficient command over the available facts. In order to have a better chance of obtaining the facts, one should reach the site of violence as quickly as possible, before the actual evidence has been removed.

Take the example of the communal violence in Meerut in May–June 1987. A team of us from *Manushi* visited Meerut a few days after the violence, when curfew had been somewhat relaxed. Since all of us were non-Muslims, we did not have automatic access to Muslims. We had to seek it out. The few contacts we had in the city were with Hindus. Muslims are concentrated in certain areas of the city, and most Hindus we met warned us against going there, telling dreadful stories about the dangers that awaited Hindu women who dared enter Muslim areas. We were solemnly told that we would never return alive. The police and administration were also extremely hostile to the idea of our entering Muslim areas. Their ostensible reason was that they would be blamed if we came to harm there. The real reason was that the law and order machinery had been actively involved in a large-scale massacre of Muslims and did not want reporters to meet the victims.

Had we gone only by the versions given by the people we spoke to, we would have been confronted with two diametrically opposed versions—one from Hindus and the other from Muslims. Simply believing the majority of those who were easily accessible to us would have meant accepting the Hindu version. Otherwise, one would have ended up in confusion, not knowing whom to believe.

Nearly all Hindus we met believed that most of the victims of violence had been Hindus and that Hindus had lost more lives as well as more property than Muslims had. Most Hindus also believed that the government was prejudiced in favour of Muslims and that had it not been for the Provincial Armed Constabulary's protective role, Hindus would have suffered still more terrible losses. This version was repeated by almost every Hindu, educated or uneducated, rich or poor, man or woman, almost as if they had memorized a tape-recorded message.

One had to be wary even of supposed eyewitness accounts. The killers often masqueraded as eyewitnesses but the inherent absurdities of the stories they told alerted us. Some Hindu eyewitnesses told bizarre stories of how Muslims had burnt their own homes in order to claim compensation, and how Muslims burnt to death accidentally and their corpses spontaneously leapt into distant wells; or that Muslims were the aggressors even in areas where only Muslims had died.

We had to adopt different methods to arrive at an estimate of the situation. First, we made a special effort to visit Muslim areas in the face of hostility and obstructionism from police and the Hindu population. As soon as we did so, we came face to face with certain inescapable facts. For one thing, we saw a much larger number of Muslims with injuries and broken limbs than amongst Hindus. Whereas in Hindu areas we mainly heard rumour-based stories of Hindu deaths, but met far fewer families of dead persons. In Muslim areas, we met numerous people who had lost family members, killed by police or who 'disappeared' after arrest.

Second, we attempted a citywide survey of damage done during the violence. In the more seriously affected parts of the city, we did a house-by-house and shop-by-shop count to see how many establishments belonging to Hindus and how many belonging to Muslims were damaged. These areas included the major markets of the city, where Hindu and Muslim shops were cheek-by-jowl. In each case, we also noted the nature and extent of the damage. The shops had not yet been cleaned up, and the wreckage was clearly visible. The results clearly showed that an overwhelming majority of damaged shops, houses and vehicles belonged to Muslims. These ranged from small- to medium-sized shops and stalls, manufactories to home-based weaving establishments and restaurants, rickshaws to buses, huts to three-storeyed houses. In comparison, the number of Hindus who had suffered losses was much smaller. In one area, a dozen large factories belonging to Hindus had been burnt and in another, a petrol pump and a few nearby shops. The factories constituted a large visible loss that made a big impact in the local papers and on people's minds.

But thousands of Muslims, most of them poor and lower middle class, had lost their means of livelihood, and many were rendered homeless. These losses were downplayed in the local Hindi press, read by most Hindus, which was violently anti-Muslim in its tone. Also, since Muslims generally lived in separate colonies, the wreckage in the interior of these colonies was not visible to Hindus, who never enter these colonies, especially at such times. Hindus dismissed the losses of Muslims with a contemptuous: 'What do those wretched rickshaw-pullers have to lose anyway?' Even on the main roads, it was clear that Muslim establishments had been targeted for destruction. Neighbouring Hindu establishments were either untouched or slightly damaged, that too due to proximity. Most Muslim establishments were reduced to ashes and rubble, while in some areas whole colonies of Muslim homes were devastated as though by war, roofless and wrecked, while the adjoining Hindu colony was untouched. Yet most Hindus seemed not to see even such visible patterns.

We tried to get a community-by-community breakdown of deaths and arrests but the administration was extremely unwilling to disclose their figures. This reluctance was understandable, given its complicity in the violence and its consequent desire to let rumours favourable to the police version of the events acquire legitimacy. After much persuasion, we were allowed to look at some of the lists for a couple of areas. A simple count of Hindu and Muslim names confirmed the impression we had formed from surveys of Hindu and Muslim areas—that far more Muslims than Hindus had died, yet simultaneously, far more Muslims than Hindus had been arrested as rioters.

If we had reached Meerut too late to see the evidence of the damage, and had been compelled to trust the versions given by the local people, the local media, the government and the press, we would have been led to believe that this was a riot between Hindus and Muslims in which Muslims had incited and led the violence. Examining the evidence with our own eyes showed us a far more complex reality.

From this experience, the realization hit us forcefully that even so-called eyewitness accounts may not serve as an adequate basis for research in a hate-charged atmosphere wherein people's subjectivity is coloured by self-interest or manipulated and distorted by politicians over so long a period and so systematically that they have lost the ability to honestly register what they see and hear, and instead merely parrot the version that is transmitted to them by their incriminated leaders and by biased media, a version that conveniently falls in with their immediate self-interest.

Even more caution in observing and listening is required when the two communities are unevenly balanced in political power and economic resources. The dominant community's hegemony in the bureaucracy, police, government and mass media makes its version the authoritative and dominant one. When the researcher's own inherited bias coincides with the bias of the state machinery and of the majority of the population, it is often no longer safe to go by the 'people's version', namely, the version put forward by the majority of the people. How the majority version becomes the received version is evidenced also in the November 1984 massacre of Sikhs in Delhi still being referred to in documents and in the press as a 'riot' even though it is clear that it was an organized one-way attack on the Sikhs by armed gangs with the support of leading Congress (I) politicians and the assurance of non-interference by police.

Therefore, any description of a riot or massacre should include a realistic assessment of the relative strength and influence of the two communities. For instance, many Hindus are convinced Muslims are a pampered minority but statistics and facts point to a situation of systematic discrimination against Muslims in most of northern India. If one does not have an accurate overall picture, one is unlikely to get facts at the ground level right.

What People Want

What then do I mean by emphasizing the need to take people seriously, when I am at the same time arguing that people's version of their own lives as recounted to an activist is often insufficient in and of itself to establish what is happening? Here, I distinguish between two kinds of information—while one needs to be sceptical, although not dismissive, about what people choose to reveal or conceal about themselves, their neighbours, relatives and friends, one needs to take people very seriously when they talk about what they want, what will improve their lives, what they need in order to live with dignity, even to survive.

We must be careful that the questions we ask regarding this last set of aspirations are relevant to the options available to a person, and not unrealistic or wholly imaginary. For instance, if a woman says she needs to have three or more children, it is wrong to attribute this to her ignorance and to insist, without careful consideration, that it is in the 'national interest' as well as in her own long-term interest to have no more than one or two children. In the case of such a conflict of interests, one must consider whether by 'nation' one does not actually mean contrary interests out to thwart the woman's own self-interest. When one seriously listens, it may become evident why she needs three, four or five children. If one reason turns out to be that she knows half of them are likely to die of malnutrition and related factors, one could begin by trying to help her fight against poverty and child disease—not as a bargaining point for a one-child family, but because that is what she needs and says she needs.

To take another example, when surveying the lives of maltreated wives, it is easy to assume that when a brutally maltreated woman says she wants to go back and live with the husband who beat her up and threw her out, this is solely because she suffers from lack of awareness and has low self-esteem or to believe that she should be persuaded, in her own interest, not to go back to him. It takes some time to realize that the woman's perception of her future, given her circumstances, could, in all likelihood, be the more realistic one, that, in many instances, she would end up leading a less dignified life in her parents' home, at the mercy of brothers and sisters-in-law, or as a single woman living on her own, than in her marital home where over the years she might have at least some slightly enhanced socially acknowledged rights and status.

Some Suggestions

The following are some tentative rules of thumb evolved from the experiences described thus far, which have the potential to help us avoid making some of the same mistakes over and over.

1. When we begin to investigate a situation, we naturally have a set of expectations or notions about what the results might be. If the research ends up so completely confirming these notions that we could have written the report without having gathered any information, we should suspect that we are likely to have made some fundamental error. We should then review the entire process—the questions asked, the observations included, the respondents chosen, and the way the questions were formulated and the answers interpreted. It is possible that our preconceptions prevented us from asking questions that were searching enough, or led us unwittingly to give the respondents some non-verbal signal that we preferred a particular type of response. We may also have excluded from the group of respondents certain relevant people who might have upset our preconceptions.
2. If at all possible, we should carefully discuss the various drafts of the report with the different groups of informants to see if it makes sense to them. Even if one believes that some of the respondents may have biases that tend to distort their opinions, we should nevertheless listen to them carefully and take them seriously. They are likely to be able to uncover complexities in the situation (including in our preconceptions) of which we were unaware.
3. We should avoid premature categorizing of anticipated or actual respondents according to preconceived categories. For example, we cannot assume that most women will primarily or automatically describe their experience from the perspective of their status as women. Other classifications may have far greater salience—for example, their religion, caste, landholding, and identity as mother, mother-in-law, daughter and wife. One has to patiently untangle the crosscutting allegiances and identities that even the most downtrodden member of a society maintains, in order to arrive at the information relevant to the category of most interest to one's investigation.
4. If the respondents do not respond in a way we expect them or would like them to respond, we should avoid assuming that the reason is that they are stupid, uneducated, ignorant or that they are at a low level of class (or any other kind of) consciousness, or that they are deliberately

trying to mislead us. While these explanations are always possible and, sometimes, though rarely, true, it is far more likely that it is the investigator who lacks mental flexibility. The unexpected and difficult answers are often the most fruitful clues to what is happening.

5. It is a mistake to think that we have a better comprehension of people's options and best interests than they do themselves. We should be particularly careful to take people seriously when they talk about what it is they consider most important to improve their lives and what is necessary for their survival. These are areas in which almost all of us end up being something of an expert, especially when regarding our own lives. We are not likely to be able to offer them greater wisdom on what their real options are, given the particularities of their own situation.
6. We should not assume that because we have some things in common with our informants, we automatically have greater insight into their lives. The investigator and the person interviewed may both be women, Dalits, teachers and mothers, but this commonality may not be the most salient factor influencing the investigation on a particular subject. The investigator's dissimilarities from the respondents may often be even more significant than the similarities. Similarities with respondents may be helpful but cannot be a substitute for taking seriously respondents' perceptions when they differ from our own.
7. We should also not assume that because we subscribe to an ideology that we believe is in the best interests of the people whose lives we are looking into, or because we genuinely believe we have their interests at heart, this will automatically give us greater insight into their situation, or that our perceptions are necessarily superior to their own, regarding the possible solutions to their problems.
8. When the people we want to help and understand are dependent on others who may want to influence their replies, we have to develop better techniques to get as forthright answers as possible. One way to do this is to inform the respondents in detail of the ways we will ensure confidentiality. We must then be compulsive in abiding by our explicit or implicit promises.

   Despite this, we need to maintain a healthy scepticism about the answers received from those respondents who are in a relatively powerless position and who could be injured by their answers becoming known to those on whom they are dependent. By the same token, it is equally essential that we cross-check the self-serving responses of the powerful who have much to gain from their version of events.

9. One of the most difficult decisions for an investigator to make is what to do with information provided in distorted, even falsified, ways, in a situation of hatred and stereotyping between groups. While discarding the falsified picture of events when trying to understand what in fact happened, it is nevertheless important to include the hateful prejudices and stereotypes prevalent as a crucial part of the situation prevailing. The existence of these hate-inducing myths is an important factor in causing a certain kind of event, for example, a so-called riot. Therefore, knowledge of these myths is vital for those who try to find ways to improve the situation.

All of this is not to suggest that we have found foolproof methods of eliciting accurate and reliable information. But we hope that what we have learnt from our experiences and mistakes over these years will help us improve the quality of our reporting and of our suggestions for change.

6

Dowry

*To Ensure Her Happiness or to Disinherit Her?**

For over a century, eradication of dowry has been a major item on the agenda of social reformers of all hues. In the last decade, it has perhaps received more attention than almost any other social issue. Yet, dowry is nowhere near being eradicated. In fact, the dowry system has flourished and spread through all levels of our society all over the country, simultaneously with the campaign against it. The reasons commonly adduced for the increase in dowry are not reflective of much serious thinking about the reasons why people give and take dowry. Until we understand how dowry actually works, we will not be able to do anything meaningful about it.

*This article appeared in *Manushi*, No. 34, May–June 1986.

Due to Growing Greed?

One argument repeated *ad nauseam* is that people in today's world have become very greedy, hence the increasing demands for dowry. Often, this 'greed' is seen as an influence of western consumerist culture, which leads people to want more and more gadgets and other consumer goods.

This tendency to view the present age as *kalyug* and the past as a golden era may be consoling, but is not grounded in fact. Early twentieth century literature, both fiction and reformist propaganda, is full of laments over the increase in dowry and the growing materialism of people. This was much before refrigerators and videos appeared on the scene.

A common theme of many social protest movements is a harking back to an earlier golden age and a criticism of the current materialist culture in comparison to the good old days. The literature of the *Bhakti* movement (the writings of Kabir, Nanak and others), or even of such an early movement as Buddhism, bears testimony to this. There is nothing new in people's desire for more and more wealth. Nor is this trait specific to any particular culture. Dowry, however, is specific to certain cultures.

If increasing dowry demands were, in fact, merely related to the aping of the materialist culture and lifestyle of the West, we might expect to find even higher dowry demands manifested in many western countries. This is quite clearly not the case. People in the West have created a thousand other terrible problems for themselves but they do not show any inclination, at present, to foster the giving and taking of dowry. This is not because people in one country are more or less greedy than people in other countries. However badly a man may currently maltreat his wife in a western country, he dare not demand a video and car from her parents as dowry, not because he is more enlightened than a husband in India but because his wife's parents will not normally entertain such demands. They do not feel that they must get their daughters married and see that they stay married at any cost. They would not consider it an unbearable social disgrace for themselves if their daughter stayed unmarried or left her husband, although they would prefer her to get married and to remain married.

The 'greed' theory would make sense only if the world was divided into two sets of families—one set which produced only boys and another which produced only girls. In such a situation, the boy-producing families would be at a permanent advantage. Despite the prevalence of various forms of female infanticide in India, our society is not yet divided into these two mutually exclusive camps. Thus, there are no permanent gainers or losers. In most families, dowries are both given and taken. Quite frequently, the same families whose daughters are harassed for more dowry themselves harass daughters-in-law in similar ways.

One of the most notable features that emerges during anti-dowry campaigns is the small number of people who are consistently either genuinely for or against it. There is hardly anybody in the country who, at one time or another, will not decry and lament its pernicious effects. Vast numbers of people are as unanimous in condemning it as they are persistent in practising it. It is common for a person to deplore dowry in one breath and justify it in the next. Some are content merely to express helplessness in breaking away from it.

The arguments generally put forward for and against dowry are in the nature of moralistic clichés rather than the results of careful analysis of our society. Why is it that even those who consider dowry transactions morally wrong and socially harmful insist that they must continue to practise it? The vast majority of parents, at the time of a daughter's marriage, appear as eager to give dowry as they are to receive it at the time of a son's marriage.

If dowry was basically the product of greed, the groom's family would not encourage extravagant expenditure on the wedding feast and entertainment of guests. In fact, the groom's family too spends substantial amounts on non-recoverable expenses connected with the wedding such as extravagant receptions, music bands and gifts to various relatives.

At a recent marriage in my neighbourhood, I observed that what the groom's family actually received in cash and kind did not exceed what they had themselves spent on the wedding of their son. The bride brought with her furniture, jewellery and other goods not worth more than Rs 60,000. This is about the amount that the groom's family had spent on their part of the wedding celebrations. A portion of the money they spent was borrowed on interest. Even though the bride's family spent twice as much as the groom's family, only a part of this money reached the groom's family in the form of durable goods, much of it being spent on celebrations. In this instance, which I believe is fairly typical, the ultimate economic gain for the groom's family does not seem commensurate with the amount they spend on the marriage.

Even a cursory study of wife harassment cases shows that taunts flung at a daughter-in-law do not relate to major demands for cash or items like videos and scooters. Much more common are taunts regarding the number and quality of *sarees* given to her, the quality of the wedding feast and the presents given to her by her natal family at various festivals. If the main motive was avarice, it would be wiser for the in-laws to demand cash for themselves rather than grumble about the number of *sarees* given to the bride. Instead of saying, 'Why only 21 *sarees* and not 31?' or 'Why cotton *sarees* and not silk?' or 'Why Indian gadgets and not imported ones?', they would say: 'Why even 21 *sarees* ? Let her manage with her old *sarees* and give us the rest of the money in cash. No need for an expensive mixer. She can use a grinding stone. We need the money.' This would also eliminate the possibility of the daughter-in-law having some basis to exercise her rights over what are supposed, in some traditions, to be her personal dowry items.

When writing on dowry-related harassment and murder, the media tends to mention failure to meet major demands such as that for a scooter or a colour TV as the direct precursor of maltreatment. However, I believe that an in-depth study of most cases would reveal that the harassment seldom ceases as and when these demands are met. The daily torture and harassment that breaks a woman down is more often related to constant taunts designed to humiliate her, make her feel a contemptible burden on the family and put her on the defensive over every conceivable matter. For instance, recently, a young woman from a fairly wealthy business family came to us in connection with her divorce case. She had been married to a well-off businessman who earns about Rs 30,000 a month. She complained that he would give her no money at all. Even if she needed to buy herself a pair of slippers, she would be told to get the money from her 'wealthy father'. In another case, the woman complained that she did not even have enough money to visit her parents' house about 10 km away. Each time she went there, she was expected to take an autorickshaw and get her parents to pay the fare so that each visit became a humiliating affair for her. In addition, the gifts she brought back from her natal family were thoroughly screened and denigrated in a way that made her feel inadequate and ashamed.

The whole process of constant humiliation is intended to demoralize a woman so that her feeling of vulnerability makes her desperately desire to somehow to carve a place for herself in her in-laws' house, however degrading the terms she must accept. She is compelled to grovel before her husband and his family in order to seek a precarious foothold. The never-ending demands and taunts make her feel perpetually insecure as she never knows which occasion may be used to demean and threaten her further.

This psychological warfare is part of a strategy to make women accept a subordinate position within the family and feel grateful for being allowed to survive at all in the marital home. The retraining of the daughter-in-law into total subordination is an essential part of her transition from the natal to the marital home.

Thus, dowry demands are as little or as much related to greed as rape is to sexual satisfaction. Both are essentially forms of violence whose primary purpose is to degrade and victimize a woman so that she retains a desperate fear of disobeying the powerful. Just as rapists frequently beat, maim or kill their victim as a further expression of their power over her, so also the taunts and abuses of a daughter-in-law may escalate into beatings, torture and even murder.

'Voluntarily' Given Gifts—Not Dowry?

One reason for the utter ineffectiveness of the campaign against dowry is the dishonesty with which even the reformers define dowry. The dominant opinion even among opponents of dowry is that anything that is given by the bride's family of their own free will, without any demands being made by the groom's family, is not to be considered dowry. Therefore, there is no need for these gifts to be considered wrong. Demands made by the groom's family are alone reprehensible.

This view is based on the idea that conflicts over dowry arise only when the groom's family is exceptionally greedy. It is assumed that whatever the bride's family 'voluntarily' gives at the time of marriage is a sign of their genuine love and concern for the welfare and security of their daughter. But demands for additional goods or money by the groom's family are the main source of trouble. This argument is a highly dubious one. In the social atmosphere of India today, it is ridiculous to talk of completely voluntary giving of dowry. If dowry is indeed an essential expression of voluntary concern for daughters, it should be a universal phenomenon—which it is not, even in India, let alone in the world. Dowry of the kind that exists among some communities in India has been prevalent in certain cultures. There is no evidence that these cultures have shown any special fondness for daughters. It frequently coexists with severe forms of discrimination and oppression of women.

Can Dowry Giving Be Voluntary?

Even when demands are not made, any marriage is contracted in a highly competitive marriage market, wherein it is assumed that boys are precious commodities and daughters a burden whom parents must get rid of, at as early an age as is feasible. It is important to remember that these are the assumptions not only of the man's family but equally of the woman's family.

One key pressure that compels the 'voluntary' giving of dowry is that among most communities, especially among the dowry-giving communities in India, marriage is just about universal, and is considered so essential that without it a woman's life is considered blighted. Parents feel duty-bound to plan and perform their daughters' marriages. It is considered a great dereliction of social duty if parents fail to perform this all-important ritual. A daughter is never considered settled if she is not married, not even if she has a well-paid high status job.

The pressure is not only to 'settle' her but to do so at the right age. The concept of the right age has varied from time to time and community to community. For the urban educated middle class today, the 'right age' begins soon after the daughter graduates, when she is about 19 years old. By the time she crosses 26, she is on the verge of losing out in the marriage market. Hence, the desperation grows and the groom may have to be compensated with a higher dowry.

Even if she has acquired more education or a better paid job, these are not always considered sufficient compensation for the age handicap. The dowry for a highly educated daughter is likely to be larger rather than smaller because the amount of dowry is calculated according to the market value of the prospective son-in-law. Since under no circumstances can a woman be married to a man younger than she is, a man in his late 20s or early 30s is likely to be better settled in his career and hence have a higher market value.

In such a situation, it is meaningless to talk of free will or voluntary giving. This is the equivalent of saying that a steep price rise of essential commodities is fine as long as the customers continue to go to the shops of their own free will and pay the high prices.

Dowry does not always have to be demanded because it is assured through other mechanisms. When marriage alliances are made, both sides take pains to display their status by describing at length their family connections and the amount of property owned. The socioeconomic status and power of brothers, uncles, grandparents, cousins, all play an important role in determining the outcome of marriage negotiations.

When the groom's family insists that the girl have a 'decent' family background, only the very naive would understand 'decency' to mean moral virtue. It is an unmistakable hint at the status of the family. This enhances the likelihood of getting dowry of a certain quantity and quality. Likewise, the groom's family displays its own connections and relatives and economic worth to hint that whatever is given should be commensurate with their status as they define it.

These status descriptions affect the calculation of a particular dowry, although dowry is also to a large extent determined by the customs in a particular kinship group. A family's 'voluntary' giving can express itself only in enhancing the dowry amount. They can certainly, if they choose, give more than what is expected. But they rarely can give less because their own *izzat* or honour is at stake. Thus, a bride from a 'decent' family is the best guarantee of a 'decent' dowry, even if the groom's family does not make explicit demands.

Is It Dowry That Causes Maltreatment?

In itself, giving of money and gifts should not become a cause of oppression for anyone. It should make the couple's life together easier. Why is it then that giving gifts and money to daughters becomes a virtual death-trap for so many women? Let us take an analogy. If a family were to offer another family Rs 1 lakh for the care of a dog, horse or cow for a period of time, is it likely that the animal would be maltreated or burnt to death as are many wives?

The form in which dowry is practised in India seems to defy all rules of rational economic behaviour and laws of supply and demand. Logic would suggest that a woman who brought wealth with her should be highly valued. And indeed we would have no reason to object to the giving of dowry to daughters if it did not lead to abuse and marital conflicts.

For a long time, reformers have perceived and projected dowry as a moral issue, as if giving of dowry itself is inherently morally flawed. This has only helped obscure the real issue, which is that women get maltreated despite carrying such enormous amounts of wealth with them to their in-laws' homes. Our form of dowry does not seem sufficient to mitigate a woman's powerlessness although it remains an indicator of the prestige and status of her natal family and of the family of the man who marries her. In economic terms, a woman who carries a dowry of Rs 1 lakh has an exchange value of minus Rs 1 lakh because her family must give this amount unconditionally to have the groom's family take this burden from them and the man who marries her is valued at plus Rs 1 lakh.

To return to the analogy of an animal handed over to caretakers, the reason an animal is likely to be well looked after is that the original owners of the animal, if paying for its future care, would object to maltreatment and say: 'If you cannot take proper care of the animal, please return it and the money.' However, most parents would rather see their daughters dead than have them get a divorce and return permanently to the parental home. Dowry is supposed to act as a bribe to the son-in-law to keep the daughter who, after she reaches a certain age, is totally unwanted in her parental home. That is why a woman's parents are ever ready to meet the continuing demands made by the husband's family, provided he keeps her in his house.

In hardly any of the cases that have come to *Manushi* in the last few years has the woman's family decisively refused to meet the escalating dowry demands and assured their daughter she was welcome back to her natal home. It is usually only when the woman is thrown out of her marital home after all attempts to placate her in-laws fail that her family will, in desperation, finally think of taking some action.

Is Dowry Really Meant for the Woman?

Despite all the fancy talk about *stridhan* (a woman's own inalienable property), dowry has very little to do with the *stri* concerned. It is essentially a transfer of wealth from men of one family to those of another, with women acting either as vehicles of transfer (brides) or as watchdogs (mother-in-law and sister-in-law). This is the most important reason for the wealth incorporated in the dowry, not empowering women.

A frequently advanced argument for the necessity of dowry is that it is a way of giving a daughter her share in parental property: 'How can a daughter be sent empty-handed from her parents' house?' The implicit assumption of this rhetorical question is that, unlike a son who is expected to outlive his parents and inherit from them, a daughter's marriage is the end of her membership in her natal family and is therefore the appropriate occasion for her to get whatever she can. But dowry is not in fact a daughter's fair share nor is it a way of compensating her for her lack of inheritance rights.

A woman has little say in deciding how much money is to be spent on her dowry and the wedding celebration. Nor does she have any real control over how that money is to be allocated. A large part of the expenditure is on the feasts, gifts, decorations and other wedding expenses. Though none of this benefits the woman in any way, she is made to feel grateful for all that is being spent—whether or not she wants that kind of wedding. For instance, a girl can rarely tell her parents that instead of spending Rs 50,000 on a five- star hotel wedding reception, they would do better to put the money in the bank as a fixed deposit in her name.

When large amounts of cash are given as part of the dowry, they are almost always given to the son-in-law, his father or other senior male members of his family. Very rarely is the cash given the daughter, in her own name.

Recently, a friend of mine was married. She was not keen on a dowry but she had no real say in the matter. To give a certain kind of dowry is a requisite for the maintenance of a woman's family's honour. They insist on giving it in that form irrespective of the woman's needs and desires. This woman felt she might have to leave her job after marriage because to commute by bus would take two hours each way every day. She could not manage this if she had to run a household. I suggested that since the family was in any case spending so much on the marriage, she could ask them to buy her a two-wheeler scooter so that she could retain her job. She replied that she did not want to impose an added burden on them by making such a demand. Could she not get them to buy a scooter in lieu of some expensive item of jewellery? To this she replied that jewellery was bought according to norms that prevailed in the community. The family purchased the dowry according to the traditions of their kinship group and her demands did not figure anywhere in the calculations except in such non-essentials as choice of colour or design of clothes and jewellery. Furthermore, if a scooter was bought, her husband would automatically assume that it was for his use. Her trying to assert a separate right over it might create serious problems at the outset of their married life.

Thus, the daughter's convenience is not the primary, seldom even a major, consideration. The transfer of goods is essentially from one family to another. This is obvious from the way money is allocated. If a middle class family in Delhi spends a total of Rs 1.5 lakh on the wedding, this is a rough estimate of how they might spend the money:

Expenses	**Rs**
Expenditure on engagement ceremony	15,000
(This would contain nothing for the woman. It consists only of gifts for the groom and his family)	
Wedding feast	20,000
Furniture, crockery, utensils	25,000
Refrigerator, television and other gadgets	20,000
Jewellery	30,000
Clothes for the bride	15,000
Clothes for groom and his family	10,000
Cash and other gifts to groom's family	10,000
Miscellaneous (including gifts to bride's relatives)	10,000

Thus, out of Rs 1,55,000 spent, not more than Rs 45,000 is spent on goods for the bride's direct use, that is, clothes and jewellery, to which she may have some claim. Although the rest is spent on her behalf, she has not even a nominal say in its allocation.

In actuality, a woman is seldom allowed to have control even over things that are supposedly for her personal use. Gold and other jewellery are traditionally supposed to be a woman's personal security but, in practice, the gold usually stays in the custody of her mother-in-law or husband. It is up to them to give her what they wish for her personal use and daily wear.

Even if a woman is allowed to keep some of her jewels in her cupboard or in a joint locker in the bank, she is more like a guardian of her husband's family wealth than an individual in possession of her own property. It would be taken extremely ill if she sold, gifted or otherwise disposed of it without their permission. And it is expected that if her husband or his family requires money, she will put her jewels at their disposal. This role played by a woman's gold is much glorified in literature and in films as a noble sacrifice on her part for her marital—never her natal—family. A woman who refused to make such a sacrifice for her husband and in-laws would be seen as selfish and heartless, but one who dared make it for any member of her parental family would be considered a traitor to her marriage.

Usually, a woman does not even exercise symbolic control over her jewels. As soon as she reaches her in-laws' house, it is taken charge of by her husband or members of his family. It is fairly common for certain items of her jewellery to be incorporated into her husband's sister's dowry.

So also with clothes. It is customary in many families for a new daughter-in-law's clothes to be displayed and for her mother-in-law and sisters-in-law to take their pick. The point of this is not so much greed to grab clothes as it is to humiliate and remind her that she can consider nothing her own, not even clothing. Many women report that in the early years of marriage, they were not allowed free access to their clothes but were given a set of clothes each morning to wear. The element of choice and control is systematically taken out of the woman's life so as to disable her and train her to have very low self-esteem.

Even more important, 'filling a daughter's hands' with household goods is a way of telling her that her life must be confined to running a household. Should she be maltreated, abandoned or widowed, those goods do not provide any kind of base for her to run a life that extends beyond that household.

In many cases that have come to *Manushi*, a woman is thrown out of the marital home and rendered virtually destitute despite the thousands and sometimes lakhs of rupees her parents spent on her wedding. Rarely is she allowed to take her personal belongings, let alone the entire dowry. Even if she manages to bring away the furniture and utensils, she has usually no place to keep them and rarely gets much for them if forced to sell them.

Her parents may reluctantly take her back but her foothold in their house remains precarious. She is there on sufferance not by right, as are sons. Part of the justification used by many families for their refusing to provide support to their daughter is that they have already done all they could for her by giving her a dowry. The fact that this dowry was of little or no benefit to her seems to be no one's concern.

We have also found that parents frequently discourage daughters from leaving tyrannical husbands because this will mean a loss of what they consider their investment. Hence their constant advice to her to 'adjust' to maltreatment. In most cases of wife murder and maltreatment, the woman feels so weighed down by the expenditure undertaken by her parents, that she feels duty-bound to present a brave, smiling face to them and never let them know that their 'investment' has proved a dismal failure.

She is led to believe that to bear maltreatment from her husband without letting her parents know of it is not only a duty she owes to him but also a duty she owes her parents, who have spent so much on her wedding. The in-laws take advantage of a girl's parents' unwillingness to take her back into their home in order to blackmail them into giving more and more money.

Most parents justify their succumbing to these demands, saying it was done for the daughter's well-being. However, the deadly quality of this peculiar brand of parental concern is obvious when we find that a girl's parents are far more willing to put even lakhs of rupees in the hands of a man or a family who torture her than to spend even 10 per cent of that money on enabling her to survive independently.

Often, it seems as if parents offer incentives to a son-in-law to keep the daughter subjugated. As he begins to maltreat his wife, her parents, instead of removing her from that situation, begin to struggle, often desperately, to find ways and means of raising money for him in order to please him. But it is almost unheard of for parents to try to solve the problem by giving the daughter a shop or a house or capital to set herself up separately so that she does not have to put up with maltreatment. Thus, the woman's parents, by putting additional resources in the hands of the groom's family, in effect enhance his power over her life, incite him to make additional demands and tilt the power scales even further in his favour.

Dowry is given, not for the daughter's happiness, as is often claimed, but to increase her dependency. That is why very few parents will spend the same amount of money to help a daughter live independently as they will to get her married and keep her married.

Nor is the dowry necessarily equal to the share of a son. Much is made of the 'huge' sums spent on dowry but rarely is the sum comparable to the sum that the son inherits from his parents. The sum spent on dowry appears 'huge' to the parents because they value their daughter at less than that sum, but the sum willed to the son, however undeserving he may be, seldom appears too much. Rarely do parents bemoan the fact that they have to leave their lifetime's earnings to sons.

In many of the cases that come to us for help, when a woman is thrown out of the house by her husband, her natal family becomes obsessed by the desire to get back the dowry. They may even fight long drawn-out court battles to this end. But in those rare cases when they do get back most of the dowry goods, this in no way helps the woman start her life anew.

The goods given in dowry are not income generating forms of property, unlike the property normally given to sons. Items such as furniture, clothes and utensils, depreciate in value very quickly and in any case are not at all comparable to the value of land, a house, a shop, a factory, farm animals, agricultural equipment or other income-generating assets that parents may have at the time of their death. It is sons who inherit the income-generating forms of property, if any. And they inherit everything in their own right. Their wives have no say in the matter.

The argument that dowry is a girl's share, is her security and is given to ensure her future happiness, is, therefore, a hollow argument. Dowry giving is an investment not in the girl's future but in her family's honour or *izzat*. The size of the dowry is talked about in the community and enhances the status not only of the groom's parents but also of the bride's parents.

Social Role of Dowry

What a man receives or does not receive in dowry usually does not make or break his own or his family's financial status. It is not as if dowry makes a poor man into a rich one. In fact, the richer a man already is, the larger the dowry he expects. Thus, a man who gets a cycle in dowry usually is able to afford to buy a cycle on his own, one who gets a scooter is normally in a position to buy one himself and one who gets a car probably already has a car in the family. The dowry is an acknowledgment of his status, not a determinant of it.

The purpose of dowry-giving rituals is comparable to that of traditional offerings to feudal overlords. Those lower down in the feudal hierarchy were expected to acknowledge the lord's suzerainty by giving him gifts on every festive occasion and celebration in either his or their own family. Whether or not these offerings made any substantial difference to the lord's actual wealth, they had to be offered as tokens of respect, in public acknowledgment of his status. Non-compliance with the ritual would be perceived as a deliberate and unforgivable insult.

So also, any omission, real or imagined, on the part of the girl's family to give gifts at appropriate times, is perceived by the boy's family as an insult to their status, and to the groom who must be treated with great deference by his in-laws. The emphasis is not on financial loss but on what they see as disrespect. Thus, it is common for a major complaint of the husband and his family to be that they were not entertained with sufficient respect by the bride's family at the wedding feast or on other occasions.

What social purpose is served by this institution of regular offerings to a man on behalf of his wife? One major purpose seems to be a constant public reaffirmation of her inferior status and his superior status.

It is important to remember that her family members bow before her husband and are humiliated on her behalf. It is repeatedly drummed into her ears that her father bows before her husband only because he is her father, a girl's father. She is made to feel guilty for her very existence as a woman, an existence that puts her parents in such a humiliating position. *Beti paida ki hai to jhukna hi padta hai* (If one has the misfortune to give birth to a girl child, one has to prostrate before her in-laws)—there are such proverbial sayings in many regional languages which convey the message that a girl's parents are destined for humiliation by virtue of having given birth to an inferior creature.

However, a girl's father, if he also has a son, plays his role as a son's father with pride and superiority vis-à-vis his daughter-in-law's father. He is not socially defined as inferior in himself. He bows only in his capacity as a girl's father. But the girl is always in one role—of deference. She bows as herself. She in and of herself is defined as inferior.

Every marriage and dowry ritual publicly places a stamp of unequal value on the bride and groom. In other transactions, such as charity, one who gives is defined as superior and one who takes as inferior. But dowry giving, like giving to a brahman or an overlord, or offerings to a god in the course of worship, is a ritual giving from or on behalf of an inferior to a superior.

Its significance is not primarily economic but political, in the sense that it defines a power relation between the man and the woman.

Are Women More to Blame?

We are often told that it is women who keep the dowry system going. Daughters are said to take pride in lavish dowries and mothers-in-law are accused of being behind many dowry demands. People often say: 'It is girls who are to blame. Despite their education, they want dowry. Otherwise, why don't they refuse?'

As already pointed out, very few women in our country have the right to decide whether or not they want to marry. There is thus no question of their deciding the terms and conditions of marriage. These are usually predetermined by the family and kinship group.

Further, daughters are well aware that they can hardly ever hope to get a fair share in the parental property, as do sons. Since they are disinherited by virtue of being female, what is the advantage to them of forgoing whatever they are offered at marriage by way of dowry, which even at its exorbitant most is much less than what their brothers will inherit by way of assets?

I am certain that if a woman were offered a choice between a dowry of some cash, gold, 31 *sarees*, furniture and utensils, and 10 acres of land or a real partnership in a family business, very few would opt for the former. If today they show an inclination for a dowry containing clothes and jewellery, it is because the other option is not really available to them.

As for the role of the mother-in-law or sisters-in-law, a closer look at dowry transactions reveals that women may be more visible as actors but they are not the directors of the drama. For instance, the amount of dowry to be given is primarily decided by how much money the male head and other important male members of the family are willing to allocate for it. After that primary budgetary decision is made, women may perhaps be allowed to choose the colour, design and number of things to be bought. Even in this, the choice of major items is more often than not left to men.

As a rule, if the groom and his father were determined not to accept dowry or determined that the bride not be harassed for dowry, even the most tyrannical mother-in-law would not dare go against their wishes. She can make demands only when she knows she has the explicit or tacit approval of powerful male members of the family.

In most families, men play a crucial role in deciding marriage alliances. The great emphasis that comes to be laid on the economic and social status of the chosen family already sets the parameters of dowry expectations. After this, women are left to sort out some of the details and to implement many of the arrangements.

The role of the mother and sisters of the man tends to get over-stressed in most descriptions because, in a segregated society, women are allowed more direct and constant contact with other women. A mother-in-law and sister-in-law can be the most consistent torturers since the bride has to spend most of her time in their company. There are strict codes governing interaction between male and female members even of the same family. Thus, much of the harassment of the daughter-in-law has of necessity to be implemented by the women of the family who are set up as her jailors.

Blaming the women as the major perpetuators of dowry is like blaming the soldiers on the battlefield for fighting. They may be the ones seen killing and dying, but only the generals and politicians have the power to declare war, although they use the bodies of others as proxies and are seldom in danger of serious harm. Dowry, as practised in India, is a war declared by men against women, using women as pawns. It is unfortunate, but not surprising, that women themselves act as soldiers and shed their own blood in a battle from which they can never emerge as self-sustaining victors, no matter how resourceful or well-placed they are on the battlefield.

Fatal Combination

The institution of dowry acquires fatal power when combined with the institution of the patrilocal family. A daughter has to shift to her husband's home after marriage. No matter how convenient it may otherwise be, a man is not expected to shift to his wife's parents' house and is often an object of pity and ridicule if he does so.

It is customary in many parts of the country to marry a daughter far away so that she does not maintain active links with her natal family. She is discouraged by both families from too frequently visiting her parents and is expected to pay the customary visits as a guest, usually chaperoned.

In her husband's house, she is surrounded by his family, his relatives, his neighbours and his friends. Thus her isolation from her earlier natural sources of expected support is complete. Should she be maltreated, it is unlikely that anyone would come to her rescue. Even if she is murdered, the evidence can easily be destroyed because no one is likely to testify on her behalf against their own people.

The institution of the patrilocal family also helps provide a convenient justification for the parents of a woman to disinherit her. They argue that she cannot be given a share in the property because she will go away to her husband's house. This 'going away' is spoken of as if it is a divinely ordained arrangement that cannot be altered. In fact, many communities even in India do not send away daughters after marriage.

Daughters are not given the choice to stay or to leave, as sons are. If they were, not many women would prefer to live in a strange family and in a strange city or village, surrounded by strangers. The ability to stay on their own turf, amongst their own people, is an important component of the power of men in our society.

Is 'Education' the Answer?

An important aspect of working out strategies for change is to know what is not likely to work, or why efforts to make things better have failed so far.

Hitherto all attempts at reform, whether by social organizations or by government have been in the direction of 'educating' people. There has been no comparable effort towards thinking out the structural changes required to change the unjust power balance between men and women in our society.

It is assumed that if people can be made aware that dowry is a social evil, the practice will disappear. This ignores the fact that even the worst of social practices have a social rationale and can be sustained only if the interests of some powerful group in society are served by these practices. That is why mere awareness campaigns without structural changes cannot accomplish long-term changes in society.

The awareness campaigns on this issue have at least a century-long history. The only visible result is that today almost everyone nominally condemns dowry and calls it a social evil even while ferociously clinging to it. Understandably, this has bred a certain cynicism.

Since the reformers failed to convince people to stop practising dowry, they had to demand that government make more and more stringent laws against dowry. This is the other side of the same coin. The assumption is that if people refuse to be educated into 'enlightenment', the government should force them into it and should punish the 'unenlightened'.

A disease like smallpox can indeed be 'eradicated'. Its potential victims would like whatever help is available to prevent them from getting it. Unlike a disease, a social practice cannot be eradicated if people continue to consider its observance vital to their interests and status in their community. Stringent laws penalizing it will only remain ineffective or, at best, make the practice assume disguised forms.

Law makers and law enforcers are not a special breed of humanity. They are as much a part of the social ethos as are those upon whom they are to enforce laws. Thus, if the parliamentarians who make laws and the police and judiciary who enforce it are all avidly clinging to the dowry institution, how can they implement the laws against it? The law is bound to remain a dead letter until there is a social base for a confrontation with the culture of disinheritance of daughters.

The Story of a Much-loved Daughter

The price that women have to pay for the severe compulsion to stay married at all costs is poignantly demonstrated by the story of Suman,[1] only daughter of Mr Malik, a prosperous businessman in Delhi. He has one son aged 28. Both Mr Malik and his wife are extremely fond of Suman, who has been a much-loved child. In 1974, she was married at the age of 21 into a well-to-do business

[1] Names have been changed to maintain anonymity.

family. The Maliks spent a total of more than Rs 1 lakh on the wedding, which in current terms would be equivalent to about Rs 4 lakh.

Soon after the marriage, the Maliks discovered that their son-in-law had no source of income and was dependent on his brother and sisters for his upkeep. After marriage, he began to use Suman as a hostage to extract more and more money from her father. He was an alcoholic and routinely beat up Suman, even during her pregnancy. For a long time, Suman and her family tried to keep this a secret in order to protect the family honour but every now and then she would be severely beaten and thrown out of her husband's house. This was a method of extracting money from her father.

For eight years, the Maliks did all they could to preserve Suman's marriage. Mr Malik says he gave about Rs 1 lakh to his son-in-law during these years, to help him set up his own business. But the son-in-law blew all the money on liquor. He never gave Suman any money to run the house. The Maliks had to pay most of Suman's household expenditure, from rations to clothing for her, her husband and children, to furnishings and linen. They also bore all the expenses for the deliveries of her two children. They spent about Rs 1 lakh on all this over these years.

When her first child, a girl, was born, everyone in her husband's family was very offended because they thought they already had too many daughters in the family. Seeing how unwelcome the child was in that house, Mr Malik brought her to his house when she was only two months old. He and his wife brought up the baby who is now a beautiful, bright little girl. Suman's in-laws seemed glad to be rid of her. Suman's mother-in-law was anxious to have a son so she pushed Suman to have another child, even though she knew her son could not afford to maintain his wife. Suman succumbed to the pressure, hoping that if she had a son, her mother-in-law would become favourably inclined towards her. When her husband discovered the pregnancy, he was furious. He came to the Maliks' house and asked them to get the child aborted, saying it was not his.

His maltreatment of Suman continued to escalate. He pawned all her jewellery (worth Rs 2,00,000) for Rs 70,000. Even the birth of her son did not improve the situation. When the son was a year old, Suman was once more beaten and thrown out of the house in the hope of pressuring her parents to give more money. However, at this point the Maliks decided to keep Suman with them since all their bribes had not succeeded in helping her get even a minimal foothold in her marital home. It is noteworthy that Suman did not walk out of her own choice, but was thrown out.

When I asked Mr Malik why he had succumbed to blackmail for so long he said, '*Maine socha kaise bhi iska ghar bas jaye*' (I hoped that somehow or other, her home would be preserved). By this, he obviously meant that he had hoped her marital status would be preserved because he could easily provide her a far happier home than she had with her husband. He recalls with pain that the day he went to fetch his daughter after she had been brutally beaten, an old man of the neighbourhood asked him: 'Baba, can't you afford to provide two extra *rotis* in your house for your daughter? Why do you leave her to suffer such torture, which makes her weep in anguish every night?'

Quite clearly, the Maliks' attempts to patch up the marriage by sending Suman back to her husband time and again did not arise from any lack of love or concern for her. Mr Malik sees all his efforts and the money he spent as manifestations of his great attachment to and love for his daughter. It is sad that love for daughters assumes such fatal forms while love for sons usually plays a more constructive role in their lives.

Today, Suman and her children are living with her parents. Both she and the children are now far happier and healthier. She is trying hard to build a new life for herself. Mr Malik says he had put such effort into maintaining Suman's marriage because 'In our culture, divorce or widowhood for a woman is worse than death', yet he admits that most of their relatives and friends are happy to see Suman back home and living peacefully. Her husband continues to make attempts to harass her, such as making obscene phone calls accusing her of being a prostitute. He has also several times rung up to apologize and ask her to return to him.

Meanwhile, Suman's younger brother has settled firmly into his father's business and was married only after he had built up an allied and flourishing business of his own.

Suman's case is unusual insofar as most fathers would not give shelter on a permanent basis to a daughter, however much the maltreatment meted out to her and her children by her husband. The parting advice to a daughter at the time of her *vidai* is meant to be literally followed: 'We are sending your *doli* (bridal palanquin) today. Let only your *arthi* (corpse) come out of that house.'

What Should Daughters Be Given?

Instead of merely urging daughters to refuse dowry and to go 'empty-handed', what is needed is an emphasis on giving a daughter her due. A woman's due is whatever she requires to construct an independent secure life of her own.

If parents invested not in a daughter's marriage but in her future as they do in a son's, if they took her education, job, business or any other form of preparation for her future security equally seriously, women would not be forced to put up with the degree of marital maltreatment that they endure today.

It is important to understand that the problem lies not in giving to girls but in the form and shape in which this giving manifests itself in India. The solution is not to stop giving but to change the form of giving.

The issue of dowry is inextricably linked to the issue of the woman's share in the family's resources, inheritance rights and the extent of her participation in the family's decisions.

Some meaningful strategies which could be adopted are as follows:

1. Instead of fooling ourselves into believing that stringent laws which punish dowry givers and takers will save women's lives, we would do better to demand a law that will prevent fathers from excluding daughters from inheritance. For instance, under Muslim law, a man cannot, by making a will, disinherit either his daughters or his sons or other family heirs. Certain fixed proportions go to them and only a certain proportion can be willed as one pleases. However, a daughter gets a smaller share than does a son. We should demand a law that makes it impossible to exclude daughters from an equal share in inheritance. A will that excludes daughters should not be considered a valid legal document.

   Similarly, a daughter should not be allowed to sign away her property rights in favour of her brothers, husband or other relatives. No such transaction should be considered valid. These measures can do much to combat the problem of dowry in a more effective manner than anti-dowry legislation. If parents cannot disinherit daughters they will have no incentive to give them dowries.
2. Giving to daughters should not be linked with their marriage. To give a daughter something at the time of her marriage, when she is most vulnerable to its being taken from her, is just a way of giving to others in her name. Daughters, on reaching adulthood, should be given a share in income-generating property as sons are, for instance, in land, house, factory, shop, machines, implements and vehicles, and should be encouraged to use them to generate an income, either individually or in partnership with others who contribute equally in resources or labour. These assets should be registered in her name. In the event of her death, the property should be inherited either by her adult children or kept in trust for her minor children.

   If she has no children, her assets should be returned to her natal family. This ensures that her husband's family is not provided an additional incentive to do away with her.
3. If an adult daughter is given cash as *stridhan*, it should be in the form of a fixed deposit in her name. Her husband and his family should be

legally disallowed from meddling with this money. She should not be allowed to sign it away to them for at least 10 years from the date of her marriage.

4. Unless her own family puts as much energy, thought, planning, money and emotional investment into her job, profession or career as they do into a son's, she cannot hope to build an independent base which will survive marriage. If her parents impose crippling restrictions on her social and educational advancement and prevent her becoming independent, it is unlikely that in-laws will behave differently.
5. If daughters acquire the right to inherit and to continue living in or near their parents' house after marriage, they are not likely to be seen as so much of a burden. Once a family stops seeing a daughter as *paraya dhan* or 'another's wealth', once they start perceiving a daughter as their own, as they do a son, they will not allow her to be maltreated.

Just as a family would not, if they could help it, allow a son to continue in a job where he was tortured, and would not advise him to 'adjust' to the torture, but would seek another job for him or even let him stay unemployed, so also if a marriage was not seen as the be-all and end-all of a woman's life, her family would be more likely to resist a man's maltreatment of her.

An important part of putting an end to humiliating and oppressive marriages is the acceptance of an individual's right to refuse to marry. Unless we get over our obsession with marriage as the most necessary and inevitable defining event in a woman's life and as the only desirable living arrangement for her, we cannot conceive of free and independent women.

If women do not feel compelled to get married and stay married at all costs, they are more likely to be able to resist maltreatment. Our society has so far had very little space for self-sufficient women, whether unmarried, divorced or widowed. We need to create an atmosphere wherein such women can live with dignity and freedom.

7

Using Women as a Pretext for Censorship

*The Indecent Representation of Women (Prohibition) Bill**

The Indecent Representation of Women (Prohibition) Bill, 1986, is so absurd a piece of legislation that it would not be worth wasting time over, were it not that it confers on government officials a number of arbitrary powers which lend themselves easily to abuse. Considering how much debate and research has been conducted in different parts of the world around the issue of obscenity, even a consultation of elementary textbooks would have enabled our law makers to draw up a less amateurish and shabby document that contains a ridiculously vague and all-encompassing definition of what is indecent and derogatory to women.

Clearly, the government's purpose is not to devise an implementable law. Rather, as with much recent legislation, the government's main purpose is to

---

*This article appeared in *Manushi*, No. 37, November–December 1986.

pretend that it is deeply concerned about an issue that is of high priority to articulate sections of public opinion. In the process, more and more poorly drafted, repressive and ineffectual laws are being added to the statute books and stay there, while the problems they are meant to resolve go from bad to worse.

Apart from being ineffective, the present law is also pernicious as are the new-fangled laws enacted for combating terrorism, corruption, income tax evasion or dowry. None of them have had any impact on the problems they were intended to solve. Instead, they end up being used to nullify the fundamental rights guaranteed to citizens in the Constitution by providing government officials new powers to subvert due process of the law.

For example, the Terrorist and Disruptive Activities (Prevention) Act, 1987 (TADA) gives the government arbitrary powers to arrest and detain anyone they choose to suspect of terrorist activity. It has been used to harass a number of innocent people, including Shahid Siddiqui, editor of a popular Urdu paper *Nai Duniya*, well known for his anti-terrorist views. He was arrested and imprisoned for 15 days for merely having published an interview with J.S. Chauhan, a London-based Khalistani secessionist, without endorsing Chauhan's views.

Existing and New Provisions of the Anti-obscenity Law

Existing obscenity laws, such as Section 292 and 292A of the Indian Penal Code (IPC) enacted by the British in 1860 in the heyday of Victorian morality already confer enormous censorship powers on the government. The IPC also defines 'obscenity' in a manner that allows easy misuse. 'A book, pamphlet, paper, writing, drawing, painting, representation, figure or any other object shall be deemed to be obscene if it is lascivious or appeals to the prurient interest or if its effect...is, if taken as a whole, such as to tend to deprave and corrupt persons who are likely...to read, see or hear the matter contained or embodied in it.'

A person found guilty of selling, hiring, distributing, publicly exhibiting or in any manner putting into circulation material considered obscene as per the vague definition cited above 'shall be punished on first conviction with imprisonment...for a term which may extend to two years, and with a fine which may extend to Rs 2,000, and, in the event of a second or subsequent conviction, with imprisonment for five years, and also with fine of Rs 5,000.'

The new law reiterates these powers, and then expands on them in further violation of citizens' rights and liberties. 'Indecent representation of women' is defined as 'the depiction in any manner of the figure of a woman, her form or body or any part thereof in such a way as to have the effect of being indecent, or derogatory to, or denigrating women, or is likely to deprave, corrupt or injure the public morality or morals' of any persons of any class or age group, notwithstanding that persons in any other class or age group may not be similarly affected.

The Bill lays down that 'No person shall publish or cause to be published, or arrange or take part in the publication or exhibition of any advertisement which contains indecent representation of women in any form.' Furthermore, 'No person shall produce or cause to be produced, sell, let to hire, distribute, circulate or send by post any book, pamphlet, paper, slide, film, writing, drawing, painting, photograph, representation, or figure which contains indecent representation of women in any form.'

A person found guilty of violating this law 'shall be punishable on first conviction for a term which may extend to two years and a fine of up to Rs 2,000. In the event of a second or subsequent conviction, the imprisonment would not be less than six months and may go up to five years, plus a fine of at least Rs 10,000 which may extend up to Rs 1 lakh.'

However, the law exempts the following categories of materials:

(*a*) Any book, pamphlet, paper, slide, film, writing, drawing, painting, photograph, representation or figure:
   (*i*) the publication of which is proved to be justified as being for the public good on the ground that such book, pamphlet, paper, slide, film, writing, drawing, painting, photograph, representation or figure is in the interest of science, literature, art or learning or other objects of general concern; or
   (*ii*) which is kept or used *bona fide* for religious purposes.

(*b*) Any representation sculptured, engraved, painted or otherwise represented on or in:
   (*i*) any ancient monument within the meaning of the Ancient Monument and Archaeological Sites and Remains Act, 1958; or
   (*ii*) any temple, or any car used for the conveyance of idols, or kept or used for any religious purpose.

(*c*) Any film in respect of which the provisions of Part II of the Cinematograph Act, 1952, will be applicable.

This is an open admission that there is much in our classical literature, mythology, temples, ancient monuments as well 'religious' texts and epics which can be called 'obscene' under present-day supposedly modern laws.

The new law gives wide-ranging powers to those put in charge of implementing the law. It says,

> any Gazetted Officer authorized by the State Government may, within the local limits of the area for which he is so authorized:
>
> (*a*) enter and search at all reasonable times, with such assistance, if any, as he considers necessary, any place in which he has reason to believe that an offence under this Bill has been or is being committed;
> (*b*) seize any advertisement or any book, pamphlet, paper, slide, film, writing, drawing, painting, photograph, representation or figure which he has reason to believe contravenes any of the provisions of this Act; and
> (*c*) examine any record, register, document or any other material object found in any place mentioned in clause (*a*) and seize the same if he has reason to believe that it may furnish evidence of the commission of an offence punishable under this Bill.

The only redeeming feature is that an offence punishable under this Bill is bailable. But at the same time, since the offences under this Bill are cognizable, it gives powers of summary arrest that are likely to be used mainly for harassing concerned persons for bribes.

Government Functionaries Owe No Accountability

The most deadly part of the law is that even if there is good evidence that an official misapplied the law, he/she cannot be called to account since 'No suit, prosecution or other legal proceeding shall lie against the Central Government or any officer of the Central Government or any State Government for anything which is in good faith done or intended to be done under this Act.'

This in effect puts vast arbitrary powers in the hands of state functionaries. These powers can be used to harass those who criticize or expose government misdoings. In India, since TV and radio are already under tight government control, the press is one of the few important channels for dissent and free flow of information. Even without obtaining the enhanced powers in the Indecent Representation Bill, we have seen a series of attacks by the government on the press, blatantly misusing existing laws. For example, an issue of *The Illustrated Weekly of India* carried a tasteless photo feature of semi-nude women. This magazine had frequently carried such features over the years and no action had been taken against it. But this particular issue happened to carry a follow up report on the sexual misdeeds of J.B. Patnaik, the then chief minister of Orissa. It was to stop that report from reaching people in Orissa that the Orissa police seized all copies of the issue to stop it from entering the state. But the pretext used was the alleged obscenity of the featured article.

A Tool for Curbing Citizens' Freedom

The new Indecent Representation Bill lends itself admirably to such persecution of the media because it defines indecency as 'anything that is likely to injure the morals of any person...' All that is required to subject an editor to a lengthy and cumbersome trial under this law is for a gazetted officer to book him for producing obscene material or for *any one* person in the country to allege that his 'morals were injured' by reading a certain report or seeing a picture in a paper. The decision as to whether this is sufficiently proved or not and as to whether the report or picture is indecent or not is left entirely to the discretion of the individual judge before whom the case happens to come up. The process is basically arbitrary, as individual judges are bound to have conflicting opinions on what constitutes indecency. The supposedly free judiciary in India has often allowed itself to be influenced by powerful vested interests, especially if they happen to be in positions of power in the government.

As mentioned above, the wide-ranging powers given to 'any gazetted officer' to come with a warrant to forcibly enter and search anyone's residence or office and seize anything he thinks is indecent, including personal letters ('writing... sent by post') constitute a serious assault on personal freedom and are prone to easy misuse. It is left to him to decide what can be exempted on grounds of being literary, artistic, scientific or religious. There is no evidence that our bureaucrats are among the most astute judges in such matters. Even if the court later decides that he was wrong in his understanding and interpretation of the law, Section 9 protects the gazetted officer from any legal action. A government officer, by virtue of being a government officer, is above the law, unaccountable to anyone for his actions. Even if the court ultimately acquits the victim, he or she would have suffered a great deal of harassment during the litigation of the case, and the confiscated articles are likely to be damaged or destroyed in police custody. The law thus provides very deadly powers in the hands of government officials to settle private scores as well as to extract bribes. As soon as a law is passed declaring a certain activity 'criminal', people who continue to engage in it are forced to operate underground. Those at the lowest level, in this case petty vendors of magazines, become more vulnerable to harassment by police. The activity, if it continues, can only continue with the active collusion of the police. Thus, the main effect such a law usually has is to increase bribery and corruption.

The functioning of the Suppression of Immoral Traffic in Girls and Women Act (SITA) is a good example of this process. SITA is used to harass the prostitute, not to reduce prostitution, and thus creates a situation wherein police can function as pimps. Police periodically raid brothels and arrest prostitutes to make a show of implementing the law. On an everyday basis, police use the threat of arrest under SITA to extract bribes, both sexual and monetary, from the mostly underprivileged women who work as prostitutes. By declaring these women criminals, SITA makes it difficult for them to claim the rights available to other citizens such as schooling for their children and medical care, thus worsening their plight.

Ladies' Compartment Approach

This law owes its origins to the aggressive lobbying by some feminist groups in a few metropolitan cities who demanded gender-specific censorship of the media to combat the 'negative portrayal of women' in the media. The limited perspective of its sponsors shows up the difficulties inherent in the ladies' compartment approach to women's issues:

1. The campaign raised only the issue of the derogatory portrayal of women without sufficient emphasis on the overall context within which the Indian media functions. The most important issue for radio and TV in India today is covert and overt government censorship that obstructs the free flow of information and opinion. However, campaigners who lobbied for this law completely ignored the issue of harmful forms of existing government controls over media. By restricting their lobbying activity merely to the demand for more women's programmes and more women producers, together with a 'non-derogatory' portrayal of women, the campaigners created the impression that all would be well with our media if only some negative stereotypes of women were eliminated and women were given more time and attention on radio and TV.[1]
2. So far, all the films and hoardings against which women's groups have agitated by picketing or blackening them out have been those which showed women in semi-nude or sexually suggestive poses. This reinforces

[1] This article was written at a time when the government enjoyed total monopoly over radio and TV.

the notion that anything sexual is obscene and that respect for women is equivalent to treating them as sexless. It also leads to ignoring other derogatory stereotypes of women, for example, those that portray them as marginal dependent beings who exist only to serve men. It disregards various cynical ways used by advertisers to manipulate people's desire for a better life.

For instance, the Regent cigarette advertisement, which showed a semi-nude woman in proximity to a male hand holding a cigarette under the slogan 'An Exclusive Affair', was widely attacked by some feminist groups. However, the cigarette advertisement showing two fashionably dressed young people under the slogan 'Made For Each Other' or the Charminar cigarette ad showing birds flying in the sky with the caption 'Taste the Spirit of Freedom' came under no criticism. Is it not dishonest and harmful to equate freedom and happiness with a product that is proven to destroy the consumers' health and might even result in untimely death?

Similarly, an ad that does not show any woman but depicts only a pink rose, and promises 'rosy cheeks this winter' if one uses a particular brand of face cream has not come in for any criticism although it misleads women into believing that a cream by itself, regardless of a woman's general state of health and nutrition, is sufficient for a blemishless, rosy complexion. The campaign has not emphasized the need for advertisers to provide essential information on the contents of a product and evidence of a scientific nature, demonstrating how that product can achieve what its maker claims.

3. The equation of indecency with nudity and sex allows all other portrayals of women to pass off as 'decent'. If a woman is clad in a *saree* but shown as a servile housewife, finding her life's ultimate fulfillment in using a particular detergent for the family wash, or a particular cooking oil to prepare meals for her husband, no one finds it objectionable.

Overmuch emphasis on the portrayal of women as sex objects and not as service objects has been picked up from some women's groups in the West, who have usually targeted mainly the former kind of portrayal for public action. It is significant that right-wing forces and church conservatives have joined a section of feminist opinion that has rallied for government controls on pornography in the West. Women's demonstrations against sexually explicit or suggestive films and hoardings have always been joined by conservatives whose version of respect for women is covering up, seclusion and segregation for 'good women' but punishment and humiliation for 'bad women,' defined as those who defy social and sexual conventions. We have seen the effects of such ideology in countries like Iran where a bare-headed woman or one caught having an extra-marital relationship can be more violently attacked than a male who purveys pornography. A milder version is visible in our country, when a woman in a sleeveless or low-necked blouse, if molested in a public place, is likely to be told she asked for it.

Asking for More State Controls

During consideration of this Bill, some feminist groups drew up a list of recommendations as amendments to the Bill, and presented them in the Rajya Sabha. These include:

1. Giving police officers the same powers of search and seizure that the Bill gives to gazetted officers. So much for all the experience of women's and other vulnerable groups in this country who have launched endless protests against the high-handed and brutal record of the police and its failure to protect citizens' rights.
2. Adding 'exhibitions, photos, plays, films, video films, slide shows, TV programmes and other shows' to the list of media covered by the Bill. This involves bringing more and more media under indirect governmental control instead of challenging the monopoly government already has over radio and TV.
3. Amending the definition of 'indecent representation of women' to include any depiction or description of a woman which has the effect of being 'violent in character' or 'derogatory to her dignity as a human being or to her status as an equal to man'.

The definition could easily be used to censor reports on injustice and atrocities against women. Anyone could allege that a particular depiction of gang rape of Dalit women is 'violent in character' or 'derogatory to the status of a woman as equal to a man'. It would also, for example, be easy for anyone to allege that reports of atrocities against women during communal massacres such as the anti-Sikh pogroms in November 1984 aroused their prurient interest and corrupted their morals because these reports described sexual atrocities, including public gang rapes of women. Such an allegation by one person would be sufficient for prosecution, seizure and confiscation of the publication to take place, if the concerned gazetted officer or magistrate decided to play along. Any description of the actual unequal status of women would violate this definition. Women's organizations that have made this recommendation may believe that they would ensure that reports of this kind are not affected. But, in thus assuming that women's groups will be able to control and monitor the implementation of law by government machinery, they are forgetting that once a high-handed law comes into existence, no one section of society can control its use and abuse by those with vested interests, far less ensure that government does not misuse it.

Significantly, no amendment has been suggested to lessen the arbitrary powers of government officers. For example, no change is suggested in Section 9 that protects the officer from being sued by genuinely wronged citizens.

Making Women Unmentionable

Bills like the present one could adversely affect many social activities vitally necessary to help women, for example, sex education programmes, so direly needed in educational institutions, particularly by girls, who are kept in greater ignorance than boys regarding how their bodies function. It could well be used, for example, to censor the dissemination of information vital to improving women's health, merely because this may sometimes have to be in a form that the censor construes as sexually explicit.

Although much of the public debate around the portrayal of women has revolved around the commercial exploitation of women's bodies in films and advertisements, the new law is far wider in scope. It covers all kinds of writings intended for circulation, not only those that are commercial. Significantly, most commercial films have been excluded from its purview, even though the film industry is widely acknowledged to be among the most active among our media in purveying sexually titillating representation of women.

There are manifold ways, for example, that classics like Kalidasa's *Shakuntalam*, Vidyapati's poems, the epic *Mahabharata*, mythological and folk literature too could be construed as indecent under the absurdly wide definition provided by this Bill and qualify for a ban if this law had not created a special exemption for literature which is used for bona fide 'religious purposes'. But how does one tell whether a person reading the *Shivapurana* is doing so for religious reasons or other kinds of interest? More modern works, particularly in regional languages and by relatively unknown authors, will be in greater danger because if objections are raised against the work on flimsy grounds, the author would find it hard to prove that the book is justified in the interest of 'public good'. In different times and places, reactionary hysteria, whether reflected in public demonstrations or in the opinions of administrators and judges, has been notorious for censoring and banning various works that have later been accepted as works of literary and artistic merit.

If rigorously applied, it could conceivably be used to ban almost any communication that refers to women in any way because all that is required to make such a reference indecent is for any one person to allege that he or she has been morally injured by it. The only way to avoid the possibility of being prosecuted under this law would be never to mention women at all. Women could thus become the unmentionables of Indian society, and a new obstacle would be placed in the way of normal discourse as well as of attempts at alleviating women's oppression. The new law thus constitutes a serious infringement of the fundamental right to freedom of speech and expression.

Who Wants This Law?

Three kinds of forces have come together to back this Bill. The first consists of certain urban feminist groups. They have taken their cue from similar campaigns in the West. Giving so much priority to the image of women in the absence of a greater effort to change the reality of their lives is particularly misplaced in India, where millions of women continue to die prematurely from physical violence, as well as the unseen violence of malnutrition, disease, overwork, deprivation and family tyranny.

The second force is the conservative lobby that wants to impose a repressive culture on people in the name of Indian traditions. In fact, their notions have little to do with our own traditions, but are directly descended from the nineteenth century British rulers' perverse puritanical Christian morality. According to this morality, sex is a product of original sin and is inherently dirty, the genitals being referred to as 'shameful parts'. The only kind of permissible, yet unmentionable, sex is that within marriage, its primary justification being procreation. The IPC with its prudish definition of obscenity was framed in 1860, the heyday of the Victorian version of morality imposed on Indians by the British through various agencies such as educational institutions, missions and legislation.

For example, Section 292 of the IPC defines 'obscenity' as that which is 'lascivious or appeals to the prurient interest or if its effects...tend to deprave or corrupt persons who are likely to read, hear or see the matter. . .' The dictionary meaning of 'lascivious' is that which excites sexual desire and 'prurient interest' as an interest in sexual matters. The Penal Code thus identifies immorality with sexual desire and morality with its repression. It is sad that instead of questioning such outdated provisions, we are instead adding even more absurd criteria in judging literary and media products.

In the course of the twentieth century, legal concepts of privacy and of the individual's liberty have greatly advanced. Many countries have introduced legal safeguards to attempt to reduce governmental violations of the privacy and integrity of the individual. No causal connection between literature and depravity has been established in any country that has liberalized its laws, nor have crime rates risen concurrently with more liberal laws.

The third force behind the Bill is, of course, the bureaucracy, which welcomes any opportunity to acquire more control over people, and would like to control not just their actions, but even their words, thoughts and desires. It is typical of our government's hypocritical style of functioning that it has responded to the issue with this law that tries to rearrange the clothing on pictorial representations of women while so many women are without adequate clothing or shelter in India.

Questions of Strategy

While there can be no doubt of the need to struggle against the negative portrayal of women in the media, a strategy that prescribes moral policing by a corrupt and tyrannical state machinery as the main way of changing societal perceptions of women is likely to backfire. It is not the absence of stringent laws that allows the denigration of women to continue and accelerate. Rather, it is the dependent status of women as a group in society that denies them the power to decide what roles are best suited to their requirements and aspirations and how they wish to be projected in the media, which allows harmful images of women to dominate public perception. This culture of dependence allows violence against women to flourish both in everyday life and in the media.

In this situation, it is important to continue our struggle to make the denigration of women in the commercial media as unprofitable as possible for its purveyors. However, there was no need to ask for a far-reaching law that has the potential to curb media and literary freedom and in the process infringe on our fundamental rights enshrined in the Constitution.

Postscript

This Bill became an Act of Parliament after it received the assent of the President on 23 December 1986. At the time it was widely hailed by leading feminists as a measure of their success in making the government yield to their concern for women's dignity. However, in recent years, when Bharatiya Janata Party (BJP)- and Rashtriya Swayamsevak Sangh-oriented women became active on such issues, the feminist lobby not only disowned this law but also attacked the BJP for being anti-women reactionaries for invoking this law. Ironically, 'obscenity' and portrayal of violence against women in the media has increased manifold since the enactment of this law. The proliferation of pornography as a full-fledged industry in recent decades through the Internet and freely available CDs of blue films make a total mockery of this law even while the police retain the power to invoke it for harassment and profit.

Part II

Battling Domestic Violence

8

Women's Organizations I

*Vengeance Squads, Firefighters or Counsellors?**

In the 1980s, there was a proliferation of women's groups in different parts of the country. Most of these urban groups have been set up in response to cases of atrocities against women—especially atrocities within marriage. In the first few years, a great deal of attention was paid to the issue of dowry-related wife murders. Most urban-based women's organizations responded to these gruesome killings by organizing protest demonstrations, both against the families in which they took place, as well as against the government machinery, notably the police, which usually went out of its way to convert such murder cases into suicides and accidents.

Gradually, women's organizations began to feel dissatisfied with their role of protesting after a woman was dead, and felt they should try and prevent such deaths. Beginning in the early 1980s, women's groups tried to meet this

---

*This article appeared in *The Indian Express*, 5 March 1987.

challenge by setting up legal aid and support groups for women in distress. They hoped that by offering timely support and help, they would be able to encourage women to resist maltreatment and walk out of violent or oppressive family situations before they could be killed or be driven to suicide.

Today, that hope is fading, not only in the hearts of those who undertook the job but also of those who welcomed the emergence of women's groups.

This is reflected even in the attitude of the media. The days of laudatory coverage seem to be coming to an end. There has been a spate of fairly cynical articles on the supposed failure of women's groups. However, neither in the earlier phase of laudatory coverage nor in the cynical phase now beginning has there been any serious attempt to understand or take stock of the situation.

In this chapter, we would like to share the experience of the *Manushi* group in this regard, in order to shed some light on the inherent limitations of what women's organizations can do, given the fact that there is no basic change in the family system in most parts of India.

The *Manushi* group began providing legal aid and other forms of support to women in distress in a purely ad hoc fashion. In our view, our primary task is to bring out the magazine *Manushi*. But a number of women in distress began to come to us for help. Most were referred to us by readers of the magazine. Since, at the time we started work in 1979, there were not many other such groups, we felt duty-bound to respond, whether the request was for shelter or for legal aid. Over the years, the process got somewhat more organized.

Family Deals

A vast majority (about 90 per cent) of cases that came to us were related to maltreatment of women in marriage. Most of them were from the urban middle and lower middle classes. Hence, the observations that follow do not reflect the experience of other sections of society in this regard. In most of these cases, the woman concerned came with some members of her natal family—usually her father, mother and/or brother. In a few cases, the woman came with a sister-in-law or married sister. But even in these few cases it was usually clear that they had been sent by the rest of the family. Very few women came by themselves without the support of the natal family.

Thus, from the very beginning, it became clear that mainly those women who have some support from their natal families are able to venture out for help. We found that the attitude of a woman's father and/or adult brothers is a key determinant. While hardly any women came on their own, there were a number of instances of a father or brother coming without the woman concerned.

It was not always easy to convince such family members that we could not offer any meaningful advice without having talked to the woman. In many cases, the father or brother would not return if we insisted that we would have to talk to the woman before offering any advice, since it was important to know what she herself wanted. Even in cases where the woman did accompany other members of her family, she was often not allowed to speak for herself.

Most of the women were not even in a position to make minimally autonomous choices. We had originally, naively, assumed that any woman who seeks intervention by a women's group must be seeking a life of independence. In fact, the cases that came to us can be broadly categorized as: those wanting reconciliation with the husband and/or in-laws; and those wanting advice and help in legal proceedings to protect the woman's rights such as maintenance, child custody, return of the dowry and an end to harassment and threats of violence after separation.

Whether the first option was being sought or the second was seldom dependent on what the woman, left to herself, wanted. It was almost totally dependent on what kind of support her parental family was willing to give her. The factor of natal family support was even more important than whether or not the woman was employed. In almost all the cases where the woman was desperate for reconciliation, despite having suffered severe forms of maltreatment, it was because her natal family was not willing to take any responsibility for supporting her in her decision to leave the husband's house.

The desire for reconciliation by the woman and her family seldom implied that they expected husband and wife to sit down together and mutually agree to adjust. Usually, it meant that they hoped the husband would agree to take his wife back with an assurance that he would not in future subject her to too much torture. It is significant that in most cases, the women reported that they had been thrown out of the matrimonial home. Hardly any had voluntarily walked out. The few who did walk out almost always did so only when they feared for their life or found life completely unbearable.

In almost no case did a woman report walking out on her marriage due to temperamental differences or because she did not 'like' the man. Most women had gone through years of severe maltreatment before they thought of doing anything about it. This was true for women of all income groups—both employed and unemployed. Only in rare cases did any of these women walk out within a year of marriage. Even fewer walked out without being subjected to violence. Several had stayed on for months even though the marriage was not consummated.

It is in this context that the desire of the woman's family for reconciliation, at whatever cost, assumes deadly significance. In many cases, parents openly admitted that they were aware that their daughter might die if sent back.

Reforming Husbands—A Viable Proposition?

Needless to say, despite our best efforts as a women's group, we could be of very little help when families wanted to make the son-in-law accept their daughter back and expected us to convince him to treat her well. This is because we have no way of influencing the behaviour of a man or his family except through moral persuasion. But, in most cases, all possible forms of persuasion and intervention by relatives, community elders or *biradari* (community) bodies had already been tried. Husbands do not usually respond to women's groups' reconciliation efforts because they see no advantage in doing so.

Many families had the feeling that organized protest demonstrations would help. Many asked us to approach some government official or some highly placed person in the police to pressurize or threaten the man. But, like most other women's groups, we did not have the government machinery at our beck and call to arm-twist errant husbands, nor did we aspire to perform this task.

Ultimately, the problem is the lack of any bargaining position for women in the present family set-up. A husband can get away with maltreating and throwing out his wife because he knows she is easily replaceable. There are enough desperate parents willing to marry off their daughters to just about any man available. The woman controls nothing in her marital family—not even the dowry. The maintenance laws are so ineffective that only rarely does a man have to part with any money when he throws his wife out. The family property is almost never jointly held nor is any significant proportion in the woman's name. So she can claim nothing as her own when she is thrown out.[1]

The attitude of most husbands is very similar to that seen in a case we came across at the Crimes Against Women Cell. The woman said she had been humiliated, confined to the house, beaten and harassed for dowry ever since the wedding. She finally left the house when her husband beat her up one day and repeatedly told her to get out. Her mother and brothers were desperate to send her back to her husband on any terms. Her mother said, 'I told my son-in-law not to mention divorce. The word is unknown in our family. I told him I was ready to eat his shit if he would only take her back.'

A few months later, when we went to meet them again, they told us the woman had returned to her husband. We visited the husband's house. We were not allowed to talk to the woman alone. Nor did she say a word during our visit except to offer us tea. Her husband lectured us at great length on the faults of her family, her folly and his magnanimity. He emphasized that

[1] The situation has changed dramatically ever since domestic violence and maintainence laws were amended, as discussed in Chapters 10 and 11.

he would not let her meet her parents frequently and gloated at her having been forced to return on his terms although she had left with what he called arrogance, 'She thought I would go and plead with her to return. But you must have heard the Sanskrit saying: A mouse after all remains a mouse.'

It was clear that the woman was compelled to return and endure such humiliation because no other place was available to her. Her brothers were not willing to continue supporting her, nor were they prepared to let her take a job, though she is a qualified beautician. They felt that this would damage their family honour.

A woman generally has no leverage to compel the husband or the in-laws to behave reasonably. She can at best try to be a 'nuisance'—to fight back with words, yell, scream and cry.

But she has no power to enforce her wishes in the way that her husband has. If she becomes too great a nuisance, she can always be thrown out. This threat acts as a most powerful deterrent. The only option she has is to walk out. But if she has no parental support, no house of her own, and is not earning an income substantial enough to support herself and her children with dignity, she cannot exercise this option. This, more than anything else, emboldens the husband's family into riding roughshod over her.

Disabling Daughters

Parents often argue that their daughter must return to her husband because she is incapable of living on her own. They seldom acknowledge that this situation is of their own making. Having disabled their daughter as far as they could, denying her any opportunity to acquire professional skills, confining her to the house and having prepared her only to work as a housewife, they then label her incapable and see her as a burden on them if she is thrown out by her husband.

The woman, already demoralized by the maltreatment she has suffered, needs encouragement if she is to learn to stand on her own feet. Instead, she is repeatedly told by all her family members that she can never survive alone. She has little choice but to accept their evaluation of her. Fearing that she will be a burden on her brothers in whose homes she might be even more humiliated and unwanted than in her husband's, she also repeats that she wants her husband to take her back. This also puts her in a morally 'right' position in the eyes of her family. She is seen as a dutiful rather than a defiant wife. This 'wish' of hers is, however, heavily influenced by all the pressures she faces in her parental home and by a lifetime of conditioning to believe that she is weak and inadequate.

Contrary to popular belief, the fact of a woman having a job and thus being supposedly economically independent does not sufficiently compensate for the lack of parental support, especially if she has children. There are several reasons for this.

The job market is structured in a way that relegates women, even those from middle class families, to lower paying jobs such as teaching, secretarial and clerical work. The income that a woman gets from such a job is rarely sufficient for her to bring up her children on her own, especially if she has no house and has to rent one. Apart from the skyrocketing rents, which most single women can ill afford to pay, the hostility of landlords towards single or divorced women is such that only an exceptionally lucky woman will find a place, even if she can afford to pay a high rent. And for the poor, the violence and exploitation that results from the lack of physical security, especially for a female-headed household, deters such a choice.

Finally, since in India most people's social life centres around the family and kinship networks, a woman finds it very hard to survive on her own if she is completely cut off from her family. There are hardly any support systems available to her outside of marriage and the family. Even childcare arrangements are hard to come by and are very expensive. Most women depend on older members of the family or on homebound sisters-in-law to keep an eye on their children while they are away at work.

Most women are not allowed to socialize independently and build solid friendships either before or after marriage. Most married women are compelled to socialize in their husbands' circles. Even if a woman is employed and has friendly colleagues, the support she can get from them is minimal. Any close contact with male colleagues will provoke censure and scandal. Female colleagues can usually provide only as much support as their own families permit. Usually a woman's friendship with a divorcee is looked down upon and virtually discouraged.

Family Support is Essential

The key to a woman's survival is her own family's attitude—not so much that of her husband or her in-laws. Only if a husband is made to realize that the woman has other viable options, that her family's support is available as and when she needs it—just as it usually is for a son—will he have to reconsider his attitude. It is only when a woman can realistically say, 'I will stay with you only if I am treated well', and actually has the ability to walk out if she is abused, that things will begin to change.

Women's groups naively believed that if they extended the moral and emotional support that a woman's own family might not be willing to provide, they could encourage a woman to break out of an oppressive situation. But it turned out that this seldom works. First, the support of a women's group cannot be lifelong. The group may or may not last very long. Its composition is in any case likely to be fluid, with old members moving out of town, marrying or losing interest and new ones joining. Most groups have to deal with more cases than they have the resources to handle. New cases keep cropping up. The volunteers are few and overworked and cannot possibly substitute for the intimate human contact that a family can provide, if it chooses to do so.

Very often, harassed fathers and brothers have come and screamed at us, 'What's the use of these women's groups if you cannot even help our daughter get a decent deal in her husband's home and save her from beatings?' The truth is that in our country even god cannot help a woman live a life of dignity if her own father would rather see her dead than divorced, would rather she died in her husband's house than have her come back and build an independent life for herself.

In India, where the family plays such a crucial and role in the life of a woman, it is foolish to expect women's groups to act as a substitute for family support.

No wonder, then, that the few cases where a woman is able to rebuild her life are invariably those where some measure of support is already available to her from her family, where her father or brothers are willing to tell her: 'Don't worry, you can always come back to us.' Most such women recover remarkably quickly no matter how traumatic their marriages have been.

In such cases, it is easy for a women's group to offer help and advice about how the woman's rights should be protected, how she should proceed to fight for maintenance, child custody or divorce. In most cases where parental support was available, the woman was not nearly as seriously affected by whether or not a court case went in her favour.

Take the case of Seethalakshmi who for eight years had been subjugated to all forms of physical and mental abuse by her husband. Finally, when she felt she could not go on any more, her father willingly supported her. Within a few months, she changed from a depressed, sickly person to a glowing, smiling one. She started to study music all over again and felt she had begun a new life. When she left her husband, she did not earn more than Rs 800 a month but the assurance of a secure shelter for her and her son made it easy for her to start afresh. It would have been almost impossible for her to rent a place, live by herself and arrange child care if her parents had refused support.

Parents often give the excuse that 'society' does not allow divorced women to exist in peace. In actual fact, this so-called society is usually no more than a woman's own family. In almost all the cases in which the powerful male members of a family decided to support and take their daughter back, they did not report any significant harassment at the hands of neighbours or relatives.

When relatives bring a woman to a women's group, they often expect the group to solve all her problems as though with a magic wand, while they themselves continue demoralizing the woman by making out that the breakdown of her marriage is the worst disaster imaginable and that her life has no value or meaning outside marriage.

If the role of parental support is so crucial even for women in big cities, where relatively many more options exist, we can well imagine how much more dependent on family support women in rural areas are likely to be, where avenues of mobility and employment for women are for more restricted.

Vengeance Squads?

Another role the women's groups are frequently expected to play is that of vengeance squads. Women and their parents who feel the police and the courts have failed to give them justice, or have delayed it indefinitely, often request women's groups to teach the husband and in-laws a lesson, to make them suffer as they made the woman suffer, or to get the dowry back by negotiation or by some variant of strong-arm tactics.

In the initial phase of agitation, some cases of public exposure of the misdeeds of husbands and in-laws and of women going in a group to retrieve a dowry received newspaper publicity. This raised people's hopes and many families began to come with the plea that a demonstration be staged outside their son-in-law's house. Often, they would offer to arrange transport. Women's groups were almost expected to be on hire for protest demonstrations as bands are on hire for weddings.

The problems inherent in this soon became apparent. First, to proceed on a demonstration merely on the basis of the woman's version of events could land the group in an embarrassing position.

Second, men's families soon developed techniques of ignoring demonstrations. For example, they could simply lock themselves into the house. If the demonstrators tried to enter the house, they made themselves vulnerable to legal action. Similarly, if a man simply denies having received dowry, there is little a women's group can do to compel him to return it.

Third, taking revenge serves no useful purpose. It may give the woman a temporary sense of satisfaction. But an obsession with revenge often prevents her from building a new life. In a way, her energies continue to centre on her husband and his family.

What is most important is that this strategy is clearly not workable on any significant scale. Women's groups cannot possibly stage a demonstration against every husband who misbehaves. Nor is there any guarantee that a demonstration will deter him from his earlier course of action.

Over the years, we have begun to feel that the ease with which our society has made social space for women's groups to exist and make noise has perhaps something to do with their being used as conscience easers. We often get phone calls from people informing us that a woman in their neighbourhood is being beaten up and asking us to come and save her. By making one such call, the neighbours feel they have done their duty. If the beating does not stop, they can assure themselves it is because women's groups are insincere or lazy.

Women's groups too have erred in building up this illusion that they can act as firefighting squads. The answer to the beating up of a woman in Shakarpur or Rajendra Nagar is not that someone from an organization in Lajpat Nagar go rushing to rescue her, but that vigilance committees be formed in each neighbourhood so that residents themselves take on the task of ensuring, through collective action, the safety of all women in the immediate vicinity.

Preemptive Measures

By thus emphasizing the role of the family and neighbours, we are by no means suggesting that women's organizations are redundant and that we can do no more than pray that families begin to support their daughters. Agitation by women's groups has had a noticeable impact on social attitudes.

Even though the number of women being beaten or burnt to death or tortured in various ways remains alarmingly high, there is a slow but perceptible change in the attitude of parents. There are relatively higher chances of parents responding to their daughter's plea for help than was the case a decade ago.

The widespread publicity given to atrocity cases has alerted parents and neighbours, many of whom are beginning to take pre-emptive action. Yet it is not enough for parents to respond when a woman is being beaten and abused in marriage. It is far more important that they prepare her adequately for life, and not just for marriage. This means:

1. Not seeing marriage as the be-all and end-all of a woman's life. Parents need to invest in a daughter's education as well as in giving her an independent economic base from which to operate.
2. This should include giving her a fair share in family resources rather than spending lakhs on a lavish wedding, which does not benefit her in any way.

3. Instead of giving dowry to her husband and in-laws, parents should give a daughter something she can call her own. Instead of giving her fancy clothes and jewellery or cash and consumer goods to her in-laws, it would be far better if parents gave her a house of her own—however small it may be—so that she will not have to put up with a disastrous marriage for fear of being thrown out on the streets.
4. Parents should allow daughters to have greater mobility and to form more autonomous alliances so that they can build an adult social life of their own from which to draw emotional sustenance and support rather than only be the shadows of their husbands.

9

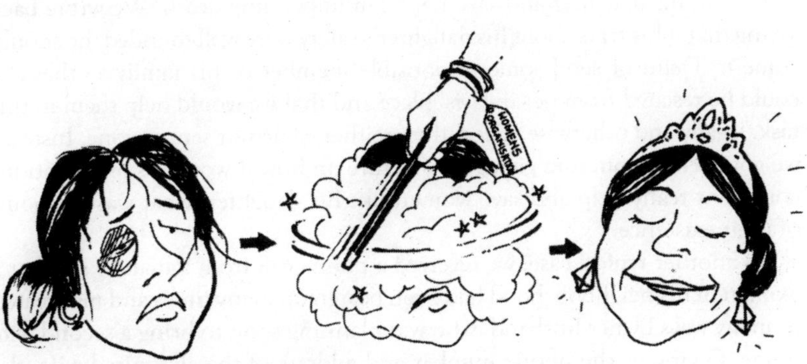

Do we have a magic wand?

Women's Organizations II

*The Pressure of Unrealistic Expectations**

'Atrocities on women are increasing. Does it not show that women's organizations have failed in their task?' The implication of this oft-asked question is that since women's organizations have single-handedly taken on the responsibility of eradicating violence and injustice against women, therefore, the continuation of this violence reveals the ineffectiveness and futility of women's organizations. Often, the question is related to a specific case of violence reported in the press: 'So-and-so woman has been killed or battered or raped. What are women's organizations doing about it?'

Let me give two specific examples of the unrealistic expectations from women's organizations. A man from a small town in Uttar Pradesh wrote to us a heart-rending account of how his daughter who was married in Delhi some five years ago was being subjected to brutal torture and violence at the hands of her husband and in-laws. He said he suspected she might be done

---

*This article appeared in *Manushi*, No. 59, July–August 1990.

to death as her husband had already attacked her murderously on several occasions. He then went on to express his inability to come to Delhi to help his daughter, saying he was prevented by some illness in the family. He asked us to help his daughter and save her from impending death. We wrote back saying that if his fears about his daughter's safety were well-founded, he should come to Delhi or send some responsible member of his family so that she could be rescued from her in-laws' place and that we would help them in this task, legally and otherwise. The father neither came nor sent anyone. Instead, we got a letter from him giving us a lecture on how if women's organizations could not really help and save women like his daughter, what was the point of their existence.

In another typical case, we received a phone call from a man to say that a woman in his neighbourhood had been beaten up many times and maltreated in many ways by her husband, who was planning soon to bring a second wife home. Giving us the phone number and address of the victimized wife, the caller asked us to ring up and offer her help. When I called the number and spoke to the woman concerned, she flatly denied that she was facing any problem and said I had been misinformed. However, I gave her our phone number and told her to call us if she ever needed help. A couple of hours later, she called to say that the information we had received was correct. Her husband had fixed a date for his second marriage, which was to take place in two days. He was determined to bring the second wife to the same house. He beat the first wife severely for protesting. She had been unable to tell the truth when I had called earlier because her husband was in the house at the time. She then asked for advice. I suggested that she lodge a police complaint against her husband for intending to commit bigamy and offered to help her with legal action to follow up the case. She expressed her helplessness to do so because if he got to know of it he would throw her out along with her children.

But did she really want to continue living with a man who put her through such humiliation? The answer was: where was she to go with her three small children? Her parents, who were living in Bihar, were not willing to take her back. She was a graduate but had no other employment skills and no job experience. In any case, under whose care would she leave her children if she went out to work? With the small salary she was likely to get as an unskilled, inexperienced graduate, she would not even be able to rent a small room, let alone have money to bring up her children. At present, her husband at least said he was willing to support her and let her continue living in the same house if she quietly accepted his second marriage. But if he got to know she was planning any kind of action against him, he would simply beat her out of the house. She then asked if we could help in any way and stop his second marriage without her coming into the picture.

We rang up the neighbour and explained the situation as the woman had described it to us and asked if he and other neighbours would be willing to help if we intervened and approached the husband. He flatly refused and said as someone who had to live in the neighbourhood he did not want to intervene and provoke enmity. He then went on to give us a lecture on how, if a victimized woman was not willing to help herself and if we, as a women's organization, could not instill enough courage into her to fight for her rights, then the moral of the story was that women deserve to be maltreated.

Thus, the onus for the continuance of the unjust situation gets to be passed on to the victims of the injustice and the women's organizations who claim to fight this injustice. The cited examples are fairly typical and routinely recurring ones.

The questions we need to ask are: Can a women's organization be expected to substitute for family, kin, neighbours or for a social welfare system? Are parents, relatives and neighbours justified in delegating their responsibility to a distant organization? A women's organization is not like a trade union that collects membership dues and purports to guard the interests of its members. Even a trade union's main function is to guard its own subscribing members, with whose employers it has some *locus standi,* not all oppressed workers. But a women's organization, functioning on limited social acceptance and a paucity of human and economic resources, is expected to guarantee the economic, social and emotional well-being of half the population, when all the power structures are weighted against that well-being, and is denounced as useless if it fails to be omnipresent like Brahma and play the guard in every home where women are maltreated.

How did the illusion arise that women's organizations must be able to rescue every maltreated woman and magically resolve her problems? It arose partly from the misconceptions of those of us who began to organize new women's groups about a decade ago. Since dominant social opinion appeared to be hostile to a woman actively resisting marital violence, women's organizations hoped to act as an alternative body of opinion, one which would reassure maltreated women that they were justified in resisting aggression, even in leaving a violent husband. In working on this assumption, women's groups tended to focus more on the emotional support needed by a woman than on the physical protection and social and economic support she needed. A few individual women who were educationally and otherwise equipped to support themselves independently–and most of whom also had the support of their natal families–were able to draw on the moral support offered by women's groups. But the most maltreated wives face immediate problems of housing, subsistence and help with child care, and also the active hostility or prejudice of both marital and natal families.

A few women's organizations set up shelters for battered women but these proved to be of limited value. They were intended as short stay homes for three to six months, as only thus could they continue to cater to more women in need. But, very often, after that time, a woman still had nowhere to go and the women's organization would be compelled to negotiate with her natal or marital family to take her back on slightly better terms than before.

Responding to the problem of marital violence by providing shelters for battered women was a product of women's movements in the West. However, the overall situation there was substantially different from that in India. In many western countries, a woman can get social security payments and subsidized housing for herself and her children. This may not be sufficient to keep her from poverty but at least allows her and her children to survive. It is also relatively easier for a woman, even one without any professional skills, to find some sort of job in the West. The shelter thus can try to function as a transition point while the women's organization helps the woman establish herself independently.

In India, however, many women, even those from middle class and lower middle class backgrounds, have been allowed to develop only the skills of domestic work. The better part of their lives has been spent on perfecting these skills—cooking, cleaning and childcare. But domestic service is a despised and ill-paid occupation in our society. It cannot support a woman and her children in a lifestyle even remotely resembling that to which she is accustomed. It is also not an occupation that her community would approve of. Since family and community approval and support are very important for an individual's mental and emotional well-being, few women desire to take up jobs that are looked down upon by their community.

It is, in some ways, relatively easier for a poor woman to cope with living on her own, because the husband's desertion may not bring about a major change in her income, given that these households often run mainly on the woman's income even when the husband is living with her. If her natal family is within reach, she may be able to resist the violence of her husband and manage to live on her own. This is one major reason for the much larger number of woman-headed households among the poor.

Our experience shows that the lack of viable options, economic and social, is a major cause for most maltreated wives being unable to live on their own, and being compelled to return to their husbands. Women's organizations end up trying to negotiate with the woman's marital family for a better deal for her. But it is not possible for the organization to mount a round-the-clock vigil to see that she is not battered again. This inability is not a measure of the failure of women's organizations. It is merely a physical impossibility. The only people who have some chance of intervening at the moment of violence are immediate neighbours who live close enough to witness maltreatment.

If it is impossible for women's organizations to substitute for a social security system, it is equally impossible for them to substitute for overall social norms which can provide a supportive environment to women. A positive social opinion refusing to acquiesce in maltreatment of women, whatever the excuse, has to be built up locally within each community and neighbourhood. Many of us tended initially to be dismissive of organizations like *biradari* panchayats and *mohalla samitis*. We assumed that they would automatically throw their weight on the side of the husband's family rather than of the victimized daughter-in-law who has no independent status in their eyes. However, it is important to try to change this opinion rather than substitute for it.

We have to try to get neighbours and the community to be at least willing to take responsibility to ensure that women of their neighbourhood are not tortured. They are in the best position to do this because they can observe more accurately, and can also exert pressure on the man, than can outsiders, including women's organizations. Protest demonstrations by women's organizations may temporarily embarrass a wife murderer but he recovers soon enough and even remarries. However, if his community boycotts him, it is not so easy for him to remarry or live a normal life. In our community-oriented society, the fear of community disapproval can deter people more effectively; status in the community is highly valued and a low opinion can be extremely harmful for a man in a multitude of areas of his life.

As a result of the activities, protests and pressure built up by women's organizations, and the very sympathetic coverage given to these and to women's rights issues in the mass media, many more people today are aware of the need to combat women's oppression. Concerned members of different communities have been emboldened to openly espouse women's rights, even to organize discussions on the subject to spread awareness in the community. This overall favourable social opinion proves useful to individual women who need help. Relatively larger numbers seem able to acknowledge that they are being maltreated and to seek redress.

We should recognize that it could be this 'speaking up' that is creating an effect of increasing violence in society. It is a case more of the violence being acknowledged, than the scale of violence actually going up, that we are witnessing. The process is still nascent and largely confined to urban areas; it needs to be encouraged further.

Parents have to be made aware of their own role in crippling their daughters, by not equipping them to stand on their own feet, and by treating marriage of a daughter as a substitute for an independent livelihood. Once parents realize their responsibility, many of them will offer support to a maltreated daughter and try to help her build an independent life rather than repeatedly bribe a violent son-in-law to take her back into his house. When a woman is well educated and skilled, the full support of her parents and siblings is often all that is needed to help her make the break.

Women's organizations have been successful in generating a widespread debate on women's situation. Today, there is a visible ferment amongst women in many parts of the country, both urban and rural, and many more men are willing to actively support work for women's rights.

Thus, generating ideas and building social opinion is an important task women's organizations must continue to perform. The popular assumption that every women's organization must provide relief to individual battered women, and that this must be the only purpose of women's organizations, is a mistaken one.

However, those organizations which choose to work in the area of relief provision to victims of violence would probably be more effective in the following situations:

1. If they attempt to establish a dialogue with community organizations in the neighbourhood where they are based. They must induce women to participate in decision making of the community bodies, and see that individual cases of wife beating are taken up by the community organization, which should commit itself to combating violence on women within the community. However slow and piecemeal this process, which some organizations have already undertaken, it is likely to be somewhat more effective in the long run in providing relief to individual women.
2. If they make it clear, to themselves as well as the public at large that:
   (*a*) Women's organizations alone cannot ensure that violence is eliminated from society, or that every perpetrator of violence is punished or restrained.
   (*b*) What women's organizations can do is act as catalysts for action to combat violence on women, and to press for the building of a more supportive environment for women to resist injustice and maltreatment.
   (*c*) Women's organizations cannot act as a substitute for the economic, social and emotional nurturing that only a supportive family, community and neighbourhood can provide.

10

Laws Against Domestic Violence

*Underused or Abused?**

The birth of *Manushi* in 1978 coincided with the unfortunate rise in reported cases of domestic violence and murder. Some of these appeared to be linked to dowry demands. When we organized one of our first demonstrations in early 1979 to protest against the police gang-up with the murderer's family by registering the death of the newly married Tarvinder Kaur as a case of suicide, nearly 1,500 people of the neighbourhood joined us in calling for a social boycott of the family. This protest received widespread publicity in the media. As a result, *Manushi* and other organizations that joined in that protest were flooded with cases of married women seeking redress against abusive and violent husbands, as also parents, whose daughters had been murdered by their in-laws, seeking our help in getting justice from the police and courts. However, the experience of approaching the police and law courts turned

---

*This article appeared in *Manushi*, No. 120, September–October 2000.

out to be a very disappointing one for most women's organizations. To begin with, the police would put all manner of hurdles in even registering cases of domestic violence, even when the victims feared for their very lives. In cases where wives had been murdered, the police were found to play an active role in destroying evidence and passing off these cases as suicides or accidental deaths—simply because they had been suitably bribed. The story in the law courts was not very different. Husbands and in-laws got away with torture and even murder because the women and their families found it difficult to 'prove beyond doubt' that they were victims of violence and extortion.

From that experience, many concluded that what we needed were stringent laws. By comparison, far less importance was given to figuring out ways of making our law enforcement machinery behave lawfully. But most important of all, domestic violence and abuse came to be seen as a one-way affair, largely because most of those whose cases reached women's organizations, police stations and law courts, happened to be wives who had complained against their husbands. Our laws do not recognize the possibility of daughters-in-law maltreating old in-laws or other vulnerable members of their husband's family.

Demand for Stringent Laws

As a result of determined campaigning and lobbying by women's organizations, significant amendments were made to the Indian Penal Code (IPC), the Indian Evidence Act and the Dowry Prohibition Act with the intention of protecting wives from marital violence, abuse and extortionist dowry demands. The most notable ones are Sections 304B, 406 and 498A of the IPC and Section 113A of the Indian Evidence Act.

However, the actual implementation of these laws has left a bitter trail of disappointment, anger and resentment in its wake among the affected families.

On the one hand, many victims of domestic violence, as well as many women's organizations, feel that despite the existence of supposedly stringent laws that enshrine the dual objective of helping the woman gain control over her *stridhan* and punishing abusive husbands and in-laws, in reality most victims fail to receive necessary relief. This is due to the unsympathetic attitude of the police, magnified by their propensity to protect the wrong doers, once they are adequately bribed.

A survey of cases in which wives had been murdered or had committed suicide carried out by Vimochana, a Bangalore-based women's organization, also indicates that the police and other law enforcing agencies are willfully avoiding use of the stringent laws against domestic violence. In most cases, even where the circumstantial evidence clearly indicates that the wife was killed, the police seemed to go out of their way to convert her death into a case of suicide. In many instances, families of victims found it difficult to register an accurate First Information Report (FIR), or have the case properly investigated. There are widespread allegations that the police usually collaborate with the murderers in producing false post-mortem and forensic reports, even destroying circumstantial evidence so that the accused can easily secure acquittal (see report by Vimochana in *Manushi*, No. 117).

Similarly, a study based on police records to evaluate the functioning of section 498A of IPC, conducted by a group of women activists associated with the Tata Institute of Social Sciences in Mumbai, indicated that 40 per cent of women were dead by the time their families came to lodge complaints against their violent husbands.

Thus, numerous women continue to suffer humiliation and battering, many even to the point of death, despite the existence of stringent laws in their favour. On the other hand, there is a growing and widespread feeling that these laws are being used by most police officers and lawyers to help unscrupulous daughters-in-law hold their in-laws to ransom.

The Tide Turns

In the first decade of *Manushi*'s[1] existence, most of those who came to us for legal aid were women who alleged abuse in their marital home. In the last few years, a good proportion of the cases coming to us involved complaints by in-laws and husbands about the misuse and abuse of laws, especially sections 498A and 406. Wherever I travel, in India or abroad, such cases are invariably brought to my notice, not only by aggrieved families and their friends but more often by members of women's organizations themselves.

Things have come to this pass, not just due to police and judicial corruption but also because the laws, as they are currently framed, lend themselves to easy abuse.

During the 1980s, far-reaching changes were introduced in our criminal laws to deal with domestic violence. Prior to 1983, there were no specific provisions to deal with marital abuse and violence. But husbands could be prosecuted and punished under the general provisions of the IPC dealing with

[1] Right from the start we went beyond reporting cases of atrocities to actually helping victims of abuse through legal aid and counselling as well as mobilizing public support to combat the growing culture of violence against women. In 1991, we created a separate entity called Manushi Sangathan to implement the activist interventions of *Manushi* on various issues.

murder, abetment to suicide, causing hurt and wrongful confinement. Since marital violence mostly took place in the privacy of the home, behind closed doors, a woman could not call upon any independent witnesses to testify in her favour and prove her case 'beyond reasonable doubt', as was required under criminal law. Therefore, women's organizations lobbied to have the law tilted in women's favour by bringing in amendments that shifted the burden of proof on the accused and instituted fairly stringent, preemptive measures and punishments against the accused.

All these amendments placed draconian powers in the hands of the police, without adequate safeguards against the irresponsibility of the enforcement machinery. The truth is that there were adequate provisions in the IPC Sections 323, 324, 325 and 326 for use against anyone who assaults a woman or causes her injury. But the police would in most cases not register a complaint against a husband under these sections, even where there was clear evidence that the wife's life was in grave danger. This was partly because, as habitual users of violence, policemen, more than any other section of our population, find it easy to condone beatings and even murder of wives by husbands. Given their track record in routinely brutalizing people who fall into their clutches, it is reasonable to assume that the propensity of our policemen to beat up their wives would be much higher than that of the average citizen. Add to this their entrenched habit of patronizing criminals as a way of garnering extra income and it would be, indeed, naive to presume that they would turn into compassionate rescuers of women in distress, simply because more stringent laws had been put at their disposal.

No new principles of accountability were added to the Police Act. The only new innovation we witnessed was that special Crimes Against Women Cells were created in select police stations to handle women's complaints. And, in some places, Family Courts were put into operation.

However, since the new police cells for women are run by the same police personnel, barring a few exceptional officers, the rest have had no compunction in making a mockery of the new laws by systematic under-use or abuse—depending upon which offers better money-making opportunities.

The New Amendments

Let us examine the new provisions to see how they facilitate this process: The IPC was amended twice during the 1980s—first in 1983 and again in 1986—to define special categories of crimes dealing with marital violence and abuse.

In 1983, Section 498A of the IPC defined a new cognizable offence, namely, 'cruelty by husband or relatives of husband'. This means that under this law the police have no option but to take action, once such a complaint is registered by the victim or any of her relatives. It prescribes imprisonment for a term that may extend to three years and also includes a fine. The definition of cruelty is not just confined to causing grave injury and bodily harm, or posing danger to life, limb or health (physical and mental), but also includes harassment and emotional torture through verbal abuse. This law takes particular cognizance of harassment where it occurs with a view to coercing the wife, or any person related to her, to meet any unlawful demand regarding any property or valuable security, or occurs on account of failure by her, or any person related to her, to meet such a demand.

During the same period, two amendments to the Dowry Prohibition Act of 1961, enacted in 1984 and 1986, made dowry giving and receiving a cognizable offence. Even in this case, where a person is prosecuted for taking or abetting dowry, or for demanding dowry, the burden of proving one's innocence was placed on the accused.

However, no punitive provisions were added for those making false allegations or exaggerated claims. There is, of course, the law against perjury (lying under oath). But in India, the courts expect people to prevaricate and lawyers routinely encourage people to make false claims because such stratagems are assumed to be part of the legal game in India. Therefore, the law against perjury has hardly ever been invoked in India.

Partners in 'Crime' Let Off

A person guilty of giving or taking dowry is punishable with imprisonment for a term ranging from six months to two years, plus a fine, or the amount of such dowry. Needless to say, no case is ever registered against dowry 'givers.' It is only dowry 'receivers' who are put in the dock. Not surprisingly, the law is invoked very selectively. The very same family that would declare at the time of marriage that it only gave 'voluntary gifts' to the groom's family, does not hesitate to attribute all their 'gift-giving' to extortionist demands once the marriage turns sour and is headed for a breakdown.

Section 406 prescribes imprisonment of up to three years for criminal breach of trust. This provision of IPC is supposed to be invoked by women to file cases against their husbands and in-laws for retrieval of their dowry.

Furthermore, Section 304B was added to the IPC to deal with yet another new category of crime called 'dowry death'. This section states that if the death of a woman is caused by burns or bodily injury, or occurs under abnormal circumstances within seven years of her marriage and it is shown that just prior to her death she was subjected to cruelty by her husband or his relatives, in connection with any demand for dowry, such a death would be called a 'dowry death' and the husband or relative would be deemed to have caused her death.

The person held guilty of a 'dowry death' shall be punished with imprisonment for a term which shall not be less than seven years but which may extend to imprisonment for life. By inserting a new section 113B in the Indian Evidence Act, the law makers stipulated that in cases that get registered by the police as those of 'dowry death', the court shall presume that the accused is guilty unless he can prove otherwise.

Under section 304B, in the case of a 'dowry death', where allegations of demand of dowry or non-return of dowry are made, the accused are frequently denied anticipatory, or even regular bail.

The burden of proof is shifted to the accused party. The basic spirit of Indian jurisprudence is that a person is presumed innocent till proven guilty. However, in cases involving allegations of domestic violence, a husband and his family are assumed guilty till they can prove themselves innocent.

In the case of the unnatural death of a woman, the state of her marriage certainly merits investigation as a potential cause of death. While shifting the burden of proof to the accused instead of the complainant may appear justified in cases where the woman is dead or has suffered grievous injuries, presuming that the husband and his family are the ones likely to be guilty in all cases of domestic discord leaves the law open to great misuse. Domestic violence laws ignore the fact that marital conflicts are frequently the result of mutual incompatibility or unreasonable demands of a wife and not just due to the tyranny of husbands and in-laws.

Misuse of Section 498A

Way back in 1988, I had pointed out, in what came to be a very controversial article, that there was already a distinct trend to include dowry demands in every complaint of domestic discord or cruelty, even when dowry was not an issue at all (see my article 'Rethinking Dowry Boycott', *Manushi*, No. 48: 10–13). The police as well as lawyers were found to be encouraging female complainants to use this as a necessary ploy to implicate their marital families, making them believe that their complaint would not be taken seriously otherwise. With the enactment of Section 498A, this tendency has received a further fillip. Mentioning dowry demands seems to have become a common ritual in virtually all cases registered with the police or filed in court.

For years after the new law had come into existence, the police would refuse to register cases under Section 498A unless specific allegations of dowry harassment were made. However, determined action by some women's organizations ensured that this section came to be used in all situations of cruelty and violence—not just confined to dowry-related violence. But, in places where there are no vigilant organizations taking up such cases, policemen and lawyers are often found encouraging complainants to add dowry demands as the main cause for cruelty. This has created an erroneous impression that all of the violence in Indian homes is due to a growing greed for more dowry. This makes the crime look uniquely Indian but the truth is that violence against wives is common to most societies, including those that have no tradition of dowry.

Often, highly exaggerated or bogus claims are made by unscrupulous families who demand the return of more than what was actually given as *stridhan*, using the draconian Sections 498A and 406 of the IPC as a bargaining tool. Sometimes the goal is reasonable—the woman wants the return of all items that legitimately belong to her—but she is encouraged to overstate her case and to demand an enhanced settlement as a pre-condition for divorce by mutual consent.

A large number of cases registered under Section 498A are subsequently withdrawn, though not necessarily because they are false. Bombay-based lawyer Flavia Agnes points out that the 'complexities of women's lives, particularly within a violent marriage, have to be comprehended beyond the context of popular ethics. The conviction and imprisonment of the husband may not be the best solution to the problems of a victimized wife.' Her limited choices and constrained circumstances often 'make it impossible for her to follow up the criminal case'. As Agnes points out:

> Since the section does not protect a woman's right to the matrimonial home, or offer her shelter during the proceedings, she may have no other choice but to work out a reconciliation. At this point she would be forced to withdraw the complaint as the husband would make it a precondition for any negotiations. If she has decided to opt for a divorce and the husband is willing for a settlement and a mutual consent divorce, again, withdrawing the complaint would be a precondition for such settlement.

Agnes adds: 'If she wants to separate or divorce on the grounds of cruelty, she would have to follow two cases—one in a civil court and the other in a criminal court. Anyone who has followed up a case in court would well understand the tremendous pressure this would exert, especially when she is at a stage of rebuilding her life, finding shelter, a job and child care facility. Under the civil law she would at least be entitled to maintenance, which would be her greater priority. So if she was to choose between the two proceedings, in most cases, a woman would opt for the civil case where she would be entitled to maintenance, child custody, injunction against harassment and finally a divorce which would set her free from her violent husband.' Thus, many women end up dropping the criminal proceedings. In most cases, criminal proceedings are quashed as a result of a settlement or compromise by presenting, with mutual consent, a joint petition in the High Court under Section 482 of the Criminal Procedure Code.

Instrument of Blackmail?

Sadly, there are also several cases coming to light where Section 498A has been used mainly as an instrument of blackmail. It lends itself to easy misuse as a tool for wreaking vengeance on entire families, because, under this section, the police may arrest anyone a married woman names as a tormentor in her complaint, as 'cruelty' in marriage has been made a non-bailable offence. Thereafter, bail in such cases has been denied as a basic right.

Many allege that such a drastic paradigm shift has lent itself to gross abuse, because arresting and putting a person in jail even before the trial has begun amounts to pre-judging and punishing the accused without due process. Although a preliminary investigation is required after the registration of the FIR, in practice such complaints are registered whether the charges are proved valid or not, and arrest warrants issued without determining whether the concerned family is actually abusive, or they have been falsely implicated. For example, there are a number of cases where the problem is of mutual maladjustment of the couple rather than abuse by the entire joint family. However, a host of relatives, including elderly parents, who are not necessarily the cause of maladjustment, have all been arrested and put in jail for varying lengths of time before the trial begins. Lawyers have cited several cases where judges have refused bail unless the accused family deposits a certain sum of money in the complainant's name as a precondition to the grant of bail.

Held Guilty Without Trial

Scared by these developments, many apply for anticipatory bail at the slightest likelihood of a wife lodging a complaint with the police. I also know of several cases where the lawyer advised his client to preempt his wife from registering a case of cruelty against him, by filing a divorce petition before the wife could reach the police. Husbands could then reasonably argue that the charges of cruelty were a *mala fide* retaliation against the husband's petition for divorce.

Thus, instead of finding redressal for her grievances, a woman ends up fighting a defensive divorce case.

The law was recast, heavily weighted in the woman's favour, on the assumption that only genuinely aggrieved women would come forward to lodge complaints and that they would invariably tell the truth. In the process, however, the whole concept of due process of law had been overturned in these legal provisions dealing with domestic violence.

Police and Lawyers Mislead

During the preliminary investigations carried out by *Manushi*, several lawyers provided us with instances of the police using the threat of arrest to extort a lot of money from the husband's family. Likewise, people allege that the police threatened to oppose or delay granting of bail unless the accused family coughed up fairly hefty amounts as bribes. Others allege that many lawyers encourage complainants to exaggerate the amounts due to them as *stridhan*, assuring them that they would get them a hefty settlement from the husband, provided they got a certain percentage as commission for their services in coercing the husband's family.

Many cases have come to our notice whereby the woman uses the strict provisions of Section 498A in the hope of enhancing her bargaining position vis-à-vis her husband and in-laws. Her lawyers often encourage her in the misguided belief that her husband would be so intimidated that he will be ready to concede to all her demands. However, once a family has been sent to jail even for a day, they are so paranoid that they refuse to consider a reconciliation under any circumstances, pushing instead for divorce. Thus, many a woman ends up with a divorce she did not want and with weaker, rather than strengthened, terms of bargaining.

Several women's organizations, with long years of experience in intervening in such cases, find to their dismay that their help was being sought in patently bogus cases. Several police officers also admit that a good number of cases are of dubious standing.

The cases in which these provisions have been exploited cover a large spectrum. In an instance brought to our notice by the Delhi-based organization Shaktishalini, a young woman who happened to have married into a much wealthier family than her own used the threat of 498A to pressure her husband into giving money to her brothers for investing in their business. In yet another case, a woman wanted a divorce because she was having an affair with a doctor from whom she was also pregnant. Yet, she sought a divorce alleging cruelty at the hands of her husband and charged him with being impotent—all so that she could coerce him into giving her a sum of money. Shaktishalini also mentioned a case they had to deal with in which a wife refused to consummate her marriage because she was involved in an incestuous relationship with her own father. Yet this father–daughter duo filed a case under 498A and demanded Rs 10 lakh from the groom's family as a pre-condition to uncontested divorce.

I personally know of instances where the main point of discord between the couple was that the wife wanted the husband to leave his parent's home or an old widowed mother and set up a nuclear family. Since the man resisted this move, the wife used 498A as a bargaining device, though without success. In one instance, the young wife being the only daughter of a wealthy businessman, wanted her husband to move in with her parents because his income allowed middle class comforts, not the luxuries she was used to. Since he did not succumb to the pressure of leaving his parents, she got both her father and mother-in-law arrested and put in jail for several days under 498A, at a time when her husband had gone visiting his sister in the US. The man himself dared not return even to bail out his parents before he got anticipatory bail from the court. Needless to say, all these cases ended in divorce rather than in the wife getting her way.

Are These Stray Cases?

The question to ask is: are these stray examples or do they represent a growing trend? Opinions differ. Some lawyers will tell you that more than 90 per cent of cases under 498A are false or are based on questionable grounds. A lawyer, who handles the cases of a feminist organization, told me that in Punjab, on any given day, 75 per cent of the cases listed for hearing in criminal courts are registered under Section 498A, and of these more than 90 per cent are *mala fide*. Sumitra Kant of Punjab Istri Sabha (the women's front of the Communist Party of India, based in Punjab) confirms that the proportion of such blackmail cases is growing fast in Punjab and cited several cases personally known to her.

Nobody has established as yet whether the abuse of these laws is as rampant as it is made out to be. Some think that the scare caused by isolated cases of misuse has caused a reaction in our society, making people exaggerate the damaging consequences of these laws. They dismiss the charges of abuse by pointing to the very low rate of convictions under Section 498A.

While it is true that very few people have actually been given sentences under 498A, there is no doubt that a large number of families have been locked up in jail for a few days or weeks, some even for months, following the registration of a police FIR. That is punishment enough for most. In many instances, out-of-court settlements are made using 498A as a bargaining point by the woman's family. Many cases do not go far because the charges are so exaggerated that the cases fall through. All these and other factors may be contributing to an abysmally low conviction rate.

However, many feminists think that Section 498A has indeed served women well and proved extremely useful as a deterrent. They argue that women may not be in a position to see their complaint through to its logical end. But this is not to deny its usefulness in bringing the husband to the negotiating table. Since the offence is non-bailable, the initial imprisonment for a day or two helps to convey to the husbands the message that their wives are not going to tolerate violence lying down.

No doubt, some women feel compelled to use this method to arrive at a speedy divorce and settlement of alimony because they feel that they will not get justice through the civil courts, given their tardy and unpredictable functioning.

But this in itself amounts to using the law as a weapon of intimidation rather than a tool of justice. I would condone its use thus, if it were true that lawyers used it judiciously to effect dignified settlements for women with legitimate complaints. But in a good number of cases, at least in metropolitan cities, lawyers are actively distorting the spirit and purpose of the law.

The basic problem with the present laws dealing with domestic discord and marital abuse is that instead of providing effective remedies through civil laws, the whole matter has been put under the jurisdiction of criminal laws, with very draconian provisions to make their implementation stringent.

This is what scares many women from approaching the police or the courts for protection, because once they put their husbands behind bars, they know then that they are in a fight to the finish. Most women are not prepared for that. Instead, they prefer to approach organizations that can mediate on their behalf and work out a better solution for them. In some cases, where the Crimes against Women Cell personnel are sensitive to their job and honest, they do perform the role of mediators well. But in most cases, the police make such cases an occasion to make money by squeezing the husband's family, in return for the woman withdrawing her opposition to grant of bail.

Need for Workable Laws

One of the tragedies of independent India is that we have not yet learnt to distinguish between reasonable and unreasonable laws, between implementable and unimplementable laws, just as we have failed to create a law enforcement machinery capable of providing genuine recourse to all those whose rights have been violated.

Through a great deal of struggle and hard work, women's organizations have won a measure of social legitimacy in persuading our society, especially law makers, to recognize the serious threat to women's lives due to domestic violence. However, if instances of manipulation of such laws become common, we will get less and less sympathy for the plight of women in our society, even for those women who are facing threats to their lives. We need to sift the grain from the chaff and check out whether the allegations of abuse are indeed genuine, or they are exaggerated or altogether *mala fide*. Those of us who are concerned about expanding the horizons of women's freedom and strengthening their rights, both within the family and in the public domain, ought to be taking note of these developments as they arise.

11

Well-intentioned but Over Ambitious

*A Review of the New Domestic Violence Act**

The new Domestic Violence Act (DVA) has made some significant improvements over the existing laws but the media hype generated around it created the erroneous impression that prior to this Act there were no civil laws to protect women's rights in the family. Astute and determined lawyers have successfully pleaded and got adequate relief for their female clients under the existing matrimonial, civil and criminal laws. But the tardiness of court procedures and judicial bias often resulted in miscarriage of justice.

The biggest shortcoming of this Act is its overweening ambition and lack of sense of proportion. Ordinarily, when handling such deep-rooted problems, sincere regimes start their interventions with a clear focus on victimized

---

*This article appeared in *Manushi*, No. 156, September–October 2006.

groups facing life-threatening situations; they set themselves realistic goals for dealing with blatant and clear-cut cases of abuse and bring the worst offenders to swift justice. For example, they direct their laws and welfare measures to those women who have suffered severe physical injuries in their homes and are recognized in their communities as abused wives.

But what the framers of this Act have done is to anticipate *all* possible ways that the law could protect *all* aggrieved females from *any and all sorts* of harm and humiliation. At the same time they have put all their faith in *all women being essentially good and honest* while they view the government and the non-governmental organization (NGO) networks as being capable of righting *all* kinds of wrongs, and in using *all* the claims of *all* women to get them justice, without worrying about proof of claims, or the current state of the society and of the government machinery. It is as if the framers of this law live in a dreamland where wishful thinking is all that is needed to protect women from all kinds of real and imagined harm. In the process, we are likely to see this law make a mockery of itself.

The Positive Aspects

A major plus point of this Act is that it acknowledges domestic violence as a problem in itself rather than keeping it forcibly tied to the *pallu* of anti-dowry laws. The previous law carried an absurd assumption that domestic violence was invariably linked to dowry demands and hence a new and exotic variety of crime called 'dowry death' was added to the statute book. Consequently, lawyers, police and even some women's organizations encouraged women to register violence cases under the Dowry Prohibition Act even when there was no basis to the allegations of dowry demands because they felt stringent provisions of the anti-dowry law made it easier for them to press charges and get a sympathetic hearing. Thus our courts came to be filled with cases with exaggerated or patently false charges of dowry demand-related cruelty, while other dimensions of cruelty got pushed under the carpet. This new law frees women from the need to make bogus dowry-related charges in order for their abuse to be taken seriously. This may enable us to know the real face of domestic violence in India and dispel the simplistic notion that dowry is the sole or main cause of violence against women.

The DVA provides for comprehensive and speedy relief within a set time frame. So far, the remedies available to a victim of domestic violence in the civil courts and criminal courts vide Section 498A of the Indian Penal Code (IPC) were limited. They could file for divorce under civil law and/or get the abusive spouse arrested and tried for cruelty under Section 498A.

Thus the earlier laws hinged mainly on threatening the use of penal provisions to get the accused arrested and jailed on registration of a complaint in order to negotiate relief with an allegedly abusive spouse. Many women learnt to use the law to arm-twist their husbands to agree to financial settlements before divorce. The new Act moves in the direction of providing positive protection of women's civil and matrimonial rights without using the threat of imprisonment under criminal laws *as the first step* towards seeking redress, as was the case with Section 498A. Under this law, imprisonment comes as a *second stage remedy*.

Earlier, victimized women found it hard to get emergency relief unless a very determined lawyer was willing to walk the extra mile and use the skillful techniques described by Flavia Agnes in an article in *Manushi*, No. 156, titled 'Making Laws Work for Women: The Potential of Existing Laws Against Domestic Violence'. But even in those cases they had to combine legal means with extra-legal ones. Since court proceedings are invariably protracted, the victim had to often live at the mercy of the abuser or walk out of the house.

A major shortcoming of earlier laws against domestic violence was that they assumed women to be abused only in their roles as wives and daughters-in-law. The new Act takes a more balanced and nuanced view of domestic abuse by including daughters, sisters, mothers, mothers-in-law, sisters-in-law and even grandmothers in its purview. A woman can also be brutally victimized by her own father or brothers. Many older women, especially widows, are also victimized by their sons and daughters-in-law.

This new Act provides for swift, time-bound and comprehensive civil remedies for maintenance, right to the matrimonial home, protection against violence as well as custody of children. It would have marked a significant improvement over the earlier civil remedies available to abused women had the framers of this law been more focused, realistic and balanced in their approach. However, it has done very little to allay the fears of all those who have witnessed widespread abuse and misuse of the existing laws against domestic violence. If anything, it has added more reasons for concern and alarm.

Beneficiaries of this Law

Section 2(a) of the Act enables a woman to seek protection against any adult male family member who has been in a domestic relationship with her. This includes her own father, brother, husband or male partner as well as his male and female relatives. However, under Section 498A a father-in-law, mother-in-law or even siblings of the husband and other relatives can be proceeded against even if they are not living under the same roof.

DVA also covers sisters, widows, mothers, daughters, women in relationships of cohabitation, single women, adopted children, and so on. The types of offences that would make fathers or brothers subject to the Act have been expanded in ways that make it much easier for the women to enter a case under DVA. While this marks an improvement, it has the potential to create very conflicting situations. For example, what if a mother-in-law is being abused by her daughter-in-law, who in turn seeks an injunction against her mother-in-law? Given that battles between women in the family tend to be no less ferocious than those between spouses, this is not an unlikely scenario. Our domestic violence law allows a daughter-in-law to sue her mother-in-law, but a mother-in-law, even if genuinely aggrieved, cannot file a case against her daughter-in-law because it recognizes only 'cruelty by husband or relatives of husband'. Moreover, men, no matter what their status, are not entitled to seek relief under this Act, which is based on the assumption that only women and children suffer domestic abuse. Thus an old father-in-law who may suffer abuse, taunts and even violence at the hands of his son or daughter-in-law cannot get relief under this law.

However, under this law, children can also file a case against a parent or parents who are tormenting or torturing them physically, mentally or economically. In case the child is not in a position to approach the court on his/her own, 'any other person' can file a complaint on behalf of the child.The law does not specify that a person has to be closely related or well known to the child in order to qualify for filing a complaint on the child's behalf.

Provisions for Speedy Relief

The following provisions meant for speedy relief can prove beneficial only if an efficient delivery mechanism is put in place. The Magistrate shall fix the first date of hearing, which *shall not ordinarily* be beyond three days from the date of receipt of the application by the court.

The Magistrate shall endeavour to dispose of every application made under sub-section (1) *within a period of sixty days* from the date of its first hearing.

A notice of the date of hearing fixed under section 12 shall be given by the Magistrate to the Protection Officer, who shall get it served by such means as may be prescribed on the respondent, or on any other person, as directed by the Magistrate within *a maximum period of two days* or such further reasonable time as may be allowed by the Magistrate from the date of its receipt.

A declaration of service notice made by the Protection Officer in such form as may be prescribed shall be the proof that such notice was served upon the respondent and on any other person as directed by the Magistrate unless the contrary is proved.

The Magistrate may, at any stage of the proceedings under this Act, direct the respondent or the aggrieved person, either singly or jointly, to undergo counselling with any member of a service provider who possesses such qualifications and experience in counselling as may be prescribed.

Where the Magistrate has issued any direction under sub-section (1), he shall fix the *next date of hearing* of the case within a period *not exceeding two months.*

These measures are indeed commendable because women who are facing grievous threats to their life require emergency measures. However, given the state of our courts, given that even cases involving heinous terrorist crimes, including those handed over to special courts appointed for the purpose, languish for decades in our courts, it seems highly unlikely that this *sultani farman* (imperial edict) will achieve its goal. But it sure provides a handle to lawyers who want to pursue the case with vigour.

Definition of Abuse

Section 3 of the law defines 'domestic violence' as any act/conduct/omission/commission that harms or injures or has the potential to harm or injure a woman or child. This law considers physical, sexual, emotional, verbal, psychological and economic abuse or threats of violence and abuse as equally serious offences. The law lists out in detail different forms of violence faced by women so that interpretation of what constitutes violence is not left solely to the discretion of the judges. Even a single act of commission or omission may constitute domestic violence. This has been done with the intention that women should not have been made to suffer a prolonged period of abuse before the law takes them seriously.

The court may conclude that an offence has been committed by the accused upon *the sole testimony of the woman alleging abuse.* Given that lying in court has never been taken seriously enough to invoke punishment, laws which presume guilt even before the trial has begun are prone to great misuse.

Physical abuse is defined as any act or conduct which is of such a nature as to cause bodily pain, harm or danger to life, limb or health, or an act that impairs the health or development of the person aggrieved, or that includes assault, criminal intimidation and criminal force.

Sexual abuse is any 'conduct of a sexual nature that abuses, humiliates, degrades, or otherwise violates the dignity of woman'. The law also covers instances where a woman is forced to have sexual intercourse with her husband against her will.

While it is important to respect a women's right to say 'No' to sex even in a marriage, it is not easy to assess whether a particular sexual act is against a woman's will or was with her consent in case of married couples, especially if there are no signs of struggle or resistance on the woman's body.

Verbal and emotional abuse has been defined as 'insults, ridicule, humiliation, name-calling, especially with regard to not having a child or a male child; and repeated threats to cause physical pain to any person in whom the aggrieved person is interested. So, for example, if the abuser were to threaten the children, or relatives of the woman, this will also be considered an offence under this law. However, putting verbal taunts or abuse at par with physical violence amounts to very shoddy thinking. For example, calling someone a 'moron' cannot be treated at par with beating them up.

Economic abuse, under the new law, has been defined as deprivation or denial of financial resources to which the aggrieved woman or child is entitled under law or custom, or which the person aggrieved requires out of necessity. A husband would be held guilty of economic abuse if he were to sell or use her *stridhan* (dowry), her jewellery and/or any other property jointly or separately held by the wife. But the law does not specify what happens if a certain asset has been alienated with the written consent of the wife but later she makes a case that it was done against her will.

Even under previous laws, a woman was entitled to seek maintenance for herself and her children from her husband. However, the legal procedures were cumbersome and poorly enforced. Consequently, too many men got away with shirking responsibility for maintaining their children and divorced wife. Therefore, women began to use the draconian provisions of Section 498A of the IPC to arm twist their husbands into offering them a one time settlement. Under the new law, civil remedies have been strengthened and economic rights of wives more clearly defined. However, the new law leaves as much scope for misuse as the previous laws whose faults it was supposed to remedy, especially since it puts short-term live-in relationships at par with legal marriages.

Live-in Relationships

The most important new element in this law is that it recognizes live-in relationships and offers the same degree of protection to a woman who is living with a man outside of marriage. According to Section 2(g), any relationship between two persons who live, or have *at any point of time* lived together in a shared household when they are related by marriage, consanguinity or through a relationship similar to marriage, or are family members living in a joint family, is considered a 'domestic relationship'. It also protects women in fraudulent or bigamous marriages, or in marriages considered invalid by law. However, the law does not make explicit whether it also applies to same sex marriages or gay relationships.

The wide-ranging definition of 'domestic relationship' may bring the needed relief for those women whose husbands dupe them into cohabitation without going through proper ceremonies and then dump them at will on the grounds that theirs was not a valid marriage. But it has cast its net so wide that it leaves enormous scope for flimsy claims with a view to harassment and blackmail.

The Act does not specify how long a couple has to have lived in the shared household in order for a woman to claim benefit under the Act. Thus, as per the letter of this law, a woman who may have lived with a man for two or three months without being married to him can *at any point* seek relief under this law, at par with a legally wedded wife. This amounts to making a mockery of laws against bigamy. The habitation rights of live-in partners in the same house in case of already married men cannot be protected in this way without serious damage to the rights of legally married wives and their children. It is perfectly legitimate to protect a woman from violence and punish a man for inflicting it on her, whether or not she is married to the man. However, to give her the right to claim maintenance and get injunctions barring her male partner's entry into his own house is going a bit too far, especially if he already has a wife and children living in that house.

No Eviction or Harassment

An important addition to the law ensures that an aggrieved wife or partner who takes recourse to the law and gets a 'protection order' or an injunction barring the entry of the husband into the house cannot be harassed for doing so. Thus, if a man is accused of any of the aforementioned forms of violence, he cannot, during the pending disposal of the case, prohibit/restrict the wife's or partner's continued access to resources or facilities to which she is entitled by virtue of the domestic relationship, including access to the shared household. If he does so he invites a fine of Rs 20,000 and/or a jail term of up to one year.

Section 17 of the law, which gives all married women or female partners in a domestic relationship the right to reside in a home that is known in legal terms as the 'shared household', is applicable regardless of whether or not she has any legal right, title or beneficial interest in the same.

According to Section 2(s), a household where the woman alleging violence lives or *at any stage or any point of time* in a domestic relationship, either singly or along with the respondent, is defined as a 'shared household'. The period of cohabitation has not been specified before a house can be considered a 'shared household'. This provision is a clear example of over-kill and leaves a lot of scope for misuse.

This applies whether the household is owned or tenanted, either jointly by the person aggrieved and the respondent, or by either of them, where either the person aggrieved or the respondent or both jointly or singly have any right, title, interest or equity. This allows even those women with whom a live-in relationship was terminated months or years ago to claim maintenance, compensation and right of residence from the male partner, thus opening the gates wide open for bizarre claims by women who at some point may have spent a few weeks living with a man before his marriage.

Sections 18–23 provide a large number of avenues for an abused woman to get relief. Courts are obliged to give her Protection Orders, Residence Orders, monetary relief, custody of her children, Compensation Orders and Interim/*Ex parte* Orders.

The law provides that if an abused woman so desires, she has to be provided alternative accommodation comparable to the standard of living she is used to. The cost of the accommodation and her maintenance has to be paid for by her husband or partner. Thus there is provision for rapid temporary rights for the woman, pending disposal of the case. This makes perfect sense as far as wives are concerned. But to put the same weapons in the hands of a temporary live-in partner amounts to letting our notion of gender justice run haywire. In effect, it means that a man has no right to break off a love affair without paying through his nose.

A woman who is the victim of domestic violence will have the right to the services of the police, shelter homes and medical establishments. She also has the right to simultaneously file her own complaint under the existing laws against domestic violence, such as Section 498A of the IPC. Thus, an accused person will be liable to have charges framed against him under both the old law and the new one. Further, the offences are cognizable and non-bailable.

No Safeguards against Abuse of Law

It is unfortunate that despite widespread complaints of misuse of earlier laws, the new Act pays scant attention to building safeguards against *mala fide* use of 498A and the anti-dowry laws. All it has done is to pile on more provisions with similar potential for misuse.

Section 498A of IPC enacted in 1983 defined 'cruelty by husband or relatives of husband' as a new cognizable offence. As in the new DVA, under

Section 498A too, cruelty was given a very wide-ranging definition to include violence that leads to bodily harm, or danger to life, limb or physical health but also includes endangerment of mental health, harassment and emotional torture through verbal abuse.

In addition, Section 498A made it obligatory for the police to take prompt action and arrest all those in her marital family against whom a woman alleges cruelty. The bail in such cases could be opposed and delayed. Thus, in many cases, those accused of 'cruelty' to wives or daughters-in-law got punished even before the trial actually began.

Given the corrupt and lawless ways of the police, this provision came to be misused and abused widely by the police to extract bribes as well as by unscrupulous women and their lawyers to blackmail the husband's family even on trumped up charges. *Manushi* has dealt with numerous cases whereby innocent men and their families have been devastated by unscrupulous wives and daughters-in-law.

It is not just men, but even a lot of women who have suffered the consequences of irresponsible use of Section 498A, who believe that it is extremely one-sided and an instrument of blackmail rather than of securing justice. On the other hand, many genuine victims of violence hesitate to seek legal redress under 498A because it would mean getting their husbands and in-laws sent behind bars. While many kids may support their abused mother in seeking divorce, most do not support their mothers in getting their fathers sent to jail even if they have personally been victims of abuse because having a father convicted and sent to jail mars and stigmatizes the life of children as well (see Chapter 10).

So deep is the reaction against this easy-to-manipulate law that in recent years, senior police officers, including women officers in-charge of Crime Against Women Cells (CAWCs), have let it be known to those handling such cases to go slow on booking cases under 498A. This means even genuine cases of abuse end up being viewed with mistrust.

Injunctions for Residence Order and Protection Order

The Magistrate may, on being satisfied that domestic violence has taken place, pass a Residence Order–

- Restraining the respondent from dispossessing or in any other manner disturbing the possession of the aggrieved person from the shared household, whether or not the respondent has a legal or equitable interest in the shared household;

- Directing the respondent to remove himself from the shared household;
- Restraining the respondent or any of his relatives from entering any portion of the shared household in which the aggrieved person resides;
- Restraining the respondent from alienating or disposing off the shared household or encumbering the same;
- Restraining the respondent from renouncing his rights in the shared household except with the leave of the Magistrate; or
- Directing the respondent to secure same level of alternative accommodation for the aggrieved person as enjoyed by her in the shared household or to pay rent for the same, if the circumstances so require.

  [N.B. However, no order can be passed directing a woman to remove herself from the shared household, even if she may be the main perpetrator of violence.]
- The Magistrate may impose any additional conditions or pass any other direction which he may deem reasonably necessary to protect or to provide for the safety of the aggrieved person or any child of such aggrieved person.
- The Magistrate may require from the respondent to execute a bond, with or without sureties, for preventing the commission of domestic violence.
- **Time-Bound Monetary Relief:** The respondent shall pay the monetary relief granted to the aggrieved person within the period specified in the order.
- Upon the failure on the part of the respondent to make payment in terms of the order, the Magistrate may direct the employer or a debtor of the respondent, to directly pay to the aggrieved person or to deposit with the court a portion of the wages or salaries or debt due to or accrued to the credit of the respondent, which amount may be adjusted towards the monetary relief payable by the respondent.
- **Right to Police Help:** While passing an order, the court may also pass an order directing the officer in charge of the nearest police station to give protection to the aggrieved person or to assist her or the person making an application on her behalf in the implementation of the order. While making an order, the Magistrate may impose on the respondent obligations relating to the discharge of rent and other payments, having regard to the financial needs and resources of the parties.
- **Right over *Stridhan*:** The Magistrate may direct the respondent to return to the possessions of the aggrieved person, her *stridhan* or any other property or valuable security to which she is entitled.
- **Monetary Relief, Compensation for Losses and Expenses:** While passing an order in favour of the woman, the Magistrate may direct the

respondent to pay monetary relief to meet the expenses incurred and losses suffered by the aggrieved person and any child of the aggrieved person as a result of the domestic violence and such relief may include, but not be limited to:

(*a*) the loss of earnings;
(*b*) the medical expenses;
(*c*) the loss caused due to the destruction, damage or removal of any property from the control of the aggrieved person; and
(*d*) maintenance for the aggrieved person as well as her children, if any, including an order under or in addition to an order of maintenance under Section 125 of the Code of Criminal Procedure, 1973 or any other law for the time being in force.

The monetary relief granted under this section shall be adequate, fair and reasonable and consistent with the standard of living to which the aggrieved person is accustomed.

The Magistrate shall have the power to order an appropriate lump sum payment or monthly payments of maintenance as the nature and circumstances of the case may require.

- **Punishment for Breach:** A breach of Protection Order, or even an Interim Protection Order, by the respondent shall be an offence under this Act and shall be punishable with imprisonment of either description for a term which may extend to one year, with fine which may extend to Rs 20,000 or both. Charges under Section 498A can be additionally framed by the Magistrate, in addition to the charges under this Act.

Implementation Machinery

Section 8 of the law provides for the creation and stipulates the responsibilities of Protection Officers (POs). These officers, to be appointed by state governments, will be under the jurisdiction and control of the court, and will be responsible to the court for monitoring the cases of domestic abuse.

The PO has to assist the court in making a Domestic Incident Report (DIR) or an application for a Protection Order on behalf of the aggrieved woman and/or child. POs will ensure that aggrieved people are provided legal aid, medical services, safe shelter and other required assistance.

POs are supposed to ensure that necessary information regarding service providers is made available to the woman or child alleging violence and that orders for monetary relief are complied with. Most important of all, the PO can be penalized for failing/refusing to discharge his/her duty, provided that prior sanction of the state government is obtained for this purpose. They invite a penalty of Rs 20,000 and/or a prison term of up to one year for failing to do their job.

Service Providers (SPs)

POs have been given the power to register SPs who are defined by the law as private organizations, which are recognized under the Companies Act or Societies Registration Act.

They will have to register with the state government in order to qualify as service providers. An organization can be registered as an SP if it has provided services to women in distress for at least two years prior to seeking registration under Section 10(1) of the DVA. In addition, magistrates who are to hear cases under DVA are empowered to appoint counsellors under Section 14(1) of the Act who are to assist the petitioner and report to the magistrate's court.

The new law, thus, recognizes the role of voluntary organizations in addressing the issue of domestic violence and enables NGOs working for women's rights to register as SPs under the Act. An SP is protected for all actions done in good faith in the exercise of the powers under this Act towards the prevention of commission of domestic violence.

The SPs will, among other things, have to record the DIR, arrange for medical examination of the complainant, and ensure that she is provided accommodation in a shelter home, if she so requires.

Unrealistic Expectations

How many NGOs, even in metropolises, leave alone small towns and villages, have the resources and capacity to provide such comprehensive services? Genuine shelter homes do not exist in most cities, leave alone in rural areas. The few government-run shelter homes that exist are often dens of corruption. Also, there is no provision for reimbursing NGOs for providing these services. Thus the responsibility for making this law work has been put on a non-existent machinery. Considering the speed with which bogus and corrupt NGOs have come up in India, it is not unreasonable to fear that a whole range of goons and anti-social elements will manage to register themselves as service providers much faster than genuine NGOs.

No budgetary allocation has so far been provided by the Centre to assist states in paying for the expenses involved in providing such comprehensive assistance to women. To insert a state-level government official, a PO, into the machinery without considering the financial burden put on the states is likely to lead to grief. Chances are that in most states, this function is likely to be added to the existing job responsibilities of government officials already on the ground without figuring out if they can handle the burden of their new job along with their other tasks. Alternatively, state governments who are usually cash- starved would find good reason to delay forever the setting up of this machinery. Some state governments have already refused to operationalize the Act on the ground that POs have not been appointed yet.

If such comprehensive services were indeed available to the DV victim as a consequence of her complaint, and these same services are difficult to obtain otherwise because of their scarcity, what would prevent poor women from filing false charges simply to avail shelter, medical help and financial support?

Giving Exaggerated Hopes?

This Act raises several new problems, repeats some of the mistakes of the old laws and raises many unresolved questions.

- The 'Rules' that define the institutional framework for the new Act came into force with effect from 26 October 2006—a full year after the DVA was added to the statute book. This delay is itself instructive and points out that the new law may remain a paper tiger or be used haphazardly since the elaborate countrywide machinery mandated under the DVA is nowhere in sight.
- The enactment of the new DVA is an open admission that the existing provisions of law against violence are a failure. If such a strong law as Section 498A proved ineffective or came to be misused widely, why should we expect that the new law will act as a magic wand to be used honestly against genuine offenders?
- As a supportive measure for 498A, provisions were made for the creation of CAWCs in every police district. They are in principle supposed to do what POs have been assigned to do in the new Act. The performance of the CAWCs depends largely on the level of commitment and sensitivity of the person heading a particular Cell. Given that their personnel are drawn from the normal police cadre, CAWCs function as well or as badly as their parent body. In many places, they have not afforded protection to women even against the most blatant and devastating forms of domestic violence. Why should we expect that the new officials would be correctly chosen, well trained and made to do an honest job for victims of domestic

violence? What is to be the role of CAWCs after the creation of new machinery as envisaged by the new Act? Will they be folded up or will they exist as a parallel system? The state governments have been given a year to work out these problems; little is known of their preparations for implementation of the Act.

- The Family Courts Act of 1984 was enacted with the purpose of providing civil remedies for domestic disputes and a more conducive atmosphere for the settlement of marital conflicts. They had the following provisions:
  - The jurisdiction for claiming maintenance was shifted from the magistrate's court to delink matrimonial matters from those which deal with ordinary criminal cases like theft, kidnapping and pick-pocketing;
  - Counselling of couples as a first step to see if their differences could be settled through negotiation and neutral but woman-friendly mediation rather than taking them straight for legal remedies which have adversarial processes inbuilt into them;
  - Reduce the role of lawyers, who tend to complicate matters by dragging out cases for their personal benefit and cut down litigation costs by allowing petitioners to argue their case in person; and
  - Club together divorce and maintenance proceedings and bring them under one roof so that women need not have to fight parallel battles in different courts for different types of relief.

Family Courts have failed to deliver because the government did not allow them the space and resources to function well. It is noteworthy that during the more than two decades since the law was passed, 18 states and union territories (including Delhi) have failed to set up Family Courts. Lawyers in many states have succeeded in stalling these institutions because matrimonial disputes have become a very lucrative business. They lose business if litigants can manage without them, as envisaged by the Family Courts Act.

Where Family Courts exist, they function poorly because the government has not provided enough resources for the required infrastructure. Nor have the costs of litigation come down. The system of counselling has also remained at best a mere formality and at worst turned into a system that forces women to accept unfavourable settlements because no serious effort has been made to train and orient the required number of social workers to support women claimants. If skilled and professional family counsellors in adequate numbers were not appointed to assist Family Courts, why do we assume that the government will somehow manage to get POs of the required calibre and commitment with the passing of DVA?

DVA in a way amounts to a step backwards because the cases will be tried in a magistrate's court along with petty criminal cases, whereas Family Courts are presided over by district and sessions judges who are higher in status than magistrates. Will the Family Courts exist as a parallel and competing institution after the coming into force of the DVA? Or will they be allowed to languish even further now that the government is required to set up a whole new machinery? Can the new DVA be operationalized if state governments fail or refuse to set up the required machinery, as happened with the Family Courts?

Though a product of good intentions, this Act is likely to open the floodgates of messy litigation even further because it is too pompous and ambitious. Furthermore, it has not provided any deterrents for litigants, lawyers and police found misusing the law with bogus allegations. Nor does it provide compensation for families who are falsely implicated and suffer the ignominy of arrests and jail terms under Section 498A without deserving to do so.

Laws are akin to weapons. Just as the best of guns cannot help win a war if the soldiers in whose hands they are placed are ill trained, irresponsible, cowardly and prone to mindless violence. Similarly, without an honest, efficient and accountable law enforcement machinery, even the best of laws become useless. In India we have not yet learnt to craft our laws judiciously because we have no experience of their honest implementation. And yet, every time a law shows signs of dismal failure, the government responds by passing yet another new law or amending the existing law to make it more stringent and/or more wide-ranging and then pretending it has handed over a new magic wand for the empowerment of women.

In the process, the government makes a mockery of its own intentions as well as its ability to deliver justice. Unless the task of introducing far-reaching police and judicial reforms is undertaken with urgency, attempts at new legislation are not likely to yield much good.

12

Destined to Fail

*Inherent Flaws in the Anti-dowry Legislation**

Even though *Manushi* played a leading role in bringing national attention to domestic violence and the role dowry has come to play in making women's lives vulnerable, after nearly 28 years of experience with these issues, I have come to the firm conclusion that the terms 'dowry death' and 'dowry violence' are misleading. They contribute towards making domestic violence in India appear as a unique, exotic phenomenon by giving the impression that Indian men are the only ones in the world to use violence based on astute and rational calculations. By this logic, it would appear that men in all other parts of the world are truly stupid because they beat and kill their wives without any benefit accruing to them, whereas Indian men attack their spouses in the expectation of extorting financial rewards from their in-laws.

Domestic violence is about using brute force to establish power relations in the family whereby women are taught and conditioned to accept a subservient status. Domestic violence is a way of trying to get women to believe that they can only live at men's mercy. It is often committed by men with low self-esteem

*This article appeared in *Manushi*, No. 148, May–June 2005.

who destroy a woman's sense of self-worth because they feel inadequate to cope with a woman who thinks and acts as a free human being with a mind of her own. Like rape, wife battering is a common predicament of women across nations, castes, classes, religions and regions.

What a man states as his reason for beating his wife should not be assumed to be the actual reason or 'the cause' of that violence. For example, if a violent incident is triggered off in a home in Germany by a man flying into a rage and battering a woman to death saying, 'You are a lousy cook' or 'You are fat and ugly', we do not call such crimes 'Lousy Cooking Murders' or 'Ugly Woman Murders'. We recognize that the ostensible reasons given by men for their violent rages are mere excuses to destroy a woman's sense of self-worth. They are not the real cause. The same logic applies to dowry-related violence. I have not come across a single case where a man battered a woman solely because of additional dowry demands and would begin to treat his wife well if his in-laws met with all his demands.

By contrast, I have come across numerous situations where a woman suffers a lot of taunts and even violence because her husband's family feels she might start considering herself high and mighty for bringing in a huge dowry. Director Vijay Anand's film *Kora Kagaz* produced in the 1970s provided a very sensitive and insightful portrayal of an otherwise happy 'love marriage' suffering a break-up because the bride's mother insists on showering her daughter and son-in-law with gifts to make up for the modest income of the latter, leading to a sense of inadequacy and humiliation in the son-in-law.

Even though I maintain that dowry per se is not the cause of domestic violence, there is no denying that dowry demands and sharp escalation in the amounts of money being spent by families in putting together dowries has contributed to viewing daughters as a burden and a consequent devaluation of women's lives (see Chapter 6).

The culture of dowry giving is spreading even to communities which had no such tradition a generation or two ago. This despite the fact that in the last two decades the anti-dowry laws have been made very stringent and draconian. Many interpret the failure of these laws to lessen dowry giving as a sign of their poor implementation. However, these laws have so many inherent flaws that their honest implementation is well nigh impossible. In fact, these laws have created more problems than they have solved. You cannot combat a 'crime' which is as ill defined as the anti-dowry laws of India.

An Ill-defined Crime

Definition of dowry: As per the Dowry Prohibition Act (originally passed in 1961 and amended twice in the 1980s), dowry is defined as 'any property or valuable security given or agreed to be given either directly or indirectly by one party to a marriage to the other party to the marriage or by the parents of either party to a marriage or by any other person, to either party to the marriage or to any other person at or before [or any other time after the marriage] in connection with the marriage of the said parties. As per this definition, gifts of jewellery, clothes and cash traditionally given by the groom's family would also be covered by the anti-dowry law and hence declared illegal.

Cognizable offence: Two amendments enacted in 1984 and 1986 made dowry giving and receiving a cognizable offence. This means, a court can initiate proceedings upon its own knowledge or on the basis of a police report, even if the aggrieved person has lodged no such complaint.

Gifts allowed: As per this law 'dowry' is forbidden but 'gifts' are allowed. The anti-dowry law cannot be invoked against the giving of presents at the time of marriage to the bride without any demand having been made 'provided that such presents are entered in a list maintained in accordance with the rules' as defined under the Anti-Dowry Act.

Presents to the groom allowed: Presents given to the groom are also exempted, provided no demand has been made and they are entered in a list and provided that 'such presents are of a customary nature and the value thereof is not excessive' in relation to the 'financial status of the person by whom, or on whose behalf, such presents are given'.

Prescribed punishment: A person found guilty of taking or abetting the giving or taking of dowry invites imprisonment for a term not less than five years and a fine which shall not be less than Rs 15,000 or the amount of the value of such dowry, whichever is more.

Legalizing the illegal: After declaring that giving or taking of dowry is illegal, the Act adds a curious rider that 'where any dowry is received by any person other than the woman in connection with whose marriage it is given, that person will transfer the dowry to the woman within three months after the date of marriage or within three months after the date of receipt. Failure to transfer a woman's dowry invites imprisonment for not less than six months and a fine of Rs 10,000. If the dowry was received when the woman was a minor, it should be transferred to her within three months after she has attained the age of 18 years.

Burden of proof on the accused: What makes this law especially draconian is that the burden of proof has been shifted onto the accused. In most other crimes, including murder, Indian jurisprudence puts the burden of proof on the complainant and the accused is considered innocent till proven guilty.

However, in the case of dowry related offences, a husband and his family have to prove that they did not make dowry demands and what was given by the bride's parents were voluntary gifts.

Dowry return: Section 406 prescribes imprisonment of up to three years for criminal breach of trust for not returning a woman's dowry, if a woman demands it after her marriage breaks down. Section 406 is one of the few clauses in the law that has proven useful for women with a genuine case because it helps in the retrieval of dowry where the husband or in-laws are unwilling to return the goods that came as dowry. If a person fails to comply with the court's direction to transfer a woman's dowry within the specified period, an amount equal to the value of the property may be recovered from him.

Draconian anti-cruelty law: In 1983, Section 498A of the IPC defined a new cognizable offence, namely, 'cruelty by husband or relatives of husband'. This is how Section 498A defines cruelty:

> Whoever, being the husband or the relative of the husband of a woman, subjects such woman to cruelty shall be punished with imprisonment for a term which may extend to three years and shall also be liable to fine. Explanation: For the purpose of this section, 'cruelty' means–
>
> (*a*) Any willful conduct which is of such a nature as is likely to drive the woman to commit suicide or to cause grave injury or danger to life, limb or health (whether mental or physical) of the woman; or
>
> (*b*) Harassment of the woman where such harassment is with a view to coercing her or any person related to her to meet any unlawful demand for any property or valuable security or is on account of failure by her or any person related to her meet such demand.

This means that once such a complaint is registered by the victim or any of her relatives, the police have no option but to take action. It prescribes imprisonment for a term, which may extend to three years, and also includes a fine. The definition of cruelty is not just confined to causing grave injury, bodily harm, or danger to life, limb or physical health, but also includes harming mental health by harassment and emotional torture through verbal abuse. This law takes particular cognizance of harassment, where it occurs with a view to coercing the wife, or any person related to her, to meet any unlawful demand regarding any property or valuable security, or occurs on account of failure by her, or any person related to her, to meet such a demand.

Punishment for 'dowry death': Women's organizations also pushed to get a new category of crime included on the statute book via an amendment to the Indian Penal Code. This crime–named 'dowry murder' or 'dowry death'–is covered by Section 304B. This section states that if the death of a woman is caused by burns or bodily injury, or occurs under abnormal circumstances, within seven years of her marriage and it is shown that just prior to death she was subject to cruelty by her husband or his relatives, in connection with demands for dowry, such a death would be called 'dowry death' and the husband or relative would be deemed to have caused her death. The person held guilty of a 'dowry death' shall be punished with imprisonment for a term which shall not be less than seven years but which may extend to imprisonment for life.

Assumption of guilt: By inserting a new section 113B in the Indian Evidence Act, the law makers stipulated that in cases that are registered by the police as those of 'dowry death', the court shall presume that the accused is guilty unless he can prove otherwise.

Bail provisions for 'dowry crimes': Under section 304B, in the case of a 'dowry death', where allegations of demand of dowry or non-return of dowry are made, the accused are frequently denied anticipatory, or even regular bail. This is understandable in cases of death because the unnatural demise of a woman is in itself likely evidence that something was seriously wrong in the marriage. But it has also meant that in all cases of a married woman's death, lawyers tend to advise the woman's family that they must build a case of dowry demands even if the murder or suicide was due to other reasons.

Basic Flaws in the Laws

Many problems arise from this fuzzy definition of crime combined with draconian provisions for punishment:

- Who decides what is a 'voluntary gift' and what is given under pressure of a demand? The very same family that often declares, at the time of marriage, that they only gave 'voluntary gifts' to the groom's family, does not hesitate to attribute all their 'gift-giving' to extortionist demands, once the marriage turns sour and is headed for a breakdown. Thus, even when marital troubles may not be connected to tussles over dowry and the marital strain is due to mutual incompatibility rather than the husband's violence or abuse, many women's families tend to seek an advantage in registering cases using the draconian provisions of the anti-dowry law when the marriage heads towards a breakdown.
- How do you decide what is 'excessive' in relation to income by way of gifts when in India no more than 2–3 per cent people declare their incomes

and those too are grossly under-reported? How do you judge the paying status of a family if most of their wealth is in black money and property holdings held in bogus names to escape taxes?

- The bride's parents rarely want to declare the true value of gifts given because the big dowry givers also put together their daughter's dowry from black money and, therefore, do not want it listed.
- When dowry giving is a crime, why would a groom or bride's family put their signature on the list of gifts being given?
- Since a good part of modern dowries consist of expensive jewellery, household goods and high-priced clothes, how do you prove whether or not these things were transferred to the bride's name within three months of marriage? For example, if a family has spent Rs 3–4 lakh on providing new furniture for their daughter's home, does it mean that all that furniture must be kept in rooms meant for the exclusive use of the daughter?
- As per the law, even dowry giving is an offence, but there is hardly ever an instance of the bride's family being prosecuted for giving dowry. The assumption is that only 'takers' are guilty while 'givers' are hapless creatures yielding to the greed and callous demands of the groom's family.
- The campaigners against dowry make it appear as if escalating dowries are solely due to the greed of the groom's family. However, as I have argued in several articles, the theory that growing greed is the cause of dowry increase would make sense only if our country had two distinct sets of families—those who only produced sons and those who produced only daughters. The 'son-blessed' families would thus be permanent gainers as dowry receivers while 'daughter-cursed' families would be permanent victims of greed and be always at the mercy of extortionist demands. This is clearly not the case because a family, which gives dowry on its daughter's wedding, becomes a recipient when its sons get married.
- This law does not take into account the rapidly changing forms of marriage transactions and mixes up the tradition of *stridhan* with modern-day marriage transactions. Even the anti-dowry campaigners attribute the problems of the modern-day dowry system to the tradition of *stridhan*, both of which are projected as a hangover of 'traditional' patriarchal norms. The present-day custom of dowry giving may retain some ingredients of the tradition of giving *stridhan* to daughters but the difference between modern-day dowry and *stridhan* is as profound as that between a horse carriage and a motorized truck. Though both move on wheels, the power that propels the two kinds of wheels is altogether different.

Dowry vs *Stridhan*

Stridhan, as per Hindu customary practice, is that portion of wealth which is the exclusive property of women and passes from mother to daughter. It includes gifts of money, property, jewellery or a share in a family business given to a woman as a daughter, sister, wife or daughter-in-law. It also covers wealth generated through her own enterprise or any other wealth accruing to her due to her own effort or by inheritance. It includes, but is not limited to, gifts or wealth given to a daughter at the time of her marriage. It also includes gifts given to her by her in-laws. A key-defining characteristic of *stridhan* is that no one in the family can touch it, except if the woman concerned voluntarily gifts a portion to someone. In the natural course, *stridhan* passes from mother to daughter and if in a contingency a male member uses part of a woman's *stridhan*, he is expected to return it with interest.

The traditional *stridhan* given at the time of a daughter's marriage was determined by predictable norms within each community and was more in the nature of pre-mortem inheritance for the daughter that usually included items such as gold, cows or even a piece of land, along with a few clothes and utensils. Up to my grandmothers' generation, community norms decided the gifts given to a daughter. By my mother's generation dowry had started emerging as a problem because marriage alliances begun to be made on the basis of a groom's potential income and status in the 'modern' economy rather than traditional notions of *stridhan*.

Traditional *stridhan* gives women stronger and inalienable rights to a portion of wealth in both parental and marital families. By contrast, dowry is a device for disinheriting daughters from parental property, as discussed in my articles, 'To Ensure Her Happiness or to Disinherit Her' and 'Dowry Calculations' (see Chapter 6 and *Manushi*, No. 78. This theme is also dealt in my film: *Dahej: Zaroorat ya Majboori?* Available on CD from *Manushi*). Modern inheritance laws also fall short of *stridhan* because they allow daughters and wives to be disinherited at will. As I have previously discussed, the provision of 'free will' was included in the Hindu Succession Act of 1956 specifically with a view to giving the power to fathers to disinherit their daughter. (For a detailed analysis, see 'Myth vs Reality: The Hindu Code Bill', *Economic and Political Weekly*, Vol. XXIX, No. 33, 13 August 1994.)

Therefore, misplaced hostility to traditional cultural norms, including those like *stridhan* that gave women strong rights, results in ill-conceived campaigns that cause further harm to women. Punishment for such a poorly defined and conceptualized law is heavy and draconian; the anti-dowry law is being widely misused by unscrupulous families, policemen and lawyers.

From Dowry to Groom Price

Unlike *stridhan*, which was the exclusive property of the woman, the present-day dowry includes gifts and wealth given at a daughter's wedding, not just to her but to her husband, in-laws and his relatives as well as household goods required for setting up the house. These vary from simple gifts of clothing and small items of jewellery for the woman to exorbitant sums in cash or expensive pieces of property to the groom and his parents.

The amount of dowry commanded by a groom has more to do with his social status, income potential and social-familial connections than with the perceived share of a daughter in her parental property. Thus that part of wealth which is given to the groom and his family has acquired the form of groom price because it is an offering for seeking an alliance with a family with lucrative potential. Not surprisingly, men in those government jobs such as the Indian Administrative Service (IAS) and the Indian Police Service (IPS) which enable them to extort high bribes and provide unlimited avenues for looting the public, robbing the public exchequer and appropriating resources such as land allotments and business contracts, command the highest dowries. If in a family one son is an IAS officer, his dowry will be substantially higher than that of his brother who may have managed to get nothing more than a school teacher's job.

Contemporary dowry is more like an investment by the bride's family in the hope of plugging into powerful connections and money-making opportunities. Marrying a daughter to such a man may mean upward mobility for her entire natal family, especially brothers, because they may secure huge benefits through this connection.

The component of dowry that still retains some resemblance to the traditional *stridhan* involves the bride's trousseau, gold jewellery, household goods and any property that her parents might put in her name. But even this does not always remain in her control, leading to bitter tussles. It is not uncommon for a groom's family to keep a part of this dowry for their own daughter's wedding or treat the household goods as offerings made to the family, rather than being reserved for the bride.

Recompense for Disinheritance

Denial of inheritance rights to daughters is justified on the ground that they inherit in their marital homes. However, the share women acquire in their marital family's property is not made in their own right, but comes to them through their husbands. Women inherit more often as widows than as daughters or wives. Because as widows they become claimants to their husband's share of property, dowry given at the time of a daughter's wedding has come to be seen as an offering to her in-laws, rather than her exclusive personal property.

Since in most cases only sons inherit parental property and family businesses, and it is only in the form of *dahej* that daughters get a share—albeit an unequal one—in parental property, most women consider dowry as their legitimate due. After marriage, even the parental home comes to be their brothers' and *bhabhis*' home. Most women feel that a dowry-less wedding does not work in their interest because it only means their brothers end up with an even bigger share of family resources.

How People Justify Dowry

Some of the commonly expressed justifications for dowry run as follows.

When a young woman enters a new family, she feels diffident to ask for basic things she needs for her daily use. If she goes to her marital home without anything to call her own, her dependence on her in-laws and husband increases, unless she has a reasonable income of her own, which most women do not have. Therefore, all the household goods and clothes parents provide their daughters are supposed to help them feel that they have something to call their own in their new home.

Since daughters in most cases are disinherited by their parents after marriage, their main security lies in strengthening their economic rights in their husband's family. However, if they go 'empty-handed' to their husband's home, how can they expect that they will be treated as equal partners? The dowry is, therefore, in part an 'investment' made by parents to secure a share for their daughter in her husband's family property.

When women go as new brides, their in-laws are also expected to provide them with expensive new clothes and jewellery. How can gift-giving be one-way? Why should women's parents not give gifts to their husband's relatives as a goodwill gesture when the bride is expected to become a claimant in the husband's income and property?

When one raises the issue of marital violence and abuse due to dowry demands many have responded with the counter question: 'Are you suggesting that women get beaten, abused and murdered only in India, and that too only among communities that give dowry? Don't women in America, Europe,

Australia, the Philippines and Africa also get beaten and killed, even though in these countries dowry giving is not an issue?' Most women are in favour of a reasonable amount of dowry being given, provided the groom's family does not put undue pressure on her natal family with additional extortionate demands.

Reasons for Dowry Increase

Those who make a case for a stringent anti-dowry law on the ground that dowry amounts are rising exponentially, forget that among many families in the dowry practising groups, standards of living have also risen dramatically. Up to my grandmother's time, dowry consisted of clothes for the bride, gold or silver jewellery, several sets of bedding, cows, buffaloes and bedsteads, cots or *peedhas* and perhaps a wooden closet. Some communities also gifted a portion of land—a tradition still common in regions like Andhra. By the time of my mother's wedding, sofa sets and dressing tables had become mandatory and dinner sets and tea sets were included along with kitchen utensils. Watches, wall clocks and radio sets also became common because by then all these items had become customary parts of middle class life. Today, refrigerators, air-conditioners, automobiles and a whole range of gadgetry are an integral part of upper class and upper middle class dowries because these families use many of these conveniences in their daily lives.

However, there is no escaping the fact that ugly tussles are becoming commonplace over dowry payments. An important reason for growing cash demands and expensive gifts for the groom's family is that parents see this as their main, if not only, chance to be compensated for the big bonanza they are offering the bride in the form of an earning son. They feel they should be recompensed for their investment in his education and upbringing since after marriage his wife may influence him not to support his own parents. As long as joint families were the norm and most parents could count on their sons to support them in old age and treat their income as belonging to a common pool, dowry demands were not as much of an issue. However, with increasing breakdown of joint families and reluctance of many women to stay with in-laws, the insecurity of parents in many families takes the form of trying to extract what they can from the bride's family at the time of their son's marriage.

The rapid upward mobility made possible due to opening of new opportunities for urban educated middle and upper class men, whose earning potential has increased exponentially, has meant that such grooms are avidly sought after. For most women, upward mobility comes through the man they marry rather than their own employment. Most families try getting higher status grooms in the belief that their daughters will find it easier to adjust in such families than if they were to marry below their status, apart from the benefits accruing in the long run to the girl's family by forging an alliance with a well-connected kinship network; the demand for such upwardly mobile men is far in excess of supply.

An important reason for the increase in domestic conflicts, rising dowry demands and the transformation of dowry from *stridhan* to groom price is that our legal enactments, administrative interventions and state policies are forcing the nuclearization of families without due attention to the fact that the only or main old age security for the vast majority of people in India are their children, especially their sons. Parents invest all they can in their son's education and career-building in the hope and expectation that sons will get jobs or other forms of earning opportunities, bringing about upward mobility for the whole family. Sons are expected to contribute to the education and marriage costs of younger siblings as well as take care of parents in their old age. In societies where there is near total absence of any other form of social or old age security, this is an understandable expectation.

However, too many parents find this expectation belied after their sons get married, especially if their sons take up well paying jobs or succeed in an independent enterprise separate from the joint family economy. Not just in metropolitan cities, but even in small towns and villages of India, young wives are increasingly prone to insist on moving away from the joint family to set up their own independent establishment, even when the in-laws are not abusive.

A man continuing to financially support his parents or younger siblings even after nuclearization of the family often finds stiff resistance from his wife. Many even stop doing so. Sometimes parents themselves withdraw from receiving such support in order to avoid friction in the marital life of their sons.

Without doubt, in some cases daughters-in-law willingly endorse their husbands' efforts to support their natal families. But the overall trend is more in the direction of moving away from taking responsibility for the in-laws.

Insecurity of Groom's Family

In recent years I have heard any number of parents tell me that marriage no more means '*kanya daan*' (gift of a daughter) but '*putra samarpan*' (handing over of son). They say that they have to be prepared for the eventuality that even occasional visits to the son's house may be resented and blocked by his wife, if she succeeds in winning him over to her side. That is why one finds many parents try to marry off their daughters before they arrange their sons' marriages because of the fear that they may not be allowed to contribute to the expenses after their sons get married. This is also the reason why dowry is increasingly taking the form of 'groom price', with parents expecting that a certain sum of money will be given to them almost as 'recompense' for their handing over the income and assets of their son to the woman who becomes his wife.

This increasing insecurity and uncertainty is at the heart of family tussles between the bride, her natal family and her in-laws. While some gracefully resign themselves to this fate and even encourage sons to set up a separate house after marriage, many fight a grim battle to keep their sons under their influence, which often means using even vicious methods to prevent the couple from enjoying a close conjugal relationship. The young bride has a formidable weapon in her armoury—her youth and sex. The old parents exploit the emotional appeal of blood bonds. This bond is easier to sever where the parents are dependent on the sons for old age support. The few families who are very wealthy may succeed in using their property as a glue to keep their married sons close to them. This anxiety and uncertainty about their fate with regard to their sons is in large part responsible for strengthening the culture of 'dowry demands'.

The fierce battles between daughters-in-law and parents-in-law are also largely due to the fact that women in most communities are conditioned to believe that their rights lie in their husband's families. Therefore, they feel extremely insecure and resentful about the claims of other members of their husband's families. Part of the solution to this dilemma, therefore, lies in giving women inalienable rights in their parental property so that they enter their marital homes with a sense of self-confidence in the knowledge that they do not have to keep the marriage going 'at all costs' and do not have to carve out a niche for themselves by curbing the rights of their in-laws.

Draconian Yet Ineffective

The anti-dowry agitationists do not take these new dynamics into account. They have relied mainly on pious outrage combined with emotive outbursts demanding that the law be made more and more stringent in their attempt to abolish this 'social evil'. However, such laws work only if people perceive their own interest in the proposed measure of reform. If a woman believes in taking a portion of her parental wealth at the time of her marriage and if her parents believe this is a necessary investment for her future happiness, how can any law stop such giving and taking? The only effect of the anti-dowry law and campaign has been that the giving and taking has become more surreptitious. Earlier, families ensured that proper lists and accounts were prepared and the groom's family was made to sign the list of things they received while the dowry itself was put on display for all the relatives to take note of, so there were numerous witnesses to the transaction. Today, no lists are signed and most of the giving and receiving is shrouded in secrecy and made known only through whisper networks within the kinship social circle. Though there is a helpful provision in the anti-dowry law making it a criminal offence if the girl's dowry is not returned to her on demand, in case of breakdown of marriage, the battles over return of dowry have become more difficult and complicated because in order to secure the return of her dowry, a woman has to first establish what was given. If there is no clear proof of what the transactions were at the time of marriage, there is ample scope for false claims and fraudulent denials.

In the first decade of *Manushi*'s existence, most of those who came to us for legal aid were women who alleged abuse in their marital home. In the last few years, a good proportion of the cases coming to us involve complaints by mothers-in-law and husbands about the misuse and abuse of laws, especially section 498A. Such cases are brought to my notice not only by aggrieved families and their friends but more often by members of women's organizations themselves (see Chapter 10).

Even the most active proponents and defenders of the anti-dowry law cannot claim that the law has been a success. Instead of fine-tuning their campaign to the realities on the ground, the anti-dowry agitators have continued to demand that the law be made still more stringent.

Even though in recent years a good number of Indian feminists have evolved far more nuanced positions on this subject, in recent years, the Dowry Prohibitionists continue to get a lot of support from some international networks that help them remain politically fashionable. Since the wide gap between precept and practice, between what they say and what they do, has never bothered these rhetorically militant feminists, not surprisingly, the heroines produced by such a 'high-on-emotion, low-on-common-sense' anti-dowry campaign have been as phony as the Dowry Prohibition Act.

Phony Laws, Phony Heroines

On 12 May 2004, most national papers and TV channels splashed the story of the 'heroism and courage' of 21-year-old Nisha Sharma for having called the police to arrest her groom and his parents on her wedding day, alleging that they had suddenly demanded an additional Rs 12 lakh as dowry from her father. Several women's organizations, including the National Commission for Women, vied with each other to give trophies and awards to Nisha Sharma, who overnight became a national icon held up as a role model for young women. Every newspaper and TV channel carried long reports of the glorious saga of Nisha Sharma. She became an instant heroine of the international media. A *New York Times* correspondent specially flew down to India to interview Nisha Sharma. However, to the allegations by the groom's family that the fracas on the wedding day was not created by them over dowry but instead was created by a former boyfriend of Nisha who came with his friends to stop the marriage by creating a scene, were given short shrift without proper investigation. Nisha's family did not deny that her boyfriend Navneet had threatened to obstruct the marriage but insisted that the fight with the groom's family was over additional dowry demands.

An unusual aspect of this conflict over dowry was that certain items like a home theatre system, refrigerator, air-conditioner and washing machine had been purchased in duplicate—one set for Nisha and her husband and a second set for the groom's elder brother and wife. The justification given for this second dowry was that the groom's mother had demanded these additional items so that the standard of living of the two brothers would not vary too much. Apparently the first brother's wife comes from a family of modest means. Therefore, Nisha's father was expected to bridge the gap in the standard of living of the two brothers. Whatever the truth of the matter on that front, neither Nisha nor her father hid the fact that the family had already spent Rs 18 lakh on buying all these goods. Thus, even as per Nisha's version, the fight was over the alleged additional demand of Rs 12 lakh, not over the giving of dowry per se. Nisha's father is reported to have told the press that they had even tape-recorded earlier phone conversations with the groom's family after they had begun making more and more demands for dowry.

Both Nisha and her father repeatedly justified the Rs 18 lakh expenditure on dowry by saying they were not against 'voluntary giving' but were opposed to 'dowry demands'. Nobody bothered to ask them by what stretch of imagination they could describe a whole range of expensive gadgets for the elder brother's family as 'voluntary gifts' for Nisha?

So elated were the anti-dowry campaigners within the media as well as among non-governmental organizations (NGOs) that even before the start of court proceedings to prove the allegations levelled by Nisha against Munish Dalal and his mother, even before anyone bothered to investigate the authenticity or otherwise of Munish Dalal's counter-allegations against Nisha regarding her boyfriend's role in disrupting the marriage, a chapter on her as an emulation-worthy role model for young women was included in the school textbooks of the Delhi secondary education curriculum.

Thus, for the public at large, Munish Dalal's family had been permanently condemned as guilty and their alleged crime turned into a moral lesson for generations to come on the basis of half-baked media reports even before the lowest court in the land pronounced its verdict. The Sharma family, by contrast, has been lionized as though they performed a great heroic deed despite the provision of the anti-dowry law that clearly states that both the giver and taker of dowry are liable for prosecution. No one wondered why they were not arrested for having offered Rs 18 lakh dowry as inducement to Munish Dalal's family. A few months later, media persons lost interest in her story as they allegedly discovered more and more holes in the version of the dispute Nisha and her family offered.

Consensus Against Extortion

The bottomline is that Nisha, like millions of other people, believes that the voluntary giving of gifts and wealth—whatever be the amount—is perfectly legitimate, while anything demanded by the groom's family ought to be treated as an offence against the law if it exceeds the paying capacity of the bride's family or goes beyond their willingness to comply. If that is the social and legal consensus, if that is how law is actually enforced, if the dowry prohibition law comes into play not when dowry is being given or taken but only when the bride's family levels charges of coercion and blackmail, then logic demands that we scrap the anti-dowry law since extortion is in anyway a criminal offence under the Indian Penal Code (IPC).

All cases of dowry-related harassment can easily then be tried under relevant provisions of the IPC as cases of extortion. Since there is a broad-based consensus that extortionist demands are both wrong and illegal, enforcing such a law will result in greater clarity and better implementation of its scope and ambit.

Today, most women end up using the anti-dowry law to book husbands for maltreatment even if dowry is not the cause of marital breakdown. Thus the anti-dowry law has not curbed the giving and taking of dowry. It has only provided a strong weapon for revenge in the hands of wives against their husbands and in-laws, whether or not their conflict is over dowry.

Lawyers and even police routinely advise families to list 'dowry demands' as the primary cause of marital violence, even if in actual fact this is not at all the case, or is only a relatively minor factor in marital conflict. We have found that when we probed deeper, women narrate far more complex stories of conflict than come out in their simplistic statements to the police and law courts about dowry being the cause of all their woes.

Harmful Emphasis

It has become politically fashionable to attribute all forms of violence and discrimination against women, including female infanticide and female foeticide, to the economic burden of dowry that a daughter is said to represent.

Dowry requirements are used as another excuse for considering daughters a burden. The anti-dowry movement, by limiting itself to the constant repetition of 'dowry abolition' as a panacea for women's empowerment and as the primary strategy for ending their oppression, has only helped give further legitimacy to the conventional belief that daughters are an economic liability.

There is little mention of exorbitant dowries causing the ruin of families in the literature of pre-British India. Ruin due to exorbitant dowry payments became a major theme in nineteenth century literature because this period witnessed an unprecedented erosion of women's economic importance and inheritance rights due to the manner in which the colonial rulers carried out land settlement operations in India.

In conformity with Victorian norms that they were familiar with in their home country, land entitlements were given to 'male heads of the family', bypassing our customary laws that allowed various categories of entitlements to women. This concentrated property in the hands of men in an unprecedented way and paved the way for the disinheritance of women. In addition, the rapacious land revenue demands drained large amounts of the economic surplus from the rural economy. It made the peasants extremely cash poor. The destruction of traditional crafts pushed large sections of impoverished artisan groups to fall back on their small landholdings and the consequent increasing pressure on land made land ownership bestow special power and status.

However, with rural society and artisan groups becoming extremely cash poor, the tradition of *stridhan* seems to have become burdensome. The traditional view of daughters as *paraya dhan* got a new and deadlier meaning. The term *paraya dhan* had the connotation of viewing women as wealth. This is an apt description in a society in which women carried their *stridhan* with them, that is, property that is theirs by right. Traditionally, the entry of a bride into her new family would be referred to as the coming of Lakshmi (*Lakshmi aayi hai*). Even today vestiges of that tradition remain in most communities. A young bride enters her marital home with *haldi* (turmeric) soaked feet, leaving auspicious marks on the floor, marks associated with Lakshmi, goddess of wealth.

As women were increasingly disinherited, daughters began to appear as liabilities. *Kanyadan*, the gift of a daughter, became not so much a matter of earning *dharmic* merit (the merit of doing one's religious duty) so much as getting rid of an unwanted burden. It is in this context of devaluation of women's lives and marginalization of their economic rights that dowry payments began to assume the form of offerings to a groom's family so that they would take a burden from the bride's family.

Thus, our modern inheritance laws have increasingly moved in favour of men and against the interests of women. All those communities that practised matrilineal inheritance, such as the Nairs in Kerala, have also been forced through legislation to move towards patrilineal inheritance. Systems that provided reasonable or adequate protection of women's economic rights have been steamrollered out of existence.

The Way Forward

The present-day dowry system in India symbolizes the disinheritance of women and the desperation of parents to push their daughters out of their homes after marrying them off, no matter how this affects their well-being. Failure to do so is considered a severe stigma on the family's *izzat* (reputation). Since the woman is being sent as a disinherited dependent, the receiving family has to be compensated.

Once women become equal inheritors, parents will not have to depend only on sons and daughters-in-law for old age security because daughters too will be empowered to take care of their parents. This will make families less male-centric and, therefore, less prone to violent tussles. We need to combat the culture of disinheritance if we wish to effectively combat the growing hold of dowry culture. For this the following steps are likely to work better than anti-dowry laws:

- Encourage parents through widespread, high profile campaigns, to gift mainly income-generating forms of property to their daughters (land, house or business shares) depending on the economic status of the family.

- Encourage those parents who can afford it to ensure that their daughter has a house, room or even a *jhuggi* in her own name so that she is never rendered homeless, can never be 'thrown out of the house'.
- Amend the Hindu Succession Act and the Indian Succession Act to make it illegal for fathers to routinely disinherit daughters through their wills unless they can provide strong extenuating circumstances for doing so.

Part III
Inheritance Rights

13

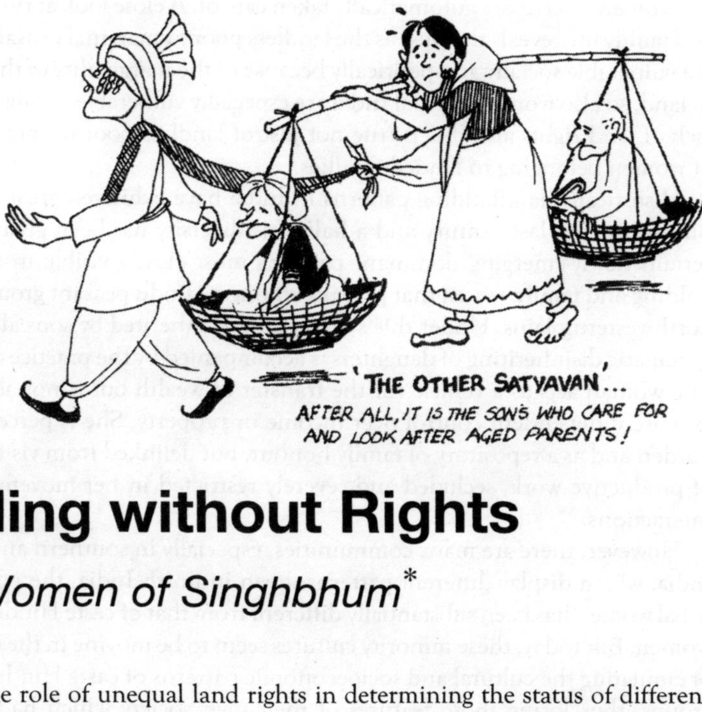

Toiling without Rights

*Ho Women of Singhbhum**

While the role of unequal land rights in determining the status of different caste and class groups in India has been the subject of much debate, their impact on women's status has generally escaped attention. This study attempts to place the issue of the denial of land rights to Ho tribal women in the context of women's daily lives, work, struggle for survival and status in the family and community.

Although the situation of Ho women has certain important exceptional characteristics, it is, by and large, typical of the situation of tribal women. The role of unequal land rights in determining the status of different caste and class groups in India is the subject of continuing debate. However, the impact on women's status of their land rights is seldom fully comprehended. That is why, on the few occasions when land redistribution programmes have been undertaken in different parts of the country, land has been given in the

* This article appeared in *Economic and Political Weekly*, Vol. XXII, No. 3, 17 January 1987.

I am grateful to my friends Ruth and Berny for their invaluable help at various stages of this study. I would also like to thank Pilar for helping me collect village data.

name of the male 'head of the household' while women have almost never received land in their own names. The patriarchal bias of the social and legal system gives rise to the assumption that once the men of a family have land, the women's needs are automatically taken care of. A close look at rural society and family life reveals that just as the landless poor or marginal peasant groups are vulnerable socially and politically because of the marginality of their rights in land, so also women in rural India are especially vulnerable because of their lack of land rights and this is true not just of landless poor women but also of women belonging to landed families.

Historically, landholding patterns in India have exhibited great diversity. But during the last century and a half, this diversity has been giving way to certain newly-emerging dominant patterns most clearly visible in the landholding and family system that prevails amongst Hindu peasant groups in the northwestern plains. Under this system, land is inherited by sons alone. The systematic disinheriting of daughters is accompanied by the practice of dowry. The woman acts as a vehicle for the transfer of wealth but is not allowed to exercise independent control over income or property. She is perceived as a burden and as a repository of family honour, but delinked from visible forms of productive work, secluded and severely restricted in her movements and interactions.

However, there are many communities, especially in southern and eastern India, which display different patterns. Even in north India, the position of tribal women has been substantially different from that of caste Hindu peasant women. But today, these minority cultures seem to be moving in the direction of emulating the cultural and socioeconomic patterns of caste Hindu peasant groups, thus losing those features of their own society which had positive consequences for women.

An indepth study of these minority cultures is very important in order to understand (*i*) the points of strength for women in different cultural traditions; (*ii*) how and why these points of strength are being eroded; (*iii*) features that make for a situation of relatively greater or lesser vulnerability for women; (*iv*) the kind of changes that have the potential to help women acquire economic and social strength; and (*v*) the special implications for women of the spread of the dominant Hindu peasant culture among minority groups.

This study of Ho tribal women will dwell on these issues and attempt to link them to the question of the denial of land rights to women.

Karonja[1] is situated in Singhbhum district, Bihar. This is one of the most richly endowed parts of India. Earlier, most land in Singhbhum was forested but today most land has been brought under cultivation or reduced to a

[1] The name of the village has been changed to protect the identity of the respondents.

rocky waste. Some forests still remain. But the area has witnessed increasing deforestation in the last century. Singhbhum is the site of very large deposits of iron, bauxite, lead, manganese, copper, limestone, sandstone, slate and other minerals. More than a quarter of the total mining activity in India is carried on in this area. A number of heavy industries are located here and major industrial townships have grown up around them.

According to the 1971 Census, Scheduled Tribes constituted 10 per cent of the population of Bihar and 7 per cent of the population of India. Yet tribals have not greatly benefited from the industrial development of the area. Many have been displaced from their ancestral lands and not given adequate compensation. Most lucrative jobs in industries have gone to non-tribals. The few tribals employed in industries work as unskilled labourers, doing the heaviest and lowest paid jobs.

Karonja is, in most ways, a typical Ho village. It has, in many ways, remained untouched by the economic expansion and upheavals caused by the industrialization of the district. It is situated in an interior area. Yet, despite its apparent remoteness, the village Karonja has been deeply affected by the happenings in the outside world. The village is inhabited almost totally by Hos who are concentrated in the Kolhan area of Singhbhum, constituting 10 per cent of the tribal population of Bihar. Hos share many common features with other tribes of the area, such as Mundas, Oraons, Santhals, Kharias and others, yet they retain a distinct identity. In the course of the last century, the process of peasantization of different tribes has been so thorough that the socioeconomic life of tribals today is in many ways similar to that of neighbouring non-tribal peasant groups. Today, the Hos are settled agriculturists. The practice of shifting cultivation, which was characteristic of tribals, has almost totally died out. They are no longer able to depend on hunting and gathering for a major part of their subsistence. The forests are fast disappearing and those that remain are out of bounds for most purposes because of increasing restrictions placed by government. Yet they continue to engage in regular gathering activities and occasional hunting to supplement their subsistence.

Karonja is divided into upper and lower regions. I conducted interviews in the lower *tola* which has about 100 families living in it. About 30 of these have converted to Christianity but most have not given up their traditional forms of worship. The only non-tribal families are a *lohar* and a *gop* family. Both are among the poorer families in the village. Most Ho villages contain a few families from artisan groups who are non-tribals.

Almost all the land in the village is still owned by Hos. An important reason for this is the lack of irrigation facilities and electricity and the consequent low productivity of agriculture. All the families grow one major rice crop a year, which they sow during the monsoon. Some families grow a second, subsidiary crop of wheat and lentils. However, when rains fail or are delayed, there is not even one crop a year. Even one year's monsoon failure causes scarcity. Often, the crops fail for several years in succession. As a result, food scarcity is a chronic problem for most families.

Land size is usually measured in terms of the amount of rice produced. The local measure is a *bandi*, roughly equivalent to 400 kg of paddy or 200 kg of rice. Most families have to supplement the income from land with other sources of income such as working on other people's land, collection and selling of forest produce and seasonal migration as casual labour in mines, construction industry, brick kilns and other worksites. The nearest train station is two hours walk away. Until recently, only two local trains stopped each day at this station. Now, one more fast train has started halting here. The village has no tarred road so there is no bus service. The nearest city is Chakradharpur, about 25 km away. There is no industry or mine within walking distance. Therefore, those who seek employment outside cannot commute daily but must migrate for employment. The nearest forest where residents go for gathering—and on rare occasions for hunting—is about a two hours' walk away. There is a primary school in the village run by one teacher. About 60 pupils are currently enrolled of whom about 25 attend school regularly. The nearest secondary school is situated at about a two hours' walk from the village.

The total number of women interviewed in Karonja was 37. However, of these, only 30 interviews were used in the analysis. Three interviews remained incomplete. Two of the three had to return to their homes to continue their work, halfway through the interview. The third refused to continue because she suspected that I might be from the family planning department, and would lure her into getting sterilized. Two other interviewees were girls aged about 12, and although they do as much work as an adult woman, I finally decided to restrict the study to adult women aged 18 and above.[2]

[2] A somewhat larger proportion of Christian women came to be included in the sample—17 out of 30. In the village, about 30 per cent of the families are Christians. But this does not seriously affect the conclusions since, from my investigations in other villages of Singhbhum, I found that the everyday life, work, marriage and inheritance patterns, even the customs and rituals of the Christian and non-Christian Hos, are very similar. Apart from interviewing the women, I also accompanied them to the market and to the forest, when they went gathering fuel and fodder, and closely observed their lives, work and interactions. Thus, I have good reason to believe that the lives of these women are fairly representative of the lives of Ho women in Singhbhum. Although the information was usually cross-checked by the observations of my interpreter who knows all the respondents and their families intimately, an important dimension is missing since I did not interview the men of these 30 families. The problems these women face are problems that lie at the heart of contemporary Ho culture.

The problems these women face are problems that lie at the heart of contemporary Ho culture. The account which follows is based mainly on women's perception of the situation.

Women and the Economy

It is no exaggeration to say that in tribal villages, the economy functions primarily on the basis of women's labour. The magnitude of the work burden may not be visible to an inexperienced outsider because the pace of work looks very unhurried, except when women are seen returning, half running, from the forest, carrying enormous loads of wood on their heads. If one made a comprehensive list of tasks performed by women and children and another of those performed by men, one would conclude that women and children perform about 90 per cent of the total labour in villages.

Among the few tasks that women do not perform is ploughing. They are ritually prohibited from touching the plough. So strict is the taboo that men do not bring the plough inside the house lest women touch it by mistake. Women are made to believe that their touching the plough will bring ill luck to the whole village, such as a drought. Women who dare break the law are fined heavily by the panchayat. In rare cases, they could even be stoned to death. Needless to say, the panchayats are composed only of men.

It is often argued that the ban on ploughing exists because ploughing is a very strenuous activity which women are constitutionally incapable of performing. However, this theory appears unsound because even 12-year-old boys manage to use the plough with perfect ease, whereas adult, able-bodied women, who are clearly much stronger, are not allowed to do so. The plough used in this area is of a very light variety, which makes no more than a two- to three-inch deep furrow. Thus, ploughing would not be a heavier task than many others that women routinely perform, such as cutting firewood and carrying huge headloads from distant forests.

Even if a woman feels capable of ploughing, she is not permitted to do so. If there is no male in the family, she has to hire a man from the village to do the job. The real purpose behind the taboo seems to be to strengthen male control over the land, even while women perform the bulk of labour on the land. The taboo ensures that women can never conduct agricultural operations on their own without male cooperation. It is very common that a woman who has no male member in her family finds it difficult to hire male help for ploughing, especially if she is in conflict with powerful men in the village. Even at ploughing time, women are busy. Not only do they carry food for the men to the field, but also walk bent double behind the plough, breaking lumps of earth with a hoe or with their bare hands. They also do weeding at this time. Men hardly ever perform these tasks, which are, in many ways, far more strenuous than ploughing. Before sowing begins, women, without any help from men, prepare manure from the cowdung that is collected throughout the year in a big pit near each house. Women make dozens of trips between house and fields carrying the cowdung compost in baskets on their heads and sprinkle it with their hands in the fields. Transplanting of rice is done exclusively by women. Threshing by hand is considered a women's job. If threshing is to be done with animal power, it is done by men. But hand threshing by women is the preferred method, because the straw can then be used to thatch roofs, while after animal threshing, the straw cannot be used for anything except fodder.

Harvesting of grain is done by women with help from men. Carrying the grain from the fields to the house is done by women, especially if it is to be carried on the head. In case a bullock cart is available, a man may help with the carrying. However, making big bundles of the harvested rice is primarily a man's job, although women help. This ensures that the man knows exactly how much grain is harvested, even though he may not have helped in the harvesting. This gives men greater control over production than they would otherwise have, considering the marginality of their labour contribution.

Men are supposed to help build embankments and take care of irrigation and water drainage in the fields. But, often, when a man is not available, women do these jobs.

In addition to fieldwork, women gather forest produce such as *sal* leaves, *datuns*, medicinal herbs, wild fruits, berries and nuts. Almost every woman has to routinely go to the forest to gather firewood and *sal* leaves (which are used as plates) for her family's use. Firewood is the only form of fuel available. Men do not help to gather fuel for the family. They help occasionally when big logs of wood are needed to build or repair a house. Men usually carry wood in a bullock cart. Men never carry firewood on their heads although they may carry it on their shoulders. Women are not supposed to drive a bullock cart.

Due to continuous deforestation, very few villages are close to forests, so forest gathering has become increasingly strenuous. A number of women also have to gather firewood for sale, especially in the lean season when less well-off families exhaust their stock of rice and depend on firewood sales for subsistence. In times of acute scarcity, women's gathering activities assume great importance for family survival.

Sometimes, the women travel ticketless by train but pay a small bribe. They also have to spend money buying food and rice beer in town. On these journeys, the women often carry with them their little babies, especially those who are being breastfed. They also usually carry some rice and a cooking pot so that they can cook a meal at the railway station on an improvised *chulha.* Women of a village usually travel in a group to the town market.

In the market, women also undertake bartering activity, exchanging grain, poultry, lentils, *mahua* fruit and oilseeds for soap, salt and oil. Since most families do not have a grain surplus, the women have to gather forest produce such as *karonji* seeds used by sweetmeat sellers in cities. One measure of *karonji* seeds is bartered for 30 measures of salt, equivalent to a couple of kilograms at most. *Karonji* sells at about Rs 60 a kg and salt for about Rs 2 a kg. Not only is the exchange unequal in value but the amount of labour that goes into gathering *karonji* is mindboggling. It takes a woman several weeks to gather about half a kilo of *karonji* while she is collecting firewood and leaves.

Women from Karonja usually do not go to the nearest weekly market because women from farther off villages go there. Karonja women go to Chakradharpur or Rourkela market. If a woman is carrying firewood for sale, it is difficult for her to travel in a train or bus because these are usually overcrowded. So they walk long distances to the market.

A noteworthy feature of marketing activity in this area is that while women conduct most of the petty trade, the more substantial trade is in the hands of non-tribal men. In the weekly markets, women sell field or forest produce or handmade goods. The non-tribal men either bring manufactured goods from outside and sell them at a profit or buy the women's produce and take them to city markets to be resold at a higher profit. Women are never involved in this level of trade, because very few women would have the capital required. Such trade also requires extensive dealings with a market economy dominated by non-tribal men who tend to be craftier in their transactions. Illiterate tribal women who have developed skills mainly for the barter form of trade would be likely to be cheated and to lose their business.

Even though Ho women are more active than men in agricultural and marketing activities, they have to do all the household work without much help from men. Although the Hos do not consider it degrading for a man to help with housework, as do upper caste Hindu peasant groups, yet such help is extended only in times of crisis, as when a woman is seriously ill. Because of the primitive nature of the economy, simple chores such as preparing paddy for consumption involve an enormous amount of work. The one job men do is thatching the roof. Like ploughing, this is taboo for women. If a woman defies the taboo, she is liable to punishment by the community. The taboo seems to be another way of ensuring that a woman cannot take care of her survival needs if she goes beyond a point in defying male opinion in the village. A house is thatched once in several years and the roof needs repair not more than once a year. In comparison, the tasks connected with the everyday maintenance of the house are left to women. Men also help in the occasional tasks of building a fence, putting in wooden doors, and so on.

Child care is mainly a woman's responsibility. She is helped by her older children to take care of the younger ones. But when infants are being breastfed, women often carry them on their backs when they go to work in the fields or go gathering in the forest. The nature of women's work does not allow for any break whatsoever. The household would starve and the village economy come to a halt, if women ceased working even for a few days. Since most families do not grow enough food for year-round consumption, women must work every day to make both ends meet, especially if the man does not have a cash income. Most Ho families are nuclear, so there may not be another adult woman to take over when the wife falls ill. Few women can afford the time to get themselves treated when ill.

Kairi Digi of Karonja has a very serious skin disease which is due to an allergy to the sun. She is unmarried, aged about 30, and lives with her old mother and a young unmarried brother in his twenties, who does nothing to earn a living. She is the main worker in the family. On her own, Kairi would never have been able to make time to go to a doctor. The woman social worker managed to persuade her to go see a skin specialist in a nearby town. But she could not continue the treatment, first, because she could not afford the Rs 50 a month it would cost and, more important, because the doctor told her to stop working in the sun for a few months.

Children's illnesses have to be similarly neglected, even when the mother is aware that such neglect will, in all probability, result in the child's death. A 13-year-old boy was seriously ill. When I asked his mother why she did not take him to the doctor, she reasoned thus: 'Children I can get any time but where am I supposed to get the time and money for his treatment? If I leave the work and go to get him treated, all the other children in the house will starve and die. It is better to let one die.' And indeed, he died in a few days.

In comparison, the few tasks that men perform, such as ploughing, building roofs or hunting game, require a one-time exertion spread over a few days, between long intervals of inaction. These jobs can easily be taken care of by hiring someone for those few days in case a son, brother or husband is not available. However, it would be impossible to substitute a woman's labour with hired help.

Even festivals do not bring much relief to most Ho women. Most writings on the Hos draw a picture of the gay abandon at festivals like Maghe Parab, as if all participate uniformly. In fact, festivals add to the workload of married women, who have to entertain guests from neighbouring villages, clean and decorate the house, and prepare extra rice beer. They may join in the dancing and singing for an hour or so in the daytime but the festival does not really mean a break from the work routine. Only unmarried women take a full part in the dancing, which goes on for hours on end throughout the day and the night. This is because festivals are the occasion for courtship and selection of marriage partners. Men, whether married or unmarried, spend all their time at the festivities.

Why Men's Labour is Peripheral

There are several reasons for men's labour contribution being so low amongst the Hos and most other tribal groups. Before the tribals took to sedentary agriculture, the major division of labour between the sexes involved hunting, warfare and clearing of forests being done mainly by men. This gave men a sort of monopoly over the means of violence. Ho women are traditionally not allowed to use bows and arrows and other weapons. This monopoly strengthened men's power over women. The Ho tribe was patrilineal and patrilocal even before the Hos became settled agriculturists, although the absence of developed forms of private property helped prevent it from being as heavily patriarchal.

However, with British conquest, inter-tribal warfare ended. The superior military might of the British and the administrative methods they developed of keeping the Hos under control resulted in men slowly losing what used to be important functions. Over the decades, new forest policies and progressive deforestation of the area entailed the imposition of restrictions on hunting. But, at the same time, men were given exclusive individual rights over the cultivable land and this gave them a new power base.

Women had traditionally taken care of agriculture, gathering minor forest produce, marketing and household work. In settled agriculture, they continued the same jobs, with one difference–their position became that of drudges on the land while men were left with little to do. In a Ho village, it is common to see men loafing around, cockfighting, drinking, smoking *bidis* and chatting, while women do all the work.

D.N. Majumdar, writing in the 1940s, had observed:

> the Ho men enjoy more leisure than women... the women toil hard from morning to night...the men have certain busy seasons in the year.... There is no continuous programme of work for men, though there are plenty of diversions. Music, dancing, visiting friends in other villages, attending Hats and fairs, and lounging in the village headman's house form the main routine of Ho men (1950, pp. 65–66).

While men's labour in today's tribal economy is truly peripheral, one must emphasise that the role of men's labour even in non-tribal societies is usually exaggerated and overvalued. In most micro-studies of non-tribal peasant societies, it has been found that women's total labour contribution exceeds that of men. The bias that makes women's labour invisible and exaggerates the importance of men's labour is in part a result of treating the nineteenth century British Victorian family norm as a ubiquitous norm. Early ethnographic writings by nineteenth century British men reflected the bias of the culture they came from, and imposed these as the norm in descriptions of societies very different from their own. These biases have been slavishly picked up by many of the Indian anthropologists and sociologists writing about tribal society.

Ho Women's Rights in Land Today

Whether they are animists, Christians or Hindu converts, Hos continue to be governed by customary law in inheritance. In many ways, this so-called tribal law, in regard to women's property rights, is very similar to unreformed Hindu law of the Mitakshara school. Under this law, women are not allowed to inherit property but, as widows and unmarried daughters, they have a right to be maintained from it.

Unlike in Hindu upper castes, where the right to be maintained means that the woman is economically dependent on males, tribal women such as the Hos, because they play the key role in production, are not maintained by the men's labour, but get the right to cultivate a portion of the land in their lifetime. After their death, it reverts to men of the family. This is called a usufructuary right.

The Hos and other tribals in the Kolhan are governed by the Chota Nagpur Tenancy Act which was passed in 1908. The purpose of this Act was to check the alienation of tribal lands by non-tribals. It prohibits tribals from alienating land by sale, gift, will or transfer except with the permission of the Deputy Commissioner. Rights in the land are 'hereditary and inalienable and must descend to his sons; and if a Ho has [no] direct male issues, the land goes to his brother or next of kin; and if no kith or kin, to the village community represented by the Munda.'[3] In practice, the last situation usually means that powerful families in the village grab the land.

[3] 'Final Report on the Kolhan Government Estate', District Singhbhum, 1898, Chapter 1, para 10, letter from R.W. Collins, officiating secretary, Board of Revenue, to the Secretary to the Government of Bengal, Revenue Department.

As soon as a daughter marries, she loses her limited usufructuary right over parental land even if the marriage turns out to be a nominal one. A married daughter thrown out by her husband cannot claim shelter in her parental home as a right, although some women are given temporary shelter by their brothers. An unmarried daughter has the right to work on and be maintained from her family's land. But she does not inherit as a son does. He has an inalienable right similar to the right of male coparceners in Hindu joint family property. A daughter is not given an equal portion of land with sons. She is usually given a piece of land, for her maintenance, which is much smaller than the ones sons get. She may live with her brothers or demand a partition of the land and live by herself. If an unmarried daughter is raped or has a sexual relationship with a non-tribal man, she loses her usufructuary right to the parental land. If she gets pregnant by a Ho man, she loses her right just as she would if she were to get married.

A widow's usufructuary right in her husband's land is similar to that of an unmarried daughter. She does not inherit the land but has a right to be maintained from it. She may live with one of her sons or she may demand a partition of the land in which case she would get a much smaller portion than a son gets. In practice, very few women's customary rights are honoured. D.N. Majumdar observes: 'The widow if she remains with a married son becomes a drudge in the latter's family! If she remarries, she loses her usufructuary right over her dead husband's land which goes to her sons, or if there are no sons, to the husband's male agnates.'

Ho women are also denied a right in other forms of family property. Daughters do not have a share in the family's cattle or house. A married woman does not even have a right to the cattle that may be given to her father or brothers as her bride price.

The Chota Nagpur Tenancy Act defines *khuntkhattidar* and *mundari* rights that create different categories of tenants, giving primacy to those who originally cleared the forests and established villages. Although it prohibits alienation of land by the tenants, it has several loopholes which have allowed land to slip away from the hands of tribals. First, land can be sold or transferred with the permission of the Deputy Commissioner. This means that significant amounts of land get illegally transferred with the connivance of the government machinery. Second, tribals are allowed to mortgage land. Two kinds of mortgage are prevalent. Under *bandhak* mortgage, a sum of money is paid and a piece of land taken in exchange. The land is returned only when the sum is repaid. Since poor tribals can rarely collect the cash to repay the debt, a *bandhak* transfer is sometimes a sale masquerading as a mortgage. Under *thika* mortgage, land is loaned for a fixed number of years in exchange for a sum of money. If the debt is not repaid, the land reverts to the original owner after the lapse of the time period agreed upon. If the debt is repaid any time before the fixed number of years has elapsed, he or she can take back the land. Tribals prefer to mortgage land on *thika* but, in times of distress, they are forced to give it on *bandhak*. Legally, tribals are allowed to give land on *bandhak* or *thika* only to other tribals, but in certain areas where there has been an influx of Hindu peasants from north Bihar, the latter draw the tribals into various fraudulent mortgage arrangements. This has led to large-scale alienation of tribal lands.

A male tribal can mortgage his family land whenever he wishes. He can do this without consulting his female relatives who have a usufructuary right in that land, because the land is registered in his name. But a woman, because she has only a usufructuary right, cannot mortgage her part of the land if her male agnates disapprove. Thus arises a paradoxical situation wherein a man may give away his family land on *bandhak* and use the money for his personal benefit, thereby depriving the women members of the family of their means of subsistence, without even consulting them. But an unmarried woman or widow will find it difficult even to give her land on *thika*, to tide over a crisis, unless her male agnates agree to her doing so—which they rarely do.

Status of a Wife

Ho women's land rights as wives are the most precarious of all. At no point of her life can a woman claim a share in her husband's land in her own right. She is only allowed to claim a right through her son, if she has one. The concept of joint property is totally unknown. The wife's status is in many ways similar to that of a landless labourer. If a man decides to be considerate, the wife may feel she is part of a joint enterprise. If not, she has no power, economic, social or political, to resist maltreatment. If he takes away all the earnings from the land, leaving wife and children without enough food, she cannot demand a portion of the land to feed herself and the children.

Of the 22 married women interviewed, the situation of 17 was, in some way or other, rendered more vulnerable because of their lack of rights over their husband's land. All 17 had problems trying to enforce their usufructuary right under customary law. Jasmani's story illustrates the dual insecurity of Ho women in relation to the land of their natal family and marital family, which makes their situation very precarious, despite their enormous labour contribution. Jasmani is about 25-year-old and very small built. She has four brothers. Her father died when she was a child. Her mother died a few years before Jasmani married. She says: 'We could not get much land from my father's family because my father's father died very young. Therefore, my grandfather's brothers took away most of the land and left a very small share for my widowed grandmother!' After her mother's death, Jasmani was compelled to leave her natal home because two of her brothers gave away the family land on *bandhak* and went away to the city. Jasmani was not consulted and her usufructuary right as an unmarried daughter was ignored. She did not get any of the money that her brothers raised through the mortgage. In anger and frustration, she left home and migrated to Rourkela. There, she was employed by a contractor working for the steel plant in the only occupation allowed to tribal women—that of a headloader. She used to earn about Rs 7 to 8 as a daily wage labourer. While in Rourkela, she met her husband, Saluka Sundi. This is how she describes their marriage:

> He used to work in the same place as a coolie. One day he came to my hut and said to me, 'I have a lot of inconvenience cooking my food. I don't even have proper utensils. Let me live in your hut. That way, I won't have to pay Rs 7 as rent for my hut.'

So they began to live together. After a year or two, he decided to come back to his village and Jasmani accompanied him. In all, she spent four years in Rourkela. When I first met her in 1981, she had already lived for about three years in her husband's village.

Jasmani and Saluka constitute a nuclear family. They have no children. Saluka has inherited three *bandi* land from his father. He has studied up to class six. Jasmani is illiterate but extremely intelligent and lively. Since she came to Saluka's village, their relationship has changed. Now she is living in *his* house, feeding off *his* land, and he spares no occasion to remind her of this. When they came from Rourkela, Jasmani brought with her Rs 400 that she had saved over the four years of working in Rourkela. All this money was spent by Saluka on repairing his house, getting a new thatched roof and buying seeds. So, Jasmani is now totally dependent on his land. He is neglectful and violent in his behaviour towards her. He beats her up often and on the slightest pretext. She dares not retaliate even in self-defence because she fears he may hack her to pieces in his anger. He actually takes out his *tangi* (sharp knife) every now and then and threatens to cut her in pieces. Once, she had a narrow escape when he came to attack her with a sharp weapon; she ran for her life and took shelter in his brother's house.

Saluka also threatens to bring another wife. She says once he brought a woman home from a fair. That morning, he had snatched all the money Jasmani had—about Rs 14 in all—to spend at the fair. Since she had at first refused him the money, he beat her severely. At night, he came with another woman and asked her to serve food to both of them. She refused, saying there was no food in the house. This was true, since she had, in protest, done no work all day.

Addressing the other woman, Jasmani said: 'You are welcome to live here as his wife. Look how he beats me. This morning, he snatched my money, beat me up and went away to a feast. Now, he comes with another woman. Do you think he will treat you any better?' The other woman got the message, quietly slipped out of the house and went back to her own home.

Jasmani does all the work on her husband's land. Often, he refuses even to do the ploughing. She had brought her brother's 12-year-old son to live with her so that he could plough the land. Her husband hates to work. Occasionally, he may thatch someone's roof and earn Rs 7 to 8 for that day. But, most of the time, he just loafs around the village and the weekly market. On the other hand, Jasmani does wage work in the village wherever she finds any. She does not want to go to the city for work as long as she can avoid it because she says they make the labourers work very hard, without holidays. Also, there is no prospect of future security there. Like most Ho women, Jasmani prefers to live in the village and work on the land. And, like most Ho women, she has no land that she can call her own. Her only chance is to try and secure some kind of foothold in her husband's land. Her problem is that he can throw her out of the house whenever he chooses. Also, he can do what he likes with the land without consulting her.

Let me illustrate by narrating an incident that occurred in June 1984. The day I reached the village, Jasmani came to see me. She was bruised and bandaged. Saluka had beaten her severely because she had opposed his plan to give a part of their land on *bandhak* to a person from a nearby village. He had given the field on *bandhak* to raise Rs 1,000 to pay a bribe to the police. The story of the bribe is as follows: Saluka's elder sister's daughter had been recruited by a local woman who acts as a *sardarni* (recruiting agent) for a brick kiln contractor in Kolkata. The young woman was molested by the manager of the kiln as a result of which she came back, pregnant, to the village. In all this, the *sardarni* had connived with the owners and had not come to the rescue of the young woman. She was also cheated out of her money both by the *sardarni* and the contractor. Saluka's family was very angry with the *sardarni* and decided to take revenge. As soon as the *sardarni* returned to the village, Saluka, his sister and a few others beat her up. She was badly injured and was taken by her family to get a criminal case registered.

When the villagers came to know that it had become a police case, they prevailed upon Saluka and his associates to go to the police station at Sonua and surrender. The reason was simple. The villagers knew from experience that if Saluka did not surrender, the police would come to search for him. Once the police entered the village, there was no knowing what they would do. They would have an excuse to indulge in indiscriminate intimidation and extortion. Therefore, the villagers thought it would be better for Saluka to go and strike a deal. When he reached the police station, he was arrested and handcuffed for about half an hour. After that, a deal was struck. Saluka would pay Rs 1,000 as bribe on behalf of himself and a relative who was also an accused party. The police would then close the case. Therefore, Saluka decided to mortgage a part of their land.

However, Jasmani felt that once the field was mortgaged for seven years, they might never get it back. Also, in the seven years, they would have much less food. As it was, they did not have enough for year-round consumption. So she told Saluka to accept the arrest and let the court case continue. Her reasoning was logical:

> At best, they will sentence you to a few months in prison. That will mean you will be fed free for several months. We will save some food in the house. So, when you come out of prison, we will have a little surplus, and, of course, the land will be intact. Better that you go to jail and come out in a few months than that we lose our land!

This logic, of course, did not appeal to Saluka. So he beat her up and went ahead with the mortgage.

Whenever I met Jasmani, she always talked about wanting to leave her husband. But she had nowhere to go. She said she was willing to leave if he returned her Rs 400. She did not want to leave without any money in hand because if she fell sick in the city and could not work for some days, she would starve. Her health has deteriorated considerably after marriage. She looks malnourished and has not enough stamina for the hard labour required at worksites. She tries to save some money for herself by hiding a part of the paddy produced in the fields and selling it behind her husband's back. But he invariably snatches away whatever money she has since he does not earn any cash himself. She says:

> He beats me up less during days of scarcity because if I were to go away, he would find it hard to fend for himself. However, when there is enough rice in the house to last a few months, as after the harvest, his beatings and threats increase and I am often asked to leave the house.

She does not want any children because, as she says: '*Apna to kuch thikana nahin hai, bacha lekar kya karega?*' (I have no security myself, what will I do with a child?). But she admits that her position might have been relatively stronger had she produced a son. 'Right now, he keeps saying, "The fields are mine, you leave my house". Then I could have replied, "The fields are mine too now." I would have acquired a right through my son!'

Son Preference and Land Rights

The fact that land can be inherited only by sons and that daughters have minimal usufructuary rights only as long as they stay unmarried creates conditions of domination by men and also gives rise to a culture of son preference, even when, in most other respects, it is far more advantageous for a woman to have daughters.

The nuclear family is the norm amongst Hos. When a man gets married, he usually separates from his parents and builds his own house on part of the family land. However, the agricultural land is often not divided among the sons until they themselves have sons. The youngest son usually remains in the parents' home and often gets a somewhat larger share of the land when partition takes place, since he has to support the parents. The assumption is that, if a man has no sons, the land he cultivates in his lifetime will revert to his brothers and their sons after his death, so land need not be partitioned. The man is assured of his right over the land in his lifetime, but his wife is in a much more insecure position. After his death, she is dependent on the goodwill of her husband's male agnates. If she has a son, she has a right over his portion of the land, which she can cultivate in his lifetime. Thus, women are forced into a situation of son preference.

It should be emphasized that a mother's right through her son is only a usufructuary right during his lifetime but is considered more secure because a son is expected to outlive his father. If, however, the son dies, the mother's right through him does not survive. Maki Bui's sons died in childhood so her husband's family did not allot the couple a portion of the land. As long as her husband was living outside the village because of his job, he did not feel the need to demand a share. After retirement, he settled in the village and was allowed the use of a small portion of land. After his death, Maki's usufructuary right has been denied to her by his male agnates.

A woman's staying power is also determined by the age of her sons at the time of her husband's death. Mukta's father died a couple of years ago of cancer. He was survived by his wife, four daughters and two sons, aged three and six. Mukta, aged about 20, is the eldest daughter. The family land has not been formally partitioned. Mukta's father's elder brother controls the land. He has allotted a very small portion of the land to Mukta's family to cultivate, instead of dividing the land into two equal portions. He has a 25-year-old son who has studied up to college level. He himself has lived and worked at Gua mines where he earned a regular salary of Rs 800 a month. The extra income enabled his family to buy farm animals and agricultural inputs. All this has made his family one of the most powerful in the village, whereas Mukta's family, with two infant sons, no regular source of income and not enough land, is among the most powerless. Whenever they ask for a formal division of the land, the uncle's family reply: 'Not yet, not yet', obviously hoping that the baby sons will die, thus rendering partition unnecessary.

Sona's case shows how having grown-up sons can help a woman keep a foothold on the family land even when her husband abandons her and remarries. Sona is about 50 years old. She was widowed about three years ago. She has two adult sons and two daughters. Her husband was in the police and lived in Tatanagar, where he took a second wife by whom he had a daughter, now aged about 20. After he retired, he returned to the village with the second wife and built a separate house for her. After his death, the second wife could not get a share in the land because she has no son. Even her usufructuary right as a widow was not honoured. Thus, it is not enough to have a legal right to land. The ability to enforce the right is even more important. Women who have only daughters or baby sons tend to be relatively powerless in the violence-charged atmosphere of the village. The land of such widows is often snatched away from them by male agnates through force or fraud.

But son preference amongst Hos does not have the kind of fatal consequences for female children that it has amongst some Hindu peasant castes. Daughters are more valued by mothers because of their work capacity. A Ho woman's work burden is killing if she has no daughters to help her. Grown-up sons rarely help their mother. Also, Ho girls fetch a bride price instead of taking a dowry so they are not perceived as a burden on the family. Therefore, the Ho type of son preference does not include a dread of having daughters. The sex ratio in the region gives an indication of the relatively more favourable position of females among the Hos. According to the 1971 Census, there were 1,041 women for every 1,000 men amongst the Hos in Bihar. In the northern plains, Punjab and Haryana (874), Uttar Pradesh (883), Bihar (956) and Rajasthan (919) have adverse sex ratios for women. Most Hindu peasant groups which manifest low sex ratios have a deep-rooted tradition of paying huge dowries to sons-in-law.

Most of the women interviewed categorically stated that they personally preferred daughters. Jasmati, when she became pregnant after several years of a fairly bad marriage, said that even though a son would improve her position vis-à-vis the land, she wanted a daughter. Her reasoning was:

> Even if I have a son, this man (her husband) may not keep me in his house. If he does allow me to stay, what do I need a son for? If our land goes to his uncles or cousins after he dies, what do I care? If I don't have a daughter, who is going to give us some affection and warmth when we are old? A son and daughter-in-law will never do that. When my mother was sick, I cared for her. None of my brothers cared for her!

Another reason for son preference is that the outside world of education and employment is extremely male-oriented and male-dominated. Therefore, if Hos have to seek a foothold in the mainstream economy, they can do so only through sons.

That the culture of son preference has largely been imposed on Ho culture by patriarchal land relations becomes evident when one considers the attitude of Hos to sons born out of wedlock. When an unmarried woman becomes pregnant, all the men of the village meet to decide who the father of the child is. Daughters born out of wedlock are not as unwelcome as sons, even in cases where the father refuses to acknowledge responsibility for the child. A baby boy whose father does not acknowledge him runs a higher risk of being killed or allowed to die through neglect than does a girl. A boy's life is not seen as worth much if he is not going to inherit land since that is seen as his most important function in life. Also, if an unmarried woman is saddled with a boy child, she will find it more difficult to get married. A prospective husband will not like another man's son in the house as a possible claimant of the land, whereas a stepdaughter, since she will grow up to share her mother's drudgery on the land and in the house, will not be a burden.

Violence Related to Land

On the surface, a Ho village appears deceptively calm and quiet. Beneath the surface simmers extreme mistrust and hostility because the relatively more powerful families are constantly on the lookout for opportunities to usurp the land of less powerful families. Single women and childless widows are among the most vulnerable. If a woman does not surrender her usufructuary right, she may become the target of different kinds of violence. One such case was that of Sumati Kui, whom I met in Chaibasa court in July 1982, where she had come for the hearing of a murder case in which she had been implicated. She is a young woman who lives with her old widowed mother Jugni Kui of Kalmia P.S. Tonto. She said she had chosen to stay unmarried so that she and her mother could live off the family land. She had an affair with Dobro Ho and gave birth to a baby which, according to the two women, died soon after birth. But their relatives accused them of having murdered the child. Most of the witnesses against them in this case are Sumati's father's male agnates. This is an extract from the testimony of Sumati's cousin, Singrai Tubid:

> Jugni Kui had filed a case against my father and brother for harvesting the paddy from her field. The case continued for some time.... It is true that my father and brother have been quarrelling with Jugni Kui for a long time. Jugni has no son. Sumati is her only child. We are her near agnates.

> If Sumati Kui were to leave her mother Jugni Kui and go somewhere, then we would inherit all her land. Ever since the land dispute started, I have not been on speaking terms with Jugni Kui.

Whichever way the case is decided, the women are likely to end up as landless destitutes, because if Jugni and Sumati are sentenced to a prison term on the charge of murder, the land will be taken over by the agnates; if, however, they are acquitted, most of the land is likely to have been mortgaged to pay the court expenses. They told me they had to spend about Rs 200 on bail and each visit to court cost them at least Rs 20. The only way they could raise this money was by mortgaging their land since they are subsistence cultivators.

Violence against women often takes the form of 'witch' killings. No systematic study has been made of this phenomenon. Most commentators attribute it to superstitious ignorance. British administrators assumed that spread of formal education would put an end to it. Wilkinson in his despatch of 1838, wrote: 'there must be spread of education to put down witchcraft and the institution of *sokhas* who make divinations and indicate someone as the witch' leading to her murder (Chaudhury 1958, p. 253). Even today, most social reformers of the area believe that it is primarily lack of modern healthcare facilities that makes tribals fall prey to the superstition that various diseases are the result of witchcraft. However, it is important to remember that it is usually against women that the so-called superstitiousness erupts.

My study suggests that often the real motivation for witchkilling is the desire to eliminate the woman and take away her land. I came across several such cases in Chaibasa court, where single women or old widows in vulnerable circumstances had been murdered by their own relatives. In one case, a man who worked as a veterinary doctor in a government hospital was accused of having murdered his two paternal aunts. The two old women were unmarried and lived together, working the land over which they had a usufructuary right. He had accused them of being witches and of having caused the death of his wife. A child had seen him murdering them with an axe but he was acquitted by the court. He inherited the land which the two old women had been cultivating.

Maki Bui, a petitioner in the Supreme Court case challenging the denial of succession rights to Ho women as being in violation of the Constitution of India,[4] was also accused by her husband's male agnates of being a witch. She felt they were preparing grounds to have her killed, and fled to her married daughter's village.

[4] A petition in the Supreme Court by *Manushi* on behalf of Maki Bui and her daughter Sonamuni was filed in 1982 under Article 32 of the Constitution of India.

Another form of violence is social ostracism. Women hesitate to carry the fight for their rights beyond a point lest they be perceived as deviants and outcasts. The severity with which such ostracism is enforced varies, depending on how much of a threat such a woman is perceived to be by the powerful families of the village. A woman who has been ostracized will not find anyone to plough her fields or thatch her roof. She will not get people to assist her in essential rituals. She will find it hard to procure food loans in times of scarcity or to buy and sell essential goods.

Women and the Family

A notable feature of marriage in Ho society is that the age at marriage of Ho women is much higher than among Hindu peasant groups. Most of the women interviewed did not know their exact age and, therefore, could not give accurate information regarding their age at marriage. But, by and large, most of them seem to have married in their twenties. This seems to accord with what is known about the age of marriage among the Hos. Child marriage is unknown and even teenage marriages are rare.

Ho society allows greater freedom of choice to women in marriage as compared to Hindu peasant groups. But this freedom is circumscribed by various customs and taboos. Even though there is relatively greater freedom in intermixing of men and women, an unspoken but strict code operates. For instance, if a woman is alone in the house, no man other than a family member will enter the house. In the course of work, men and women observe an unstated kind of segregation. Women usually go in groups to the forest, field or market. An unmarried woman will never go with a man to gather fuel, but sometimes a man may accompany his wife to fetch heavy logs.

There are regular occasions when men and women intermix. The most important are the weekly markets held in each area. Rice beer is sold and consumed, and men and women are expected to court each other. At festivals such as Maghe Parab, which is celebrated soon after the winter harvest, many restraints are dropped. Unmarried women sing, dance and drink with abandon. Men are expected to openly woo women and many marriage alliances are formed at this time. Such a self-arranged marriage is known as *Jisuku.*

Men and women do not enter into any other form of alliance except that of marriage. Ho society has no space for casual or serious friendships between men and women. Long-drawn-out love affairs or betrothals are also rare. As soon as a man and woman show interest in one another, they are expected to start living together as man and wife, provided that neither family has strong objections to the match. Sometimes, a man and woman who enter into a *Jisuku* marriage have a prior acquaintance by virtue of being from neighbouring villages. But, sometimes, a woman will go with a man she has met for the first time at a market or festival. If she finds, on reaching his house, that he is very poor or already has a wife, she may leave immediately. But even if she leaves a few hours after going to his house at his invitation, she may be considered married and may lose her usufructuary right in her parental land.

Self-arranged alliances also take place between men and women working at brick kilns or mines, away from their villages. Women enter in these alliances without informing their families. It is significant that though women have the right to accept a proposal without consulting their families, the proposal, in all the forms of marriage, must come from the man or his family. Neither the woman nor her family are expected to make marriage proposals. If one asks an unmarried woman why she has not married, the answer often is: 'No one has called me yet!'

Marriages arranged by families are known as *andi* and *diku andi*. These are held in higher esteem than other types of marriages. Negotiations over bride price play a large part in them. The village headman and *killi* elders are supposed to be consulted before an *andi* marriage is finalized. The *andi* is the traditional form and the *diku andi* is borrowed from the Hindus. P.C. Roy Chaudhury observed in 1958:

> Recently among the manki-munda class a peculiar form has come into vogue known as *diku andi*. In this form of marriage, in addition to traditional tribal customs, some local Hindu rites have also been added, such as participation of a Brahmin priest and the employment of the Hindu barber (p. 248).

It is mostly well-to-do families living in close proximity to caste Hindus who have adopted these rites and ceremonies. But, even in such marriages, traditional observances have not been entirely given up,

Of the 22 married women in our sample, 17 (about two-thirds) had self-arranged marriages. Five reported that their parents or other relatives had arranged the marriage. Of these five, three women considered their marriage good and attributed this to the fact that it was family-arranged. Of the 17 self-arranged marriages, 12 women seemed to be having a tough time.

Two other types of marriages mentioned by anthropologists are *opertipi* and *anader*, but these are not common today. *Opertipi* is marriage by abduction. Sometimes, the abduction takes place by mutual agreement of the couple. But even when a woman has been abducted against her will, she is often forced to accept the marriage for fear of social ridicule. *Anader* is when a woman forces herself into her lover's household as his wife, against the wishes of his family.

Hos are usually expected to marry outside the village. This custom is strengthened by the taboo against marrying within the *killi* or clan. Some villages are dominated by one *killi*, in which case it becomes necessary to marry outside the village. Men and women of the same *killi* are supposed to be cousins and marriage between them is considered incest. But in villages like Karonja, which have a population comprising different *killis*, marriage within the village is not uncommon.

One cannot help noticing the great contrast between Ho women and women of non-tribal peasant groups in India. Ho women do not have to take their parents' permission or approval in order to accept or reject a marriage proposal. Even when the family arranges a marriage for a daughter, she has a right to refuse and her wish is supposed to be respected. But, if the family is under pressure from more powerful families, they may push her to marry. Frequently, an unmarried woman may be pushed into marriage by her brothers, especially if they have wives to labour in the fields and do not need her labour.

Does this mean that Ho women get a better deal in marriage than do women of non-tribal communities? In some ways, yes. They do not enter into marriage in the same spirit of self-abnegation as women of most other peasant groups in India. They are not brainwashed into expecting a husband to be a protector and provider. They are much less caught up in romantic myths of marriage, and openly talk of it being a bad deal which they are compelled to enter into for survival. They are fully conscious that they will have to work like slaves in the husband's home, can expect to be beaten and cannot expect security as a right. Thus, in many ways, they are mentally better prepared to fend for themselves, whether or not the marriage breaks down.

Women neither get nor expect much emotional sustenance from their husbands. If one asks a woman whether her husband 'loves' her, she normally understands this to refer to sexual relations. The only word in use for 'love' in the Ho language is '*dular*' which usually refers to affection for children. I was told that even this word is rarely used in everyday conversation.

In general, all a Ho woman asks is that her husband not actively maltreat her and not throw her out of the marital home. Most Ho women cannot get even this minimum consideration because they do not have the power to enforce their customary rights as wives, even though these are upheld in principle by their society.

Distance from Natal Family

The denial of equal land rights to women amongst peasant groups in India, including the Hos, is often justified on the grounds of patrilocal family structure. It is argued that because a woman shifts to her husband's home and village on marriage, she will not be able to cultivate land in her natal village, so there is no use her inheriting parental land. It is also argued that she, as a wife, acquires an unwritten but real right in her husband's family land, from which all her needs are met.

However, my study indicates that while a man in Ho society strengthens his economic position through marriage, acquiring a worker on his land, a woman's position becomes more tenuous. She loses the usufructuary right she had in her parental land, but the process of gaining even minimal rights in her husband's land is an uncertain and hazardous one.

Most marriages amongst the Hos are self-arranged and since these alliances are made at local festivals and weekly markets, people tend to marry either in their own village, or in nearby villages. This is because people normally attend only the markets and festivals at villages within walking distance of their own village or, at most, an hour or so away by bus or train. This clearly emerges from my village sample. Seven of the 22 married women interviewed had married in their own village. The natal villages of six others were less than three hours' walk away. One woman's natal village was one hour's walk away. Eight women's villages were more than three hours' walk away. Of these, the natal village of one was 40 km away and that of another was 1 to 1/2 hour's walk and half an hour's train journey away.

Thus, most of the women are reasonably close to their natal villages. The distance, in most cases, is much less than the distance they routinely cover to gather firewood or to procure salt and soap from the market. So if a woman had land to cultivate in her natal village, it would be possible for her to manage it. Therefore, there is no justification in denying women land rights on the ground of their moving out of the parental home after marriage. In fact, there is good reason to believe that if women had secure land rights they would tend to marry even closer to their parental homes than they do at present.

When parents have no son, they may invite their daughter and son-in-law to live with them and cultivate the land. There is no stigma attached to a son-in-law living in his wife's parents' house comparable to that which prevails amongst most Hindu peasant castes. But the woman's father's male agnates will perceive her presence as a threat to their inheritance rights and will exert tremendous pressure to get rid of her and her husband. For instance, Maki Bui, petitioner in the Supreme Court case, was keen that her daughter and son-in-law live with her in her village and cultivate her deceased husband's land over which she had a usufructuary right. But she dared not keep them there for fear that they may be attacked, even murdered.

Marriages outside the Tribe

Hos are not allowed to marry outside the tribe and inter-community marriages are supposed to be punished with social ostracism. But, in fact, this code has been relaxed considerably for men. Men who go to work in mines and industries outside the village occasionally contract marriages with women of other tribes. The man is not usually ostracized when he comes back to his village with a woman from another tribe. But she is never allowed to forget that she is not a Ho, and is not allowed to feel an integral part of the village.

Marriages between tribals and non-tribals are very uncommon. When women go to work in mines and kilns, non-tribal men often keep them as mistresses and exploit them sexually in various ways. Ho society has a strict code governing male–female relations but it is strict in different ways from that operating in non-tribal societies. When a Ho woman enters into a regular sexual relation with a man, they are considered married in Ho society. But by the standards of morality prevailing in Christian and upper caste Hindu culture, such a woman is considered a mistress or a prostitute and is despised, although the man is not similarly treated. This conflict of cultural norms has led to much abuse of Ho women by non-tribal men who see these women as promiscuous and treat them as easy game. Such women are usually ostracized when they return to their village, especially if they have children by the alliance. Those women who are economically vulnerable are usually treated with greater severity than those who are better off. It is extremely rare for a non-tribal man to marry a tribal woman except for fraudulent purposes. There have been several cases of non-tribal men marrying tribal women in order to get tribal land on *bandhak*.

When a woman is declared *kajomesin* or ostracized for having a child by a non-tribal, she is not allowed to draw water from the village well or to join in village rituals and festivities. Nor is she allowed access to the portion of the house where ancestral spirits are worshipped. No one will talk to her, accept food or drink from her, or give it to her. Her family, too, is ostracized in the same way unless they make her leave their house and also ostracize her. When she dies, her dead body cannot be touched by the members of the *killi* nor put in the *sasan* (burial ground) (Majumdar 1950). An ostracized woman is accepted back as a member of the community only if she pays a heavy penalty such as Rs 500 in cash, a goat, a chicken and several pots of rice beer. Often, her brother will pressurize her to pay or quit his house. Since very few women have the money to pay such a heavy fine, most have to leave the village and migrate for employment.

While the Hos consider marriage or alliance with a non-tribal illegitimate, it is significant that they have no concept of illegitimacy of a child. Amongst the Hos, as long as the father is a tribal, a woman is not stigmatized for the birth of a child outside marriage, as she is among Hindu, Muslim and Christian groups. Even if a child is born after a brief affair without the parents having lived together, the child is not considered illegitimate. The men of the village hold a meeting and ask the woman to name the father and give some evidence of her relationship with him. She is not cross-examined as in a court of law. Her statement is given due weight. The man she names as the father is expected to take responsibility. With the gradual breakdown of the internal cohesiveness of the tribe, it often happens that men do not honour their commitment. If this happens, the woman is left to bring up the child on her own, but she is not despised or ostracized, nor is it impossible for her to marry another man, as would be the case amongst other peasant groups. Sometimes, she finds a way to shift the burden of the child on to the father. When the man who had fathered Sona's child publicly denied it, she quietly went away to Kolkata to work at the brick kilns, leaving the child on his doorstep.

The influence of Christian missionaries and of Hindu peasant groups has had a very negative influence on the relatively egalitarian sexual morality among the Hos. Educated tribal men, especially when living in close proximity to Hindus or Christians, become somewhat enamoured with modelling their family life on the pattern of land-owing Hindu peasant groups as a proof of their upward mobility. Their ideas of legitimacy and illegitimacy of children are catching on. Educated Hos in white-collar jobs are beginning to aspire to have house-bound wives as a mark of higher status. They are also adopting repressive marriage traditions from Hindus and Christians, even though in many ways, Hos have been able to resist the process of cultural assimilation relatively better than certain other tribes such as Mundas and Oraons.

Bride Price versus Dowry

Among the Hos, a family has to pay *gonong* to a woman's natal family, represented by her father, brothers or other male agnates, as a price for a wife for their son. This usually consists of cattle and some cash. They may also give goats and poultry. The custom is partly an acknowledgement of the value of a woman—both to the household she is joining and to the household she is leaving.

When the marriage is arranged by the families, they usually try to come to an agreement in advance about the amount of *gonong*. The paying capacity of the groom's family and the social status of the girl's family seem to be the chief determinants of the bride price. But a girl who is healthy and known to be a sturdy worker is likely to fetch a higher bride price, while a woman in ill health is not likely to get many marriage offers.

It is not unusual for bride price agreements to be violated. Often, the groom's family promises to pay a certain amount later, but after the bride has gone to their house, they either default altogether or pay less than the amount agreed. In such cases, the girl's family seldom insists beyond a point lest that become an excuse for the man to throw the wife out. The ability to insist and extract more also depends on the social and economic status of the girl's family in comparison to that of the man's.

If a woman wants to leave her husband and remarry before he has remarried, the custom demands that the husband be compensated for the bride price by the man willing to marry her, or that her natal family returns the payment made to them. This may be one reason why it is not very common for women to remarry, and even rarer for them to remarry before the husband does so.

Of the 22 married women, 13 had received *gonong* at the time of their marriage. Nine out of 22, that is about 40 per cent, had received no *gonong* at all. Of the six who were 40 years of age or more, all but one had fetched bride price. Of the nine women under 30 years of age, six had received no *gonong* whatsoever. In one case, the *gonong* was much less than the full promised amount. This suggests that bride price has been on the decline in the last few decades. Of the nine families that did not give any *gonong*, four did not do so because of poverty. Naguri Surin and Panpati Sundi explained that their husband's family had only one pair of draught animals. If they gave away even one animal, they would not be able to plough their own land. This would further jeopardize their precarious economy.

In a self-arranged or runaway marriage, where the woman goes to the man's house without prior negotiations, her family is likely to insist on an appropriate bride price. If the boy's family does not agree, the girl's family may sometimes threaten to take her back, but the threat is rarely executed. Of the 17 self-arranged marriages in our sample, 10 women had fetched no bride price at all. In one case, only a small part of the payment agreed upon was made. In contrast, in all of the five parent-arranged marriages, *gonong* had been paid and was usually more substantial. Even though it seems that payment of bride price is relatively less likely in self-arranged marriages, our sample shows that in those cases of self-arranged marriages where a bride price was paid, the amount was not very different from that paid in family arranged marriages.

Over the last few decades, there has been a general trend of decline in the practice of bride price. In 1935, D.N. Majumdar did an informal survey of marriages in a particular village. He found that in 44 of the 53 marriages, bride price had been paid. The amounts paid were much higher than those in our sample. The five highest bride price amounts were as follows:

1. 40 cattle and Rs 50
2. 32 cattle and Rs 30
3. 40 cattle and Rs 30
4. 25 cattle and Rs 45
5. 25 cattle and Rs 45 (Majumdar 1950, pp. 147–152)

In our sample, the women interviewed reported much lower amounts. The five highest bride price amounts were as follows:

1. 10 cattle and Rs 100
2. 5 cattle and Rs 400
3. 5 cattle
4. 5 cattle
5. 4 cattle

The lower number of cattle given could in part be explained in terms of a reduction of the amount of grazing land available because of increasing land scarcity in this area. But it is significant that the decline in the number of cattle given has not been accompanied by an increase in the value of other forms of payment in cash or kind.

It has often been made out that the custom of bride price, like dowry, has harmful consequences. It is supposed to result in a large number of women remaining unmarried because many families are unable to offer the requisite payment for a bride. It is said that men from poorer families cannot find wives easily and end up remaining unmarried for life. As far as my information goes, this theory is not based on facts. It is much influenced by the personal prejudices of the colonial administrators. Christian missionaries and upper caste Hindus have found the practice unacceptable because it openly acknowledges women's economic worth–a notion alien to their own culture. Dalton and Risley observed:

> In no other country [part] in India are spinsters found so advanced in years and in many of the best families grey-headed old maids may be seen whose charms were insufficient to warrant the large additions to the usual price called 'Pan' imposed in consideration of the high connection that the union would confer!

Captain Haughter even proposed the abolition of bride price but it was Hayes who in 1868 initiated some measures to combat it. He convened a meeting of tribal leaders and made them 'agree' that at least a reduction should be brought about. It was resolved that in future bride price was not to exceed 10 heads of cattle and that, if one pair of oxen, one cow and seven rupees were given, it should be received as an equivalent of the 10 heads. For the poorer classes, bride price was fixed at Rs 7. Commenting on this, C.P. Singh concludes that these 'built-in malpractices could not be swept away by merely passing resolutions. The bride price continued to undermine the social structure of the Hos' (Dalton and Risley cited in Singh 1978, p. 147).

Majumdar refers to it as a 'social inequity'. He condemns the practice because it leads to 'a general lowering of the standard of morality within the tribe' and to much 'premarital licence' and 'irregular unions'. In his view, this has led to a high number of men and women among the Hos remaining unmarried' (Singh 1978, p. 148). Tribal practices, such as bride price, even when they are more egalitarian and beneficial for women's lives, are despised by other hegemonic groups simply because they are associated with the culture of a subjugated group.

The spread of education among tribals has further intensified attacks on bride price. As tribal youth begin to move out of their villages into nearby towns for education and employment, they come more easily under the influence of Hindu upper caste norms as well as the ideology of Christian missionaries. It is from among this group of tribal youth that occasional campaigns against this supposed social evil have emanated even—though experience shows that when bride price does die out, it begins to be replaced by dowry, which proves far more harmful for women. The few college-going Ho girls I met confirmed that when they marry there is little likelihood of bride price being paid because they will marry men with white-collar jobs in urban areas. They were certain that their parents would give them various household goods as dowry.

Another important reason for the decline in bride price even among village-based Hos is the increasing land hunger among the Hos. This has resulted in increasing devaluation of women's labour. Land is now considered the prime possession. This encourages the feeling that a wife who is brought in to labour on the land can easily be replaced. Since another wife is readily available, there is a tendency to avoid payment to her family.

In recent years, there has been greater stratification within the tribal community. The more powerful families in the village are able to indulge in open land grabbing from poorer and weaker families with the connivance of the government machinery. Thus, Ho society has come a long way from the relatively egalitarian land distribution which characterized tribal society. The better-off families are unwilling to pay bride price, especially when they get daughters-in-law from relatively poorer families. In such a situation, the woman's family may not insist much on receiving the payment because they feel the alliance with a better-off family will benefit them in other ways. In addition, their daughter is less likely to go hungry and search for wage labour.

In my sample, I found that payments do not play as crucial a role as is made out to be the case. There were four marriages where the boy's family expressed inability to pay because they had no extra animals. But no fuss seems to have been made because the bride's parents realized that by taking away the one pair of animals owned by the groom's family, they would jeopardize their daughter's future. Even in cases where families were in a position to pay, I did not come across any case where the parents broke off the alliance due to default in payment.

A large number of Ho women stay unmarried, especially if they feel more secure in their natal family (of this more later). Thus, a certain number of men would have to stay unmarried, especially since a number of men have more than one wife and women do not remarry as often, nor do they have more than one husband at a time. Fewer non-tribal women are likely to be available to tribal men for marriage. Thus, bride price is not likely to be the reason for a number of Ho men and women remaining unmarried.

Bride price is not an unmixed blessing for women. As with dowry, women do not get anything for themselves. The payments go to their fathers, brothers or male kin who inherit the family land. Even if a woman is thrown out of her husband's house, she cannot claim the bride price from her father or brother, although she has lost all rights in the natal family land by virtue of her marriage. Dowry has at least the pretension of being part of *stridhan*. The practice of bride price does not allow any space for this pretence. Ho women, like caste Hindu women, get to be used as vehicles for the transfer of wealth from men of one family to those of another rather than becoming owners of income-producing assets in their own right.

Yet, bride price ensures that a woman is not seen as a burden on her parents and thus allows women better survival chances. The progressive disappearance of bride price is a sign of the erosion of women's bargaining position. Even though among the Hos this erosion has not yet given way to the widespread practice of dowry, the dowry system is catching on among some other tribes in the area, especially among the educated and better-off families. This is likely to have adverse consequences for women's lives.

Of the 22 married women interviewed, seven had co-wives. Of these, three continued to live with their husbands while four had separated from or been thrown out by their husbands. One of these men has four wives. Only one of the 22 women had remarried. She had done so only after she was compelled to leave her first husband's house.

Polygamy is permitted among Hos but not polyandry. Customarily, a man can have more than one wife only if he has some justification for remarrying, such as infertility of the first wife or her inability to work due to sickness. Another acceptable reason for a man to remarry is if the first wife has not produced a son. It is not unusual for the first wife's family to offer their second daughter without a bride price, as a compensation for the 'failure' of their first daughter to provide her husband with an heir. My informant told me that she knew of hardly any case in the village where under 'normal' circumstances, a man would get himself a second wife while the first one was around. It is considered 'outside' the custom.

However, many of the customary safeguards for women have broken down because of migration. Men feel justified on the grounds that they need one wife to take care of the land in the village and one to minister to their needs at the workplace in town. Often, the two women get to know of each other's existence only when the man returns to the village with the second wife. If the man continues to live outside, and visits the village infrequently, the first marriage usually subsists because the first wife continues using the land for her and her children's subsistence. But, if he chooses to return to the village, a conflict usually results, leading to one of the wives being pushed out. He may build a new house so that the two wives can live separately. He can do this if he has enough land to feed both wives and their children. Otherwise, the one who has less power, who is older, for instance, or who has no sons, tends to get pushed out.

Outside the village, customary restraints cannot be enforced on men. Even within the village, the traditional arbitration machinery is slowly breaking down and men are able to openly defy the norms. This is truer for men of better-off families.

Sukmaru was 'called' by her husband from Maghe Parab. She had no idea that he had another wife in his village. The first wife was a much older woman, therefore, the man invited Sukmaru to live with him and forced the first wife to leave the house. Sukmaru says she would never have gone with him if she had known he had a wife already. Once she had gone with him, it was difficult for her to leave him because she would have had to face social ridicule and criticism.

Divorce is generally an informal affair. Unlike men, very few women walk out on a marriage for the sake of another relationship. A woman will quit her husband's house only if she is severely maltreated. Since a married woman usually has no other source of economic security, she tries to stay on as long as she can in her husband's house. That is the only way she can fight for her usufructuary right in his land. If he tries to throw her out, she may bring the matter before a group of arbitrators headed by the *mukhia*. A few women even end up fighting lengthy court battles when all other efforts fail.

Women with ceremonially arranged marriages are no more secure than those with self-arranged marriages. The only difference is that it is relatively more difficult for a woman to 'prove' a self-arranged marriage before a court or panchayat, especially if the marriage took place outside the village. It is difficult for a man to deny a ceremonially arranged marriage. However, that does not at all ensure that he behaves more responsibly towards his wife and children.

While Ho men remarry with relative ease, there is no stigma attached even to women remarrying, unlike among non-tribal Hindus and Christians. After a certain age, it is difficult for a woman to find a second husband, especially if she has children, yet it is not rare for separated women to remarry. In the last few decades, Christian missionaries have been trying to steer Ho society towards monogamous marriages and discouragement of divorce but they have not been able to influence men much in this direction.

It is extremely rare for a woman to have an extra-marital affair with another man while living in her husband's home. My informant told me that throughout her stay in Karonja, she had heard of only one such affair. A middle-aged woman was found having an affair with a young unmarried man. Her husband, who lived outside the village, already had two other wives. A few village men, who suspected her of having an affair, wrote to her husband about it. One night, they went to her house, forced her to open the door and caught the young man inside. They compelled him to take her to his house as his wife but his family refused to accept her because she was already married and had two children by her husband. She was forced to migrate to Kolkata to seek work, since her husband's family would not allow her to cultivate the family land. Their desire to get her land may have been an important motive behind their conspiracy to expose her.

When I asked Ho women why polyandry was not permitted while polygamy was, the reply often was: 'It is convenient for a man to have two wives because he gets two slaves to work for him. But if I have two husbands, I will have to work in two men's houses and fields, when I can barely manage the work of one man's household!'

When I asked women who had particularly bad marriages why they did not remarry, the answer almost always was: 'When this man with whom I have lived for so many years, and have had children by, does not treat me well, how can I expect another man will be better?' Another reason cited was that they had nowhere to go. Ho women continue in bad marriages only as long as they do not have any other option. Those who can find even a precarious foothold elsewhere do not stay to take the beatings. Seldom do they stay on from a sense of wifely duty, which is so deeply engrained amongst upper caste Hindu, Muslim and Christian women.

If land was communally utilized by the tribe and if women had equal land rights, a woman's life would not be negatively affected by her marriage breaking down because there is no stigma against divorce and remarriage. But, today, in the context of men having nearly exclusive control over land, a woman is compelled to have a heavy stake in the continuance of her marriage. For men, marriage means getting hold of a bonded labourer. In a situation of land scarcity, men's bargaining power in procuring a woman to drudge for them has been considerably enhanced.

Men as Absentee Landlords

The problems arising from women's precarious rights in land are aggravated by men's increasing tendency to seek jobs outside the village. Often, men end up living much farther away from their village land than women do after marriage. Men leave their wives to work on the land while they migrate to cities; it is usually daughters-in-law, not sons, who cultivate the land.

It is rare for a man regularly to send money home to his wife and children. Usually, a man spends most of his earnings on his personal consumption or on maintaining a second family in town. Of the 22 married women in my sample, eight said that even when their husbands earned, they did not contribute to feeding the family. Almost all of what a woman earns is spent on family subsistence. Apart from soap, oil and an occasional *saree* or blouse, a woman buys almost nothing for herself. But men spend not only on drink but also aspire to buy a bicycle, a watch, a transistor–things a woman rarely dreams of buying for herself.

Although most men who find jobs outside the village do not contribute to work on the land, they manage to keep control over it by virtue of their near exclusive rights over it. An unmarried sister or a wife continues the subsistence agriculture in the village while the brothers or husband function somewhat like absentee landlords. The land is an important source of security for men. They can return to the village during periods of temporary unemployment. Most Ho men prefer to return to the village after retirement. The cash income from their pensions, combined with the produce from the land, makes a relatively comfortable old age possible for them. A woman rarely, if ever, can attain such security on her own.

If men could not leave their land in the charge of wives and sisters, they would find it much harder to retain a firm hold on it while they lived in the city. Loaning or renting the land to a relative, neighbour or even a brother is not as safe because in the present situation of acute land hunger, anyone who acquires *de facto* rights over land actively resists parting with it.

However, a woman, even a wife, seldom comes to acquire such rights. Even if she has worked on the land for many years, she cannot resist being thrown out by her husband, let alone claim a share in the land. When a man returns, he can easily take over the land from his wife, sister or daughter, because the village community supports the man's right.

The division of labour releases men to explore other possibilities which further consolidate their power over women. A man who has a steady job in town is at a much greater advantage vis-à-vis his wife than one who lives in the village and is dependent on his wife's labour on the land.

Return to the Natal Family

After being pushed out of her husband's house, a woman may find a refuge in her parents' house only if the family needs an extra worker. Jasmati Sundi's story is an instance of this. Jasmati's natal family fetched her, taking her back to their house although she has, by marriage, forfeited her usufructuary right in their land. The main reason they brought her back is that they require her as a worker on the land. She has two married sisters. Her one brother, a failed matriculate, does absolutely no work. He wants a city job but is unable to get one. Twice, he got involved in police cases for attempts to murder someone with whom he got into a fight. He even attacks his parents violently.

They have about 11 *bandi* land which will be inherited by the son. Jasmati works on the land single-handedly with the help of hired labour. She fears that when her brother marries and the sister-in-law takes over work on the land, her position will become more insecure. Jasmati cannot remarry until her husband remarries, because, if she does, her family will have to return the cows they received as bride price. If a woman's family already has adult women to do the work, she is not likely to be welcome there, especially if her parents are dead. Generally, brothers and their wives do not want an extra person living off their land. Barti at the age of 30 has come to precisely such a dead end. Barti's husband migrated to Assam some years ago. She was neglected and ill-treated because she had little value as a worker and her in-laws saw her as a liability. When she was very sick, her mother took her back for some months but sent her back to her in-laws. She would prefer to live at her parental house but her brother and his wife do not let her stay there even though they are fairly well-off.

Women who are able to earn a substantial amount of money by their labour are likely to be allowed to stay in their parental home. A woman whose parents are landless is also likely to be accepted back because she can contribute financially by her wage labour. Gurbari is one of the few who had no problem returning to her natal family when she was thrown out by her husband. An important reason seems to be that her family is landless, having lost their land when her father died 17 years ago and his brother grabbed the land that should have been inherited by Gurbari's brothers who were then small children. Gurbari's sister, Hire Kui, is also staying in their mother's house with her two daughters. Hire Kui and Gurbari now run their mother's household economy, so their brothers exert no pressure on them to leave.

Although many widows do not get their usufructuary right on their deceased husband's land, and are thus in an insecure position, a woman's situation may improve after her husband's death if she manages to hold on to her usufructuary right. This happened in the case of Panderi Devi who was widowed about a year ago. Her husband, a school teacher, had studied up to intermediate. He had inherited some land from his father, half of which he gave away on *bandhak*. Now they only have a small piece of land which produces two to three *bandis* of rice. Panderi has a son aged about four, one daughter aged 11 and another who is one year old. She continues to cultivate the land by herself, as she did in her husband's lifetime. She is under pressure from some of her husband's male agnates to surrender her usufructuary right in the land, but is determined to hold on to it. Thus, in many ways, a widow with sons is better-off than a woman whose husband is alive and maltreats her. As a widow, a woman has a usufructuary right in the land and can demand that a portion of land be allocated to her for separate cultivation, in case she does not get along with her sons. She may not always get this in practice, but, in theory, the customary law does protect her right. However, as a wife, she does not have such an independent usufructuary right. If her husband throws her out, she cannot demand that she be given a portion of land to cultivate separately.

Sons and daughters-in-law may neglect a widowed mother but she is seldom beaten, as wives routinely are, with no intervention from the community. As a widow, a woman faces the possibility of violence outside the house in the form of attacks by her husband's male agnates. But, as a wife, a woman has to face everyday violence and may be rendered destitute if the husband does not need her to labour on his land.

Among non-tribal peasant groups, women are seldom allowed to decide whether or not they want to marry. Consequently, almost no women are left unmarried at 30. Even among other tribal groups in Bihar, none show such a high proportion of unmarried women as do the Hos. According to the 1971 Census, approximately 11 per cent of all Ho women 45 years of age or above had never married (Census of India 1971). A similar figure has been reported ever since the census operations in India began. This is an incredibly high percentage for any community in India. In contrast, the all-India percentage of tribal women above 45 years of age who had never married is less than 1 per cent, approximately the same as the all-India figure for all communities.

So far, there has been no large-scale, systematic study of the reasons for this unusual phenomenon. The data gathered from my study of Karonja village suggests that the causes are likely to be far more complex than the prevalence of bride price, which is often cited as the cause.

Of the 30 women interviewed, eight are unmarried. Five of them seem to have stayed unmarried by choice. In a Ho village, these five women, who are 30 years of age or older, would be considered above the age of marriage although Ho women sometimes get married even in their forties. A Ho woman who does not want to marry may face certain socioeconomic pressures from her family; but there are no cultural pressures comparable to those prevalent among Hindu peasant groups. Among the Hos, even if a family enters into marriage negotiations for a daughter in response to a proposal, she has the right to say 'no' and expect her choice to be respected. The fact that this option, although constricted by a complex web of social pressures, is available to Ho women, gives them a rare advantage over women of most other communities in India.

The reasons these women gave for their unmarried status throw light on the nature of the social and economic compulsions they confront and the way marriage tends to make their situation more vulnerable. However, circumstances in their parental families do not allow most of them to act on the basis of this reasoning. Rani, who is 35 and has chosen not to marry, is in an advantageous position right now because she is the main worker on the family land. She lives with her young unmarried brother and old mother, both completely dependent on her. The land is shared between this family unit and her other brother who is married. Rani's brother has passed the middle school exam but has no job. He does no work except to plough the land before the sowing season. The situation may change if he gets married and gets an able-bodied wife to do the work that Rani does. So Rani would have to move out if her sister-in-law wanted her to go. But as long as parents are alive, unmarried women have better protection. Parents usually prefer to live with daughters because they take better care of them than do sons. So an unmarried daughter could set up house separately with her parents and not be dependent on her brother and his wife. Rani has an added advantage insofar as her mother wants to live with her. This will enable the two women to get a portion of the land allocated to them for separate cultivation as their usufructuary right. She is not likely to find even as much security as this if she marries. Staying single definitely seems more advantageous.

Jano, aged about 40, explains why she chose not to marry: 'I was frightened of being hungry and left to starve. At my parents' house, no one can get angry with me. After marriage, they beat you so. Here, at home, I feel more happy and free!' Jano has two sisters and four brothers. Three of her brothers are working as skilled or semi-skilled labourers outside the village. One brother lives in the village and works for the forest department. The father died several years ago. The land has been divided up among the four brothers and Jano has been allotted one field much smaller than the others' for her maintenance. Even with this unequal share, Jano has been able to carve out a better deal for herself than most married women manage. She lives by herself and has hired a boy from the village to help her with the work. She has also worked out a deal with one of her brothers who works in Chiriya mines. She looks after his fields in his absence, for which he pays her a small amount.

Often, young women are pushed into marriage, much against their wishes, by male relatives who wish to grab their land. Mukta's case is an example of this pattern. When I interviewed Mukta in 1983, she was unmarried. Some time in July 1984, I got a detailed report from the village about how she had been forced into marriage. Mukta, about 22, was the main earner of the family. Her father had died four years ago. She has two brothers, aged six and three. Her father's older brother and his son refused to divide the family land equally and apportioned a small share of land to Mukta's family. Mukta did wage work to supplement the family income. One day, Mukta went with her cousin Laxmi to a fair in another village, where she stayed in a relative's house. Suddenly, without obtaining her consent, these relatives put *sasan*, the symbol of marriage, on her. Later, her wedding feast was celebrated. She kept weeping loudly and bitterly as women usually do at a burial, and had to be literally pushed by relatives to leave her parental home. Now that Mukta has to live in another village, she cannot cultivate her natal family's land. The family has no other grown-up child to do this work, so they will be forced to mortgage the land and take loans from their better-off relatives—those who arranged Mukta's marriage. Mukta's marriage may well have been arranged by her male relatives as a way of grabbing her family's share of the land.

Often, such pressure comes from a woman's own brothers, and if she refuses to marry, she may be forced to migrate. This is what happened to Kuni Sundi, aged about 30, who has chosen not to marry. Kuni did not want to live with any of her three brothers who live in the village. Kuni's parents are dead. Her mother had allocated two fields to Kuni which yield about two *bandi* rice. Her brothers insisted that she live with one of them. She appealed to the panchayat, which decreed that she stay with her oldest brother. Kuni does not find this arrangement satisfactory so she seldom stays in the village. In her absence, her oldest brother ploughs her land and keeps the crop. For all practical purposes, he has taken over her land. When she stays in the village, she is allowed to live off the rice from her fields but not allowed to sell any portion of that rice. So, when in the village, she has to work as a labourer in other people's fields to earn some cash to buy soap and oil. She once tried living with her younger brother but left his house after a quarrel because he refused to give her any of the rice from her fields.

It seems that when parents clearly leave a particular piece of land for an unmarried daughter's use, she has a relatively stronger position in the family and the village than when she has to depend on her brothers' goodwill. Many women say that when an unmarried woman grows old or falls sick and is unable to work, she becomes particularly vulnerable. This means that she may be pushed off her land by her male agnates.

Generally, male agnates make sure that the old woman is not allowed to live on her own. It becomes particularly difficult for her to resist this pressure if she has no brothers living in the village and willing to take her side.

A widow may also face the problem of unavailability of helping hands in the fields. The popular notion is that in most villages, especially tribal villages, there is a good deal of reciprocity, with families helping each other out *gratis* in times of difficulty. The *Singhbhum District Gazetteer*, 1958, comments: '... there is a good deal of cooperation in economic matters. Exchange of agricultural labour is very common and communal hunting and fishing with equitable distribution of the spoils indicate their collective spirit!' (Chaudhury 1958, p. 243). But this seems, by and large, to be a matter of the past. Most families are so close to the brink that they have very little to give others by way of labour or food. Childless old women are often left to their own efforts, eventually to starve and die. This happens also to younger women who live alone when they fall sick. Even close relatives seldom help out, except for a consideration. If a widow wants her brother to plough her land, she has to pay him at the prevailing wage rate, either in cash or kind. At times, labour may be bartered for labour.

There are also cases when families pressure a woman not to marry for a while, and her marriage may even be delayed indefinitely until she grows so old that she is not considered marriageable. Jabani, aged about 18, is unmarried and is being made to act as caretaker of the family land until her little brother is old enough to inherit it. Jabani's father died about seven years ago. His widow, who was much younger than he was, then married a man from another community. She was ostracized by her family and lost her usufructuary right. Jabani has four married sisters and her brother, aged 10, lives with one of them in Rourkela. Jabani, as an unmarried daughter, is the only one with a right to cultivate the land. So she is made to live alone in the village and take care of the land so that male relatives do not grab it before her brother can take it over. She hires help to plough the land, and her sister pays for this.

Thus, women in Ho society suffer from different levels of economic insecurity. The most enviable state is that of a married woman whose husband does not maltreat her and allows her some control over the family income. This kind of security cannot be acquired through a woman's own efforts but is dependent on chance. Hence, there is a certain scepticism among Ho women about seeking security through marriage.

The second best alternative for a woman is to live as an unmarried daughter. She has a right to subsist on her parents' land and will not be beaten. But once her parents die, her brothers or male cousins may want to push her off the land. She cannot hope to strengthen her position by having sons, as a married woman can. It is this hope which pushes many women into marriage. It is thus very likely that the higher proportion of unmarried women in Ho society as compared to other communities is due to the definite advantages detailed earlier, as well as the important fact that there is no social stigma attached to being unmarried.

Given the remarkably clear-headed rationality that Ho women display in making decisions such as the decision to marry or not to marry, or to migrate and take a job for wages, it is likely that if the options available to them expanded, for instance, if they acquired equal rights in land, they would know how to make the best of these options. They do not seem to be prey to the self-delusory humbug regarding marriage, dependence on men or their own disabilities that is characteristic of most non-tribal women's perception of their situation, including that of most urban, educated women.

Ho women attempt to arrive at the best possible deal under adverse circumstances. This is not at all to suggest that they are crafty and calculating. In fact, their clear-headedness about marriage and their relationships with men is often accompanied by a surprising degree of naiveté in dealing with the outside world, especially when cash transactions are involved. Panpati's life is a good example of the extraordinary resilience and resourcefulness of Ho women. Panpati is about 50 years old. She was married about 25 years ago to Sado and had three children, of whom one died. She now has one unmarried son and one married daughter. She left her husband's house after he brought a second wife. Panpati came to her natal village. Her brother had inherited about 20 *bandi* land. For a couple of years she lived in his house, worked on his fields as a wage labourer and did most of the housework. But her brother would keep getting angry with her children and say: 'How long can I go on feeding them?' Her children felt very upset and could not study.

So she moved out and made a separate home. Slowly, she saved some money from selling rice beer and doing wage work. With this, she got two small fields on *bandhak* from one of the families in the village. This produces about two *bandis* of rice. She keeps one *bandi* for consumption and gives the other on loan. Her son has studied up to matriculation. He failed about three times before finally passing, and is now looking for a job. He is of no help to her.

Aged about 20, if he occasionally gets some wage work, he spends most of the money on himself. He is now demanding his share of land from his father and is involved in a dispute.

Even though Ho women strongly resist violation of their rights, this resistance does not take aggressive forms, not even the form of loud protestation. They are gentle and dignified in their resistance, which is expressed mainly through actions such as quietly leaving home or going about their business without succumbing to a particular pressure. Refusing to cook for the husband or withdrawing from him sexually after a fight are common forms of protest. Even in their dealings with exploitative outsiders, Ho women retain their dignity. They do not beg or grovel before authority or plead for favours in a self-demeaning fashion. Throughout my travels in these villages, I do not remember even one occasion when any woman begged for any favour, no matter how poor or desperate her circumstances.

Power Structures Outside the Family

Even though Ho women have far fewer restrictions on their physical mobility than most other women, their access to education is severely restricted. The disadvantageous position of Ho women in matters of education is reflected in my village sample. In the sample, 27 out of 30 women are totally illiterate. In contrast, over one-third of the husbands of the 22 married women interviewed were educated up to matriculate level. Only about a quarter of the husbands were without any schooling. Two out of three of the husbands could be assumed to be literate and about half of them had passed middle school. The educational gap between unmarried women interviewed and their brothers was also very wide. Not one of the unmarried women had had any schooling while all four of their adult brothers had studied up to class eight or further. The three brothers who are still youngsters are attending school.

The illiteracy rate for Ho men in this sample is much lower than the general rate of illiteracy for Ho men as given in the 1971 Census (Census of India 1971). This may in part be due to the presence of good mission schools in a nearby town. However, in my sample, Christian men are not more literate or better educated than non-Christian Ho men nor do they have better jobs than the latter. Nevertheless, Ho men in Karonja seem to have obtained a somewhat higher level of education and relatively better employment than Ho men in the rest of Bihar. This factor should be kept in mind while reading these descriptions and analyses of men's education and employment. However, the illiteracy rate of Ho women in my sample is not substantially different from the general illiteracy rate among Ho women in all of Bihar according to the

1971 Census. Whatever the factors are that have helped Hos to achieve more education in this village, they seem to have favoured men while not affecting women much.

The gap between male and female literacy levels is likely to grow in the coming decades if the present trend continues. It is similar to the all-India pattern which shows that in 1981 approximately two out of three illiterates were women. According to the 1971 Census, 94 per cent of those Ho tribals who have studied up to matriculate level or above are men, and only six per cent are women. Ho women seem to have somewhat less access to education than women of other tribes in Bihar. Tribal women are recorded as 10 per cent of all tribal matriculates in Bihar. The 1971 Census records only five Ho women graduates or above in all of Bihar. The total number of male graduates or above was 184.

Among most Hindu peasant groups, women's unequal access to education is related to the culture of *purdah* and imposition of heavy restrictions on women's mobility. Amongst Hos, these factors do not exist. Yet, after a certain age, there are restraints on male–female intermixing. Since most of the village schools are mixed, parents do hesitate to send their daughters to school after a certain age.

But there are important economic reasons for not sending girls to school. Since young boys are not expected to contribute to household labour in any substantial way, their schooling has a better chance of continuing uninterrupted for a relatively longer period. Little girls are expected to begin taking on major household responsibilities from a very early age. Many of them begin doing regular wage labour by the time they are 12 years old. So valuable is their labour for the survival of the family that very few families are able to send daughters to school. Thus, while very few girls manage to study beyond class two or three, boys have a somewhat better chance of continuing their education if they are interested in it.

Among most communities in India where female education has made some progress in the last century, the major incentive for the education of women has been the demand for educated wives by men who have taken to higher education and entered the professions or upper echelons of the business community. While a number of Ho men study up to intermediate level, very few go beyond and even fewer find a place in middle class professions and almost none in business. The number of such men is not substantial enough to create a widespread demand for educated wives. Therefore, among the Hos, education for women has not yet become an important qualification in the marriage market.

Another possible reason for such a high level of illiteracy amongst Ho women could be that an urban-based, middle class population has not yet emerged amongst Hos. It is from this group that women are recruited for white-collar jobs which become an incentive for families to educate women. Even when Ho men migrate to towns and get jobs there, they prefer to leave their wives to work the land in the village. There is, therefore, a strong feeling amongst Hos that education will make women unfit for and resistant to the hard work on the land that is expected of them. Unless young girls are trained from an early age to work even harder than farm animals, they will not develop the requisite stamina. If they are allowed education, some of them might begin to think of other options and be less inclined to pour all their energy into agricultural work, as they are compelled to do for survival when left uneducated and unequipped for any other job.

Sometimes, even when a family wants to educate a daughter, the pressure of powerful men in the village acts against it. Maki Bui reported that she was forced to withdraw her only child, a girl, from school after she had studied up to class seven, because some village men threatened to 'spoil' her. Such threats work easily against poorer or vulnerable families, especially those with no adult sons. Currently, three girls from Karonja are studying at the nearest high school and nobody dares threaten their families who are relatively better-off and powerful. However, even when such families educate daughters, it is almost never with a view to improving their employment chances. A Ho woman is rarely educated beyond intermediate or higher secondary level. Only 157 Ho women were matriculates or above in all of Bihar according to the 1971 Census (Census of India 1971).

The few better-off families who educate their daughters are beginning to impose restrictions on women which are alien to Ho culture. Savita Sinku, one of the very few Ho women to be educated up to B.A., is from a relatively well-off family. She told me that her family does not allow her to go out of the house alone, even to the market. Her family lives in a small town where her father has a government job. Even when she goes to her village, she is not allowed to go to the forest like other village women or to visit her relatives in Ranchi by herself. The government hostel for tribal girls at Chaibasa where she was living when I met her, represents the new restrictive culture that Ho society is being pressured to adopt. Girl students are allowed out of the hostel only twice a month for a couple of hours on every alternate Sunday. Even then, they have to go together in groups of five or six. Thus, the process of interaction with the supposedly more advanced outside world with its repressive morality has pushed Ho women backward and, in many ways, has had the effect of reducing their ability to cope, instead of enhancing it.

The labour of Ho women plays a pivotal role in the village economy while men's labour is, by and large, peripheral. But when Ho men and women move to the outside world, the situation is reversed. Women get the lowest paid and the most peripheral kinds of employment while men, because of their relatively higher literacy and education levels, move into relatively better paying jobs, including a few white-collar jobs.

When tribals migrate to urban areas, they operate in a situation of general discrimination against them as tribals. Although the government describes industrialization of Singhbhum as development of a tribal belt for the benefit of tribals, various studies have shown that tribals are, in fact, not the primary beneficiaries of the new employment opportunities created by the industrialization of the region. They are, by and large, confined to the lower rung, lower paid jobs, most of the better jobs being cornered by north Biharis and non-tribal migrants from other parts of north India.

But, though Ho men are at a disadvantage vis-à-vis men of other more powerful communities, they fare far better than the women of their own community. Since the government's reservation policy for Scheduled Tribes does not include a sex-based reservation component, men corner almost all of the regular and permanent jobs which fall within the quota for Scheduled Tribes. The gap between male and female employment opportunities is reflected clearly in our sample. Among the husbands of the 22 married women interviewed, half of the total had jobs in the organized sector. The nature of the jobs held by them is also revealing. Three were employed in the army. Later on, one of them joined the police and another worked as a security guard. The other men have held jobs as school teachers, worker in malaria eradication department, worker in a government co-operative, supervisor of contract labour at Tatanagar, permanent worker in the Gua mines, clerk in the forest department, and so on. Only two of the men who work in the organized sector have jobs as casual labourers. They work for the forest department. Undoubtedly, all these jobs are considered low level jobs in the hierarchy of the organized sector, yet they are evidence of an element of upward mobility for the men.

Of the men in the unorganized sector, one repaired houses, another ran a ration shop and a third worked as a driver of a lorry in Kolkata. One had migrated to Assam and another to Kolkata for employment. Only six of the men were supposed to be assisting their wives with work on the land. Their attitude ranged from giving seasonal help to total indifference.

On the other hand, not one of the women interviewed had a job in the organized sector. The 1975 figures show that only 9,597 women were employed in the factories of Singhbhum district, that is, only a pitifully small number of women had jobs with some minimum protection of labour laws. Only 153 claims for maternity benefits are recorded for the entire year 1975 throughout Singhbhum (*Bihar Statistical Handbook* 1978, p. 251). Needless to say, only a tiny fraction of this pitifully inadequate employment would have been available to Ho women.

Women's interests are grievously neglected in the few jobs available, including those created by government. For instance, in 1984–85, 600 jobs were created in an afforestation programme in the Karonja area. The wage was Rs 10 a day. Not one woman was employed in the programme. It was not for lack of time or inclination on women's part that they were excluded. During this same period, I visited Karonja and saw the eagerness with which women flocked to a private worksite near the village where a big well was being dug. The monsoon was round the corner and the well had to be completed fast, otherwise it would cave in. Therefore, work was going on in three shifts. Most of the women were working two shifts at a stretch, that is, 16 hours a day, and seemed cheerful because this wage work was available to them.

But very little such wage work is available in the village on any continuing basis. Wage work is available in the villages mainly at sowing and harvesting times. In these seasons, a woman may find work at the rate of Rs 3 a day in the fields of a family which has a deficit of adult females to manage the work. This wage rate was prevalent in 1982–83. Often, the family that hires the woman is as poor as she is, and, therefore, no one can demand or get the government fixed minimum wage.

In the town too, women, unlike men, can never hope to get a job other than one which involves heavy manual work. Very few occupations are open to Ho women in the outside world. They can work as headloaders or stone-breakers on construction sites, at brick kilns, stone quarries, mines, railways or dams. These are casual daily wage jobs and some of them are available only during certain seasons. Women constitute the lowest rung of employment even in these fields, and cannot hope to move into better paid, skilled or physically less strenuous jobs. None of the jobs that women get provide them with any modicum of security or with benefits like provident fund, gratuity, pension, medical care or paid leave. Very few families educate their daughters up to the level necessary for getting such jobs, but, even if they did, the women are likely to be discriminated against by employers.

Patterns of Migration

Broadly, there are two categories of men who migrate in search of employment opportunities:

1. Uneducated men of poor families who migrate, either alone or with their wives, because their land in the village does not yield enough food for year-round consumption or because they are victims of land alienation. Such men usually end up in low paid occupations with harsh working

conditions, for example, as unskilled labourers in mines, quarries, brick kilns, or as agricultural labourers in surplus producing regions.

2. Men with some education, who move out of the village to improve their prospects by getting a permanent job in a government or private enterprise which ensures them regular, year-round cash income and other benefits. There is great hunger for these jobs. Men of this category are likely to be from somewhat better-off families and can afford to wait around in the village until a satisfactory job comes their way. During this period, their wife's or sister's labour on the land usually provides for their needs.

Since the kind of job one gets in the outside world often depends on one's bargaining position, that is, one's ability to wait for a good offer, men who migrate in distress situations usually fare much worse in the employment market than those who can afford to look around for a suitable job. Jasmani's husband, educated up to class eight, worked for a couple of years as a casual labourer in Rourkela. After he returned to the village, he has done virtually nothing. He says he is waiting for a job. Two of the other women interviewed have sons who are matriculates but do no work. These women continue to do wage work to feed the family. Thus, women's labour enables men to acquire upward mobility which does not necessarily extend to the women concerned.

By and large, women migrate only in distress situations, such as crop failure, or if they are thrown out of the marital home, unlike men, who often migrate to better their prospects. In the months after harvest, when very little wage work is available in the villages, a number of women go to nearby towns such as Rourkela, Tatanagar or Kolkata in search of seasonal employment.

This option is usually taken only if no other employment is available within walking distance of the village. Women tend to prefer work in and around the village, even at lower wage rates, to the work available in cities.

Despite the great lure of urban employment for men, those men who have substantial amounts of land and some source of cash income in the village prefer not to go and work outside. Ho men are not used to being ordered around or to doing hard work on a sustained basis. In the village, they work during certain seasons and the rest of the year only as and when they please. Those who can afford to avoid it would rather not be subjected to the discipline of a regular job.

Suru's husband, who is from one of the most powerful families in the village and has a regular cash income, has never tried to get a job outside the village, even though he is a matriculate. Often, men who migrate for a job come back in a few days, having thrown up the job because they could not get used to working fixed hours and obeying orders. At least five women reported that their husbands had either left or disrupted a fairly well paid job. Sukmaru's husband had a job in the malaria eradication department. She says he went 'mad' and lost the job. He did not like working so he roamed around for about 10 years. Now he earns about Rs 5 a day making *bidis*.

Women who migrate for work usually end up working under far more exploitative conditions but seldom complain on return. Whenever we asked a woman: 'How was *paiti desham* (land of work)?', she invariably said that she found it very good. This, despite the fact that few of them received the statutory minimum wage. A woman who has been out working for six months may come back with no more than Rs 50 as savings given to her by her employer just before she left the worksite, while she got no more than Rs 20 to 25 a week for her rations during her stay, in return for about nine to ten hours of work a day.

This marked contrast in male and female reactions to work outside is related to their respective lives and work patterns at home. Women have to work so hard and so constantly at home that working fixed hours at a worksite seems easier in some ways. However bad the working conditions, they do not have to walk long distances to fetch basic necessities such as water and fuel as they have to in villages. In contrast, men find life at home easier.

Only seven of the 22 married women had migrated for seasonal employment. They had gone to the usual places—Rourkela, Jamshedpur, Kolkata and Patna. But most of the women interviewed clearly said that they prefer to live in the village and do not like to migrate for work. There are several reasons for this. Some of the women fall sick when they migrate. In comparison to the clean homes and villages of the Hos, living conditions are extremely unhygienic at city worksites. More important is the fact that seasonal migration as daily wage labour cannot provide any security for old age to women, as jobs with pensions and provident funds can for men. Hence, women desperately cling to their usufructuary right in the family, which alone has the potential to provide some measure of security in old age and sickness. Prolonged absence from the village could lead to the loss of woman's precarious rights in the land.

Further, at almost all the city worksites where tribal women find seasonal employment, various forms of sexual exploitation are rampant. Many are compelled into sexual relations with contractors and supervisors, and are vulnerable to unwelcome advances from fellow workers. It is not uncommon for an unmarried woman to return from a worksite pregnant or with a child. Such a woman is subject to social ostracism in the village and loses her usufructuary right in her father's land. Sometimes, a young woman who gets pregnant in this fashion will stay away for years, and return to the village only if the child dies.

Women's migration follows certain routine patterns. While a man may migrate on his own when he gets a government or other comparable job, women who go in search of seasonal employment always migrate in groups to areas where some of them have been before or where they know that some people of their community are already employed. Labour contractors also recruit women through village women who act as sub-contractors. Thus, even when women move far away from the village, the watchful eyes of their community members are on them and it is difficult to cover up any indiscretion such as an alliance with a non-tribal man, especially if it leads to pregnancy.

Women whose families have enough grain for year-round consumption and are considered to have high status in the village are averse to migrating, unless pushed by personal circumstances such as a serious conflict over their usufructuary rights. Of all the women in the sample, Moni expressed the strongest aversion to moving out of the village. At present, her family has both land and status. She is the only able-bodied woman worker in the family and is not in danger of being denied her usufructuary right. Her father has a small cash income and her unmarried brother is dependent on her labour. There is thus no incentive for her to leave the village.

Although Ho women would rather stay in the village and work on the land, they are exceptionally independent when they do migrate. Since the family structure is not as rigidly hierarchical as among non-tribal peasant groups, women are not dependent on the permission of the male head of the family to move around. Unmarried women are even freer in this regard. When an unmarried woman decides to migrate, she does not necessarily seek the approval or permission of male members of the family. Though the reason for a woman to migrate is usually economic hardship faced by the family as a whole, the decision is often the woman's own. She may suddenly hear of a group of women being recruited at the marketplace and may decide to join, then and there. She would send a message home that she is migrating to a particular place. But it is not uncommon for men to push women of their families to go in for seasonal migration, while they themselves hang around the village. A young woman may also decide on seasonal migration, following a quarrel in the family or, occasionally, even from a desire to see the city and earn some cash. Occasionally, the father or brother of a young woman may go and try to fetch her back, if her labour is needed at home or if they fear she may return pregnant. But, by and large, unmarried women take and execute their decisions with a kind of independence that is extremely rare among women in non-tribal peasant groups.

A married woman, especially if she has children, cannot migrate as easily. She would need to obtain her husband's consent because, if he got angry, he could use this as a pretext to get another wife and throw her off the land. A married woman cannot risk migrating after a quarrel unless she is willing to risk a total break with her husband and her right in his land. In my sample, only one woman reported having migrated in search of employment against her husband's wishes. This was Sukmaru who had never migrated before her marriage because there was enough to eat in her parental home. After marriage and the birth of her three children, she went to Assam and Kolkata at different times because there was no money in the house for basic needs. Her husband opposed her going but she went with a group from the village, risking his displeasure.

Considering the relatively greater mobility of Ho women, particularly unmarried women, in conjunction with their relatively greater freedom of choice in marriage, there seems to be reason to believe that if they had more access to educational and employment opportunities, they would be able to take advantage of them with relatively greater ease, since they suffer from fewer familial and cultural restraints than do women of non-tribal peasant groups.

Decision-making Patterns

The precariousness of women's rights in land helps make them peripheral to the political power structures in the village. Land ownership is the basis of political power in Ho villages as in most peasant societies. The families that have relatively more power and influence in the village are invariably those who have acquired more land than others. Such families usually also dominate the political structures such as the panchayats.

It is likely that even before the Hos got peasantized, and land ownership became vested in the hands of individual men, women were kept out of the political decision making processes. When Hos practised shifting cultivation combined with hunting, the clans or *killis* operated as groups trying to exercise control over particular territories. Since warfare and hunting were mainly male monopolies, clear leaders would have been men and control over territory would have been collectively exercised by men. This would have created the basis for making women peripheral to political decision-making. The imposition of patriarchal property following the settlement operations carried on by the British after 1837 further consolidated this pattern.

The disinheritance process was carried on step-by-step, not as a wilful conspiracy. It occurred as a result of colonial rulers imposing certain institutional forms and structures resembling those of their own society. It took decades for women's rights to become as marginalized as they finally did. C.H. Bompas, Deputy Commissioner of Singhbhum, observed in 1897:

> The rights of the unmarried daughters are also uncertain. If they equal the sons in number, each son may take one to support, but if they all live with one brother, he will get extra land for their support, and then

> the question arises whether he is entitled to retain this after their death. I hope to find time to draw up a definite set of rules on these and other points and get the mankis to agree to them. At present, the panchayat decides each case on its merits, and when disputes arise the courts often have no fixed rules to guide them (*Bihar Statistical Handbook* 1978, p. 251).

It is clear from this that the courts were directionless because they were setting new precedents on the matter, many of them against the grain of tribal traditions in landholding. The language of the Settlement Report tries to hide the fact that many of the rules were being freshly created by the British, borrowing from their own culture as well as from the practices of certain Hindu communities. The process seems to have been similar to what the British did to the vast variety of practices prevailing among Hindu communities when they rigidified them in favour of men in the process of codifying the Hindu law.

Not much is known of the political organization of Ho society before the British came to this area. But from the writings of British administrators it appears that it was not a very stratified society and no definite ruling class had emerged. The *mankis* and *mundas* were supposed to be the traditional heads of villages but even they did not exactly constitute a ruling elite. Regarding the tribal *mankis*, the Kolhan Settlement Report of 1919 says: 'In the Kolhan it appears that before the British occupation of the country there were headmen only in those parts which were under some control from the neighbouring chiefs and which paid rent or taxes for each village' (Majudmar 1950, p. 13). Lieutenant Tickell, assistant political agent, Singhbhum, in a letter dated 1 February 1842, to the governor general's agent, on the subject of assessing the Kolhan, writes:

> These border tracts had their chiefs or mankis who were elected on paying a *salami* for the distinction by the zamindars and who used to present the amount of tax required. But in the interior, the Kolhan from the first presented, and indeed does in measure still present, the anomaly of a people living together without an acknowledged head or ruler of any kind whatsoever (quoted in Majudmar 1950, p. 13).

The British pretended that they would leave intact the internal organization of the villages even while they superimposed their rule in the area. However, since the traditional structure was expected to become a willing tool in the hands of British administrators, it slowly evolved into a mere arm of the empire at the village level:

> the old village system of the Hos was maintained by the recognition of the *mundas* or the village headmen and of the *mankis* or the headmen

> for groups of villages... The rent was collected by the *mundas* and paid by them either direct or through the *mankis*. The *mundas* and *mankis* were allowed to keep a commission of l/6th or l/8th as their wages (Chaudhury 1958, pp. 356–57).

The practice of allowing the *mundas* and *mankis* a commission led to their developing a vested interest not only in collecting as thoroughly as possible but also in enhancing the revenue. A family which defaulted in payment forfeited its land, which then came under the jurisdiction of the *munda*, who was considered by government as the person responsible for the proper conduct of the village. He thus developed an interest in keeping certain families in such a state of poverty and dependence that they would sooner or later be forced to surrender their land. The *mankis* and *mundas* were entitled to settle the village wastelands and forests on resident *raiyats* and fix a rent for them, on which they got a commission. These powers could be grossly misused because the *mankis* and *mundas* were no longer accountable to the community. The 1898 Settlement Report states:

> the *mankis* and *mundas* have abused their power in many instances; by appropriating the lands of tenants; by evicting defaulting tenants from their holdings... by settling the holdings of defaulters with foreigners, ignoring the claims of the resident Ho tenants to the vacant jotes.[5]

The *manki* was liable to fine and dismissal only by the Deputy Commissioner and that too for disobedience of his orders or for breach of the terms of his *patta* (Chaudhury 1958, pp. 363–64). The British said a man chosen for the post of *manki* was to be one 'who exercises greatest degree of local influence' (Singhbhum Old Records 1958, p. 33). But the *pattas* the *mankis* were made to sign made them into stooges of the government machinery and destroyed their role as community leaders. Majumdar quotes from one of these *pattas* signed in 1828:

> If the revenue of your *Ilaka* is not paid in proper time you will be held responsible for it and it will be realised from you. You will work with heart and soul and render help.... You will carry out all orders. You will receive a separate *patta* that you will get one tenth of the total revenue of your *Ilaka*. If you show negligence in the discharge of your duties this *sanad* will be taken away from you and given to another man (Majumdar 1950, pp. 13–14).

---

[5] 'Final Report on the Kolhan Government Estate', District Singhbhum, 1898, Part II, Chapter 1, para 182.

Another patta states the further implications of their role:

> You are to assist in person and with your followers in apprehending all offenders against the authority of government... and in the suppression of insurrections in every part of the jurisdiction of the assistant governor general's agent or other authority... in which your services may be called for (Singhbhum Old Records 1958).

The *mankis* and *mundas* were entrusted with police functions such as reporting crime and getting people arrested. Armed with arbitrary and repressive powers, they emerged as a new rural elite owing allegiance to the oppressive government outside.

In most other areas of India, when the British took over from the existing ruling elite, they also inherited the state machinery. But as this area had no previous history of being firmly under any ruling elite, it had no need for an elaborate state machinery. As we follow step by step the process of the setting up and consolidation of the institutions of the state under the British, it becomes clear that it comes into existence not to protect and benefit the people, but to drain wealth from their land and exploit their labour.

The key assumption behind the new state machinery is that the state has ultimate and total sovereignty. The rulers are able to determine according to their own interests what provisional rights people should have. In return, the state can arbitrarily demand whatever it chooses from those over whom it rules. It can arbitrarily impose and enhance land revenue or decide to lease out someone's agricultural land with no concern for the people who are treated as mere tenants of the state. The revenue imposed was raised every now and then, not just to extract more surplus but to drive home the point that the state had ultimate sovereignty. The governor general's agent justified it thus in 1851: 'it is expedient the Coles should continue to feel that the authorities have unrestricted control in such matters' (Ricketts 1853, p. 67).

Post-Independence Developments

The political institutions superimposed upon the Ho society have after national Independence carried even further the process of consolidating male control, encouraging internal stratification and reinforcing arbitrary powers of the state machinery.

The functions of *mankis* and *mundas* were traditionally partly hereditary, but also involved an element of community consensus. In 1947, the government appointed a committee, on whose recommendation it decreed that 'the posts of *manki*s and *munda*s should be made elective and that their educational qualifications should be insisted upon as far as possible' (Chaudhury 1958).

Today, the traditional panchayat system, much altered and stunted, operates parallel to government-sponsored political structures, such as the elected panchayat headed by a sarpanch which also exists in non-tribal villages. The traditional *munda*s and *manki*s do not have the powers they once enjoyed unless they also latch on to the government-sponsored political institutions.

Members of the panchayat, the *sarpanch* (head of this panchayat) and the *mukhia* (traditional headman) are all supposed to be elected by the adult villagers. But people in Karonja do not remember elections for members of the panchayat ever having taken place in their village or in nearby villages. The only elections which take place are those for the *sarpanch* and *mukhia*. Once these men are elected, they choose a set of their cronies who function as the panchayat. Although both men and women vote in the election of the *sarpanch* and the *mukhia*, no woman has ever stood for either post in Karonja. The situation is not likely to be very different in other villages.

Since these elections are held at the behest of, and conducted by, the government, the *mukhia* and *sarpanch* hold themselves accountable to government officials above them and owe practically no accountability to their fellow villagers. Power is bestowed on them by the government rather than the people, even though it is ostensibly based on elections by the people. But the institutions they represent and the functions they perform are not of the people's making.

The *mukhia* is supposed to act as intermediary between the village and the government administration at the block level. He is in charge of getting government programmes implemented at the village level. This involves handling substantial amounts of money. The functions of the *sarpanch* include keeping in touch with the local police and reporting anything unusual that happens in the village. The household of the *mukhia* is usually identifiable by the large number of goats and fowls it possesses. He is supposed to distribute these to poorer families in the village but usually appropriate them for himself.

In Karonja, a meeting of the village panchayat is a meeting of the *mukhia*, the *sarpanch* and a few of their friends and relatives. At these meetings, they work out matters of common concern to villages, such as getting funds to repair a well or build a road. But it usually ends up as a lobby of powerful men who try to grab whatever resources they can for their own benefit. This pattern extends outside the village. Each cluster of a dozen or so villages is supposed to have a joint panchayat which, in practice, consists of the *mukhia* and their close friends.

The government-sponsored panchayats do not arbitrate disputes between families. Such arbitration is handled by the traditional decision-making structures which are, in some respects, nearly extinct today. Whenever two or more individuals or families are involved in a dispute, they first try to resolve it by calling a meeting at which both sides ask people they trust to be present as arbitrators. The *mukhia* or *sarpanch* is usually also present. Both sides present their case and the arbitrators are supposed to work out a mutually acceptable solution. In most cases, the relative power or powerlessness of the parties concerned is likely to decide the outcome of this arbitration process. A powerful family is likely to have the support of other powerful families of their *killi* and hence would tend to bulldoze others into accepting disadvantageous deals. If one party does not feel satisfied, they may resort to court action, provided they have the resources to do so.

Women are completely excluded even from the village-level arbitration machinery. They are not supposed to attend such meetings unless a woman is party to a dispute or is required as a witness. If a widow like Maki Bui seeks the intervention of the arbitration machinery, she will, in all likelihood, be the only woman present amongst several men, so that an anti-women bias is built into the system and women seldom manage to get a fair deal from it. Women-headed families are less likely to be powerful because in a Ho village, as in most villages, apart from the amount of land owned, the ability to wreak violence is an important component of the power of a family. This ability is largely determined by the number of able-bodied adult males a family has.

Another important factor that determines the amount of political influence exercised by a family is the amount of steady cash income that flows into it. Since the better paying and regular income yielding jobs are only accessible to some men and not at all accessible to women, families with earning male members tend to acquire more influence in village affairs. Their cash income, apart from giving them prestige, enables them to buy the favour of the local police and administration. They are in a better position to extend patronage to other villagers who feel beholden to them and dare not oppose them. Most *mankis* and *mundas* belong to such families, which are also the ones involved in landgrabbing, whereas the families from whom land is grabbed are usually those which have only very old men or infant males, or consist of widows or single women.

A poor woman who is in conflict with men of a better-off family may try to get her brothers or other male kin to be present at the meeting on her behalf, but in her marital village, people are unlikely to support her against her husband and or his male agnates. A woman's ability to mobilize support for herself is further hampered by the institution of the patrilocal family. By virtue of having shifted from her own village to that of her husband's, she is effectively isolated.

In Conclusion

The British gave strong encouragement to the myth that tribals would benefit by being brought into contact with the outside world under the benevolent authority of the Raj. This myth is even more passionately supported by the inheritors of the Raj. The Indian government uses the rhetoric of national development. However, most attempts at tribal development have essentially meant furthering their subjectation and pushing tribal society into a completely male-dominated, hierarchical mould. Many of the disabilities from which Ho women suffer are not a consequence of their traditional customs, as is often claimed. On the contrary, their traditional strengths are being eroded and new strengths have not been allowed to emerge. Ho women's present plight is due to a combination of the following factors:

- British land settlement operations created a new system of peasant proprietorship with increasingly partilineal forms of inheritance that destroyed the tradition of land being held collectively by the clan.
- Tribal areas were opened to exploiting outsiders such as mining and industrial companies and Hindu peasant groups, with greater resources and know-how. This led to increasing land alienation. The resultant scarcity of land changed the power balance between Ho men and women. It allowed the Ho men, who control the land, to subjugate the women, who provide almost all the labour, in ways never before possible.
- External political structures, owing to their allegiance to exploitative, hierarchical government machinery with a virulent bias against women, fostered a far less egalitarian and far more repressive social structure, with women at the very bottom of the pyramid.
- The Hos are forced to practise non-viable subsistence agriculture. The destruction of the fertility of the land and the lack of irrigation and other agricultural resources make it impossible for Ho women to feed themselves and their children adequately.
- Discriminatory marriage customs such as polygamy and easy discarding of wives has led to an acceleration in the pace of the disinheritance of women from rights in the land.
- Ho men's tightening control over the land and other income generating economic assets permits ever increasing exploitation of Ho women despite women's far greater contribution to the family's livelihood through never-ending drudgery.
- Ho women are denied access to formal education and secure employment in the organized sector–the few opportunities that are now available to tribals are a male monopoly.

- The lack of viable alternatives for women to enable them to earn a living in the outside world makes them very vulnerable to economic and sexual exploitation whenever they are compelled to migrate from their villages in times of scarcity and distress.
- The government's forest laws make previously available forest produce such as fuel and fodder more and more inaccessible, making women's lives much harder.
- The exclusion of women from all meaningful decision-making, especially within the village or kinship panchayat, as well as at the district- and state-level bodies, ensures that women are not able to offer organized resistance when they are discriminated against.
- The male monopoly over organized violence, due in part to their traditional involvement in hunting and warfare, has been strengthened because the institutions of state violence, such as the police, are in favour of male control in case of any conflict of interest between Ho men and women. Women can hardly ever hope to get support and protection against violence from the police, the courts, or any other part of the government.
- The central and state governments' pretensions of fostering tribal welfare and 'development' actually help strengthen the stranglehold that outsiders maintain on most of the wealth of this rich region. From the Tatas to the local policeman, they extract everything possible, but provide little or nothing in return.
- The influence of the anti-women, rigidly hierarchical culture of dominant non-tribal groups in surrounding areas has encouraged Ho men to reject much of their relatively egalitarian tribal culture.

What Needs to be Done

So far, most of the pitifully few efforts to provide help to tribal women have focused on the terrible conditions under which tribal women and men have been exploited as migrant labourers. There have been numerous campaigns for the release of bonded labourers and for improving their working conditions in mines, brick kilns and other worksites. While this is important, the key to improving the situation of tribals is first to stop and then to reverse the forced or fradulent alienation of tribal lands. Without this necessary first step, all of the tribal development schemes are meaningless deceptions.

Even if some land were to remain in tribal hands, it would not necessarily benefit women unless they obtain secure and independent rights in the land. Without that as a base, they cannot negotiate a better deal for themselves in the family, the village and the outside world.

In addition to bettering Ho women's lot, measures to secure their rights will also assist in halting the process of alienation of tribal land. Ho women are the primary cultivators of the land. They are less inclined to mortgage or sell the land and move to the cities. The disinheritance of women is culturally determined rather than due to any inability to cultivate the land.

Giving women rights in the land will not undermine tribal culture, as is often argued. On the contrary, giving women secure and equal rights in land will help halt the ongoing disintegration of the tribal culture and society, because they are the ones who have the greatest stake in the survival of their culture and society.

The underlying principle behind much of the land reform legislation in India was that the land should be owned by those who actually cultivate it. Unfortunately, the principle has never been extended to women. If it were, Ho women would have a case for more than equal inheritance rights, since they are the primary cultivators in their society. Even if we do not take the principle of 'land to cultivator' to this logical conclusion, there seems absolutely no justification for denying Ho women equal land rights. To this end, the Chota Nagpur Tenancy Act needs to be amended to enable women to become full inheritors. But mere amendment of the Act will not be enough. It is equally important that the government rapidly moves to take the responsibility for entering women's names in the record of land rights, and to give women *pattas* to confirm their ownership.

In order to ensure that non-tribals do not come and grab tribal lands through fake marriages and other fraudulent deals, we need to ensure that the present provisions incorporated in the Chota Nagpur Tenancy Act to prevent the alienation of tribal lands are further strengthened. When a tribal man or women marries a non-tribal, the latter should not have the right to inherit tribal land after the spouse's death.

Right now, the government has vast arbitrary powers that allow the sale or takeover of any amount of tribal land. This power has been grossly misused and needs to be curbed drastically.

With women's land rights as the starting point, certain additional measures are required to strengthen their position. The transition from below-subsistence level agriculture to self-sustaining agriculture needs to take place speedily. These women require adequate credit to enable them to obtain irrigation facilities, better varieties of seeds, farm animals and other agricultural input.

No less urgently required is the reversal of the tide of decades of cultural imperialism so as to enable Ho society to retain the more egalitarian and humane aspects of its traditional culture. It is unfortunate that Hos are emulating the deadly anti-women biases which have devastating effects on the lives of most non-tribal women. It is absolutely vital that we do not view tribal society and women's situation in it merely to offer them suggestions for improvement from our supposedly superior vantage point. There are many things we could usefully learn from Ho women, such as their spirit of independence, their ability to get around by themselves, and their refusal to accept the ideology of subservience including the widely prevalent practice of treating men with godlike deference.

References

Bihar Statistical Handbook. 1978. Directorate of Statistics and Evaluation, Government of Bihar.

Chaudhury, P.C. Roy. 1958. *Bihar District Gazetteers, Singhbhum*. Patna: Gazetteer Revision Section, Revenue Department, Bihar.

Census of India. 1971. Series 1, Part V-A (ii). Special Tables for Scheduled Tribes.

Majumdar, D.N. 1950. *The Affairs of a Tribe: A Study in Tribal Dynamics*. Lucknow: Universal Publishers Ltd, pp. 65–66.

Ricketts, H. 1853. *Report on the District of Singhbhum*. Calcutta: Bengal Military Orphan Press.

Singh, C.P. 1978. *The Ho Tribe of Singhbhum*. New Delhi: Classical Publications.

Singhbhum Old Records. 1958. Secretariat Press, Bihar, Patna.

14

Inheritance Rights for Women

*A Response to Some Commonly Expressed Fears**

In 1956, in the course of the parliamentary debate on the Hindu Succession Bill, Ammu Swaminadhan, Member of Parliament (MP), arguing in favour of the Hindu Succession Bill providing of equal inheritance rights for women, said:

> I would ask the hon. Members to turn to Kerala.... If you will only see what is happening and what has happened there all these years when women have had equal rights, I am sure that you will agree that... nothing terrible will happen in this country if they had equal rights.

Yet, many today continue to fear that terrible things will happen if women actually (not just on paper) get an equal share in inheritance. The arguments

*This article, co-authored with Ruth Vanita, appeared in *Manushi*, No. 57, March–April 1990.

put forward against daughters inheriting parental property equally with sons are the same arguments that were put forward over 50 years ago, when the Hindu Succession Bill was first mooted. The Bill, when it finally became law, gave women very unequal rights and even those remained largely on paper. Hence, today, we still need to work for actually getting women equal inheritance rights, as the majority of women in our country, even those of wealthy families, do not own income generating property independently in their own right and are disinherited by their fathers for no reason other than their gender.

We shall here attempt to deal with some of the fears commonly expressed regarding women's inheritance rights.

Land Fragmentation

In India, the chief form of income generating property is agricultural land. The Hindu Succession Act, by denying women equal rights in ancestral property, effectively denies them a share in most agricultural land. In addition, the various state governments have resorted to a number of legal stratagems to further obstruct women's ownership of land.

That giving a share in family land to daughters will result in excessive fragmentation, making each holding uneconomical, is a favourite and longstanding argument for denying women a share in this form of property. However, no one argues that giving a share to all the sons will also result in fragmentation. It would be more logical to argue for primogeniture (the eldest child, most frequently, the eldest son, alone inheriting).

Denying women their rights is no answer to the problem of fragmentation, as is evident from the persistence of the problem today, despite such denial. The cause of fragmentation is overpressure on land. A disproportionately large ratio of the Indian population is compelled to depend on land for subsistence. This is a sign of an unbalanced economy. Neglect of agriculture and of rural areas, and draining of agricultural surplus for the benefit of the elite in the urban population, has increased the misery of the land-dependent peasantry.

A part of the answer to this problem lies in making agriculture more viable and providing larger sections of the rural poor population with alternative sources of income generation. Denying women a share in land means making them the most powerless section within the already powerless poor peasantry. Certainly, if a piece of land can be divided between three sons, there is no reason why it cannot be divided between two sons and a daughter.

All of the arguments usually adduced against daughters' inheritance rights, especially in agricultural land, were raised in the Parliamentary debate on the Act. Some members defending the Act cogently countered these arguments, for example, Shri Venkataraman (Tanjore) argued '... it is urged that we must exclude agricultural lands. Most property in India is agricultural land. It is another way of refusing inheritance to women. If we say so, that would be more honest.... Instead of that, you may say that you allow them to inherit water, air, and some natural resources!'

Shri B.C. Das from Ganjam South also spoke in the same vein from the experience of his home state where women enjoyed property rights.

> The law which is enacted to stop fragmentation of land should apply to sons as well as daughters.... If you say that it will apply only in the case of daughters, that is not right. It is axiomatic that those who are economically independent are really independent.... If the wife comes to the husband's house as the heir of some property she can claim some respect from the husband. She is an economic entity and she is entitled to claim some respect. That is the reason why the daughter should inherit the property of the father.

The Daughter Goes Away

Another favourite argument is that since the daughter marries and goes to her husband's house, which is often far away, she cannot cultivate her parental land, live in her parental house or run her parental business, so these properties should be inherited by her brothers. A subsidiary argument frequently put forward is that since the woman becomes a member of her husband's family, she should be restricted to inheriting a share of his parental property.

This argument assumes that marriage and going away from the parental home and village are as inevitable as water flowing from a higher to a lower level. But this is not the case. In our own country, many different communities have widely different arrangements. In some tribal communities, where women do most of the land cultivation and where singleness is not despised, a number of women choose to stay single and to remain with their parents, cultivating the land. In several other communities which are matrilineal, married women continue to live in their parental home where their husbands either join them (without being despised as *ghar jamais*, as in the north) or visit them.

In many more communities, women are married within the same village or into neighbouring villages. This is the case both in communities where cross-cousin marriage is practised and in some others. Yet, women do not inherit land in these communities and such is the power of ideology that the same argument of women going away continues to be used to deny them equal inheritance rights.

The injustice of this denial of rights to women is particularly apparent in tribal communities since women do about 80 per cent of the agricultural and related work, including gathering forest produce, marketing and cultivation. They are the mainstays of the family and the economy. Yet, they have no independent foothold on either the father's or the husband's land, and this makes them vulnerable to abuse and violence, including such violence as witch-hunting which is often used by men to get rid of a single woman or widow whom they perceive as obstructing their rights to the land. In most parts of the country, what is known as the customary law of tribal people (who form 7 per cent of India's population and who belong to different religions, some being animists and ancestor worshippers) is very close to Hindu uncodified law. Property, which is now mainly land since most tribals have settled down as cultivators, passes from father to sons in the male line. There are matrilineal tribes in the north-east, however. In the patrilineal tribes, women are excluded from inheritance. An unmarried daughter has a right to sustain herself from her father's land. A married daughter, however, loses this right and does not regain it even if divorced or widowed. A widow is supposed to have a right to sustain herself from her husband's land, but if she has no sons, she is usually pushed out by her husband's brothers, nephews and other male kin who are the heirs. If she has adult sons, she may be somewhat better protected. *Manushi* in 1982 filed a petition in the Supreme Court, along with two tribal women from Bihar, challenging the denial of land rights to Ho tribal women of Bihar and, by implication, to other tribal women (see *Manushi*, No. 13, 1982).

When the argument that daughters cannot manage land because they 'go far away' after marriage was used to counter the petition filed by *Manushi* and two tribal women in the Supreme Court to demand equal inheritance rights in land for women, our study of a Ho village in Bihar (see Chapter 13) showed that of a sample of 22 married women interviewed, seven had married in their own village, six lived less than three hours' walk away, eight were more than three hours' walk away. Thus, most of the women were reasonably close to the parental village and land. They routinely cover much longer distances on foot for subsistence activities such as gathering and marketing of forest produce. Yet as soon as they marry these tribal women are denied the right to cultivate parental land.

That this is not a reason but a pretext for disinheriting daughters is clear from the fact that however far sons may go from the parental home, they are almost never disinherited on this account. It is as common for sons to migrate from villages to cities, even go abroad in pursuit of employment and career, but they rarely relinquish their claim on parental property. In fact, this claim acts as a bond, encouraging them to visit during vacations, lease out the land or the orchard, claim its produce, even plan to return to the family home after retirement. The claim acts as an important form of security, financial and emotional, for the son. However far away, he continues to be acknowledged as a family member, who must be consulted before property is sold or altered, while a daughter, even in the next village, is treated as a member of another family.

This crucial difference in status is a key factor in women's overall powerlessness in society. It is idle to imagine that a daughter-in-law can be treated as a full member of her marital family with an equal share in its property, after she has been totally disinherited by her natal family. The powerlessness of the daughter and of the daughter-in-law are two sides of the same coin. A culture which uproots its daughters and in fact sees this uprooting as the pivot of a woman's life, which labels a daughter from birth 'a stranger's wealth', 'a migrant bird', and 'a guest' in her father's house, views its daughters-in-law at best as bringers of wealth, themselves the wealth of their husbands and parents-in-law, but not as independent owners of wealth.

A woman who has full rights in her parents' property will relate to her husband and in-laws from a position of relative strength. She will have more of a chance to be viewed as an entity in her own right, not as a helpless creature whose only chance of survival and identity lies in 'adjusting' to her husband's and in-laws' demands and whims.

Parents who refuse to recognize their own daughter's full membership in their family and equality with their sons, have no reason to expect that her in-laws, to whom she is a complete stranger, will automatically treat her as an equal inheritor with their sons.

Sons Look after Old Parents

This argument runs: since sons, not daughters, support and look after parents in their old age, sons should inherit the parents' property.

First, we should note that the implication that sons inherit property as a compensation or reward for supporting old parents is not correct. Even if parents die young or in early middle age, fully self-supporting sons still inherit and daughters do not. Further, many old parents are 'supported' by sons from the property or family business that the parents have built up. If the daughters inherited, they could as well support their parents. Significant numbers of women now earn an income and could support their parents. Even women who do not have a job contribute crucially to household income by their work in the fields and the home and should have the right to support their old parents.

A second, very important, dimension of the situation is that since 'looking after' old parents is not just a matter of financially supporting them but of serving and nursing them, the actual care is generally provided by the woman, not the man, that is, in our dominant family set-up, by the daughter-in-law, not the son. The daughter-in-law, who is forbidden to care for her own parents, is expected to channel her emotional energy into serving her parents-in-law. Every lapse of hers is noted, more severely than a daughter's lapse would be. Old parents themselves often acknowledge their need for their daughter, but this need is denied and thwarted. This family set-up therefore places strangers in intimate proximity while cutting off from each other those who have been close for years. The resultant frustration, friction and misery, not just for daughters-in-law but also for old parents, are visible in almost every home.

Especially when a very old and ailing mother is in need, she is often treated as having no rights in the property, now perceived as her son's, and is neglected by the daughter-in-law. The present set-up is conducive neither to the welfare of old parents nor of women, whether as daughters or daughters-in-law, but to the welfare of adult sons, who virtually take over parental property in the lifetime of the parents. The culturally unquestioned right of even a misbehaving son over the property of parents he may neglect or maltreat places the old in a powerless situation just as it does women. Indian literature teems with examples of how old parents are sidelined, neglected and allowed no say in matters affecting their own lives and the property they have helped build (see for example, Munshi Premchand's story 'A Mother of Sons' in *Manushi*, No. 42–43).

It will be argued that for married daughters to live with their parents and care for them is 'against our culture'. But this assumes that our culture is a monolith. The taboos on eating in—and even drinking water in—a married daughter's home are restricted to certain communities in certain parts of the country, where discrimination against women is most severe. The prevalence of such taboos exposes the fragile rights of a woman in her husband's house. How can a woman who cannot entertain guests of her choice hope to claim a share in the property of her marital home?

But in many other parts of the country, in most of the south and parts of north-east, for instance, such taboos do not prevail. In some communities where it was formerly customary for married daughters to remain in the parental home, there is still a tendency, even after that custom's demise, for old parents to go and live with their married daughter in her marital home, rather than to live with their son.

If both sons and daughters inherited equally (after parents' death rather than in their lifetime) it would not be as easy for a child simply to take over parental property and then treat parents as a useless burden. It would also mean that parents could choose to live with the child to whom they feel closest and who they think will look after them best. They could even, as some parents do, live with their children by rotation. The decision regarding which child to live with should not be determined arbitrarily by the child's gender, but rather by the parents' and the child's preference, on the basis of their mutual relationship.

Brother–Sister Love will be Destroyed

Another argument often used against giving daughters property is that it will breed animosity, even litigation, between brothers and sisters, destroying the harmonious and beautiful brother–sister relationship.

The flaw in this argument is that it is based on untenable generalizations. Not all brother–sister relationships are beautiful any more than are all brother–brother or sister–sister relationships. Those that are truly so are unlikely to be disrupted merely because the sister gets her due. If the beauty of the relationship is based solely on inequality, on the brother's full endowment and the sister's deprivation, it is a beauty of a questionable kind.

Sisters' one-way dependence on brothers is occasioned by the powerless and insecure position of those sisters. The status of a woman in her in-laws' house is affected by how much concern her brothers demonstrate, how often they invite her and how many gifts they give her. These visible demonstrations of concern serve to remind her in-laws that she is not altogether friendless and cannot be maltreated with absolute impunity. A woman cannot call on her married sister's support as easily, not because sisters care less for one another but because married women are not usually expected or allowed to shelter or financially help their sisters. A brother, however many his marital problems, does not need his sister's support in the same way because his survival and well-being are not at his wife's mercy, as the woman's are at her husband's. Thus, the brother–sister relationship in many communities is structured by the power of men and the powerlessness of women. It does not make for mutual support but compels the brother to be a perpetual giver and the sister to be a perpetual taker. This is very likely to breed resentments, especially between sisters-in-law. The brother's wife is forced to forever give, often at her own cost, even from her own dowry, to her husband's sisters. Such one-way giving cannot be conducive to the development of friendship or amity between women. Instead, it sets them up as rivals.

If brothers and sisters inherited equally, better, more equal, relationships could develop between brothers and sisters—and also between sisters, who would be better able to help out one another in times of crises.

Dowry is the Daughter's Share

This is a red herring that should nevertheless be considered because of its wide prevalence.

Dowry cannot be considered a daughter's share because:

(*a*) it is not in her control, as property is in the son's control;
(*b*) it functions as a bribe to her in-laws to keep her in their house, while property enhances the son's independent standing; and
(*c*) dowry generally consists of extravagant display which enhances family status and of cash and items which are expendable and do not appreciate in value; while property often comprises income-generating assets such as land, house, tools and machines. Thus, property provides or enhances a son's livelihood, while dowry enhances a daughter's total dependence for survival on marriage and on her husband.

Dowry often provides an incentive for a man to ill-treat his wife and throw her out of the house. Knowing that she has no culturally sanctioned right to stay in her parents' house and will be viewed as a burden there, he can demand and extract more and more from her parents as the price for keeping her in his house. The flow of dowry is dependent on her remaining married to him.

Conversely, if she owned certain assets in her own right and if these assets were legally nontransferable by her, this would be an incentive for the husband to treat her well and keep her in his house. As an owner of property, she would not be viewed solely as a burden by her brothers either. Knowing that she could go to live in her parental home or even live on her own, the husband would be aware that he shares the use of her property only if she lives with him. Thus, ownership of property would strengthen a woman rather than weaken her as dowry does now.

If equal inheritance by women became the rule rather than the exception, the pattern outlined above would be greatly furthered.

She will Inherit Doubly

It is often objected that a woman will end up getting double rights—inheriting both from her father and from her husband. However, in the natural course of things, as many men would also inherit doubly—from their parents as well as from their wives. Since today in our country men have a longer life expectancy than women, it is even possible that more men outlive their wives than vice versa, though this may be partially offset by the disparity of age at marriage between men and women.

The law should provide that if a woman dies under suspicious circumstances, her property inherited from her parents should revert to her parental family. The husband would inherit only if she died a natural death. The sons and daughters would inherit both parents' property equally.

Women Cannot Manage Property

It may also be objected that since women in most parts of the country have historically less experience of managing property, and lack the alliances and mobility in the outside world that men have, and also since women do not have the resources to use violence in defence of property that men have, especially in violence fraught areas of the countryside, effective control of property nominally inherited by a daughter will pass on to her husband and his male kin. It is true that members of any group which has historically been deprived and oppressed will take time to assume full control of any resources they may get. This is true, in different ways, of such groups as Dalits, the landless poor and women. However, this is not a reason for continuing the deprivation. Rather, putting resources in the hands of oppressed groups is a step towards making the overall culture more egalitarian and, hopefully, in the long run, less violent.

In the short term, especially as long as women who own resources are isolated individual exceptions, or in pockets surrounded by a culture of women's deprivation, it may be true that their husbands will wield more control over their property than they will. But even a nominal acknowledgment of the woman's ownership rights or semi-control by her will be an improvement over the present situation in which exclusive male ownership is not only the practice but the norm. For example, in matrilineal households in certain communities in Kerala, property was passed from mother to daughter but was often controlled equally or more by the mother's brother. Yet, women's status was relatively better in terms of greater autonomy, mobility and better rights in marriage, than in communities where women are disinherited.

We are not, by any means, arguing that inheritance rights are a magic wand, which will single-handedly empower women overnight. But these rights are one important form of empowerment which, especially if achieved on a sufficiently large scale, could help move the culture in the direction of greater equality and freedom for women.

What about the Propertyless?

Another objection frequently raised is that the entire debate on inheritance rights applies only to the propertied sections of our society.

This is true, but property and assets are not in most cases the equivalent of great wealth. The middle and lower middle classes, the middle and poor peasantry, and even the labouring poor, generally have some asset—a piece of land, a dwelling, trees, animals, implements, a vehicle, a small family trade. Many have an occupation or profession—also an important resource—that can be passed on to a child. The absolutely propertyless or destitute section is significantly large but in the total population it would be a distinct minority. Further, all those concerned to better the lot of the poor, do wish for and work for the poor to get control over more assets and independent resources such as land and housing. Our government has a policy of giving small groups among the very poor sections of society different kinds of assets—whether in the form of land to the landless, reservations in educational institutions and in jobs to those categorized as Scheduled Castes and Scheduled Tribes, housing to slum dwellers, or loans and subsidies, cattle, trees, implements and vehicles to those who cannot afford them. Too often, the government, influenced by the dominant cultural norms, gives these resources to the male 'head' of the family, wrongly assuming that this would take care of the needs of the whole family. In fact, this often further reinforces the inequality between men and women in the family. Even in reserved categories, there is no special reservation for women.

If we are committed to improving the condition of the poorest and the most oppressed, these are inevitably the women in each oppressed group. Ensuring that they are endowed with assets is also the most likely way of ensuring that the benefits actually reach whole families, as women spend a far larger proportion of their income on the other members of their family than do men.

As more sections of society move in the direction of acquiring assets, they tend to follow the norm set by those sections who already own assets. This trend is visible in the spread of dowry practices from upper caste groups to upwardly mobile lower caste groups, imitating those higher up in the social scale. Thus, changing the norm of inheritance and making it more egalitarian between men and women is a crucial part of making the whole society and its culture more egalitarian.

Legal Provisions among Different Communities

Hindu Law[1]

The majority of India's people, including all those defined as Hindus, Buddhists, Sikhs and Jains, are governed by what is known as Hindu law.

Before the British rulers attempted to codify Hindu law or put it into the form of a Parliamentary enactment, communities in different parts of the country were governed by widely differing systems of law, such as the many schools of Mitakshara in different parts of India, the Dayabhaga in Bengal, the Marumakkattayam, Aliyasantana and other kinds of matrilineal law in certain parts of the south. A number of legal treatises including the *Smritis* and various commentaries on them, ranging from about the second century BC to the eighteenth century AD, were recognized as authoritative in different regions. Local customary practice was also an important factor in determining law. Hindu law was thus a flexible and dynamic set of rules and practices.

A characteristic feature of Hindu law was the concept of property as owned by an extended family or household. The idea of a birthright is endemic to Hindu law, as to most cultures' early laws. However, the idea that an individual, by making a will, can decide in advance how property shall be disposed of after his or her death, is a concept unknown to Hindu law.

Every individual had the right to enjoy the property of his or her family and thus the family was supposed to function as a sort of social security system for the aged, orphans, disabled and others not able to earn. All had the right to live in the family house and to be sustained and educated from the family funds. A child could not be disinherited or deprived of its right to sustenance even by its father. Many early texts lay down in great detail the rights even of those who would in modern terms be called illegitimate children.

While the joint family consisted of both men and women and all had a right to sustenance, control of property was differently vested in different regions. Under patrilineal systems like the Mitakshara and the Dayabhaga, women, because of the patrilocal nature of the family, were not given a full birthright as sons were.

Under Mitakshara law, joint family property was vested in males in the male line alone. Thus, a man, his sons, grandsons and great-grandsons constituted a coparcenary which meant that each of these males acquired an equal right from birth, even from conception, in the family property. Decisions regarding disposal of family property were to be taken collectively although many powers were vested in the *karta* or male head of the family who was supposed to administer the property in the interests of all members. Although notionally

[1] The Hindu Succession Act was amended in 2005 to give women coparcenary rights (see p. 329).

each male had an equal share in the property, expenditure was not to be apportioned only to males, but the collective good was to be kept in mind. Expenditure on women members' needs, gifts and endowments for pious and charitable purposes, or expenditure on the special needs of some members, were to be undertaken from the common funds, and no coparcener was entitled to complain that more had been spent on another member than on himself. Females, such as a daughter or a son's daughter, and males in the female line, such as a daughter's son, were not part of the Mitakshara coparcenary.

Under Dayabhaga law, sons do not become coparceners at birth. They do not have equal rights in family property during their father's lifetime. However, at his death, they immediately become coparceners.

Under Marumakkattayam law, prevailing in what is now called Kerala, the family was joint and property jointly owned. However, the family was matrilineal and matrilocal. A household consisted of a mother and her children, with joint rights in property. Lineage was traced through the female line to a common ancestress. Daughters and their children were thus an integral part of the household and of property ownership.

Survivorship and Succession

Under the Mitakshara system, joint family property devolved by survivorship within the coparcenary. This meant that every birth or death of a male altered the share of every surviving male. If a coparcenary consisted of a father and his two sons, each would own one third of the property. If one of the sons had a son, automatically the share of each male became one fourth.

Mitakshara law also recognizes inheritance by succession but only to property separately owned by an individual, male or female. Females are included as heirs to this kind of property by almost all schools of Mitakshara law, but some schools recognize more categories of females than do others. Under the Bengal, Benaras and Mithila schools, only five females can succeed as heirs to a male, namely, his wife, his daughter, his mother, his father's mother and his father's father's mother. The Madras school recognizes, in addition, the son's daughter, daughter's daughter and the sister as heirs. The Bombay school, which is, in many respects, the most liberal to women, recognizes a number of other female heirs, including a half sister, father's sister and women married into the family, such as stepmother, son's widow, brother's widow, and also many other females classified as *bandhus*. Some Mitakshara schools allowed a wife to act as a *karta* in her husband's absence, while others did not.

Under Dayabhaga law, since the coparcenary comes into existence when a man dies, succession rather than survivorship is the rule. If one of the male heirs died, his heirs, including females such as his wife and daughter, became members of the coparcenary, not in their own right, but representing him. Since females could be coparceners, they could also act as *karta*, and manage property on behalf of other members.

Partition under Mitakshara took place when one male member declared his intention to separate and took his share. He and his sons then set up a separate coparcenary. Under Dayabhaga, partition could take place when sons succeeded to the property, if they so desired. Under Marumakkattayam law, inheritance was by survivorship. Partition was not allowed. The head of the household was a male, the mother's brother, or, in his absence, a female.

Stridhan

The concept *of stridhan* (women's wealth) or female-owned and inherited property coexists uneasily with the concept of the Mitakshara or Dayabhaga coparcenary and was considered the most complicated part of these laws. It is not known to Marumakkattayam law since there, women were full owners of family property, like men.

Different schools defined *stridhan* differently. But it usually included any gifts made to a woman by her natal family or by strangers, and anything earned by her. Under some schools, it also included gifts made to her by her husband or his relatives.

Just as a male's separately owned property passed by succession to certain defined heirs whom he could not disinherit, so too *stridhan* passed to certain defined heirs. The set of heirs to *stridhan* was substantially different from that of heirs to a male's property. This list differed from school to school, but, generally, a woman's child figured first. In some schools, daughters were preferred to sons and unmarried daughters to married daughters, this being suggestive of *stridhan* as a possible hangover from a matrilineal system. The husband and his heirs came next, and the woman's natal family last. However, most schools laid down that if the *stridhan* was originally gifted by the woman's natal family, it reverted to them.

Most Mitakshara schools held that property inherited by succession by a woman from a man did not become *stridhan*, but reverted to the original owner's heirs after her death. But the Bombay school held that property inherited by a woman born into the family (daughter) became her *stridhan* and passed to her heirs, while property inherited by a woman married into the family (widow) was held by her in her lifetime and reverted to the original owner's heirs on her death.

Women's Limited Estate

Under pure Hindu law, all estate is, in a sense, limited, as the concept of willing away one's property (absolute estate) is unknown. Property, whether ancestral, descending by survivorship, or separate, descending by succession, whether patrilineal or matrilineal, goes to certain sets of heirs and it is not in the individual's power to alter the arrangement and leave the property according to his or her will, or to disinherit anyone he or she may not like.

However, since men were full members of the coparcenary in Mitakshara and Dayabhaga, while women were not and since men were entitled to act as *karta* in their own right while women were not, men under these systems had much greater control over family property than did women.

The concept of a will was gradually introduced into Hindu law and this right to make a will was acquired only by men. Under Dayabhaga, men were allowed to make a will in respect of all property, while under Mitakshara, they were allowed to make a will in respect of separately held property (which generally consisted of self-acquired property) but not in respect of ancestral property or of their share in it.

However, when women, as widows, acquired a right over their husband's share in ancestral property, they continued to have only a limited estate in it. How far they could dispose of it by gift, mortgage or transfer was a subject of much dispute, as was the question of whether women could will away *stridhan*. Different schools held different opinions on this. The Bombay school held that property inherited by a woman from a woman became her absolute property.

Codification Process

In their attempts to impose countrywide uniformity, first the British rulers and later the nationalist reformers and legislators tried to devise one legal system for all those classified as Hindus, however different their family systems. The process took a long time and proceeded piecemeal by the passing and amendment of several laws. These statutes were based partly on interpretations of certain texts to the neglect of others and partly on British law. British law was itself undergoing reform throughout the nineteenth century. That it served as a model is clear even from the titles of statutes, for example, the Married Women's Right to Property Act in England was followed by the Hindu Women's Right to Property Act in India.

Perhaps the most important new factor introduced by British rule in the shaping of law was that of legal precedent. Decisions of different courts became binding on other courts and acquired the force of law. The judges often claimed to be guided by the 'spirit of the law' or the 'reason of the thing' or 'general principles' which were often fine names for their own predilections. A heavy bias in favour of British law and of the northern schools of Mitakshara is visible throughout the process.

The process of codification culminated in the Hindu Succession Act, finally passed in 1956 in a highly watered down form, after over 20 years of fierce debate both inside and outside Parliament.

Hindu Succession Act: Provisions

1. The Act applies to Hindus, Buddhists, Sikhs, Jains and to any other persons who are not Muslims, Christians, Parsis or Jews, unless it is proven that they would not have been governed by Hindu law or custom.
2. Scheduled Tribes are excluded from the Act, and are to be governed by their customary law.
3. The Act overrides all earlier prevailing laws, rules, texts and customs.
4. When a male Hindu having an interest in a Mitakshara coparcenary property dies, his interest in family property shall devolve by survivorship and not by succession, on the other coparceners.

   But if he has any female relative or male relative in the female line specified in class one of the schedule attached to the Act, then his share in the Mitakshara property will be separated, and will devolve by succession on his heirs. The heirs in Class One of the schedule are: son, daughter, widow, mother, son of a predeceased son, daughter of a predeceased son, son of a predeceased daughter, daughter of a predeceased daughter, widow of a predeceased son, son of a predeceased son of a predeceased son, daughter of a predeceased son of a predeceased son, widow of a predeceased son of a predeceased son.

   (Thus, if a man has two sons, but none of the other above heirs, on his death the two sons will remain coparceners, with half a share each in the coparcenary property. However, if he has a wife, mother, daughter and two sons, then on his death, the property will be divided up into five equal parts, each heir taking one part, unless he makes a will specifying that his two sons are to inherit, or unless his wife and mother sign away their rights in favour of the sons.)
5. However, a man may make a will leaving his interest in coparcenary property to anyone he likes. This is an altogether new provision introduced by the Act, which did not exist according to any earlier text, custom or law.

6. When a Hindu to whom the Marumakkattayam or Nambudri or Aliyasantana law applies dies, his or her interest in the property is separated and descends according to intestate succession on the heirs in Class One of the schedule and not by survivorship.
7. The separately owned property of a male Hindu devolves either according to his will or, if he dies without making a will (dies intestate) it devolves first on the heirs in Class One of the schedule, and, if there are none, on the heirs in Class Two of the schedule (father, grandchildren, brother, sister, nephew, niece, grandparents, and so on) and if there are none of these either, on relatives through males known as agnates, such as cousins on the male side, and lastly, on relatives through females, known as cognates, such as cousins on the mother's side; those more closely related being preferred.
8. All property owned by a Hindu woman is her absolute property. The Act abolishes the concept of limited estate. However, a man may in his will create a limited estate, for example, leaving his property to his widow only for her use during her lifetime, or to his daughter only as long as she remains unmarried.
9. The property of a Hindu woman who dies without making a will devolves on a different set of heirs, in the following order, each category inheriting only if no heir in the earlier category exists:
   (*a*) her children and husband, taking equal shares. If any child has died earlier, leaving behind children, these grandchildren between them take one share, that of their dead parent;
   (*b*) her husband's heirs;
   (*c*) her parents;
   (*d*) her father's heirs; and
   (*e*) her mother's heirs.

   However, if the property was inherited by her from her parents and she has no children or grandchildren, the property shall be inherited by her father's heirs. If the property was inherited by her from her husband or father-in-law and she has no children or grandchildren, the property will be inherited by her husband's heirs.

10. In the case of people who were earlier governed by Marumakkattayam or Aliyasantana law, a special provision has been made, in recognition of the matrilineal system under which they lived, that agnates (relatives related through males) shall not be preferred to cognates (those related through females) in the list of heirs to those dying intestate. Further, a

woman's heirs in these communities are the following, each category inheriting only if one does not exist in the earlier category:

(*a*) her children and her mother, taking equal shares, and any children of predeceased children taking between them one share, that of their deceased parent;
(*b*) her father and husband;
(*c*) her mother's heirs;
(*d*) her father's heirs; and
(*e*) her husband's heirs.

11. Posthumous children have the same rights as other children in inheritance.
12. When a Hindu man or woman dies without making a will and leaves a house occupied wholly by members of the family, if he or she has both male and female heirs specified in Class One of the schedule, then the female heirs have the right to live in the house but do not have the right to demand partition of the house until the male heirs decide to divide it. If they do divide it, each female heir gets her share; if they do not, she does not get a share. But a married daughter has no right to live in the house unless she is separated, deserted or widowed. This clause does not apply to persons who would have been governed by Marumakkattayam or Aliyasantana law. Women of those communities have a right to demand partition; and married daughters have a right to live in the parental house.
13. Under certain earlier schools of law, persons physically and mentally disabled, suffering from leprosy and certain other diseases, were barred from inheriting property. This Act removes all such bars. Only the following are excluded from the right to inherit: the widow of a predeceased son or grandson or the widow of a brother who has re-married; a person who has murdered the owner of the property to be inherited; children of a person who has converted from Hinduism to another religion.
14. The Act allows any law contravening its provisions to be passed with the purpose of preventing fragmentation of agricultural holdings or of fixing ceilings or for devolution of tenancy rights. As agricultural land is a state subject, the states have passed different laws in these respects.

Curbs on Women's Rights

The Hindu Succession Act was framed with two express purposes: to create a uniform codified law for all Hindus; and to give women equal rights in inheritance in accordance with the constitutional guarantee of non-discrimination between the sexes before the law.

It appears, however, that in the process of the Act's evolution, the former purpose took precedence over the latter. A uniform law was established, eradicating many other schools of law largely in favour of one particular school of Mitakshara law, but neither were females given equal rights nor were the limited rights conferred on them adequately protected.

By establishing a new right to will away property, the Act gave a new weapon to men to deprive women of the rights they earlier had under certain schools of Hindu law.

The main limitations of the Act so far as women's rights are concerned, are:

1. The retention of the Mitakshara coparcenary without including females in it means that females do not inherit ancestral property as males do. If a joint family gets divided, each male coparcener takes his share and females get nothing. Only when one of the coparceners dies does the female get a share as his heir. In the case of a brother and a sister in a joint family, on the death of their father, the brother would get his own share in the property and also a share out of his father's share, whereas the sister would only get a share in her father's share. This is usually considered the most serious flaw in the Act because most immoveable property in the country is ancestral property.
2. The married daughter has no right to live in her parental house. Even her nephews and grandnephews have a right to live in her parental house, but not she. This is the case even if the house belonged to her mother. This clause clearly discriminates against women.
3. The Act allows different states to make laws relating to agricultural land, and does not specify that these laws should not discriminate against females.
4. The Act, while it claims to abolish the limited estate of females and to treat them on par with males, still discriminates in terms of heirs. The heirs of a male's property and of a female's property are different. A man's mother inherits equally with his wife and children, while a woman's parents inherit only after her husband's heirs, that is, if she has no in-laws. Thus, even a woman's self acquired property bought from her own earnings would be inherited by her in-laws in preference to her own parents, while a man's wife's parents figure nowhere at all in the list of his heirs. This discrimination is clearly an outcome of the *stridhan*

concept which was part of the patrilineal system wherein a woman was viewed as losing membership of her natal family after marriage. The retention of a woman's mother as her heir along with her children in communities which were governed by Marumakkattayam law clearly reveals the anomaly, and also shows that Mitakshara law was being treated as the norm by the law makers. There is no other reason for the privileging of the male line (agnates) over the female line (cognates) in the list of heirs.

5. The Act allows for the retention of the Mitakshara coparcenary–if there are no female heirs or male heirs in the female line, the coparcenary remains unaffected by the death of male members. However, the Act lays down that the Marumakkattayam and Aliyasantana households are broken up as soon as a member dies, and the property devolves by succession, not survivorship. Thus the Act heavily privileges the Mitakshara patrilineal system over the matrilineal systems. The latter have nearly died out in Kerala today due to a variety of reasons. By introducing the right to make wills, the concept of partition unknown to Marumakkattayam and demolishing the principle of survivorship, the Act virtually decrees the dissolution of a system wherein women had better rights and imposes on them an alien system which puts them at a relative disadvantage–for no reason other than 'uniformity'.
6. By far the most far-reaching change introduced by the Act was the right of a man to will away his interest in joint family property. The legal right of Hindus to will away property was statutorily conferred by the Indian Succession Act, 1925, which was a law based on British law and passed mainly for the benefit of the British in India and Indian Christians. None of its clauses apply to Hindus except those relating to the right to make wills. However, even this Act allows Hindus to will away only self-acquired property.

The Father's Will

Under all systems of Hindu law, women had certain inalienable rights in ancestral property, which differed from one region to another. Widows had a right to live in the dwelling house and generally had a right to manage their husband's share of the property. Unmarried daughters had a right to live in the house and to be maintained. This was a birthright like the son's birthright. The only difference was that sons had greater powers of management and disposal. Under Dayabhaga law, widows and daughters could even become coparceners and heads of households. Under Marumakkattayam, property passed in the female line and daughters could not be disinherited. They had full right to live in the house even after marriage, and so did their children.

By giving men the right to make wills, the Hindu Succession Act allows them to disinherit anyone they choose. Given the prevailing bias in favour of sons and against daughters, this power is generally used to disinherit daughters in favour of sons. There are very many cases even of highly educated men disinheriting daughters in favour of brothers' sons. Thus, all that the Act gives with one hand, it takes back with the other. No restriction by way of a safeguard of women's rights has been laid on men's power to make wills. A man can give his female heirs only a limited estate in property or can lay down any unreasonable conditions for their enjoyment of property, for example, that his widow or son's widow not remarry. In ancestral property, the Act allows the sons an inalienable share as coparceners; therefore even if the father disinherits them he can disinherit them only from a share in his share of the property. But since daughters are not coparceners they will get no share in ancestral property if the father disinherits them from their share in his share. Thus, the birthright they earlier had is lost. This is particularly injurious in the case of communities that were earlier governed by Marumakkatayam. When the Bill was debated in Parliament, the proponents of women's rights repeatedly pointed out that:

1. Either females should be made coparceners on an equal footing with males, or the coparcenery itself should be abolished. The initial pilot of the Bill, Dr B.R. Ambedkar, India's first law minister, had abolished the coparcenary altogether, but this met with much opposition in Parliament and the Bill was referred to a joint committee which restored the distinction. The retention of two kinds of property—ancestral and self-acquired—puts females at a disadvantage. Andhra Pradesh and Karnataka have recently partially remedied this by making daughters coparceners (see *Manushi*, No. 17), but certain disabilities still remain.
2. Men should not be allowed to will away ancestral property. Although this was hotly opposed at the time, H.V. Pataskar the law minister in whose tenure the Bill was finally passed, argued:

> the father is the best man to judge, with respect to his property, as to who should get what.... There have been suggestions made that the daughter should be considered as a coparcener .... I cannot imagine of a family, which can go on smoothly by the addition of a daughter, their heirs and so on.

He even blatantly pointed out that a father could use the will as a means to deny the daughter's rights:

> Supposing the daughter D has been married. . . and that daughter is well placed, A can under the new provision. . .make a will. . .and provide that she shall have no share in his interest. The joint family will continue as before even after A's death, without being affected in any way by any of the provisions of this Act. It is thus clear that those who want to be governed only by the existing rules of the Mitakshara system even after the passing of this Act have been given the choice to do so.

Mr Pataskar's suggestion was followed by too many fathers. Some MPs even declared in Parliament that they had made wills disinheriting daughters.

We know today that not only do fathers use wills in a discriminatory manner, but also women are generally compelled to sign gift deeds transferring their share both in ancestral and in self-acquired property of their parents to their brothers.

Unfortunately, because the power to make wills is undisputed in western countries whose jurisprudence (particularly British) is the most dominant influence on our own, this right is today no longer the subject of debate but has been accepted as a *fait accompli*.[2]

[2] The Hindu Succession (Amendment) Act, 2005 came into force from 9 September 2005 through a notification by the Government of India. It aimed at removing some of the blatant gender discriminatory provisions mandated in the Hindu Succession Act, 1956 and gives the following rights to daughters under Section 6:

- The daughter of a coparcener shall by birth become a coparcener in her own right in the same manner as the son.
- The daughter has the same rights in the coparcenary property as she would have had if she had been a son.
- The daughter shall be subject to the same liability in the said coparcenary property as that of a son and any reference to a Hindu Mitakshara coparcener shall be deemed to include a reference to a daughter of a coparcener.
- The daughter is allotted the same share as is allotted to a son.
- The share of the pre-deceased son or a pre-deceased daughter shall be allotted to the surviving child of such pre-deceased son or of such pre-deceased daughter.
- The share of the pre-deceased child of a pre-deceased son or of a pre-deceased daughter shall be allotted to the child of such pre-deceased child of the pre-deceased son or a pre-deceased daughter.

After the commencement of the Hindu Succession (Amendment) Act, 2005, no court shall recognize any right to proceed against a son, grandson or great-grandson for the recovery of any

Christian Law

The Indian Succession Act

The Indian Succession Act, 1925, stated to have been passed to consolidate the law relating to testamentary and intestate succession, was intended to apply to British citizens domiciled in India and to Indian Christians. It has special sections on the law applicable to Parsis. It also has sections enabling Hindus to make wills. It was originally to have applied to the property of those married under the Special Marriage Act, 1954, but by a later amendment to the latter, two Hindus marrying under it were to be governed by the Hindu Succession

---

debt due from his father, grandfather or great-grandfather solely on the ground of the pious obligation under the Hindu law, of such son, grandson or great-grandson to discharge any such debt. The amendments abolished Section 23 of the Hindu Succession Act which denied a woman the right to seek partition of an inherited 'dwelling' unit/house if other male heirs are residing in it and further restricts her right to reside in the inherited residence unless she is a widow or has been separated from or deserted by her husband. However, the proposed changes are not comprehensive enough and women will still be subjected to unequal property rights in agricultural land as Section 4(2) of the Hindu Succession Act allows for special state laws to address the issue of 'fragmentation of agricultural holdings', 'fixation of ceiling' and 'devolution of tenancy rights' in these holdings. For example, state laws existing in several states including Delhi, Uttar Pradesh, Madhya Pradesh, Punjab and Haryana deny women equal rights of succession in tenancy rights. Further, certain other Sections of the Hindu Succession Act discriminate against women through the discriminatory order of succession for male and female heirs. The proposed Amendments to the Mitakshara Joint Family Property laws making women equal coparceners are sought to be made applicable only to women who are not married at the time the law is passed and is thus patently unjust also.

Section 6 of Hindu Succession Act contains another instance of gender bias. It states that the property of the deceased in the Mitakshara Coparcenary shall devolve by intestate succession if the deceased had a female heir or a male heir who claims through such female relative. The gender bias creeps in the rules of devolution of interest under Section 8 of the Hindu Succession Act. In this Section there are only four primary heirs in the Schedule to class I, namely, mother, widow, son and daughter. If, however, for example, the son or daughter has already died, their children can inherit the property. The principle of representation goes up to two degree in the male line of descent; but in the female line of descent it goes only upto one degree. Accordingly, the deceased son's son's son and son's son's daughter get a share but a deceased daughter's daughter's son and daughter's daughter's daughter do not get anything. A further infirmity is that a widow of a pre-deceased son and grandson are class-I heirs, but the husbands of a deceased daughter or granddaughter are not heirs.

Most important of all, the right to 'will away' one's property has not been curbed even though it is well established that it is used mainly against daughters. Therefore, the likelihood of daughters being persuaded or coerced into signing away their rights in favour of their brothers remains high. Moreover, the right of a father to disinherit his daughters in his self acquired property also remains intact.

Act and not by the Indian Succession Act. However, the Indian Succession Act applies to two Muslims marrying under the Special Marriage Act and also to intercommunity marriages under the Special Marriage Act.

The rules of succession applying to a man and a woman are the same.

If a person dies without making a will, the property is divided according to the following rules:

1. If there is a spouse and children, the spouse gets one-third, and the remaining two-thirds is divided equally between the children. If there is only one child, he or she will get two-thirds. If there are grandchildren but no living children, the grandchildren will divide the two-thirds equally between them.

   If some children are living and others have died, leaving their children, then the two-thirds is divided in such a way that the children of each deceased child divide between them the share of their parent. The same rules apply correspondingly to great-grandchildren.
2. If there is a spouse, but no children, grandchildren, or great-grandchildren, the spouse gets half the property and the other half goes to the persons kindred in the following order: father; mother and siblings dividing equally; nephews and nieces shall inherit if their parents have died, on the principle of all of a dead parent's children together representing him or her; brothers and sisters equally dividing half the property between them. If there is only a spouse, but no children, parents or siblings, the spouse inherits all; so also, if there is only a mother or only siblings.
3. If none of the aforementioned relatives are alive, the next of kin inherit according to rules laid down in the Act.

Limitations

The most glaring discriminatory provision is that the father is preferred over the mother. If a person is unmarried and childless, and both parents are alive, the father inherits all. If a person has a spouse but no children and both parents are alive, the spouse gets half and the father half. But if the father is dead, the mother has to share with the brothers and sisters. Under this scheme, a daughter inherits equally with a son. This is the only law in India under which this is the case. Therefore, the law makes no provision for a widow of a son or grandson to inherit the father-in-law's property. However, the law allows a person to make a will and disinherit anyone he likes. If daughters are disinherited by this means, they will not get any share in the father-in-law's property either, if they are widowed.

Parsi Law

Sections 50 to 56 of the Act deal with the Parsi law of succession. The laws of succession are different for a man and a woman.

1. If a Parsi male dies without making a will, the widow and each son get a share double that of the daughter. If there is no widow, each son gets a share double that of each daughter. If his parents are alive, the father gets a share equal to half the share of a son and the mother a share equal to half the share of a daughter.
2. If a Parsi woman dies without making a will, her widower and children get equal shares of her property. If there is no widower, the children get equal shares. Her parents get nothing if she has children.
3. If there is only a spouse but no children or grandchildren, the spouse gets half and the rest is divided among heirs listed in the Act. If there is a spouse and also the widow of a child or grandchild, the former gets one-third and the latter one-third, and the rest goes to other heirs. If there is more than one widow of children or grandchildren, they divide one-third of the property between them.

The remaining part of the property is divided among heirs in such a way that each male gets double the share of each equally closely related female. The list of heirs places parents first, next siblings and then paternal relatives before maternal relatives.

If there are none of the these relatives, then the next of kin, listed in the schedule, take the property in order of closeness. The principle of males taking double the share of females who are equally closely related is followed.

It is evident that this law is clearly discriminatory against women. Even though a daughter is assured a share, she gets only half what a son gets, and this principle is followed with regard to all male and female relatives. Only a woman's property gets to be equally divided between her children. A man's parents share along with his wife and children, but a woman's parents do not.

Muslim Law

There are five major schools of Muslim law, of which the Hanafi school is followed by a majority of Muslims in India. The five schools were founded by five great jurists: Imam Jaffar, 765 AD, Imam Abu Hanifa, Imam Malik, 795 AD, Imam Shafei, 820 AD and Imam Hanbal, 855 AD. The first is followed by the Shias and the rest by the Sunnis. In India, any Sunni case may be decided in accordance with the opinions of any one of the four jurists.

The Koran and the *hadith* or traditions of the Prophet are the chief sources of law, but *ijtihad* or consensus and local traditions also play a large part in the interpretation of law. There are important and substantial differences in the laws applicable to Muslims in different countries today. In India, its evolution has been greatly influenced by British colonial rule. For example, in pre-British times, Wahabis were the most influential sect in India, but since they were also among the leaders of the 1857 revolt, the British persecuted them and deliberately eradicated their influence from the interpretation of law.

Inheritance

A saying ascribed to the Prophet is: 'Learn the laws of inheritance, and teach them to the people; for they are one half of useful knowledge.' In pre-Islamic Arabia, property passed primarily to male heirs in the male line. These are known as agnatic heirs. The Koran, while sanctioning the right of these heirs, adds 12 more categories of heirs, of whom eight are female. These are known as Koranic heirs. Thus, the prescription that women must be able to read the Koran would ensure not just literacy and religious knowledge, but also knowledge of their inheritance rights.

We are not here going into all the complexities of the complete system of inheritance which basically operates by ratios. The main heirs under Hanafi law are the spouse, the parents and the children. A husband gets double the share that a wife does; a son double the share of a daughter. The father and mother get equal shares (one-sixth) as Koranic heirs but the father may also inherit as an agnatic heir and would thus get more. These provisions clearly discriminate against females. The principle of representation is not recognized–thus a dead son's son will not get his father's share.

Under Shia law, if a man has only daughters and no sons, they inherit more than they would under Sunni law.

Wills

While persons may gift away all their property in their lifetimes, they can only will away a maximum of one-third of their property. The rest must be divided among the agnatic and Koranic heirs. A person is, of course, not required to make a will. As with most traditional customary laws, Islamic law is not inclined in favour of disposition of property by will.

The origin of the permission to Muslims to make wills is a very telling *hadis* of the Prophet: a man who had a lot of property but only one daughter to inherit it, asked the Prophet if he should bequeath two-thirds of it in charity. The Prophet said, 'No.' When asked if half should be bequeathed in charity, he again replied, 'No.' He then told the man to bequeath one-third if he wished to and added that even one-third was 'much' for it is better to give one's heirs security than to leave them in want. Thus, the desire to disinherit the daughter is clearly frowned upon.

Another very important principle of Muslim law is that none of the legal heirs can be given anything in the will. This means that the one-third bequeathed can go only to charity or to a friend, but not, for example, to a son.

However, if two Muslims in India marry under the Special Marriage Act, or even, much after their wedding, get their marriage registered under this Act, then the Indian Succession Act will apply to their disposal of property. This means that they will be able to make a will, leaving all their property to anyone they want, for example, to a son, excluding the daughter.

The anomalies of the law thus tend to operate in favour of male heirs. Two Hindus marrying under the Special Marriage Act continue to be governed by Hindu succession law, so that their daughters and other female heirs are deprived of the more egalitarian rules of intestate succession under the Indian Succession Act. However, the principle of Muslim law which does not allow a daughter or a wife to be totally disinherited by a father's will can be evaded by a Muslim father simply by registering his marriage under the Special Marriage Act.

Dower *(Mehar)*

Dower is a sum of money or other property which the husband at the time of the marriage ceremony gives to the wife (known as prompt dower) or promises to pay her on demand (known as deferred dower). It is a settlement on the wife as a token of respect for her. Even if no sum is mentioned in the marriage ceremony, the wife has a right to 'proper' dower fixed by the court, which she can claim. Unfortunately, today, the dower fixed is usually a nominal sum. However, if the wife and her family are able to get a substantial sum fixed in the *nikahnama,* she will be legally entitled to it.

When the husband dies, the wife is entitled to claim her dower from his estate, and it is treated as an unpaid debt at par with other unpaid debts, which must be paid before the heirs get their shares. The wife gets her dower in addition to her share as a Koranic heir. The dower can be increased at any time by the husband. So the dower is an effective instrument for endowing one's widow. This means that the widow is the only heir whose share can be increased at will.

Making of Wills

Theoretically, a person making a will is supposed to have complete freedom to leave his or her property to whomsoever he or she wills. In a society where sons and daughters were more or less equally valued, wills would tend to be made fairly equally in favour of both, except when a parent's relations with a particular child were strained, a consideration not determined by the child's gender. In our society, however, the cultural assumption that sons are the naturally privileged heirs generally overwhelms all other considerations. Wills are used to disinherit daughters on account of their gender alone, and to keep assets in the hands of men as a group. One has only to look at land records to see how rarely women's names figure there, or to glance at business establishments' signboards to notice how frequently '... & Sons' or '. . . Brothers' occurs, with the female variant rarely if ever in evidence.

One may compare the situation with that caused by the current misuse of sex determination tests selectively to abort female fetuses. In a society where daughters and sons were more or less equally desired, sex determination tests would present no serious problems; however, in our society it assumes problematic, even threatening, dimensions. So also, with the use of the will as a weapon to disinherit daughters.

It therefore becomes necessary to take certain steps to redress the situation so as to empower women whose present powerlessness has serious adverse consequences for their lives and for society as a whole. It is for this reason we would suggest that any will that disinherits daughters in favour of sons should be treated as a *legally invalid document*. This could be a temporary measure, tried on an experimental basis.

Fears have been expressed by some that in such a situation parents would resort to female infanticide rather than allow daughters to inherit. While it is possible that this may occur as an exceptional aberration, it is unlikely to happen on a wide scale. More likely would be attempts to evade the measure by other means. In any event, in certain regions of the country even today, neglect of female children to the point of death is not unknown, as is evident from the imbalanced sex ratio amongst infants in these regions. Available data from different regions and countries suggests that infanticide and neglect of female infants are characteristic of those societies where women are disinherited and perceived as a useless burden, while in societies where women inherit and are perceived as full members of the family, the proportion of women in the population is significantly larger. The high sex ratio (larger numbers of women to men) in Kerala and in certain parts of the north-east is evidence supporting this interpretation. So, trying to right the imbalance in inheritance is one way of trying to change the overall imbalanced man–woman relationship which renders women powerless.

Challenges of Implementation

While it may not be at all easy to implement such a measure, especially given the failure of our administrative machinery to implement almost any measure successfully, it would be worthwhile for the state to commit itself more unequivocally to the principle of women's equal inheritance rights. This would involve changing the laws governing inheritance to remove the inequalities contained in them. It would also mean passing laws to render any will that disinherits female heirs in favour of male heirs a legally invalid document, and forbidding the gift or transfer of immoveable property by a father in his lifetime to his sons alone; and in the event of a sale, enforcing equal distribution of the proceeds amongst all children. If, however, parents wish to disinherit all children equally in favour of some third unrelated party or a charitable institution, this would be permitted. Property inherited by a married woman should be non-transferable by her.

Even if the measures are not fully implemented at once, they will have some advantages over the present situation:

1. Serious efforts by the state machinery to combat the culture of disempowering women by building an effective implementation machinery and legal provisions to discourage the practice of disinheriting daughters through wills and offering them protection from violence in cases where their demand for equal inheritance endangers their lives. At present, the state machinery actively supports the passing of property from father to son, and the exclusion of female heirs. Even if the state is not able to halt this, it should withdraw its support.
2. Building effective safeguards for women to retain control over inherited assets rather than meekly pass the ownership on to their husbands.
3. This will encourage individual women who are in a position to demand their rights to fight for them, unlike at present when they are disinherited by legal means.
4. Just as certain land reform laws endow not just individual landless persons but a whole section of the landless poor with land rights, even though only a few individuals may be able to take advantage of the measure, so also, such measures as outlined above will endow women

as a group with certain rights, and throw the weight of the law in their favour, so that if they organize to assert their rights over time, the number of women able to claim their rights may grow.

While it is true that these suggestions are fraught with difficulties and complications, this is one possible way to try and make some change in the present situation of near total disinheritance of women, which causes untold large-scale oppression and suffering. In the long run, the full endowment of women will not only improve their lives but also those of men, who will be freed of the anxiety of having to marry off dependent daughters and sisters, and then having to ineffectively intervene when they are maltreated after marriage.

Part IV

Challenges of Politics and Organization

15

Nature of Women's Mobilization in Rural India*

This chapter examines various rural movements—the factors that have facilitated the participation of women, the extent and quality of their participation, and the limits to their involvement.

Since the early seventies, there has been a new upsurge in the mobilization of rural women as participants in various movements. They are being mobilized in large numbers, and participating in more militant actions within a wide variety of rural movements as well as around a wider variety of issues. These mobilizations have often been described as rural women's movements. However, in my view, these sporadic mobilizations of rural women within

*This article appeared in *Economic and Political Weekly*, 24–31 December 1988.

various larger movements do not amount to evidence of the existence of rural women's movements.

At a minimum, rural women may be said to be mobilized when they begin participating in social action outside the family even sporadically—and with some, even slight, intensity. However, for any group's mobilization to acquire the character of a movement, certain minimum pre-conditions must be met, of which the following would seem to be most important:

1. A perception by the group not only of the injustices faced in common, but also of a commonality of interests, and the ability to organize them into a set of common issues intended to be resolved by collective action.
2. An ability of the group to act as a coordinated constituency, asserting its combined strength toward the fulfillment of its aims.
3. An ability of the group to independently sustain its own organization and to struggle over an appreciable period of time with the intention of achieving a satisfactory settlement of its demands.

If these criteria are accepted, it is premature to talk of rural women's movements in India today. In this chapter, I will try to examine the nature of women's mobilization within various movements—the factors that have facilitated the participation of women, the extent and quality of their participation and why it stops at the points that it does. My attempt is not to belittle the importance of existing efforts to mobilize rural women but to learn from them how it may be possible to move on to a further stage towards building rural women's movements.

Whatever systematic information we have on the mobilization of rural women is mostly confined to reports of movements that are composed primarily of men. These movements can be categorized as follows:

1. The struggle of poor, marginal peasants and landless labourers, most of whom are usually Dalits, against social and economic oppression.
2. The struggle of village communities, many of them tribals, to defend their traditional rights over land and other natural resources against exploiting outsiders.
3. The struggle of rural artisans and rural labourers in small industries for better wages.

In recent years, activist development agencies have also mobilized women in these categories in certain small localities. However, the more large-scale mobilizations of the rural population consist primarily of the following:

1. Traditional political parties using local rural leaders within each of the rural strata (especially those from the dominant middle peasant castes) as intermediaries and these rural group leaders exchanging their vote blocks for personal and group influence and patronage. Congress, Telugu Desam and Lok Dal are only a few examples of such parties.
2. Mobilization around ethnic, religious, language, caste and other identity questions, such as the Akali Dal, the Dravida Munnetra Kazhagam (DMK), All India Anna Dravida Munnetra Kazhagam (AIADMK) and Jharkhand Mukti Morcha.
3. The new peasant movements such as those led by Shetkari Sangathana and the Bharatiya Kisan Union (BKU).

Participation of Women Encouraged During Crises

A necessary pre-condition for women's mobilization is the general and usually prior mobilization of the men in the rural community. Movement leaders have seldom, almost never, begun by mobilizing women as an integral part of their rural organizations. In almost all cases, their organizing efforts have initially focused primarily on men—whether the organization is of the peasantry or of the landless poor. However, as soon as the organization undertakes mass actions and gets into a state of confrontation for getting its demands met, women often come out spontaneously to lend support to the movement, especially at moments of crisis.

This is true, to give just a few examples, of the movement of tribals and landless poor in Shahada, Maharashtra, of the struggle of landless field labour led by the Chhatra Yuva Sangharsh Vahini in Bodhgaya, Bihar, the Communist Party of India (Marxist-Leninist) (CPI-ML)-led struggles of the landless poor and poor peasantry in Andhra Pradesh and Bihar, and the mobilization of landed peasant women by the Shetkari Sangathana, the Bharatiya Kisan Union and the Akali Dal.

Sharad Joshi admits that when he started building the Shetkari Sangathana, he did not think of drawing women into the organization. However, from very early on, women would spontaneously come out in large numbers for mass action such as *rasta roko*s (road blocks). It was through this experience that the leadership slowly became aware of the potential that women represented.

The same pattern was visible during the BKU agitation in Uttar Pradesh. Women are reported to have been present in significant numbers during the month-long *gherao* of the Meerut commissioner's office, and seem to have helped keep the agitation peaceful and orderly during a very trying period. This, despite the fact that the BKU has not so far evolved any special programme for women.

Even though women tend spontaneously to join movements during phases of militant action, it has been found that in most cases, the leadership begins to make a special appeal to women to join when the movement is facing a crisis like government and police repression or a backlash from opposing forces. At such times, the leaders call on women more easily because the community is compelled to suspend the normal rules of behaviour in order to cope with the emergency and the men become more willing to encourage women's participation. At such times of crisis, women too tend to perceive their participation as a duty to the family and the community.

For example, in the Akali-led landed peasant movement in Punjab, rural women's participation was dramatically enhanced during the Emergency and later, during the eighties—the two periods when severe repression had been unleashed. The Akali Dal, then led by Longowal, had launched a protest movement wherein on every single day of the Emergency, *jathas* or teams of volunteers would start out from the Golden Temple and other gurudwaras in Punjab, raise slogans against the Emergency and court arrest. Slowly, the numbers grew from 50 to 100, then 200 to 1,000. The team would recite a prayer and take a pledge not to turn back until the Emergency was lifted—regardless of what kind of government repression they might have to face. As the repression intensified and volunteers were beaten, arrested and sometimes tortured, women began to come out in larger numbers in response to Longowal's call for their help.

I interviewed several women, including some *jathedarnis* (women team leaders) from Punjab villages, who had taken part in the struggle. These women had not only organized supplies of food and clothing for volunteers but also done propaganda work, moving from village to village, and led women's teams to court arrest as well as participated in the later *rasta roko* agitations of the early eighties. Many of them had been jailed more than once.

In all their accounts, what came through clearly was their fervent dedication to the cause identified with their community and its leaders—even though the movement had nothing to offer women as women. The repression unleashed on the men of their families and community was a more important causal factor for their participation than any of the political demands. They repeatedly said they had joined the movement to do *sewa* or service, to 'give' rather than to 'take'. For example, Bibi Beant Kaur, aged 62, from a village in Sangrur district, described her initial motivation in this way: 'On the first day of the anti-Emergency movement, five Singhs courted arrest. After that, I dedicated myself to Sant Longowal. I said: "You take whatever *sewa* you want from me."'

Another woman in her forties recited a poem she had composed when Longowal advised her to go home to her children, saying he would summon her when she was needed. The whole poem is built around one idea that she cannot sit at home when the men of her community are suffering repression. The solidarity family members feel for one another was extended to the larger community. Here is a prose summary of the poem, translated from Punjabi:

> Our community is in dire straits. How can I sit at home at such a time? ...My sons, brothers and nephews have been sent to prison, have been oppressed, beaten, and framed in false cases.... When 34 Singhs were killed by a train at Tarn Taran (during the *rail roko* agitation), I was sitting in my kitchen; when I heard about it, I started weeping; an arrow seemed to pierce me, I was filled with anger and I could not distinguish between home and the world; I came to go to prison, forgetting all my other chores. I am ready to wear a necklace of the hangman's noose, I am ready to go to prison... Listen, my father, so far I have never contradicted you, But Harwant can never turn back and sit at home at such a time...

An unquestioning obedience to leadership, a do-or-die spirit was also evident during the *jail bharo* agitation. There was such massive inflow into jails that the government was forced to improvise new jails in schools and other public buildings not just for men but also for women. Finally, the government started releasing the prisoners unconditionally, as the expense and responsibility of maintaining them in custody became unwieldy. Several Akali women narrated how women's *jathas* had refused to leave the jails even when the government tried to force them out. They said they would only leave when they received orders from their leaders to that effect. Forty-five year old Beant Kaur of Khanpur village narrated how she and the 150 women of her team locked the prison doors from within and stayed there for 12 days after their official discharge:

> We refused to leave the jail because our leader had not yet ordered us to do so. Some of the women had small children with them.... We asked the jail staff to leave, and took over the jail; we locked it from inside. All of us stood guard, ready to fight if anyone came to discharge us forcibly. We were afraid the policemen might attack us or take our honour. So we collected brickbats and got ready to fight. The jailers stopped supplying us rations. For two days, we stayed hungry; then our brothers from villages nearby sent us food.

It was only after Longowal gave the order to leave the jails that the women did so. Even then, instead of returning to their villages where their families were anxiously awaiting them, they proceeded straight to Sant Longowal to receive further instructions. Women also participated in large numbers in the *rasta roko* agitations in the eighties. They blocked traffic by squatting on the roads, singing *bhajans*, and faced police *lathis* with courage.

The Akali women were able to become a significant presence in the movement despite the fact that in normal times the political participation of women in rural Punjab is particularly low. Women normally live extremely secluded and restricted lives and are not allowed political participation even at the gurudwara level. The participation in this movement became possible because the men of the community were willing to release the women from their normal routine workload. Many women described how their husbands offered to release them from domestic responsibilities in order that they could add strength to the movement in a time of crises.

In the Shahada struggle too, despite constituting a large percentage of the landless poor labourers, in the initial years 'the mass of women remained outside the activities of the Shramik Sangathana'; they hardly participated in the night meetings where movement-related issues were discussed and decisions taken. The crisis brought about by the 1973 drought enhanced women's participation in various struggles demanding adequate relief measures from the government. At this time, women came to participate almost equally with men in *morchas* and *gheraos*. Apart from protesting against atrocities on women by landlords and the police, the women repeatedly came to the rescue of men who were being attacked by these forces. In the 1972 strike of agricultural labourers for higher wages at Pariwaraha, the militancy of the few women who took part played a crucial role. Despite the presence of the police, they managed to persuade the strike breakers to join the struggle. Likewise, when activists were arrested, the women spontaneously came to the men's rescue.

In a struggle of Dalits against Maratha landowners, in Ramegaon, Maharashtra, it was found that women spontaneously came to the rescue of male activists who were being attacked by Maratha men. These women normally never spoke in the meetings of the organization. Yet, as an activist of the area reported:

> To quote some of the women: 'the moment our men saw the upper caste men approaching, they lifted their *dhotis* and ran'. The women ran towards the activists and tried to protect them by covering them with their *sarees* and getting beaten up in their stead. Later, the organization demanded that government land be given to the landless. Towards this end, the organization decided that the Dalits would plant a crop on the surplus land which the Maratha men were trying to claim as their own. They were afraid of reprisals from the Marathas. So, it was felt that it would be better for only women to do the planting, because the upper

caste men might hesitate to attack women. The women also said that, unlike the men, they would not get excited or angry, but would complete as much of the planting as possible.... After discussion, all the women agreed to the idea. Many of them said: 'Our men make a lot of noise, but during the fights they ran' (Lalitha et al., 'When Landless Women Organize–Case Study of an Organization in Rural Andhra', *Manushi*, No. 15, p. 22).

The role played by women here was the openly confrontational arm of the organization, not because women are supposed to be better at combat than men, but because they take beatings more courageously.

Women Bring a New Militancy

Mahatma Gandhi had once commented on the inspirational quality of his first encounter with womanpower in South Africa. Women's militant entry into the movement had made him realize how women could 'become the leader in Satyagraha which does not require the learning that books give but does require the stout heart that comes from suffering and faith' (*Harijan*, 24 February 1940).

Leaders of very diverse movements have repeatedly paid tribute in highly emotional terms to rural women's fervour and dedication. To quote one example from many, a leader of tribal agitation against drought in Rajasthan, writing from jail about women's *dharnas* outside the jail:

> Hundreds of tribal women have not gone home, not seen their children, not eaten and not slept. Their affection and firmness in this struggle have not only been an eye-opener but filled me with a deep sense of humility. The bravery and steadfastedness of these simple, illiterate women...has been the main strength of the whole movement (*Manushi*, No. 50, 1987, p. 6).

This, despite the fact that this organization has not made any special efforts to organize women qua women.

Women's entry into a movement usually brings with it a new militancy and inspirational quality. To begin with, the very idea that women have had to come out of their homes and join the struggle heightens the sense of urgency and crisis; the community feels it has reached a crisis point. Sharad Joshi of the Shetkari Sangathana narrates an instance of this galvanizing effect when, during the onion agitation of 1980, after he had addressed a public meeting in Nasik district to mobilize support, an old woman stood up and said she wanted to speak. Everyone was surprised at a woman daring to speak in such a huge gathering. Addressing the men, she said: 'If men don't want to join the agitation, we offer them our bangles to wear and sit at home. We women have decided to join the agitation anyway.' According to Joshi, this was an important turning point in the area. Because of women's massive support, Nasik district became a major stronghold of the organization.

He describes what he considers a particularly inspiring example of women's courage. During the 1981 cotton agitation at Nipani, a woman who was a widow lost two of her young sons during two separate incidents of police firing on agitators. When Joshi, after his release from jail went to condole with her, she is reported to have said: 'Two of my sons have died. But I still have one son left. I am ready to send him wherever the Sangathana needs him for its work.'

The spirit with which rural women often come into a movement is well exemplified in a Shetkari Sangathana woman activist's description of women's participation in a 1982 *rail roko* agitation:

> The women who were sitting on the rail tracks faced beatings and *lathis* and said: 'We have told our families that we are setting out to die' and I have seen that when a woman comes prepared to die, she can do anything. The movement was successful because of women (taped interview).

Women Put in the Front Line

Most mass movement leaders have paid similar tributes to women's greater capacity for suffering and faith. Throughout the freedom movement, Gandhi encouraged and exhorted women to be in the forefront of various mass actions, including picketing, because he believed that women's presence in sufficient numbers would help keep the movement disciplined and non-violent. But it was not his intention that men begin to use women as a shield against repression and beatings. It was to avoid this kind of abdication of responsibility by men that he was against taking women on the Dandi march, since he expected the government to react with violence to this agitation:

> Just as Hindus do not harm a cow, the British do not attack women as far as possible. For Hindus, it would be cowardice to take a cow to the battlefield. In the same way it would be cowardice for us to have women accompany us (1930, *Collected Works*, Vol. 43, pp. 12–13).

However, most leaders of mass movements today, including many of those who profess to use Gandhian tactics, have been far less scrupulous in this matter. Often, women are deliberately put in the front line to face the brunt of repression. Often, this is justified on the grounds that the police or other attackers may behave with relatively greater restraint when faced with women protesters and that, even if they do not, women will face the attacks more valiantly than men.

In the Bodhgaya land struggle, women were encouraged to take a leading part in one of the most risky actions–that of reaping the disputed crop on land owned by the *matth*. An activist reports: 'More women participated in the harvesting action than in any other action because most families felt that the larger the number of women who went from their family to participate in the harvesting, the larger would be the share they could carry home, and thus the larger the share their family would get. Once again, in many villages women were used as a means by the men.'

Needless to say, this strategy does not always result in less repression. It often results in women bearing the brute face of repression. The strategy has often been used in the agitations of the Jharkhand Mukti Morcha in Bihar. For example, following a militant tribal agitation for the reclamation of forest lands in 1980, the government had unleashed brutal repression in tribal villages in Singhbum district. The Bihar Military Police was sent to raid villages and as usual went on a rampage. When we went to investigate police atrocities in the area, we found that in most of the raided villages, men had run away to the forests, leaving women, children and the old behind. In some villages where men joined in resisting the police, they openly admitted that when they had to stall police entry into the village, they would put women in the front. The reasons they offered were:

1. Women do not lose their cool as easily as men do and are able to resist without unnecessary violence. This forces the police to be relatively restrained.
2. If the police start using force, women do not run away as men tend to do. They often fight to the last to protect their men and children.

The leadership of Shetkari Sangathana categorically asserts that while movements of Dalits, tribals and other marginalized groups may use women as a shield, the culture of the peasantry will not allow them to make such use of women. However, traces of this thinking are evident in the important book that lays out the strategy and organizational principles of Shetkari Sangathana. While discussing how to effectively resist the government and co-operative society officials when they come to forcibly recover loans from indebted peasants who have no resources to repay the loans, Sharad Joshi writes:

> The question arises, what will we do when the society or bank jeep comes to the village to seize the goods of the defaulters. In every village, all

> the women should be collected together. Every woman should carry a broom. They should collect outside the house of the family whose goods are being seized. The men should simply stand near the women and say 'You are not to touch the bodies of our women.' If we follow this strategy, they will not able to seize anything (*Kisan Sangathan Vichaar aur Padditi*, p. 104).

In the same book, Joshi also describes how volatile the situation can become during an agitation when the police physically misbehave with a woman.

In the Akali movement described earlier, Harwant Kaur, secretary, Stree Akali Dal, narrated how when she, along with 125 women, was in jail, the Akali men who were staying in the nearby Ludhiana jail sent a message to ask them whether the women would come to the men's help in case the police tried forcibly to beat the men out of jail. She says they sent back an assurance. 'As long as we are alive, we will not let them open the door of your jail. They will have to kill us first.' And they did exactly as they promised. As soon as they got to know that the government was going to forcibly release the Akali men, the women prisoners spread a rug outside the men's prison, sat there and defied the police to drive their trucks over them. They thus successfully prevented their men becoming victims of police atrocities.

Atrocities on Women Made a Symbol

While women victims of police and other attacks are often projected as heroines and martyrs, their own husbands and communities often reject and ostracize them should they suffer sexual assault while defending the community. In the aforementioned case of police atrocities in tribal villages of south Bihar, the leaders were full of stories of how the women had valiantly resisted police attacks and had suffered various injuries and indignities while defending their villages. Yet, no woman was willing to say she had been a victim of sexual assault. We were puzzled, until we discovered the reason for this silence. We learnt that any woman who admitted having been raped would be ostracized by the community, denied her maintenance rights in the family land and not even allowed to offer water or to participate in any ritual. Many rape victims had been compelled by this ostracism to leave the villages and migrate to towns to seek work. One woman who was selling her meagre assets to bail out her husband from jail following his arrest in the agitation was unsure whether he would keep her in the house or throw her out once he heard that she had been raped by the police.

Similarly, before the Bodhgaya movement fitfully began to take up the issues, 'the landless men had never thought of the continuous attacks on women by government officers and *matth* functionaries as attacks on women, but rather primarily as attacks on their own honour. Women were held responsible for bringing this dishonour on men. Therefore, the men thought they were in the right to insult and humiliate the women who were thus attacked' (*Manushi*, No. 14, p. 4)

Even while the victimized women seldom receive support or sympathy from family and community, atrocities on poor rural women by the rural elite and the police have often become symbols of the community's wrongs around which women are inducted into protest actions. An attack on women is seen as an attack on the community's honour and ultimately as a challenge to the men. It is in this sense that rapes of lower caste women are frequently viewed by the Dalit or tribal movements–not primarily as an act of violence against women but as a weapon of caste or ethnic oppression primarily aimed at the men. In Andhra Pradesh, for example, where Ryotu Coolie Sanghams of Dalit, landless and poor peasants were leading an agitation against illegal land-holdings, extraction of compulsory labour by landlords and for higher wages, women participated in large numbers. They were reported to have been organized in 'Mahila Sanghams which had been fully participating in the programmes and meetings of the Ryotu Coolie Sanghams' but '...the women's organizations appear(ed) to be ancillary to the peasant organizations' (*Manushi*, No. 2, 1979, p. 7). The only specifically women's issue mentioned as having been taken up by the Mahila Sanghams was sexual exploitation by the landlords.

So also, in a report on the CPI-ML struggle of landless peasants in Bihar under the aegis of the Bihar Pradesh Kisan Sabha (BPKS), women are only mentioned as victims of sexual exploitation when this victimization becomes a symbol for an agitation: 'In May 1981 the wife of Ram Pravesh Thakur (a barber) was raped by Tuntun Singh and co-villagers of Raj Kishori Singh of Masaurhi block. The landlords managed to hush up the matter and police also refused to record the case. In retaliation, the landless peasants decided not to work at the farm plot of Tuntun Singh which remained barren throughout the year' (*Economic and Political Weekly*, 2–9 January 1988, p. 52). The victim here seems to be the husband rather than the wife whose name is not even mentioned, as the report goes on: 'the landless peasants, in support of a barber, refused to work in the field of the landlord' (ibid.). A mention of dowry in the same report relates it not to women's status but to the lives of middle peasants, which are said to be 'ruined' by such 'modernization of old rituals' (ibid.). In the BPKS manifesto, only the last of the eight resolutions mentions women, and that too only in passing, relating to their being used as one element of the organization's fighting arm: 'To develop such organizations of the people as village self-defence corps, volunteer forces, resistance squads of women, etc. to enable them to defend themselves against the attacks of the police, military and the goondas' (*Economic and Political Weekly*, 2–9 January 1988, p. 55).

It is no coincidence then that by and large the participation of rural women in movements has been very sporadic and mainly confined to attending demonstrations, *dharnas* and *morchas*. Very few women are able to be consistently active and there are therefore hardly any instances of rural women becoming an effective part of the decision-making process in any rural movement. According to Sharad Joshi, 'the few women who are able to assume some kind of leadership role are not even mobilizers of other women, let alone able to become leaders of the movement as a whole. More frequently, they are simply ideal contacts or symbols.'

Women's Wings Formed by Male Leaders

Since so far rural women have by and large participated in movements more in the spirit of coming to the rescue of their men in crises than out of a determination to acquire any clout as women, there are hardly any instances of rural women having pressurized movement leaderships to ensure that women share the gains of the movement. In some movements, leaders respond to women's participation by organizing women's wings. But these women's fronts remain auxiliaries, playing a purely supportive role—like the Ryotu Mahila Sanghams vis-à-vis the Ryotu Coolie Sanghams. Even though the women may respond enthusiastically to the formation of women's wings, it is significant that the pressure for their formation rarely comes from the women. These wings are formed usually when the male leaders make an out-of-the-way effort to create a special space for women.

An important reason why male leaders tend to encourage the mobilization of women for their movements seems to be that women provide a relatively docile mass base. They seldom get into the kind of power struggles that men do. While they may compete with each other, women do not in any way pose a threat or offer any competition to the male leadership.

In the Bodhgaya land struggle, for instance, rural women had been mobilized for vanguard action, for rallies and protests. They had faced police repression and gone to jail. Yet, when the Vahini activists took the initiative to hold an all-women camp, they found that women were kept in the dark by their men about the progress of the land struggle. The men only notified them when their presence was required at a rally and often did not even explain what the rally was for. Some women activists suggested the formation of women's committees so that women could be more active in decision-making but this suggestion could not be implemented due to a paucity of outside women activists to organize them.

The Stree Akali Dal was formed at the initiative of the Akali leaders and not of the women members. Harwant Kaur, a secretary of the Stree Akali Dal, described its origins thus:

> Our Stree Akali Dal was started by Sant Longowal. Just as we used to think he was our father and mother, so he too had great regard for us, women. He started the women's wing after the Emergency. During the Emergency, the women had spontaneously done a lot of *sewa* (service). Many of them had courted arrest and done *sewa* of those who were in jail. That is when Sant Longowal thought that *stri jati* (womankind) can work with great dedication, so we should organize them. That is how he came to establish the Stree Akali Dal (taped interview).

Likewise, in the struggle of the landless poor in Shahada, the women themselves did not pressurize the organization leadership to address itself to their specific problems as women: 'The group of men and women activists of the Sangathana discussed how the mass of women could be involved in the struggle.' They decided to plan for a camp where women from different villages could come together and discuss their problems: 'Women's committees were set up to look after various organizational aspects of the meeting–to collect grain, to persuade women to come, to arrange drinking water.' It was the organizers of the Sangathana who decided to centre the meeting on questions of alcoholism, wife-beating and women's self-defence. In order to consolidate and further increase women's participation, a women's camp was organized. When the men resisted sending women to the camp, Sangathana activists took the initiative to persuade them. It was the effort to provide a special space for women to air their grievances that led to women taking some initiatives of their own, such as the anti-liquor campaign and resistance to wife beating and sexual abuse by rich peasants. Before they made this extra effort, women tended to stay away from the organization.

Similarly, the decision to organize a women's front came at the initiative of the male leadership of the Shetkari Sangathana without any pressure whatsoever from peasant women. The women seemed quite ready to work whole-heartedly for the organization's general programme without demanding any special attention to their problems as women. The booklet entitled *The Women's Question* published after the Chandwad conference in 1986 noted:

> It has taken the Shetkari Sangathana full six years since its inception in 1980 to form a palpable women's front and to organize deliberations on the problems specific to women.... Though the women's question has been on the agenda of all the sessions of the Sangathana, starting from

> the very first at Satara in January 1982, the deliberations concerned ways and means and need to mobilize women to strengthen the agitations rather than problems specific to women. The women who thronged there themselves did not seem to look upon the Sangathana for the redressal of their own specific grievances (*The Women's Question*, p. 1).

In other words, it was not pressure from women which made the Sangathana leadership turn its attention to women's issues. It so happened that the leadership decided the movement would be incomplete if it did not take a stand on the question. The booklet states: 'The new peasant movement has a historical and theoretical responsibility of pronouncing itself on the women's question' (ibid.: p. 4).

A woman activist described how at one of the earliest women's meetings called by Joshi, when he asked the women to express their problem, they went on talking only about unremunerative prices and other economic problems faced by peasant families. Finally, she says, Joshi said: 'Look, leave all these questions of prices and agricultural produce to us, men. What problems do you have as women?', but again we did not talk about our problems. For another whole day, we continued talking about government policy and industrialists and the labour of peasants going unrewarded. There was only Sharad bhau and a couple of other men in the hall and about 150 women. The doors were closed and the loudspeaker was removed. He said: 'Forget that anyone is listening and say what is in your hearts.' In a little while, every woman started telling her problem–someone's husband used to beat her, someone's husband was a drunkard, someone's husband refused to let her have any say in the financial affairs of the house. Many women started crying...' (taped interview).

And yet the women's identification with Samagra Mahila Aghadi, the women's front created by Shetkari Sangathana leadership to deal specifically with women's issues, remains hesitant and uneasy. While they identify enthusiastically with the Shetkari Sangathana, many of the women feel the existence of Samagra Mahila Aghadi is superfluous. Part of this resistance could stem from the inability to identify with the urban feminist leadership that has been imposed on Samagra Mahila Aghadi in an attempt to form a united front of all women. An equally important reason is their hesitation to assert the need for a separate political space for women in a situation where they know that the space they have today comes not so much from their having demanded it as from the Shetkari Sangathana leadership having given it to them.

Family Permission Crucial for Participation

Even this limited and hesitant expression of women's grievances was made possible because the men of the community had placed their trust in Sharad

Joshi and were willing to bring their women out of the homes when he asked them to do so. For example, the activist quoted earlier first came to the meeting on the insistence of her husband's elder brother. Her account:

> My brother-in-law said: 'Come on, Sharad Joshi is holding a women's camp at Katol. Many women are coming.' I said: 'I am not interested. I have to send the kids to school. I am the only woman in the house. I can't go out of the village'. But he insisted, saying: 'No, you go. You are an educated woman. If you go, about 20 to 25 other women from the village will also go.'

Most rural activists confirm that the few women who are able to take an active part in movements are wives of men already involved, who are therefore agreeable to the women getting activized. Women who come against the wishes of the male members of the family are seldom able to sustain their involvement over a long period of time. In Punjab, almost all the women I interviewed confirmed that it was because their men actively supported their participation that they could be as active as they were. Joshi also confirms that almost all the rural women activists of the Shetkari Sangathana have husbands who are either devoted workers of the Sangathana or at least active supporters. He knows of only two women who tried to be active against their husbands' wishes. Both women had to soon give up their involvement. One of these women had initially come into the movement because her husband was involved in it. After a while, he joined a political party. When his wife tried to continue working for the Sangathana, he began to slander, abuse and beat her. It was not just the male leaders of the movement who felt reluctant to allow her to be an active mobilizer, but also other women who refused to work with a woman whose husband accused her of being a loose woman.

Linked to the crucial need for family permission is the age factor. In most rural movements, while a number of male activists are unmarried youth, young unmarried girls are seldom allowed to participate. An important reason is that parents fear a girl's reputation will be ruined if he she is exposed to the world and mixes with men in a public domain. Explaining why the task of organizing women had to be done mostly by men, a report from SUTRA, a development agency doing mobilization work in Himachal Pradesh, says:

> Few local families are initially prepared to allow women to join as workers. The work involved traveling long distances...staying away from home at night, and coming in contact with men. In an area where few women travel, let alone work outside their villages, the set-up was seen as damaging to the moral status of women. Young unmarried women face problems because their chances of marriage could be ruined if

> they got a bad reputation because of their work. For older women, this was a lesser problem, but they faced the double disadvantage of being heavily weighed down with work and being illiterate (*Manushi*, No. 39, 1987, p. 34)

I have also repeatedly been told, in different rural areas, that young married women may more easily get permission if respected older women of the village are already involved and can act as escorts of sorts.

Women Participate to Serve Family Interests

If in political movements which face repression, women get moblized as auxiliaries to the male-led community effort, even rural development agencies, whose work involves taking up economic issues through some degree of political mobilization, can mobilize women only by convincing men that women's involvement will serve family interests. A leading activist of Self-Employed Women's Association (SEWA) reports on the rural wing's work in 30 villages of Ahmedabad district where the attempt was to organize rural poor women, mainly of the lower castes, into dairy co-operatives. They faced a great deal of hostility from private dairies and milk traders who had influence over the local bureaucracy.

In addition, men of the women's own families also often oppose the idea. Initially, when the activists asked the men's permission to take the women for three-day training camps to Ahmedabad, many men said that women were illiterate and brainless and it would be better to train men who are the 'real farmers'. When the co-operatives were being formed, the leading activist, who was from the urban area, had to visit each member's family to get the men's consent. The men insisted on attending the meetings. They had to be 'reassured about their continuous status at home and in community. Only, instead of their names, those of their wives and mothers will be changed (sic) in the co-operative structure. They even could recommend committee members "after all, the milk-income is going to be used for your whole family. So, what difference is it going to make if your wife or mother come to collect milk money, or the buffalo account bears her names?" we argued' (Anila Dholakia, 1986, *Rural Women in White Revolution*, p. 12. Ahmedabad: SEWA).

In every village, meetings were held to reassure the male dairy farmers that 'we were not starting a parallel dairy, that we are not against men and husbands.... All we wanted was to have women's active participation in milk production and income earning' (ibid.: p. 13). The attempt was to merge the two types of co-operatives. The men ridiculed the women, saying they were illiterate and like buffaloes and the women agreed with this assessment. Men insisted that they would continue to manage it all. SEWA had to give up the idea of all-women co-operatives as the village women members supported the choice of influential men of the village as members and secretaries, later explaining that one cannot survive in the ocean if one makes enemies of crocodiles. Later, when some male secretaries turned out to be corrupt, SEWA activists were frustrated to find that the same women members who had complained of these men's malpractices, stood up and declared that they would resign from the co-operative if these men were asked to leave. This was obviously because they feared that the vindictiveness of these men may endanger their safety.

The activist concludes in her reports that their ability to handle men tactfully was crucial to their success since if the men had been antagonized, they would not have allowed SEWA to even begin its work. She describes how she convinced the men of her own sincere belief that although the women's co-operative 'directly upsets the balance of the man–woman relationship in the village' this is only a means to another end—the good of the family: '...for the time being let women share a part of the development process. Ultimately, the additional assets or income will go in for the family only, as Indian women are conditioned by their value system to sacrifice everything for husbands and children. This has won males' support to SEWA movement' (Anila Dholakia, 1986, *Rural Women in White Revolution*, p. 45).

Similarly, when an agency called CROSS, working in Bhongir, Andhra Pradesh, began to organize separate women's Sanghams to enhance the participation of women in the already ongoing mobilization of Dalit labourers and poor peasants, the women were initially allowed to come because the agency was seen as 'an intermediary institution that helped to get funds for buffaloes, wells, general stores, vegetable vending and other small income generating projects...' (*Manushi*, No. 15, 1983, p. 12). As the Sanghams developed, women activists of CROSS held all-women meetings and camps where they also raised women's issues such as wife beating and property rights for women, apart from the general issues of poor peasants and lower castes. Even though women's issues remained largely confined to discussions, the mere fact of their being talked about in public fora aroused male hostility. Some men beat up their wives for having talked in public about their family problems. Yet, men continued to tolerate the women's mobilization, which remained largely confined to winning welfare measures for the community from the government, because 'the men who formerly had protested when the women wanted to attend meetings and weekend camps realized that in their own dealings with the landlords and other dominant groups, they could get more support from the organized women than formerly from their oppressed, individualized wives' (ibid.: p. 13).

Another revelatory example is provided by the report from Madhu Sarin, who was involved in the campaign to popularize smokeless *chulhas* in villages of Haryana. She entered the villages through a regreening project which involved the whole community through its male leadership. The women never attended village meetings and when, after a lot of persuasion by her, some of them did, they sat huddled in a corner, did not speak and soon left to attend to their domestic chores. In private conversations with her, however, they were articulate about their predicament, of being heavily overworked and yet having next to no decision-making power over their lives: '...they say their lives are no better than those of the animals they tend' (*Manushi*, No. 35, 1986, p. 26). The Gujjar peasantry of one village was fairly prosperous, and women's labour is a crucial contributory factor in this prosperity. Yet, no woman could decide on her own to buy the subsidized *chulha* for about Rs 25, without asking her husband's permission. The old *chulha* was not only a serious health hazard but also added considerably to the women's work burden by badly blackening the cooking pots. Yet, several husbands refused to pay for the new *chulha*. Sarin reports that the initial success of the *chulha* in this village had much to do with the fact that it was introduced just before the marriage season. 'Negotiations for marriages were going on in the villages. In this context, the new *chulha* became a status symbol even for the men. As one man remarked, outside parties coming with marriage proposals could be shown the new *chulha* as a sign of the family's progressiveness' (*Manushi*, No. 35, 1986, p. 29). But even those homes which purchased the *chulha* could not maintain it for long because the women could not spare the little time needed to keep it in good repair, their own convenience being a low priority in the list of domestic chores to be done.

The activist also found it next to impossible to recruit a couple of Gujjar women to become *chulha mistris* even though this was a paid job. The men would not allow women to move from one quarter of the village to another and to visit homes to repair *chulhas*. One young woman who dared begin the training was violently beaten up by her father and prevented from continuing. Sarin found that her work with women was acceptable to the men only as long as they could see the immediate benefits to the family without challenging the power of men. Women could not think of entering into activities of which men would, or even might, disapprove. For example, when Sarin proposed that the women begin to market the traditional rugs they wove for their daughter's dowries as a way to earn an independent income, the women would not even consider the possibility because they said their husbands and fathers would object to accompanying Sarin to town to set up a marketing network. After she had dropped the idea, a male villager approached her and offered to supply as many rugs as she wanted, on a commission basis. In her words:

> I asked him how he could get so many rugs produced when the women had spare time only during two months of the year. His spontaneous

> reply was: 'Oh, the women don't do anything. They can produce as many rugs as necessary.' I immediately saw how this could end up making the women's lives much worse than they are at present. Their men would start pressurizing them to produce more rugs even though they were already overburdened with work. And the cash income would still be controlled by men. I dropped the idea like a hot brick (*Manushi*, No. 35, 1986, p. 28).

SUTRA, mentioned earlier, also reports having had to shift its emphasis more towards procuring loans for buffaloes for women and training them in veterinary skills, after the hostility by men towards the anti-liquor campaign launched by the agency. It has been a common experience of rural development agencies that it is easier to mobilize women for some kind of veterinary training, so that they can tend their family animals better, than for health training for themselves. This is largely true even in tribal peasant societies where women have relatively fewer restrictions on their movements. These women not only shoulder most of the agricultural work, including marketing, but also seasonally migrate in times of scarcity, often unaccompanied by men of their families. Yet, political activists working in tribal areas have found it hard to organize women except by bringing them to the fore during confrontations with the state machinery. This is how a woman activist from a tribal area of Bihar explained the reasons for the very peripheral role played by women in tribal politics, despite their mobility:

> They are free to move around as long as it relates to their family responsibilities. Going to the local market to sell surplus produce or to the forests to collect fuel, or migrating in times of scarcity are all seen as part of working as the husband's slave. They are doing all this for the upkeep of the family, which is seen as primarily the woman's responsibility. But anything that is unrelated to that is an absolute no. For example, it is almost impossible to find a tribal woman who can work as a village health worker, let alone be a political worker (taped interview).

A telling example of the tendency to keep women's involvement within the parameters of male family members' approval is provided by the following account from the Bodhgaya struggle:

> In Piparghati village, in 1980, a *sathi* called Prakash Pran, with the help of some others, opened a school for adult women, especially those who were active in the struggle. The villagers felt the necessity for literacy because they were wholly dependent on city activists for negotiations with the authorities, drafting leaflets, and giving press releases. At that

time, there was no school for adult men throughout Bodhgaya, so that men were indignant at the idea that the first school opened should be for women. They thought the women were getting too smart and were trying to get ahead of the men, so they began to make life difficult for the women. Though these men were conducting the land struggle on principles of non-violence, they readily used every weapon from teasing and ruffianly behaviour to downright physical violence against the women. They would waylay the women on the way to school and would abuse and harass them. Several women were also beaten up at home by brothers and husbands who forbade them to step out of the house. The attendance dropped off and the school had to close.

Women Do Not Determine the Agenda

Since the prior approval of men of the community is an essential condition for women's participation and the initiative for forming a women's front too comes usually from the male leadership, the issues chosen for the women's fronts also have to be those which seem to strengthen the organization as a whole and do not alarm the men. More important, even when certain specific women's issues are raised, the initiative for doing so generally comes not from the rural women participants but from male leadership. Therefore, how far the issues are carried through in action depends on the will and the judgement of the leadership. There are hardly any examples of rural women being able to determine the agenda of the women's wing, let alone make a substantial dent in the agenda of the movement as a whole. For example, the Stree Akali Dal did not raise the question of oppression of women because this was not on the agenda of the Akali leadership. Sant Longowal's message to women as reported by Harwant Kaur was: 'Do not harm anyone. Live in peace and love with all. When you go to you in-laws' house, love everyone there. Serve your husband. Have no relationship with any man other than your husband.' The Akali leadership even proposed curtailing women's rights by introducing a personal law for Sikhs that would have deprived women of whatever legal inheritance rights they had and legally legitimized the practice of levirate. Despite rural women's militant contribution to the movement, no protest against this move emerged from the Stree Akali Dal. Whatever protest was voiced came from urban women's groups in Chandigarh and Delhi, even though the question of land inheritance primarily affects rural women. When we talked on a on-to-one basis with Akali women, many agreed that women should have property rights, but this sentiment of theirs did not find organized expression, not even in the form of a request to the leadership to reconsider the decision.

Even in the Bodhagaya struggle led by the Chhatra Yuva Sangharsh Vahini, which has a relatively better record of giving importance to women's issues, women came to play no more than a subsidiary role. Women activists felt that:

> Vahini men were more interested in women participating in large numbers in action programmes, but were less interested in their developing an independent identity. As a result, while women came and participated in a big way in demonstrations, and were often in the forefront, they could not come to have a decision making role because equal effort was not put into involving them in decision making meetings. The accepted policy was that the leadership of the movement should be in the hands of those whose movement it is. However, when it came to women's issues, leadership and decision making were not in the hands of women. True, it was recognized in principle that sympathetic men would play a supportive role. However, in practice men played not a supportive but a decisive role (see '*Zameen Kenkar, Jote Onkar*: The Story of Women's Participation in the Bodhgaya Struggle', *Manushi*, No. 14, p. 11).

It is significant that the rural women themselves did not take the leadership to task for underplaying women's issues.

The Shetkari Sangathana is one of the large-scale mobilizations of rural women in recent times to have tried to give rural women an agenda of their own. Yet, this seems to have happened without pressure from rural women, as discussed earlier. The way issues have been picked up for action by the Sangathana illustrates this further. The Chandwad resolutions had laid stress on increasing violence and ruffianism in the countryside creating insecurity, especially for women.

The resolution picked up for intensive action by the Sangathana proposes to put up all-women panels for zilla parishad elections. This is indeed a remarkable step, considering how peripheral a role women have so far been allowed to play in village and district level politics. This radical measure seems to have been accepted by the men of the Sangathana because the leadership has presented it as part of *rananiti* (combat strategy) to defeat the corrupt and *goonda* politics led by the Congress (I). Even though men are convinced that right now, women candidates, even if they manage to win seats, will not be in a position to work effectively without guidance from Sangathana men, they are enthusiastically willing to campaign for women candidates because they see this as a way of strengthening the base of the Sangathana. They also hope that women will be far less corrupt than men. Even though many women in rural Maharashtra have responded with great enthusiasm to the measure, at the couple of meetings I attended where the organization was assessing how many women it could put up in different districts, the reporting and assessing was done mainly by male activists. It was clear from the tenor of discussion that the men were assuming responsibility for finding women candidates and campaigning for them. Although the strategy of establishing all-women panels may have far-reaching consequences in the long run, it would be a mistake to see the move itself as an assertion of woman power in rural areas. Had the leadership decided that women would be given 5 or 10 or 20 per cent of the seats instead of 100 per cent, it is unlikely that women would have asked for and gotten more seats on their own strength.

The Telugu Desam is another example of the leadership unilaterally making certain important concessions to women without adequate preparation of women to defend them. NTR came to power with a big mandate from rural women. He made many pledges to women and has redeemed some of them by introducing 30 per cent reservation of government jobs for women, registration of all government housing in the women's names, nutrition programmes for pregnant women, pensions for poor widows and, most important, extending co-parcenary rights to women in their parental property, including ancestral property. However, when the Andhra Pradesh legislature passed the important amendment to the Hindu Succession Act to give near-equal rights to women in ancestral property, and the central government delayed presidential assent for over a year, there was no sign of protest from rural women in Andhra to demand that the Centre not interfere with their rights. Even after the Bill became law, the secretary of the Telugu Desam's women's wing reports that:

> Very few women have actually been able to take advantage of the Law: and that what in fact develop are clashes between a woman's husband and her brothers over land, in which 'no one thinks of the woman's right'. From this, she draws the very important conclusion that '...not only those who give rights but also those who are to take them must have a certain power.... It will take time to empower women so that they can claim their rights' (*Manushi*, No. 42–43, 1987, p. 37).

Need for Continuing Outside Support

Thus, how far and in what manner women's issues get taken up usually depends on the male leadership's inclinations and ideological bent. Rural women's mobilization can acquire an organizational and sustained character only when support, both moral and material, is forthcoming from outside the village. For example, in the Bodhgaya land struggle, it was only in villages where there were outside women activists, or especially sympathetic male activists of the Vahini, that women's issues like wife-beating and men's drunkenness, got taken up. The organization as a whole failed because of resistance by men and the feeling that they might distract energies from the struggle for land. A woman activist reported:

> The effort to stop wife beating did not have much impact because very few people openly and consistently spoke against it.... Someone made a suggestion that men who beat up their wives should not be allowed to join the organisation or the struggle. However, this suggestion could not be implemented... in general, the struggle against wife-beating was not taken up in as systematic a way as was the land struggle. As a result, the wife-beating issue is now completely buried (*Manushi*, No. 14, 1983, p. 5).

Despite women's crucial contribution to the struggle through such vanguard action as reaping the disputed crop and carrying it home in the face of hoodlum and police oppression, they could not consistently mobilize to put an end to wife-beating. The few men who gave up wife-beating were reportedly those who, being more sensitive, realized that it was wrong. The anti-liquor campaign in this area, too, began not as spontaneous action by rural women but from a women's camp organized by Vahini women activists. It remained confined to the dozen or so villages (out of a total of about 130) where these women activists happened to be working. The campaign reportedly died down when these activists left the area.

Even when it came to sharing the gains of the land struggle, it is clear that the rural women would not have been able to insist on their right to land had the outside women activists not taken up the question within the Vahini and the male leadership of the Vahini not assented. While the rural women did complain in private conversations that it was unjust for land to be distributed only in the names of men, they were not in a position to collectively oppose and reverse this process. They said they had not even been informed by the men of the rules whereby land was being distributed. Land was distributed in men's names in several villages before the Vahini women activists realized what was happening. It was only when, at the Vahini state-level conference in 1982, the women activists pressed the issue and a decision was taken by the

Vahini to accept land in women's names, that this decision was implemented. It was communicated to and debated by the villagers who agreed to it. It seems unlikely that the villagers would have been in a position to reject decisions arrived at by the Vahini, whose dedicated work among them had been the crucial factor in their success in getting rights to land at all.

Further, the government had not yet handed over the land in many villages and the Vahini activists were the chief intermediaries for negotiating the hand-over. It is significant that in those villages where the land had already been given in the names of men, women were not able to press for the transfer of land in their names. As in the case of SEWA cited earlier, here too, men seem relatively readier for assets to be in women's names when that seems the only feasible way to fight for or to get them from government, but much less willing when the transfer is to be effected within the family.

Women's movements in Uttarakhand, such as Chipko, for saving trees and against liquor consumption, have been projected as supreme examples of rural women's independent initiative. However, in this movement too, the role played by male leaders and outside activists seems to be the crucial determinant for the sustenance and continuity of the movement. Women of Uttarakhand have at times spontaneously acted to save trees from being felled. However, these spontaneous actions were often with the tacit or explicit support of the men since many villages in this area have decades-long traditions of community protection of forest resources through such techniques as collectively employing watchmen, rotating gathering activities, and so on, these efforts being usually male-led. In villages where men were hostile towards the women's efforts, the intervention of prominent male leaders from outside the village was the crucial factor in protecting and supporting the women. For instance, when Gaura Devi, a widow, led 27 women of her village to protect trees from felling, men of the village turned against her and socially ostracized her. They made their wives abandon her and put all the blame on her. When she was in dire straits and completely isolated, Chandi Prasad Bhatt, 'who had spread the message of Chipko in the village' and whose meetings her son had attended, came to her support:

> Three days later, Bhatt came to the village, complimented Gaura Devi on her action and assured her that he would take full responsibility and would face all the consequences. After this the tide turned in her favour. For a month, people from different villages came to express solidarity with her and to protest against the tree felling. The government appointed a committee to look into the matter, and accepted its recommendations (*Manushi*, No. 7, 1981, p. 23).

It was support and acclamation of the movement, based outside the village, that made Gaura Devi a heroine, not local rural women, who were pressured by their families to isolate her.

Although women in Uttarakhand have participated in large numbers in agitations against government policy on forest and liquor, the movement was not organized or led by them. The umbrella organization that has spearheaded the anti-liquor agitation in recent years was founded and led by men: 'In 1977, Uttarakhand Sangharsh Vahini was organized at Gopehswar by the joint efforts of many organizations. Men like Chandi Prasad Bhatt, Shamsher Singh Visht, Vipin Tripathi, Kunwar Prasun, Yogesh Bahuguna, Sachidanand Bharti, Puran Chand Tiwari, Pradip Tamta, were founding members of the organization' (*Manushi*, No. 24, 1984, p. 3). Reports also show that men outnumbered women in many demonstrations against liquor policy, and that though women came in significant numbers, the movement cannot be said to be organized and directed by women:

> In the course of the movement, many women's organizations have come into being, like Mahila Sangharsh Samiti in Almora, Mahila Mangal Dal in Ramgarh, Mahila Morcha at Ranikhet and Mahila Morcha at Ranital. Though not very strong organizationally, women have played a major role in the movement (*Manushi*, No. 24, 1984, p. 7).

Yet this does not imply that women could sustain the anti-liquor campaign on their own strength, nor that they have acquired any decision-making powers in the protest actions.

In Himachal Pradesh, SUTRA's efforts to raise awareness against alcoholism were centred on women. Men were rather antagonistic to these efforts. Despite a long drawn out campaign for prohibition, the women have not yet been able to get a single liquor vend closed. One important problem was that men prevented their wives from joining the protests. It is noteworthy that in this region, the alcohol-related problem is not one of deaths due to badly brewed liquor but of men squandering family income on drink and of domestic violence following drinking. Even when men did not outright forbid women to participate in the campaign, they would not take over the workload to free the women for a few days. So, only those women could participate who had another woman, such as a sister-in-law, at home willing to take over the work for a few days. When a demonstration was organized at Shimla, many husbands would not give their wives money for bus fare to and fro, so the rally had to be organized as a *padyatra*. Even for this, the infrastructure had to be heavily subsided by SUTRA, by making arrangements such as trucks to carry the bedding, cooks to prepare meals and places to stay for the night, although some Mahila Mandals along the route did organize hospitality for the demonstrators. The number of women who turned up was far less than expected and less than those who wanted to come because many had been prevented by their families. The activists in this struggle were also men, mostly from outside the villages, and it was difficult to find enough local women ready and able to work as activists, even for pay (*Manushi*, No. 39, 1987, pp. 28–37).

Women's Mobilization: Why Seen as Movements?

It is understandable that those who would like to see a rural women's movement in India tend to interpret the excitement generated by women's mobilizations as evidence of the existence of such a movement.

Movements whose leaders and interpreters use a leftist, feminist or the current development terminology, are able to project women's mobilizations, however limited their scope, as women's movements. But women's mobilizations within general movements which use traditional or religious terminology, or which are led by traditional political parties, tend to receive much less attention from progressive writers and social scientists. Thus a large-scale mobilization of rural women in Punjab by the Akalis receives much less attention than much smaller scale mobilizations by left-inclined groups or agencies in other parts of the country.

Sometimes, the writer-activists even shape the rural women's words to make them fit in better with their own ideological persuasion. Thus, a rural women activist is reported to have commented on the urban situation: 'liquor drinking, especially in the cities, is difficult to attack as an isolated issue. It is connected with a great many problems—low wages, unemployment, the routine yet hectic life of the working population', while another comments: 'It is necessary not only that we deal with the women's question in the context of general class issues, but also that we relate to oppressed women and their struggles wherever they are taking place' (*Maunshi*, No, 13, 1982, p. 34).

Decisions and activities are often made to sound more spontaneous than they actually are by the use of the passive voice in reporting. This is done without actually indicating who the subject is, for instance. 'It was decided', 'It was agreed', 'It was proposed'. The reader gets the impression that the initiative was taken by the rural women whereas in fact it was often the activists from outside, or the male leaders of the general movement. By failing to acknowledge their own role in the mobilization, the leaders may communicate a picture of the mobilization as being more self-sustained than it actually was.

Many reports also tend to treat discussion of women's issues as almost as equivalent to action on the issues, For example, a report on the mobilization of Dalit women concludes: 'The Dalit women of Ramegaon have organized themselves and become militantly united to improve their status in society first as women and second as Dalits.' But a close reading of the report shows that the Dalit women acted as buffers in the general Dalit–Maratha conflict over land, coming to the rescue of the men, and that women's issues were confined to discussions in the course of women's literacy classes (*Manushi*, No. 15, 1983, pp. 22–23).

Another factor that contributes to the projection of a mobilization of rural women in exaggerated terms is the dramatic impact that rural women's presence tends to have on the observers and leaders. Not expecting women to be present at all, observers tend to see even a symbolic presence of women as highly significant, while the larger presence of men is treated as normal and routine. Sharad Joshi explains this by saying that a rural woman has to make a much greater physical and mental preparation to get out of the house and join a movement, so one rural woman's presence is equivalent to that of 20 men. While this may be true in terms of the individual woman's effort, such mathematics is hardly a sufficient measure of strength of women as a group within the movement.

Women's excitement in participating in a new type of activity often gets communicated as a sign of greater militancy. Most agitations in which women participate follow the practice of putting the women, even if they are a handful, into the front row, with the result that they get into the photos and are seen as a key part of the vanguard. The line of distinction often gets blurred between putting women in the forefront as a strategy or symbolic statement and women actually constituting a vanguard in terms of leadership.

What Women Gain by Participating

All this is not at all to deny the importance of women's participation in larger movements in rural areas. There is no doubt that, despite the auxiliary role that they play, rural women who are mobilized for different actions gain significantly in terms of self-confidence, mobility and a chance to see the world outside the village, to deal with external agencies and authorities and to interact with other women. Again and again, rural women who talk about their participation in movement activity, mention these as major gains for themselves.

For most rural women, not just the political but even the physical mobilization is pervaded with a sense of excitement. Women who participated in the Himachal anti-liquor campaign, when asked what they had gained from their *padyatra* to Shimla, where their demonstration had not resulted in any concrete success, emphasized the importance of the march in having given them a break from drudgery and a chance to see the world outside the village. In reports on rural women's mobilizations, one repeatedly comes across the statement that many of these women, some of them middle aged, had never moved out of their villages before they went for some sort of protest action organized outside. A middle aged woman who stood for panchayat elections in a Maharashtra village in 1986 remarked that, although she lost the election, one gain was that during the campaign, she, for the first time, visited certain parts of her village that she had never before seen (*Manushi*, No. 42–43, p. 44).

The knowledge that they played an indispensable part in the movement's success helps women build a more positive self-view. This is simultaneous with the greater respect that comes to be accorded to women as a group within the community as a result of their participation. Women's heroic actions became part of the movement lore and some individual women may emerge as role models that are different from the more normal model of woman as server and giver within the family.

Mobilization of women gives them a chance to come together with many other women outside of family networks and around concerns other than the domestic. This space may become available to them for self-organization of some kind and for the development of newer aspirations, more or less articulate. Even if they get pushed back into the domestic sphere once the crisis is over, each phase of participation represents an irrevocable step of some kind and does change somewhat the collective consciousness of women. They become, at the least, conscious of their ability to emerge and to act in the public political domain.

Factors Inhibiting Growth of Rural Women's Movements

One arrives then at the conclusion that there are hardly any instances of rural women's movements in India today, if a movement is defined as it is at the beginning of this paper. Nor have women been able to incorporate their specific issues in the agenda of general rural movements. However, this is not to suggest that individual rural women lack awareness of their situation or that there is no discontent amongst them. What is lacking is that they are not in a position to organize as a constituency. I have found rural women, even those who are illiterate, far more realistic in describing their predicament than are most urban educated women. The inability of rural women thus far to generate movements is primarily due to a lack of basis requisites, primarily the following:

1. Rural women in most parts of India have no independent means of support and little control over family income even when they make major contributions to it. They are typically dependent on men of the family for sustenance and therefore for approval of any activity they undertake. In such a situation, it is difficult to develop a sense of group identity with other women, as separate and distinct from identification with the family unit. As long as women's participation in an activity is perceived by the family as supplementing her family roles and serving the family interests, she too feels justified in undertaking it. If it appears unconnected to family interests, it is difficult of her to sustain her involvement. And if it appears to go against the interests of the powerful members of the family, it is a next to impossible for her develop a stake in it.

   Any movement requires some sort of independent loyalty and commitment on the part of its members which is not wholly subordinated to family loyalties. This can only be developed if the members have a life outside the family, which they perceive as important in its own right, in which they develop extra-familial bonds and in which arena the movement has an impact. Rural women, by and large, are not allowed to develop such a life. They usually have to subsume all other interests in family interests. Even their ability to have a remunerative worklife is largely dependent on family fortunes, the tendency in many regions among large groups being to withdraw women from remunerative work as soon as family prosperity permits this.
2. Women in most parts of India, particularly in north, north-west and central India, are not allowed to develop alliances outside the family. Alliances with men are presented as being liable to compromise the woman's and the family's reputation, while alliances with women are also discouraged unless they are part of larger family alliances. After marriage, a woman who maintains strong alliances, even with members of

her natal family, is frowned upon and often penalized. In this heavily patrilocal culture, the woman is cut off for the best years of her life from any independent alliance. She has to make a place for herself in her husband's family, usually as a subordinate, with unremitting service of her in-laws as the only way to win their approbation.

For people to join a movement presupposes their having some sort of network of alliances. Only on the basis of such mutuality and solidarity can an organized movement take shape.

3. Another very important factor is the simple fact that most rural women are so heavily overworked that they have next to no time and energy to put into building a movement except when men, in the interests of larger community-based struggles, decide to relieve the women of some household responsibilities and free them to join in specific and limited movement activities.
4. Most rural women are deprived of elementary skills required to keep a movement alive, such as literacy, numeracy, and some information about and exposure to the world outside. For example, women are often ignorant of how the government machinery works—or rather, fails to work. They are also excluded from decision-making bodies in the village and community, through which most men receive some sort of rudimentary training in how to organize and take decisions. Therefore, when a movement grows, it is unlikely that women will acquire leadership positions, participate in decision making or even see this as something appropriate for women to do, unless a very special effort is made to get them to do so.
5. Since activists from outside rural areas frequently play a crucial role in sustaining and building organizations of the rural poor and in mobilizing support from outside for these organizations, the greater paucity of women activists as compared to male activists has also much to do with the stuntedness of mobilizations of rural women. Few rural women can choose to work full-time for a movement or organization. And few women even in urban areas have the freedom and the wherewithal to go and work in rural areas. Therefore, the task of providing assistance to rural women's organization and sustaining them over a period of time is even more neglected.

Need for Sharing

Meaningful strategies for moving on to a further stage towards building rural women's movements can emerge only from a more widespread sharing and discussion among various people involved in rural women's mobilizations. Something that might help take the process of mobilization a step further are:

1. To distinguish between those women's issues which are merely symptomatic of women's powerlessness, such as sexual violence against women, and those that have the potential of providing an independent social and economic base for women, such as acquiring land rights. While both types of issues are important, action on the latter has a more long-term strengthening effect for women and can help them to develop their own base.
2. To emphasize the importance of reducing women's drudgery. Reduction of rural women's drudgery is crucial to their being able to get together on their own issues in a sustained way and acquire skills required for organization building. For example, provision of clean drinking water in every home and easily available fuel should be priorities for rural movements that are concerned to provide a base for women to organize.
3. To create women's fronts within general movements is a necessary step to allow women to raise their own issues, but to try and involve women in decision making and leadership processes of the general process should be simultaneous as far as possible.
4. Those movements which have tried to create a separate space for women in the form of women's meetings and camps, have found that women respond very positively to the new experience of some time and space away from domestic responsibilities and of interaction with other women, and ask for more such activities. It is important that movement leaders put moral pressure on men to concede women such space and time which is a pre-condition for them to reflect and debate on issues that concern them. This should be more institutionalized and integrated into the movement process on a continuing basis.
5. It has been found that women tend to respond positively to a moral appeal, for instance, when called on to come to the rescue of the family or the community. On the other hand, they tend to feel somewhat inhibited about demanding rights for themselves, this being seen as somehow ignoble and selfish. This ideological bias facilitates women's energies being used by movements without being rewarded with any concrete gains as women.

It is important that movements consciously try to build the belief that it is immoral for women to be used solely as a means to some end that does not include their own participation in deciding their own best interests.

Women need to understand that it is legitimate for them to work for their own rights, even at those points where these are not necessarily subsumed in some supposedly 'larger' interest.

[This paper is not a comprehensive survey of all rural women's mobilizations in the country. I have selected a few representative examples that illustrate the general pattern as I see it. I have concentrated on women from agricultural families, including the peasantry and the landless poor. My sources of information are various reports sent to *Manushi* over the last decade. I am grateful to the participants and leaders of the various movements who have shared their experiences with me in the course of these interviews.[1]]

[1] While many of the generalizations I have made in this essay remain valid, substantial changes have come about in women's political participation in rural India since the enactment of the 73rd and 74th Constitutional Amendments, which mandate 33 per cent reservation for women in village panchayats and zilla parishads. However, within social movements, they have yet to acquire decision-making roles. The space and the importance given to women-specific issues in rural movements are still largely dependent on the importance given to these by urban, educated, outside activists.

16

The Logic of Quotas

*Women's Movement Splits on the Reservation Bill**

After much fireworks, the Bill to provide 33 per cent reservation for women in Parliament and state legislatures has been put on the backburner, which is exactly where it belongs. The pro-reservation lobby is determined to keep the issue alive. Just as well. It is good to keep it alive as an idea, as an issue to be resolved. However, it would have been disastrous if that foolishly conceived scheme of reservations had actually become part of our electoral law.

For a long time, any legislation that claimed to be pro-women, no matter how stupid and harmful in substance, sailed through Parliament because any legislative initiative claiming to help women enjoyed a moral aura. This moral vantage ground has unfortunately been severely eroded thanks to the short-sighted, thoughtless politics of many of our leaders, both women and men.

My focus here will be on the women politicians. Since the early 1980s, a small coterie of politically prominent women, acting in concert with some

*This article appeared in *Manushi*, No. 107, July–August 1998.

high profile NGOs, has taken it upon itself to push for ever new laws, as well as far-reaching amendments to existing laws, all in the name of strengthening women's rights. Most of these laws are carelessly drafted, with little thought given to their actual implementation, without any thought as to whether they are enforceable, or even if they will actually help women.

The Women's Reservation Bill is the latest, the most serious and the most ambitious of their legislative interventions. If enacted, this measure will send our already tottering political system into an even more devastating tailspin.

I have pointed in two earlier essays ('Out of the Zenana Dabba: Strategies for Enhancing Women's Political Representation' and 'Women's Marginal Role in Politics', *Manushi*, Nos 96 and 97, respectively) that the Women's Reservation Bill, in its present form, has serious, indeed fatal, defects. One-third of total parliamentary seats to be reserved for women are to be selected through a lottery system. This implies that at random at least 180 male legislators will be uprooted from their constituencies in every election. In their place, 180 women will be assigned those constituencies. Then, at the time of the next election, when the new list of 180 reserved constituencies is declared in the same manner, these 180 women will not be able to contest from the seats they are holding at that point of time because the same constituency cannot be reserved twice in succession under the Bill's rotation system.

Thus two-thirds of our legislators will be uprooted at every election, while the remaining one-third will be left hanging until the last moment, not knowing if their constituency will form part of the one-third randomly chosen women's reservation lottery and thus require them to scramble at short notice to find another seat to contest. Moreover, it takes away any incentive or motivation that female representatives might have to nurture and be accountable to their constituencies since after each election they will be expected to move to a different constituency.

The Bill, as presently drafted, jeopardizes the possibility of sensible planning to contest a political constituency for both men and women. It is amazing that our women leaders do not seem to have fully grasped the implications of such a vast change proposed for our electoral process as it will create special difficulties for women. Since very few women politicians have a strong electoral base, this uncertainty about where they will be fielded from will make them even more dependent on male bosses of their party to win elections. In such a situation, it becomes necessary that the influential male leaders be convinced of the advantages to the party leaders of these changes or else they will either sabotage women contenders as revenge against their getting pushed out or they will spend all their political capital helping their women relatives to corner the reserved seats. A likely strategy for them to adopt would be to bring in their wives and daughters as proxies to keep the seat 'safe' for them until the next election when they would be likely to be able to reclaim their seats.

Furthering Male Agendas

Being a politician's wife or daughter ought not to be a disqualification in itself. Nor would one object to their having a natural advantage, just as the children of lawyers and doctors often inherit their father's practice. However, we know that most female relatives are brought in as proxies, whose only task is to safeguard the political interests of the men of their families. Like Laloo Yadav's wife Rabri Devi, they will be brought in as rubber stamps and sent home after their usefulness is over.

I, for one, am convinced that we cannot afford to pack our Parliament and state legislatures with a larger contingent of Rabri Devis. Apart from other disabilities, they act as very negative role models for women because they enlarge the compass of the ideology of female slavery, which is most prominent in the domestic realm, into the public and political domain as well. The one and only agenda these women have is to do all that they can to save their husbands' seat or protect them from being put on trial for looting the public exchequer. They do not even bother to pretend otherwise. How does such a woman serve the cause of women or empower other women?

The *biwi–beti* brigade, in fact, acts as a definite block against the emergence of independent-minded women who wish to make a space for themselves on their own strength in the public domain. For example, it is a common phenomenon in India that the women's fronts of various political parties are headed by wives, other female relatives or mistresses of prominent male party leaders. These posts are given to these women like a *jagir* (fiefdom) for as long as their men retain their clout in the party. Such women do not easily make space for other women with merit. Any woman who enters the party, no matter how talented, has to play a subservient role to these dependent women. The political initiative of most women thus gets curbed rather than encouraged in the party women's fronts.

Because of the familial connection between the main party and the women's fronts, the politics of the women's front remains subservient to the party. They are left to tackle the colourful variety of women's issues as a side-show rather than being involved in defining over-all party policies or even strategies and tactical alliances of the party.

All too often the main purpose of the women's fronts turns out to be narrowly partisan on women's issues. For example, if a rape is committed by people associated with the Congress Party, the women in Opposition parties are used to let loose a tirade against the Congress. But the same women seem helpless to bring redressal for victimized women when their own party colleagues indulge in crimes against women. Even sadder is the spectacle of these party women attacking each other to protect the male leaders of their respective parties.

For example, during the last parliamentary elections, Mamata Banerjee of Trinamul Congress raised a big hue and cry about the violence unleashed by the Communist Party of India (Marxist) (CPI-M) cadres on women, including cases of rape, in order to obstruct the conduct of free and fair elections in West Bengal. The CPI-M women responded in characteristic style and hurled the choicest of political abuses at Mamata, instead of offering to conduct a joint enquiry, at least into the cases of atrocities on women, to verify the authenticity of those charges.

If the Bharatiya Janata Party (BJP) men are accused of gangrape, as happened recently in Rajasthan, women of that party are not known to make common cause with the non-BJP women protesting against those cases of sexual abuse. No wonder our country has not yet witnessed the emergence of women-centric politics on women's issues.

Intolerance of Dissent

However, the pro-reservation feminists have consistently refused to address themselves to this shortcoming, among others, and refused to allow a genuine debate on the merits and demerits of their reservation scheme. Instead, anyone who points out these and related flaws and suggests improvements has only met with hostility and is accused of furthering patriarchal agendas.

Even those who have had a long history of working on women's issues have been denied a hearing. When the Parliament appointed a select committee headed by Geeta Mukherjee to review the Bill, the pro-reservationists ensured that most of those who wanted to see improvements in the Bill were not even invited to present their opinion and to engage in dialogue. A few dissenters were invited, who failed to make any dent. The Bill was presented to Parliament without any modifications whatsoever. Mostly, those who were willing to rubber-stamp the Bill were given a hearing.

When some of the newspapers and magazines gave space to those few who dared to criticize the Bill's shortcomings, a slander campaign was let loose.

Just to give one personal example among several: one of the key persons in the pro-reservationist lobby, Brinda Karat of CPI-M, went as far as telephoning concerned journalists and editors asking them not to carry my critique of the Bill because, according to her, I had joined the Rashtriya Swayamsevak Sangh (RSS)! This accusation, in fact, has been a major theme of a concerted campaign against me ever since I took an open stand insisting on improvements in the existing reservation scheme. This typically Stalinist way of handling disagreements is nothing new among feminists in India.

My point in mentioning this absurd allegation is because such tactics raise more fundamental questions regarding the legitimacy of democratic dissent: do RSS women not have a right to be heard on these issues? Even if I were an RSS member, can my arguments against the Bill be dismissed with contempt simply because I do not profess the current politically fashionable version of Marxism common to many Indian feminists? In India, the left party women, in particular, and socialist feminists, in general, behave as though they alone have a monopoly over defining the agenda of social and political reforms. Because they use typically male weapons like slander to put down all dissent, feminism in India is often guilty of promoting *bhed chaal* (herd mentality). Very few women activists dare dissent openly or refuse to toe their line.

The same kind of intolerance was witnessed in Parliament. The pro-reservationists would not have invited such anger and wrath against themselves had they not insisted that this important Bill involving a constitutional amendment be passed without a debate. This is indeed unacceptable, undemocratic behaviour. What is the purpose of having a Parliament if a proposed legislation cannot be debated and discussed? Their ostensible justification for denying a discussion was that three of the major parties—the Congress, the BJP and the United Front—had committed themselves to enacting this law in their respective party manifestos. However, none of the regional parties, who are important constituents of the present coalition government at the Centre, had made any such commitment. Should they all be denied their democratic right to deliberate upon the Bill? If so, why not just wind up the whole *tamasha* (façade) called Parliament?

Moreover, as is well-known, none of our party bosses take their manifestos seriously. Even leading Members of Parliament (MPs) and party office-bearers are not consulted before drafting these manifestos. Voters hardly ever get to see, leave alone read, manifestos before casting their ballot. In such a situation, do we want to compound the farce by not allowing even a formal debate on the subject, especially since an overwhelming majority of MPs are against the Bill for a whole variety of legitimate and not-so-legitimate reasons? Can such a momentous decision be taken without winning over a section of the legislators on to the women's side—especially considering how very few women are in any position to win elections without support from their male colleagues?

Confrontation sans Strength

The pro-reservation lobby has invited the first serious male backlash on a women's rights issue in the history of independent India largely because of their ham-handed approach and undemocratic behaviour in dealing with even well-meaning dissent. So far we have had a strong tradition—thanks in part due to the legacy of the nineteenth century reform movements and the Gandhi-led freedom struggle—of significant numbers of men not only joining but even leading women's rights struggles in India. We were fortunate enough to rarely witness polarization on gender lines on women's rights issues. Despite this history, the feminist reservationists have needlessly created an atmosphere of gender warfare, alienating even those among our male politicians who could be valuable allies in the struggle for getting women their due share of political power.

The confrontationist attitude of the pro-reservation lobby is especially absurd since they do not have much of a mass-based support among women for this measure.

An Alternative Proposal

I have already discussed an alternative Bill ('Out of the Zenana Dabba: Strategies for Enhancing Women's Political Representation', *Manushi*, No. 96) in which I suggested multi-seat constituencies for those who are enamoured with 33 per cent reservation, whereby one out of every three candidates elected from a combined constituency would be a woman. However, even at that time I indicated that my own preference is for a 50 per cent reservation for women involving dual seat constituencies. This is how it would work.

Every constituency would be represented by two people—one of whom must be a female. She would be elected on the basis of securing the highest number of votes among women candidates. However, if no male candidate got as many votes as the two top-ranking women candidates, both seats could go to women. In order to ensure that the reserved women's seat went to a credible candidate, it could be stipulated that the winning female candidate (as also the male) has to secure a certain percentage of overall votes, failing which there be a second round of elections. This system will allow a larger range of choice to voters.

Some people have expressed doubts about this scheme by pointing out that it will make our legislatures too big and increase the costs of the whole enterprise. An interesting proposal in this regard has come from Mani Shankar Aiyar of the Congress Party who suggests that we could instead abolish the Rajya Sabha for it serves no real function except provide a forum for accommodating all those who fail to get elected to Lok Sabha. In any case, there is serious talk of delimiting constituencies because there has been a manifold increase in the size of our population since the first general elections when the present strength of Parliament was fixed at 544. With our population having reached the one billion mark, many of our constituencies have become truly unwielding. Therefore, increasing the numerical strength of our legislatures in keeping with the growth in population has become necessary. The proposed system of dual member constituencies thus solves two problems in one go.

However, this Bill will only take care of the quantitative aspects of women's representation. It is not enough to send a certain number of *saree*-clad persons to the Parliament. It is far more important that people who reach there—whether men or women—act with responsibility, and do not use their office merely as a licence to loot. In order to move towards that outcome, we need to work on a comprehensive agenda of political reforms aimed at decriminalizing politics, reducing the role of illicit money and making our legislators genuinely sensitive to popular aspirations and have the necessary competence to undertake the complex task of legislating for one billion people. Women ought to play an active leading role in this process rather than leave the entire exercise of defining the rules of the game to men while we only stay confined to demanding a small playing ground for women. This amounts to ghettoizing women's politics. However, genuine women-centred politics can begin to emerge only when women as a group acquire sufficient economic power to take part in politics in their own right. Their political marginalization cannot be effectively combated without combating their economic marginalization, within the family and the society.

When the Bill was unceremoniously torn to shreds in Parliament, there were no spontaneous protests by women even in Delhi, let alone in other parts of the country. The most successful of the pro-reservation demonstrations have never witnessed participation by more than a few hundred women. Most of their protests and *dharnas* (protest sit-ins) are attended by no more than a few dozen women. Most important of all, they have not made the slightest headway in organizing women as a cohesive vote-bank. Most of those leading the pro-reservation lobby could not win a municipal election on their own strength, let alone a parliamentary one. The enthusiasm of many of our feminist NGOs for reservations is particularly puzzling since most of them have virtually no roots in their own neighbourhoods or community—two essential prerequisites in the electoral arena. Their dependence on international aid money tends to estrange them from social sentiment and much of their work consists of attending national and international conferences of like-minded NGOs, unlikely venues for garnering votes.

It is noteworthy that the few among women politicians who have an independent political base are not very enthusiastic about reservations for women. No wonder the male parliamentarians have called the bluff of the women supporters of the Bill; they have realized that apart from projecting them as die-hard chauvinists in the international media and a section of the Indian press, the collective might of the feminist lobby cannot make the slightest dent in even one-quarter of a constituency in India, let alone succeed in making this an important electoral issue all over the country. That is the main reason their claims are not taken seriously within their parties.

It is naive for the pro-reservation women politicians to think that they can muster a majority vote in Parliament in favour of their Bill without winning over a significant number of their male colleagues in their respective parties. Nor has the track record of many of our women parliamentarians been such as to give this move much moral legitimacy.

Feminist Myths

The whole debate on reservations centres on the following myths:

- That a greater presence of women will be a step towards empowerment of Indian women.
- That women's larger presence as a result of this Bill will change the very nature of politics, make it less corrupt, more sensitive to women's needs and generally more democratic and compassionate.

Reserving one-third of the seats in our legislatures would undoubtedly bestow special powers and privileges on the approximately 180 women who would make it to Parliament and many more to state legislatures on the strength of the quota system. It would also create new aspirations among women at large. But I fail to understand how it will 'empower' ordinary women citizens.

Has the presence of 500-plus male legislators in Parliament empowered the men of India? Do most men in India not have to grovel, cringe and bribe for every little thing from a water connection to buying a railway ticket? Have these MPs facilitated men's freedom from abuse and harassment? From hunger and malnutrition? Do men feel secure and safe in today's India? Far from it. Even the mighty male business magnates have to act like hapless supplicants in our country in order to carry out routine aspects of their business. Most citizens, male or female, feel powerless and vulnerable when dealing with the government machinery.

If most men in this country have not benefited from the preponderant presence of male parliamentarians, why should we naively believe that 180 women in Parliament will change the fate of women in India? Given the current political structures, it seems far more likely that those women who reach the legislatures will join the loot brigade like Mayawati, Sheila Kaul and Jayalalitha, or emulate an authoritarian power seeker like Indira Gandhi.

So far in India, we have not witnessed women politicians bringing a superior vision into politics. In the last 50 years, there is no evidence that women politicians have taken a stand any different from that of their party bosses on any issue of importance or introduced any new, worthwhile issues on the political agenda, apart from making noises to get a bunch of ineffective or harmful laws passed, ostensibly for the protection of women. For instance, no woman politician from the Congress Party opposed the imposition of the Emergency. No woman politician stood against the extra-constitutional power centre that Sanjay Gandhi and his brigade came to represent. No Congress woman politician (worth her name) condemned, either within or outside the party, the massacre of Sikhs carried out at the behest of the party high command in 1984 or the various anti-Muslim riots instigated by the party as part of its electoral strategy.

Similarly, no BJP woman leader stood up to condemn the bloodshed that accompanied Advani's *rath yatra.* None of the BJP's female stalwarts have taken a stand any different from the most jingoistic of the male BJP politicians on the nuclear weapons issue. Nor have any of them raised the banner of revolt against the growing corruption and criminalization of their party.

The record of women from the Janata Dal and the various communist parties is no better. In what way then, is a larger presence of women in Parliament going to bring about greater accountability in our political system? The supporters of reservation respond to such concerns with typical disdain. Their position can be summed up as follows:

- 'Why are people raising the issue of political corruption and institutional breakdown at the same time when we are raising the issue of women's representation? This is proof of bad faith, establishing an alibi to scuttle "women's empowerment".' 'So what if the political system is corrupt and dysfunctional? We want our due share of power even if it means plunging in the sea of corruption.' To quote one of their leading proponents: '*Is sadi gali vyavastha mein bhi hamein hamara hissa chahiye*' (We want our share of the pie, even if the pie is rotten). Is this to be the Indian variant of 'Women must hold up half the sky?'

- 'Women's entry will uplift politics and improve the functioning of our legislatures. It will bring more probity into public life.'

I, for one, find these two arguments very inadequate.

Politics of the Ghetto

Political corruption and the crying need for electoral reforms have been the key issues on the national agenda for nearly a decade now. The countrywide lionization of T.N. Seshan, who as Chief Election Commissioner tried to curb electoral malpractices, demonstrates how much urgency even the ordinary citizens attach to this subject. It is one of the most hotly debated issues in our public life. It speaks of the serious marginalization of women lobbyists for the Women's Reservation Bill that none of them is actively involved with struggle over this issue. No meaningful suggestions for changes have come from them in the ongoing public debate on electoral reforms.

Their campaign for nothing more than cornering a quota for women at a time when our polity is facing grave threats from criminalization of politics and misgovernance is proof of tragic short-sightedness. It is like a daughter clamouring for her name to be included as an equal inheritor with her brothers in the parental home and property at a time when the whole house is on fire or seized by dacoits. A daughter who can lead the firefighting operation or successfully combat dacoits is more likely to be a serious candidate for her share. Even if she is short-changed, she will have more legitimacy and strength to fight it out with her brothers out to disinherit her. Can one ever imagine an Aung San Suu Kyi needing to fight from a reserved seat for women? The subcontinent needs many of the Aung San Suu Kyi variety of women who would dare to be leaders of men as well, rather than stay confined to the women's ghetto.

The *zenana dabba* (ladies compartment) mentality cannot take women too far. The ghettoizing of women's concerns to narrowly defined issues will keep them forever marginalized and fighting among each other in the typical *saas–bahu* (mother-in-law–daughter-in-law) style. Most important of all, why should the task of thinking through meaningful, overall electoral reforms be left to men while women confine their attention only to securing a share of the pie without examining whether the pie is worth eating at all? Are we then not accepting that the rules of the game will inevitably be set by men? Women would only appear as bit players— that too in the 'reserved' category.

Those who argue that a large presence of women will cleanse politics need to be made aware that women, unfortunately, have not been bestowed with any divine powers or magic wands whereby their very presence would improve things. In our subcontinent, at least, we have seen women outdoing men in corruption, crime and authoritarian politics as the career graphs of Benazir Bhutto, Indira Gandhi and the many Jayalalitha clones show. Even in the police, bureaucracy and professions, women have taken to corruption with ease and gusto.

Before women made a substantial entry into public life, many people naively believed that women's entry into public life would help cleanse it because it was believed women were intrinsically more honest and compassionate than men. Unfortunately, we have been cured of such naive and romantic notions by looking at their actual conduct in positions of power.

Women appear more moral only when they are under special familial and social constraints, which deny them wider opportunity for corruption. But when they are acting in unison and are partners in corruption with men of their family, they are not affected by social opprobrium of the kind that women indulging in immoral practices on their own initiative experience.

Most important of all, if winning an election to Parliament or state legislatures involves spending a few crore rupees, it is inevitable that such persons will try to get returns on their investment through dubious means since as legislators they are denied legitimate ways of making money. Women have succeeded in playing a creative role in politics only in those societies where political parties already function more or less according to established norms and traditions, where there is a substantial measure of accountability in public life. But where the overall politics is criminalized, women tend to join the men in corruption and crime with ease rather than attempt to establish new norms, as shown by the examples of Benazir Bhutto, Imelda Marcos and our own breed of women politicians like Mayawati.

Quotas within Quotas

The whole reservation debate has acquired many absurd and comic dimensions. The groups that are resisting it the most—male leaders of certain Backward Castes—are the ones most likely to benefit from women's reservations in comparison with most other groups and parties. They began by first trashing the very idea of women's reservation on the ground that it would strengthen upper caste hold over politics alleging that only the upper caste, upper class women would benefit from the quota because of the social and educational advantages they have acquired. Since their opposition was expressed in rather crude and derogatory terms (*Yeh par kati mahilaon ko hum dekh lenge*–We will deal with these short-haired women–sort of rhetoric), it led to widespread condemnation of the Other Backward Caste (OBC) leaders for what was rightly seen as their uncouth behaviour and nasty male chauvinism. They retreated for a while but regrouped with a fresh offensive demanding a quota within a quota for OBC women as their strategy. They were soon joined by a section of Muslim male leaders demanding a similar quota for Muslim women as well. Even the Scheduled Caste (SC) leaders are demanding their share of quota for their SC women members, unmindful of the fact that the provision for the latter already exists in the proposed Bill. Or perhaps it is a strategy to corner extra seats for SCs from the women's quota rather than yield seats for women of their communities from the existing SC quota.

In characteristic style, the pro-reservation lobby has reacted with pious outrage declaring: 'Please do not try dividing us. Women are all one; their interests are common.'

By polarizing the issue on gender lines, the pro-reservationists have actually exposed the weakness in their own ranks. They claim to speak on behalf of all of India's women. Yet OBC and Muslim women prefer to go along with their men's politics, no matter how chauvinistic, no matter how dishonest, than with the feminist lobby. When the Bill suffered a humiliating defeat in Parliament amidst very ugly scenes by OBC and Muslim MPs, none of the OBC or Muslim women leaders stood up to defend the Bill or claim solidarity with the pro-women's reservation lobby.

In fact, the male OBC and Muslim leaders were successful in getting a few known women of their respective parties and communities to endorse their stand. For a while it looked like only the supposed 'puppet' women politicians had come out with that divisive stand at the behest of their male colleagues. However, within a very short period, even within the feminist NGOs, strong voices have arisen from among Muslim and OBC women echoing the stance of OBC male leaders that there be a caste and community-based quota within the women's quota. Otherwise they will oppose the Bill. Still more interesting, certain important voices within the Muslim community are arguing that the Muslim women's quota be further reserved for the lower castes among Muslims.

They have a fairly legitimate argument as far as the logic of reservations go. They claim that caste is as deep-rooted and entrenched among the subcontinent's Muslims as among the Hindus. They allege that so far Muslim politics has been dominated by upper castes among Muslims who tend to jeopardize the safety of the poorer sections by taking very obscurantist positions on various issues, thus pitching the scales of confrontation with the right-wing Hindu community leaders. The lower castes among Muslims accuse their upper caste leaders of promoting fundamentalist politics which has kept the Muslim community trapped in backwardness and illiteracy. Therefore, they demand that the benefit of Muslim women's quota should go to the lower caste Muslim women so that the most oppressed among them are heard and represented.

This demand for reservations within reservations demonstrates how the very logic of reservations can be stretched endlessly, especially given a situation of high fragmentation within our society, existence of gross inequalities within every group and the general dysfunctionality of democratic institutions so that virtually every group feels aggrieved.

But most important of all, the manner in which this issue has divided women's organizations and whatever goes by the name of a women's movement in India shows that on most issues women's loyalty to their caste and community is far stronger than their commitment to gender-based solidarity. Even without being physically present in women's organizations, men easily dominate women's thinking and perceptions on most issues. How else does one explain the fact that the demand for a quota within the women's quota has gone only as far as the limits so far set by men?

If the logic is that the oppressed groups among women should have special provisions, why just talk of the OBC women? Why not the women of those listed as Most Backward Castes (MBCs)? Why not extend the reservations to still more marginalized and oppressed women of those communities whom the British viciously branded as criminal tribes simply because they had a long history of resistance to British rule? Even today they are treated worse than a sub-human species and face the most brutal forms of violence and exploitation. Why not a quota for physically handicapped women, as well as for women who are afflicted by leprosy, for they are treated worse than pariahs? For women beggars? For prostitutes? The list of marginalized groups is indeed endless.

Yet, why are women's organizations debating only the representation of OBC and Muslim women? The answer is simple. Men of these communities have put the issue on the agenda. So far, women's organizations in India echoed the politics of left parties in its broad contours because they claimed to be the progressive voices of society. Now with caste and minority politics of a certain hue having become another fashionable issue, women's organizations are split vertically along those lines.

Even if we were to leave aside the new complex issues emerging out of the reservation debate, is the demand for a quota for the OBC and Muslim women justified? The two actually cannot be clubbed together, for they represent altogether different realities. Let us consider them one by one.

It is noteworthy that those who are raising the issue of a quota for the OBC women are altogether silent on a quota for the OBC men. The reason is simple: because of their numerical strength, OBCs have today come to dominate most state legislatures as also our Parliament. For example, from Tamil Nadu, only two upper caste MPs could get elected. All others are from OBC, SC or Scheduled Tribes (ST). It is a similar case in the Tamil Nadu state legislature. If there was to be a population-based quota, the OBC would not qualify for a quota at all because the heterogeneous castes that get clubbed under the OBC nomenclature constitute 52 per cent of our population. Thus they cannot claim to be a political minority even while, as a socially and educationally deprived group, they do qualify for a job quota in the government. No wonder they do not raise the issue of OBC quota for men!

Granted that OBC women are among the most deprived women in India. However, they are being held back by the men of their communities rather than by caste prejudice. The OBC women's primary battle lies within their own families and communities. In fact, they would have a definite advantage over upper caste women in an electoral battle because of the numerical strength of their community. It is altogether unlikely that upper caste women would be able to win from OBC-dominated constituencies. Therefore, there really is no merit to their demand for a separate quota for the OBC women.

The Muslim quota case is the very opposite. The proportion of Muslims in our Parliament and state legislatures does not match their numerical strength in the population. But then the whole idea of communal electorates was rejected by the Indian leadership because that demand had culminated in the partition of the subcontinent. In any case, can we consider a quota for Muslim women without conceding a quota for Muslim men? It is obvious that Muslim male leaders are bringing in the issue of religion-based quotas through the backdoor using their women as a sword rather than fighting their battle on their own strength.

The idea of a women's quota is based on a secular principle that historically women have had specific disabilities imposed on them as a group, no matter which caste or community they belong to. To inject the idea of caste and communal quotas into a women's quota is essentially to delegitimize the idea that women as a group have common interests. Thus, the very demand for a women's quota becomes infructuous.

As discussed earlier, the quota system will inevitably unleash unending demands for further reservations within the quota. After all there are at present only 544 seats in Parliament in a country of one billion people situated in thousands of communities. The faults of our representative institutions cannot really be corrected through the quota mechanism. Other, more radical, remedies are required involving far-reaching electoral reforms.

17

Indian Politics

*Encourages Durgas, Snubs Women**

It is a truism that India is a land of mind-boggling diversity. Yet stereotypes about India which reduce the Indian reality to a unidimensional monolith hold powerful sway.

One such powerful stereotype is that Indian women are brutally oppressed, denied a voice in their family and community, and marginalized in politics as in other power structures. Without doubt, there is much truth in this stereotype. But how, then, do we explain the current political scene? A few women are holding the entire political establishment of India to ransom. How else does one describe the machinations of Sonia Gandhi, Jayalalitha, Mayawati and Mamata Banerjee that have caused enormous upheavals in our polity and brought about the fall of the BJP government? Powerful politicians dance to the erratic tunes of these women and are ignominiously subservient to them.

Many will try to explain Sonia's clout within the Congress party by ascribing all of it to her dynastic advantage. It certainly explains a lot. Similarly,

---

*This article appeared in *Manushi*, No. 111, March–April 1999.

many will attribute Jayalalitha's rise to power to her relationship with M.G. Ramachandran (MGR) and Mayawati's clout to her being patronized and groomed by Bahujan Samaj Party (BSP) founder Kanshi Ram.

The Furious Mamata

But Mamata Banerjee did not have the same advantages. She comes from a very ordinary, lower middle class family and has built her political career on her own strength. She challenged powerful Congressmen in West Bengal and emerged as an independent power from that battle. For years she had been sidelined and humiliated by fellow Congressmen who felt threatened by her mass appeal and aggressive populist politics. At the same time, the Communist Party of India (Marxist) (CPI-M) did their best to browbeat her because she emerged as their main opponent in their power base in West Bengal. They have met her persistent attempts to organize an anti-CPI-M front with brutal attacks. On numerous occasions, she was beaten up by the police. A couple of times she even received near fatal injuries, but she refused to be frightened or retreat.

When her own party tried thwarting her efforts, she quit the Congress-I and founded her own Trinamool Congress. She is the first woman to successfully found and lead her own party. It has emerged as the main opposition in West Bengal, shoving aside Congress-I stalwarts, many of whom now actively woo her to let them fight elections on her party ticket. Even those who disapprove of her politics are in awe of her raw physical courage and organizational skills. In recent years, she has emerged as a major player on the national scene as well. Even before the fall of the BJP government, if Mamata sneezed, Vajpayee got a cold. This, despite the fact that her gender, her class, her sensational political style and her hysterical temperament all went against her being taken seriously in the money, muscle power and male-dominated world of Indian politics.

The Vindictive Amma

By conventional wisdom, Jayalalitha had even more disadvantages in acquiring a powerful position in the political world. She was the daughter of a character actress and comes from a fairly modest family, which was so hard up for money that she was withdrawn from school at an early age by her mother and pushed into acting in films. From a very young age she provided substantial financial support to her family. She eventually became the mistress of MGR, a more prominent fellow film star who later founded a political party and subsequently became the chief minister of Tamil Nadu. He found her a convenient prop but maltreated and exploited her for years. She was reportedly spied upon and allegedly even beaten up by him.

After his death, the male leaders of the party tried to sideline her because they resented the clout she had acquired on account of her intimacy with MGR. They even tried to use MGR's wife Janaki to obstruct Jayalalitha from taking over the All India Anna Dravida Munnetra Kazhagam (AIADMK) after MGR's death. Janaki was put up as a candidate against Jayalalitha. Her party backers expected MGR's wife to have an advantage over his mistress in inheriting his political empire.

Instead, Janaki suffered a humiliating defeat at the hands of Jayalalitha, who since then has established herself as the reigning queen of the AIADMK. She commands even more fear and exacts even more grovelling obedience from her party members than did Indira Gandhi from hers. There are many temples in the state where she is ensconced as the presiding deity. She is deified by her followers as Mother Mary, Shakti and even Bharat Mata.

It is customary for her party colleagues to routinely touch her feet and do *sashtang namaskar* as a mark of obeisance. At the same time, her penchant for corruption is legendary and her vindictiveness frightening. Her greed for money and tendency for gross display of wealth would put Imelda Marcos to shame. The numerous court cases filed against her by the rival Karunanidhi government are merely the proverbial tip of the iceberg of corruption that characterized her tenure as chief minister. During her reign as chief minister, there were numerous physical, even murderous attacks on those who dared stand up to her. The victims included journalists and lawyers. A bureaucrat, Chandralekha, had acid thrown on her face at allegedly Amma's behest. Even when out of power, she has been involved in physical attacks on those she imagines have wronged her, including her own auditor, whom she beat up with her sandals, assisted by her female companion Sasikala. The remarkable fact is that she gets away with all such outrageous acts. Rather than being demonized for such vicious behaviour, she has added to her aura of being Shakti incarnate. The prime object of her fury is M. Karunanidhi, the present chief minister of Tamil Nadu. She brought down the BJP government primarily because they did not oblige her by dismissing Karunanidhi's government at her bidding.

The Fearsome Mayawati

Mayawati comes from a poor Dalit (chamar) family and though she possesses a law degree, she seems to have none of the feminine qualities expected of 'respectable women'. With Kanshi Ram as her mentor, she helped him build the BSP. Within a relatively short period, she emerged as the public voice of the party that claims to speak for the Dalit (Scheduled Caste [SC]) community in India. She is reputed to be abusive, unscrupulous and extremely ambitious. She is known to have treated all the state bureaucrats with utter disdain when she was the chief minister of Uttar Pradesh. They virtually trembled before her and took all manner of humiliation. She filled all key posts with officers willing to assist her in looting the public and the exchequer and blindly follow her whimsical orders.

But her arrogance and disdain are not reserved for the upper castes and upper classes only. Her own party men and SC members get even worse treatment at her hands. For example, in BSP meetings, she and Kanshi Ram insist that everyone sit on the floor—including their party MLAs—while these two deities alone sit on chairs.

The arrogance and disdain she displays toward fellow Dalits surpasses that of most upper caste people. Even in giving party tickets, Mayawati and her mentor Kanshi Ram have often shown a marked preference for selecting upper caste candidates to fight elections on their party tickets because upper caste candidates remain totally dependent on them for mopping up Dalit votes. They have systematically marginalized any of their own Dalit cadres who show the slightest sign of developing an independent political base or agenda. In addition, Mayawati outshines any man in her talent for robbery and extortion and has amassed enough wealth to last her for seven generations.

Mania for Sonia

Even Jawaharlal Nehru as the prime minister of India and leader of the Congress party had any number of critics and opponents. But hardly anyone in the Congress of today, created by Sonia Gandhi's mother-in-law, dare criticize or oppose Sonia openly. Without doubt, there are some disgruntled leaders like Sharad Pawar in the Congress. But their unhappiness is mainly due to her sidelining them from her *durbar* and choosing others to be part of her coterie. If she loses out to a mere man like Sharad Pawar, it will be the end of her political career. However, if she can outmanoeuvre him, she will be far more fearsome than even Indira Gandhi was for the Congress satraps. Even senior Congress leaders shake in fear before Sonia and lack the guts to challenge her claim to be the undisputed leader of the party and inherit the prime ministership. She has been able to manipulate the entire machinery of the historic Congress party into promoting her personal agenda even though until very recently she was a total novice in politics and has no political track record. In addition, she has the handicap of being a 'foreigner', someone who despite living for 30 years in India, cannot effectively communicate in any Indian language. She lives in haughty seclusion and runs the affairs of her party as though from an imperial *durbar* where a select few are allowed *darshan* (granted an audience) or called in for consultation as and when she pleases.

Their Special Clout

How do we account for the extraordinary clout these women, who came to power in such different ways, have acquired within their parties, the awe they inspire among fellow politicians and the enormous hold they have over the popular imagination?

One common characteristic that Jayalalitha, Mamata, Mayawati and, to a much lesser extent, Sonia Gandhi share with each other is that they act as though no one could get away with trying to intimidate them. They have demonstrated extraordinary resilience and cunning in the face of heavy odds.

The mesmeric power these women exercise over our political life provides us with interesting insights into the Indian male psyche. While Indian men have made it fairly difficult for ordinary women to feel comfortable as equal participants in the political domain, they tend to succumb easily to the demands of women who have the shrewdness and determination to grasp some dynastic or other leverage that provides them with the crucial opportunity to demonstrate that they are stronger and more resilient than the entire range of men in our politics, that they are courageous, fearless and hard to browbeat. In many other parts of the world, women who fortuitously find themselves in positions of power and who possess or demonstrate extraordinary strength tend nevertheless to be ridiculed and treated like aberrations. In India, the response is the opposite. Such women find greater acceptance than ordinary women who are looking for mere equality.

This is a variation of our family scene wherein many men find it hard to deal with wives desiring equality. But the very same man has no difficulty in accepting his mother as an authority figure before whom he must show unconditional deference and respect, or even a wife who begins to assume matriarchal authority. Most women, trapped in dependency, do not often get to be taken seriously. However, when they manoeuvre themselves into a superior position, whether as mothers, elder sisters, grandmothers, aunts or even well established wives, they acquire numerous advantages that accumulate, including certain well-defined rights to order and command. Such a family upbringing for most Indian men, combined with the tradition of goddess worship, provides a good training ground for men to be psychologically subservient to strong women who assume charge of the family and act like matriarchs.

As pointed out very elegantly by A.K. Ramanujan, in India, we have two kinds of goddesses—the benign consort goddesses like Parvati and Lakshmi, whose shrines and status are subordinate to those of their spouses Shiva and Vishnu. People revere but do not fear them. By contrast, there are far more numerous non-consort goddesses who are far more powerful. Every village worships its own.

> Their myths tell us of ordinary human women who are cheated into marrying untouchables or raped by a local villain or killed or buried by cruel brothers. Out of such desecrations they rise in fury, grow in stature to become figures that span heaven and earth, with powers of destruction that terrify the village into submission, sacrifice and worship. Theirs are not myths of descent or *avatara*, but of ascent from the human into divine forms.
>
> These non-consort goddesses 'represent the other side of the mother' who 'punish, afflict people with plague and pox, and when propitiated heal the afflicted. They are deities of crisis; they preside over famine, plague, death and madness' (see *Manushi*, No. 69, p. 10, 'Who Needs Folklore?').

As with all the ferocious goddesses of Indian mythology and village lore, Jayalalitha justifies her authoritarian ways and her vindictive politics as the legitimate response of a woman long wronged and exploited by men, till she rose in fury and decided to give tit for tat, and gave ten kicks for every one she received. Mamata has built her political career more in the tradition of an avenging deity than a politician. She presents herself as a victim of the CPI-M's dictatorship who will not rest until she has destroyed their power. Mayawati does not use any personal history of persecution but claims to be avenging the collective, historic insults heaped upon the entire Dalit community.

Acting at Own Behest

It is also not a coincidence that all these four women under discussion are single or widowed. As long as Sonia Gandhi acted the role of a mere wife, nobody in India paid much attention to her, except as a colourful presence by her husband's side. She never became an important icon like Jackie Kennedy or a power centre like Hillary Clinton. But after her husband's death, as soon as she began to quietly and skillfully manipulate the Congress party bosses into kowtowing before her, the entire national media and political establishment became mesmerized by her. She should, properly speaking, have been resented and discouraged from becoming an extra-constitutional authority. Instead, the sight of powerful Congressmen falling at her feet and stammering nervously while bending and bowing before her enhanced her importance. The more imperiously she behaves, the more arbitrary her actions, the more awe she seems to inspire.

Similarly, as long as Jayalalitha was an MGR consort, she was merely tolerated for his sake. She was neither respected nor feared. That is why, after his death, most of her party men were not willing to entertain her claim to be MGR's political inheritor. On the day of his cremation, she was forcibly removed from the carriage carrying his dead body to the cremation ground. However, it was only when she proved her mettle by emerging triumphant in the electoral battle against her opponents who had propped up MGR's wife against her, and successfully outmanoeuvred all those politicians who were desperate to ease her out by building an independent political base, that she acquired the aura of an invincible *amma*. She became a matriarch to be feared rather than a mere woman who could be put down. If her greed for money had not run amok and her lust for power not turned altogether destructive, she would have been even more potent a force. She has millions of devotees and followers in Tamil Nadu. It is not surprising that, surrounded with so many awe-inspired devotees, Jayalalitha grossly miscalculated her clout in the latest political crisis she created all so that she could compel the central government to dismiss the Dravida Munnetra Kazhagam (DMK) government in Tamil Nadu, install her in power and withdraw proceedings in the numerous cases going on against her.

Mamata has chosen to stay unmarried and in her single-minded pursuit of power has not allowed herself the luxury of a significant personal life or relationship. This in a way adds to her aura of invincibility because she is not dependent on any man; she is neither wife nor mistress but a universal *didi* (elder sister) to her followers. But she has had to struggle much harder than any other woman politician because instead of getting the backing of a powerful man, she has had to challenge male power, both within her party and outside.

Mayawati has also remained unmarried. Even though she is believed to have an intimate relationship with Kanshi Ram, within a short time she has projected herself as someone playing her own power games rather than acting as a mere rubber stamp or puppet in Kanshi Ram's hands.

Gender Advantage

To sum up: in India, women who prove themselves stronger and more commanding than men are able to use their gender to their advantage rather than it becoming a liability for them. The mesmerising hold Indira Gandhi acquired over the Indian imagination is largely due to her ability to frighten and manipulate male politicians and make them act as her minions. Indian men do not seem to feel embarrassed or resentful falling at the feet of such women but they can be both clumsy and aggressive with most women who clamour for equality or appear vulnerable and dependent.

This applies in all fields, including power relations in the family, politics and public life and in spiritual and religious sects. The popularity and power of sundry mother figures like Ma Anandmayi and Ma Nirmala Devi, who command huge followings among men, demonstrates the wide sway of this phenomenon. In politics, women who have the added advantage of a dynastic connection or patronage of a powerful male figure have a better chance to reach the citadels of power and can get there much faster than those who struggle it out on their own. But thereafter, only if they establish themselves as independent and autonomous do they come to wield real power and get to evoke fear and reverence. Those like Rajmata Scindia who remain dependent on men or are seen as acting at men's behest do not get to be taken very seriously. Even Indira Gandhi lost some of her sheen when people came to believe that her son Sanjay Gandhi had come to wield too much influence on her.

Lust for Power

However, for all the adulation, awe and reverence these four women have received, we cannot afford to overlook the fact that all of them have shown they are not serious about any agenda except lust for power. Two of them—Mayawati and Jayalalitha—have far outshone most men in corruption, nepotism and sheer, greed. These two queens of corruption cannot even be embarrassed in the way someone like Rajiv Gandhi was, who sometimes felt defensive about the Bofors bribes. They have been ruthless in putting down opponents, attacking journalists who fail to show them proper deference and punishing officials who fail to assist them in their ruthless strivings for loot and power. They have systematically practised the politics of blackmail on any vulnerable opponent.

Sonia Gandhi has undoubtedly behaved with relatively greater restraint and sophistication in her style of combat. But she too has indulged in a good deal of covert blackmail to protect herself from charges of corruption associated with her or her friends and relatives. Of these four, Mamata is the only one relatively free of major charges of personal corruption. However, none of them are genuinely associated with any positive programme or vision for improving the awful state of affairs in the country. Even Mamata, for all her fiery self-righteousness, has no programme, no principled agenda, except for a pathological hatred of the CPI-M and the desire to see Jyoti Basu out of office.

Similarly Mayawati, for all her pro-Dalit expressions of resentment and militancy in browbeating her upper caste opponents into yielding more concessions to her, has shown very little sensitivity to the real needs of the Dalits.

Equally important, none of these women have attempted to bring women's concerns into mainstream politics. Nor have they tried mobilizing women into a political force, which can then pressure our political system to be more sensitive to women's agenda. Their career graphs are good proof that when a polity turns as corrupt as ours, when anti-social criminal elements have come to dominate politics, the women who survive in politics are invariably those who can match or outdo men in cunning, corruption or crime. Therefore, they neither serve the cause of women as a disempowered group nor help society become more sensitive and responsive to ordinary women's needs and aspirations.

18

Enhancing Women's Representation in Legislatures

*An Alternative to the Government Bill for Women's Reservation**

Forum for Democratic Reforms

The ugly scenes and stalemate over tabling the Women's Reservation Bill in Parliament have had a very beneficial effect. They have finally brought the grim truth into sharper focus that politics has proven to be very inhospitable for women in independent India. What we are witnessing today is a worrisome

---

*This article, co-authored by Madhu Purnima Kishwar (CSDS, Delhi), Jayaprakash Narayan (Lok Satta, Hyderabad), Dhirubhai Sheth (Lokayan, Delhi) and Yogendra Yadav (CSDS, Delhi), appeared in *Manushi*, No. 116, January–February 2000.

phenomenon of further decline in the participation of women not only in our legislatures but in many other of our political and public spaces.

Most countries in the world have failed to give due space and representation to women in political life. Women are moving in the direction of near equal participation in only a handful of countries such as Germany, Sweden, Norway, Denmark and Finland. In these societies, women have begun to seriously alter the very nature of politics, making enduring and substantial gains in every field. However, in all other countries, including the supposedly advanced democracies of western Europe and north America, where women exercise certain freedoms and have acquired the wherewithal for economic independence, female presence in legislatures remains small and relatively insignificant.

In India the problem for women is more serious for several reasons. While in many other countries women are inching forward bit by bit, in India, the participation of women in politics has actually declined since the days of the freedom movement, both in quantity and quality. Government and politics are more important factors in the economic, social and power structures in India than in most other countries with stronger civil societies, and so, the effect of women's marginalization in politics is even more detrimental here.

The increasing violence, sexual harassment and victimization of women at the ground level in many of our political parties have made their participation extremely hazardous now.

There were many more outstanding women leaders and workers in the Congress Party at all levels during the freedom movement than are at present in all parties put together. In states like Maharashtra and Gujarat, virtually every neighbourhood and most villages could boast of at least one effective woman leader, even into the 1950s. But as politics became more centralized as well as criminalized, thus undermining all other institutions of civil society, women were pushed out of leadership positions to function on the margins, at best relegated to the domain of social work at the local level. Even that tradition eroded from the 1970s onward.

The setback to women's participation is even more severe at the state level than in Lok Sabha (see Tables 18.1 and 18.2). This is clearly evident in Bihar, which had 14 women elected to the Vidhan Sabha in 1952, 31 women in 1957 and 26 women in 1962. But in the 1967 elections, women won only 11 seats. Their number declined to four in 1969. Thereafter, it reached a plateau, levelling at a mere 13 during the last state assembly elections.

The representation of women in the Lok Sabha has basically remained stagnant. It reached a 'high' of 8 per cent in 1984. This figure has not been improved on since. Thereafter, it has showed some decline rather than register an increase. This, despite the fact that every major national party in recent years has declared through manifestos that they would implement 33 per cent reservation for women in all legislatures.

One of the most puzzling features of this depressed level of women's political representation in our legislative bodies is that it seems to have no direct correlation with literacy and other seemingly related indicators. A comparison between the states of Kerala and Rajasthan, whose literacy rates are at opposite ends of the spectrum, demonstrates this clearly. In Kerala, the overall literacy rate is reportedly 90 per cent, with 86 per cent female literacy. By contrast, in Rajasthan, female literacy is a mere 20 per cent and only 12 per cent of females are literate in rural areas. Kerala has a matrilineal tradition in which women have a much larger measure of autonomy and freedom of movement. Kerala's women also tend to marry at a much later age compared to women in other states. Most women in Rajasthan live far more restricted lives in aggressively patriarchal communities that still practise *purdah* and perform child marriages. But the cultural and educational advantage that women in Kerala have, does not translate into higher political participation as compared to Rajasthan. The percentage of women in the legislative assemblies of both states is low. In Kerala, this figure rose from less than 1 per cent in 1967 to 6 per cent in 1991. However, in Rajasthan, the representation of women was 4 per cent in 1967 and reached 8 per cent in 1985–90, slightly more than in Kerala, but not significantly greater. Since then it has been going down.

Table 18.1: Women's Representation in Parliament 1952–98

	Lok Sabha			*Rajya Sabha*		
Year	*Seats*	*Women MPs*	*% of Women MPs*	*Seats*	*Women MPs*	*% of Women MPs*
1952	499	22	4.41	219	16	07.31
1957	500	27	5.40	237	18	07.59
1962	503	34	6.76	238	18	07.56
1967	523	31	5.93	240	20	08.33
1971	521	22	4.22	243	17	07.00
1977	544	19	3.49	244	25	10.25
1980	544	28	5.15	244	24	09.84
1984	544	44	8.09	244	28	11.48
1989	517	27	5.22	245	24	09.80
1991	544	39	7.17	245	38	15.51
1996	543	39	7.18	223	19	08.52
1998	543	43	7.92	245	15	06.12
Average	**527**	**31**	**5.91**	**239**	**22**	**09.11**

Source: CSDS Data Unit.

Table 18.2: Declining Representation of Women in State Legislatures 1952–97 (% of Women MLAs)

State	*1952*	*1957*	*1960–65*	*1967–69*	*1970–75*	*1977–78*	*1979–83*	*1984–88*	*1989–92*	*1993–97*	*1998–99*	*State Avg.*
Andhra Pradesh	2.9	3.7	3.3	3.8	9.1	3.4	4.1	3.4	3.7	2.7	9.5	4.6
Arunachal Pradesh	****	****	****	****	****	0.0	3.3	6.7	3.3	3.3	1.7	3.0
Assam	0.5	4.6	3.8	4.0	7.0	0.8	0.8	4.0	4.0	4.8	****	3.2
Bihar	3.6	9.4	7.9	2.2	3.8	4.0	3.7	4.6	2.8	3.4	****	4.3
Goa	****	****	****	6.7	3.3	3.3	0.0	0.0	5.0	10.0	5.0	4.4
Gujarat	****	****	8.4	4.8	3.2	****	2.7	8.8	2.2	1.1	2.2	4.0
Haryana	****	****	****	7.4*	6.2	4.4	7.8	5.6	6.7	4.4	****	6.2
Himachal Pradesh	0.0	****	****	0.0	5.9	1.5	4.4	4.4	5.9	4.4	8.8	4.2
Jammu & Kashmir	****	****	0.0	0.0	5.3	1.3	0.0	1.3	****	2.3	****	1.5
Karnataka	2.0	8.7	8.7	3.2	5.1	4.0	0.9	3.6	4.5	3.1	2.3	4.3
Kerala	0.0	4.8	3.9	0.8	1.5	0.7	3.2	5.7	5.7	9.3	****	3.6
Madhya Pradesh	2.1	10.8	4.9	3.4	5.4	3.1	5.6	9.7	3.4	3.8	8.1	5.4
Maharashtra	1.9	6.3	4.9	3.3	9.3	2.8	6.6	5.6	2.1	3.8	4.2	4.6
Manipur	****	****	****	****	0.0*	****	0.0	0.0	1.7	0.0	****	0.3
Meghalaya	****	****	****	****	1.7	1.7	0.0	3.3	****	1.7	5.0	2.2
Mizoram	****	****	****	****	0.0	3.3	3.3	2.5	0.0	0.0	0.0	1.2
Nagaland	****	****	****	0.0	****	****	0.0	1.7	****	0.0	****	0.5

Orissa	9.6	3.6	1.4	3.6	1.4*	4.8	3.4	6.1	4.8	5.4	****	4.0
Punjab	2.2	5.8	5.2	1.0*	5.8	2.6	5.1	3.4	5.1	6.0	****	4.0
Rajasthan	0.0	5.1	4.5	3.3	7.1	4.0	5.0	8.0	5.5	4.5	7.0	5.0
Sikkim	****	****	****	****	****	****	0.0	0.0	6.3	3.1	3.1	2.5
Tamil Nadu	0.3	5.9	3.9	1.7	2.1	0.9	2.1	3.4	9.0	3.8	****	3.6
Tripura	****	****	****	0.0	3.3	1.7	6.7	3.3	****	1.7	****	3.0
Uttar Pradesh	1.2	5.8	4.4	2.8*	5.9	2.6	5.6	7.3	3.3*	4.0*	****	4.1
West Bengal	0.8	3.6	4.8	2.9*	1.6*	1.4	2.4	4.4	7.1	6.8	****	3.4
Delhi	4.2	****	****	****	7.1	7.1	7.1	****	****	4.3	12.9	7.3
Pondicherry	****	****	6.7	3.3	0.0	0.0	3.3	3.3	1.7	3.3	****	2.6
Period Average	**1.8**	**6.3**	**4.9**	**2.9**	**4.4**	**2.8**	**3.8**	**5.3**	**4.5**	**4.0**	**6.0**	**4.1**

Source: *CSDS Data Unit.*

Notes: Table entry stands for % of women MLAs elected to state legislature in the relevant elections

**** States did not exist/no elections held in that year/period.

* Two elections held during this period. The figures given here is an average of the two.

The figure given here are based on name recognition and hence liable to under-reporting of women representatives.

Similarly, the state of Manipur, which has a tradition of women playing a dominant role in both the family and the community (again due to a matrilineal heritage), never produced a single woman legislator till 1990—when it elected its first. Nagaland and other north-eastern states which have less repressive cultures for women have similarly low levels of women's representation. By contrast, take the proportion of women in politics in Uttar Pradesh, Bihar, and Madhya Pradesh. Though these states are known for their low education levels and repressive cultural norms for women, they have not only sent a relatively larger proportion of women to the Lok Sabha than those from the north-east, but have also elected relatively more female MLAs.

In independent India, pervasive gender discrimination has resulted in sidelining even veteran women politicians. It is difficult for women to establish a foothold without patronage from powerful men in the party—that too through close personal relations, as wives, daughters and sisters. This is indeed a matter for serious concern because the level of political participation among women in any society acts as a reliable barometer of the health of its democracy.

It is significant that stagnation and/or decline in women's political participation rates run contrary to trends in many other fields.

Women in India have made major inroads in various male-dominated professions, including the governmental bureaucracy. In the fields of business, medicine, engineering, law, art and culture, women who were given opportunities to acquire the necessary skills and education have proven themselves capable of holding their own, without availing of any special measures to facilitate their entry. But they have failed to gain ground in the field of politics. Moreover, the agenda of women's empowerment seems to have lost the kind of moral and political legitimacy it enjoyed during the freedom movement, as was evident from the ugly scenes in the aftermath of tabling the Women's Reservation Bill in Parliament. Such a response would have been inconceivable in the India of the 1920s to the 1940s.

All these trends indicate that women's representation in politics requires special consideration, and cannot be left to the forces that presently dominate our parties and government. Today, even the best of our female parliamentarians feel sidelined and powerless within their respective parties. The few women in leadership positions have not been able to encourage the entry of greater numbers of women in electoral and party politics, and are an ineffective minority within their own respective political groupings.

The very same male party leaders who compete with each other in announcing their support of special reservations for women have shown little willingness to include women in party decision-making, or even to help create a conducive atmosphere for women's participation in their own organizations. In fact, women's marginalization is even more pronounced in the day-to-day functioning of almost all political parties than in the Lok Sabha. Therefore, it is urgently required that we take special measures to enhance women's political participation in ways that help them influence decision making at all levels of our society and polity. Our democracy will remain seriously flawed if it fails to yield adequate space to women.

Given this worrisome scenario, the national debate and efforts to provide constitutional and legal mechanisms to enhance women's participation in legislatures are welcome and long overdue.

Problems with the Present Bill

The 85th constitutional Amendment Bill, introduced in Lok Sabha in December 1999, includes the following key provisions:

- One-third of all seats in Lok Sabha and Vidhan Sabhas shall be reserved for women. Such reservation shall also apply in case of seats reserved for Scheduled Castes (SCs) and Scheduled Tribes (STs).
- There shall be rotation of seats so reserved for women.
- Such rotation shall be determined by draw of lots, in such a manner that a seat shall be reserved only once in a block of three general elections.

This Bill is seriously flawed, insofar as it mechanically provides for entry of women members to fill one-third of vacancies in Lok Sabha and the Vidhan Sabhas. Such mechanical reservation and rotation suffers from serious defects:

1. One-third seats are reserved, and such reserved seats are rotated in every general election. This rotation will automatically result in two-thirds of incumbent members being forcibly unseated in every general election; the remaining one-third will be left in limbo until the last moment, not knowing whether or not their constituency will form part of the one-third randomly reserved seats and thus require them to scramble at short notice to find another seat to contest.
2. There is already resentment about reserved seats for SCs and STs being frozen in the same constituencies over a long period of time. Inevitably, there will be vociferous and justified demands for rotation of seats reserved for SCs and in some cases STs, where their population may not be very large. This will trigger off further instability in our polity.
3. The population of SCs and STs is now estimated to be around 16 per cent and 8 per cent respectively, on an all India basis. In certain states,

their combined population is much higher, reaching 35 per cent or more. In the event of rotation of all reserved seats (women plus SCs, STs) with one-third seats reserved for women, every single seat will be rotated in every general election. This means that practically every member of a legislature will be unseated in every single general election (see Table 18.3 and Figure 18.1).

4. Such compulsory unseating violates the very basic principles of democratic representation. It jeopardizes the possibility of sensible planning to contest and nurture a political constituency for both male and female candidates.
5. As legislators do not have the incentive to seek re-election from the same constituency, loot and plunder of public money will increase,

Table 18.3: Rotation of Seats

	Now (%)	*From 2001 (%)*
Reservation for SCs	15.0	16.0
Reservation for STs	07.5	08.0
	22.5	24.0
Balance Seats	77.5	76.0
Reservation for Women 33.30%	26.0	25.4
Open for Men	51.5	50.6

Figure 18.1

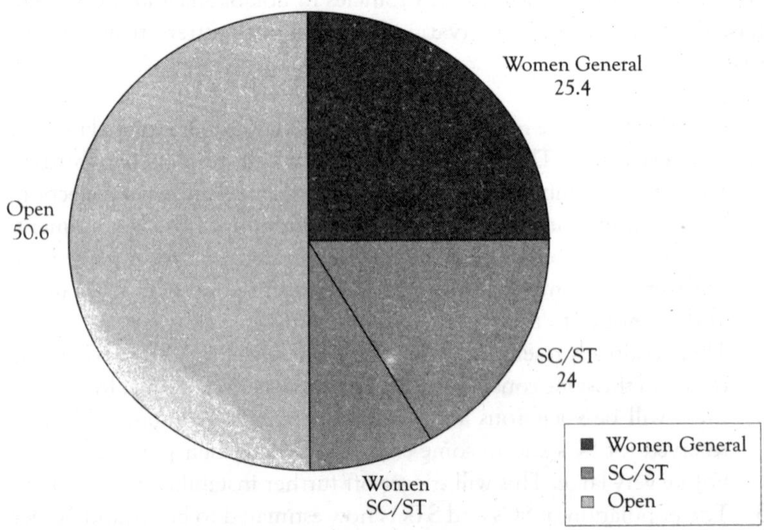

and politics will be even more predatory and unaccountable. This will contribute to a more unstable political process, and make it difficult for women to build their long-term credibility as effective representatives, since they will not be able to contest twice from the same constituency.

6. If seats are reserved exclusively for women in every election through territorial constituencies, voters in such reserved constituencies would have no choice but to elect women only, violating the basic principles of democratic representation.
7. In such a situation, there is likely to be greater resentment against women, undermining the very objective of the Bill. Those men who get pushed out of their constituencies or who see their allies sidelined will either sabotage female contenders in revenge, or spend much of their political capital helping their own female relatives in cornering these reserved seats. Such proxies would be expected to keep the seat 'safe' for the men until the next election, when they would again try to reclaim their seats. Such women would lack legitimacy in the eyes of the voters.
8. Women elected in reserved constituencies will be contesting against other women only and will lack the legitimacy and opportunity needed to prove their ability and acceptability. Leadership acquired in such a manner will be seen as unnatural, artificial and foisted.
9. Women legislators, when elected, will not be able to nurse their constituencies on a long-term basis, and thus will be deprived of a strong political base and will forever be regarded as lightweight politicians. This in effect will make their presence in legislatures ornamental, and will not lead to a more effective participation in politics.
10. This Bill does not address the more fundamental issue of inadequate participation of women in politics and their much greater marginalization within the political parties.
11. The experience of fixed quotas in a few countries where it has been tried, such as Nepal, the Philippines and the erstwhile Soviet Union, has not produced very successful results for women's political participation.
12. While this Bill provides for election of SC and ST women as legislators, it does not adequately address the issue of participation of Backward Castes (BCs) and minorities. As parties have no choice about the seats reserved for women, they will be unable to nominate women candidates from these under-represented sections in constituencies where they stand a reasonable chance of success.
13. Even though there will be no legal bar on women standing from general constituencies, it is highly unlikely that any woman will obtain

party tickets to run for office outside the reserved constituencies. This same pattern is evident with SCs and STs who have been permanently ghettoized to fixed reserved constituencies.
14. This Bill is completely silent about women's representation in Rajya Sabha and Legislative Councils.

Given these serious infirmities, it is necessary to design better models for enhancing women's representation in legislatures. Therefore, we present an alternative model which will address many of the flaws listed thus far.

The Proposed Alternative Women's Reservation Bill

The important provisions of the proposed Alternative Bill are as follows:

1. A law should be enacted amending the Representation of the People Act, 1951, to make it mandatory for every recognized political party to nominate women candidates for election in one-third of the constituencies.
2. Each party can choose where it wishes to nominate women candidates, duly taking local political and social factors into account.
3. Among seats reserved for SCs and STs also, one-third of the candidates nominated by recognized parties shall be women.
4. To prevent a party from nominating women candidates only in states or constituencies where the party's chances of winning election are weak, and to ensure an even spread of women candidates, the unit for consideration (the unit in which at least one out of three party candidates shall be a woman) for the Lok Sabha shall be a state or union territory; for the State Legislative Assembly, the unit shall be a cluster of three contiguous Lok Sabha constituencies.
5. In the event of any recognized party failing to nominate one-third women candidates, for the shortfall of every single woman candidate, two male candidates of the party shall lose the party symbol and affiliation and all the recognition-related advantages.
6. A law amending Articles 80 and 171 of the Constitution should be enacted providing for women's reservation of one-third of the seats, elected or nominated, to Rajya Sabha or Legislative Councils. Corresponding amendments need to be made in the Fourth Schedule of the Constitution and the Representation of the People Act, 1950.

Advantages of this Model

1. Parties will be free to choose their female candidates and constituencies depending on local political and social factors. Parties will nurture women candidates where they can offer a good fight rather than in pre-fixed lottery based constituencies, where they may or may not have viable women candidates. Thus there will be flexibility and promotion of natural leadership.
2. Though seats are not reserved, there will be a large pool of credible and serious women candidates in the fray. This is so because the real contest in elections is only among candidates nominated by recognized parties. Table 18.4 clearly shows that the role of Independents in our elections is marginal and declining. In Lok Sabha elections, as many as 99.7 per cent of Independents are in fact losing their caution deposits.
3. A woman candidate will be contesting against both female and male candidates of rival parties. Therefore, the democratic choice of voters will not be restricted to compulsorily electing only women candidates.
4. As women members will be elected in competition with other candidates–without reserving seats–they will be seen as legitimate representatives in the eyes of the public and not just beneficiaries of charitable measures.
5. A winning woman candidate will have been elected on her own strength, backed by party support. She will not be a mere proxy or political lightweight.
6. There will be no need for rotation of reservation. Therefore, the elected women and men can nurture their constituencies and emerge as major political figures in their own right, with an independent power base.

Table 18.4: Independents Elected to Lok Sabha in Successive General Elections

Year	*No. of Seats Filled*	*No. of Independents Elected*	*Percentage of Independents Who Lost Deposit*
1952	489	38	66.6
1957	494	42	60.1
1962	494	20	79.0
1967	520	35	86.2
1971	518	14	94.0
1977	542	09	97.2
1980	529	09	98.9
1984	542	05	99.7
1989	529	12	98.9
1991	534	01	99.5
1996	542	09	99.7
1998	542	06	-

7. At the same time, in the absence of reserved seats, there will be healthy competition for nomination for a particular seat between male and female politicians.
8. Parties will be able to nominate women from Backward Castes (BCs), minorities and other communities for elective office in areas where there is electoral advantage to them. This obviates the need for a quota within quotas—an issue which has blocked the existing Bill. Those who are concerned about the representation of BCs and Muslims need not settle merely for one-third quota for BC women within the 33 per cent women's quota as they are demanding now. They can field as many BC or minority community women as they think appropriate.
9. This method is mostly likely to find favour with political parties and incumbent legislators, as there will be no fear of being uprooted at short notice by draw of lots. Both compulsory reservation and regular rotation are avoided.
10. Unlike with the lottery system of reserved constituencies, in which women's presence is likely to get ossified at 33 per cent since there would be resistance to letting women contest from non-reserved constituencies, this model allows for far greater flexibility in the number and proportion of women being elected to legislatures. If women are candidates for one-third of all seats contested by each party, theoretically they could even win the vast majority of seats—all on merit.
11. This model also provides for reservation of seats for women in the upper houses.

Given the present state of affairs, it is likely that, to begin with, about one-third of the contested seats will be won by women. But this percentage is likely to grow over time as women gain more confidence and strength. It also ensures that their presence in legislatures reflects more closely their actual electoral strength so that they are not seen as mere recipients of charitable measures.

Plugging Possible Loopholes

A party may be tempted to nominate women from constituencies where it is weak. However, by making the unit of consideration the state or union territory for Lok Sabha, and a cluster of three Lok Sabha constituencies for the Legislative Assembly, this risk is avoided. Parties will be compelled to nominate women in all states and regions. No serious party seeking power can afford to deliberately undermine its own chances of election on such a large scale. It is also mandatory to nominate women in one-third constituencies because otherwise twice the number of male candidates of the party will lose party nomination.

In the absence of actual reservation of seats, there could be fears that women may not be elected in one-third constituencies, as the voters may prefer a male candidate over a female candidate on account of gender bias. However, evidence so far suggests that women candidates of parties have not suffered any gender discrimination at the hands of voters. In fact, very often, the percentage of success of woman candidates is higher than that of male candidates. Table 18.5 shows that the success rate of women candidates in Lok Sabha elections has been uniformly higher than that of their male counterparts in every general elections. It is possible to argue that the few women who contest are more often party candidates, and therefore, their success rate is exaggerated. However, Table 18.6 clearly shows that even among candidates of recognized political parties, the success rate of women candidates is higher than that of men. While 32.53 per cent of women candidates of recognized parties have been elected to Lok Sabha since 1984, the success rate of male candidates is only 26.5 per cent. This trend is seen in all general elections since 1984, except in 1989. Therefore, it is reasonable to assume that women will be elected in large numbers, and that, in fact, their presence in Lok Sabha will exceed one-third in many cases. In any case, past evidence suggests that in at least a quarter of the constituencies, women are likely to get elected if recognized parties nominate them in at least one-third constituencies.

It is noteworthy that women's participation has increased dramatically, to near equal or even higher than equal participation, only in countries like Sweden, Denmark, Finland, Germany and the Netherlands, which have implemented party-based quotas of the kind we are proposing.

Other Necessary Measures for Enhancing Women's Participation

While it is necessary to institute a system of reservation for women as spelt out earlier, this or any other system of ensuring women's presence in legislatures is not by itself sufficient if our objective is to make women equal partners in democratic politics. The problem is not just that women in the political arena are denied tickets by political parties. The fundamental problem is that given the nature of electoral politics today, the system itself creates insurmountable obstacles for women. Proposals for reservation for women must therefore be a part of a larger package of general reforms in electoral politics.

Table 18.5: The Gender Advantage

Year	No. of Seats Available	Total No. of Contestants	Male			Female		
			Contested	*Elected*	*% Winning*	*Contested*	*Elected*	*% Winning*
1952	489	1,874	*	*	*	*	*	*
1957	494	1,518	1,473	467	31.7	45	27	60.0
1962	494	1,985	1,915	459	24.0	70	35	50.0
1967	520	2,369	2,302	490	21.3	67	30	44.8
1971	520	2,784	2,698	499	18.5	86	21	24.4
1977	542	2,439	2,369	523	22.1	70	19	27.1
1980	542	4,620	4,478	514	11.5	142	28	19.7
1984	542	5,570	5,406	500	9.2	164	42	25.6
1989	529	6,160	5,962	502	8.5	198	27	13.6
1991	521	8,699	8,374	492	5.9	325	39	12.0
1996	543	13,952	13,353	504	3.8	599	39	6.7
1998	543	4,750	4,476	500	11.2	274	43	15.7
Total			52,806	5,450	10.32	2,040	350	17.16

Source: The Times of India, New Delhi, 14 September 1999.

Notes: Though the number of women elected to Lok Sabha has not been very impressive, their success rate (% of contestants getting elected) has always been higher than the male aspirants.

* Gender-wise data for 1952 not available.

Table 18.6: Performance of Candidates of Recognized Parties in Lok Sabha Elections—Gender-wise

Year	Total Party Candidates Contested	Elected	Percentage	Male			Female		
				Contested	Elected	% Winning	Contested	Elected	% Winning
1984	1,394	510	36.59	1,327	469	35.34	67	41	61.19
1989	1,523	498	32.70	1,437	474	32.99	86	24	27.91
1991	2,319	516	22.25	2,180	479	21.97	139	37	26.62
1996	2,269	530	23.36	2,153	493	22.90	116	37	31.90
1998	1,964	488	24.85	1,831	451	24.63	133	37	27.82
Total	9,469	2,542	26.85	8,928	2,366	26.50	541	176	32.53

Source: Compiled by Lok Satta from Statistical Reports on General Election, Election Commission of India, New Delhi.

The following general measures of electoral reform would go a long way towards making politics less intimidating for women:

1. Measures to check criminalization of politics:
   (*a*) The list of offences where a conviction leads to disqualification from contesting election should be expanded as per the recommendations of the Law Commission.
   (*b*) Disqualification should not be conditional upon final conviction. It should come into operation as soon as the judge has framed charges with reference to offences specified above.
   (*c*) A candidate should be required to make a declaration of all the cases pending against him or her, involving charges of criminal conduct or corruption, at the time of filing nominations. This declaration should be made public. False declaration should be a ground for disqualification.
2. To bring about internal democracy within political parties, all the recognized (national or state) political parties should be required to include in their respective constitutions:
   (*a*) Rules governing the membership of party and a Register of Current Members that is open for inspection by any member or the representatives of the Election Commission of India.
   (*b*) Provisions for a periodic and democratic election of all the office bearers and the highest executive body by the members of the party.
   (*c*) Procedures for selection of party's candidates for elections to legislatures.
   (*d*) Procedures for deciding upon various policy documents including the party's election manifesto.
   (*e*) Internal mechanism for adjudicating any dispute, including those concerning the interpretation of the party constitution.
   (*f*) The Election Commission shall review the party constitutions for their compliance with the aforementioned requirements, and also serve as a court of final appeal against any decision of the internal adjudicating authority in every party. The failure to comply with the Election Commission's instructions or decisions will invite de-recognition of the party.
3. Measures to curb the influence of black money in politics:
   (*a*) Every candidate shall make a declaration of his/her income and property at the time of nomination. False or incomplete declaration shall invite disqualification.

(*b*) All citizens and corporations shall be exempted, up to a certain limit, from paying income tax on donations made to registered political parties.

(*c*) The candidates and political parties shall be required, after the completion of elections, to file a detailed statement of account. Non-disclosure or false declaration should result in disqualification of candidate and de-registration of political parties.

(*d*) While the current ceiling on electoral expenses needs to be revised, certain items of expenditure (direct inducements in cash or kind to the voter, or expenditure to bribe officials or hire hoodlums) shall be considered illegal.

(*e*) Every candidate who secures 2 per cent or more of the valid votes polled in a constituency shall be reimbursed a reasonable sum of, say, Rs 10 for each vote secured.

(*f*) It shall be compulsory for all registered political parties to get a statement of income and expenditure audited annually. The statement shall be a public document.

4. Measures to curb electoral malpractices:

(*a*) The local post office shall be in charge of maintaining and revising electoral rolls on a regular basis. At present, most citizens have no access to electoral rolls, and the procedure for additions, deletions and corrections are ineffective in reality, though the law is eminently sensible. There is evidence to suggest that in urban areas the electoral rolls are flawed up to 40 per cent.

(*b*) It should be mandatory for the Election Commission to provide voter identity cards to every citizen who figures on the electoral rolls. Once this process is completed, the voter identity card or other means of identification should be made compulsory for voting.

(*c*) If the proportion of 'tendered' votes in a polling booth is greater than 1 per cent of the total electorate, a repoll shall be ordered in the booth. A tendered ballot is given to a voter in whose name a false vote was already cast, and who establishes identity. Therefore, a tendered vote is indisputable proof of impersonation and rigging. At present a tendered ballot is kept in a separate cover and is not counted, while the false vote cast is counted! If this repoll provision is incorporated and publicized, people will then avail the facility of tendered vote, and rigging will be self-limiting for fear of a repoll.

19

Lack of Gender Solidarity

*Systematic Degrading of Women Politicians**

Women's organizations and women parliamentarians have spent a great deal of energy during the last decade fighting to secure 33 per cent reservation of seats for women in Parliament and state legislatures. Fighting for a larger presence is no doubt important. It is a happy development that women Members of Parliament (MPs) were able to build an inter-party alliance on this issue. However, it is no less important to ensure that women who succeed in finding a place for themselves in politics are treated with respect and not sidelined, that they do not face discrimination as women in the allocation of ministries and that merit is given due recognition.

It is curious that women's organizations as well as women parliamentarians have rarely come to the defence and support of women politicians when

*This article appeared in *Manushi*, No. 130, 2002.

they are subjected to ridicule and humiliation simply on the basis of the bias against women in politics. The absence of such gender-based solidarity among women politicians is an important reason why party bosses find it easy to snub women and keep them on the fringes of politics. Mutual rivalries between male politicians are no less deadly, but one of the reasons why men outdo women in grabbing power positions is that they know when and how to close ranks, to lobby for each other and form interest groups. Unfortunately, at least in India, women politicians do their best to pull each other down rather than lend support to each other.

Lack of Mutual Support

By and large, women are allotted much less significant portfolios and kept in junior positions and minor ministries because, while each may lobby for herself, they rarely lobby for each other as a group. Therefore, as a group, women remain weak and insignificant. While women's organizations have begun putting pressure on political parties to give tickets to women candidates, they have never campaigned to have women gain positions controlling key portfolios. There are several examples from the recent past where gender-based solidarity was called for but failed to materialize.

Take the case of the Communist Party of India (Marxist)'s Gowri Amma, who is among the most unjustly treated woman politicians. She had emerged as one of the most popular mass leaders of Kerala and was considered a prime candidate for the chief minister's post. Yet, when she was insulted, sidelined and finally thrown out of the party on flimsy grounds, neither women leaders nor women's organizations in Kerala registered anything resembling a protest. Similarly, when Najma Heptullah was bestowed the rare honour of being elected as the chairperson of the International Inter-Parliamentary Union, she was felicitated by politicians of rival parties, but women from her own Congress Party maintained a studied silence as though her election was an embarrassment they had to hide. It is well known that while her achievements are never celebrated by her female colleagues, some of them do work hard to sabotage her chances of holding key positions in the Congress Party. She was expected to be a serious candidate for the post of Vice-President of India at one stage. However, there was no enthusiasm among Congresswomen to strengthen her claim.

For many years, Mamata Banerjee was persecuted by her own party bosses because she has been successful in building a solid mass base for herself on her own strength. I do not remember any women Congress leaders of any stature ever fighting alongside her for her due place in the Congress Party when she was a member. Even when she broke away in frustration and formed the Trinamool Congress, some important male leaders joined in a common cause with her, but not Congresswomen. Jayalalitha received even worse treatment within the AIADMK after the death of her mentor, until she effectively challenged the party leaders electorally. But, even when she was physically attacked and her *saree* torn in the state assembly, women politicians did not think it important to protest against this Draupadi type of humiliation. One does not have to support Jayalalitha's politics to protest against attempts to disrobe her publicly.

The media have consistently derided Uma Bharati as a 'sexy *sanyasin*' and taken much more interest in her real or imagined love affairs than in her politics. Yet, women politicians in the Bharatiya Janata Party (BJP) have never protested against the frivolous coverage she gets in the media and the shoddy treatment she has to endure. In fact, her own party women contribute to a good deal of gossip about her instead of protesting her denigration. Even a consistent opponent of the BJP like Mani Shankar Aiyar says that Bharati is among the most effective parliamentarians. Information on this aspect of her career rarely reaches the public. She is among the few BJP leaders with a mass appeal and plays a key role in BJP's electoral campaigns. Yet, when it comes to portfolio distribution, she is given a very minor portfolio as minister of state for sports. Why have women leaders of the BJP never cared to lobby to get her a more substantial portfolio?[1]

Maneka's Track Record

Yet another example of the sad absence of meaningful solidarity among women politicians is the total silence of women's organizations and women MPs of the National Democratic Alliance (NDA) at the unceremonious sacking of Maneka Gandhi, first as minister for culture and later as minister for animal welfare. Whatever her real or imagined faults, no one can deny that she is one of the few politicians who seriously engages with issues of importance. Even those who differ with her way of defining issues and solving problems cannot deny that she is extremely task-centred, obsessed with making a difference and producing results, in contrast to most other ministers. She is one of those

[1] Worse still, when Uma Bharati quit the BJP in protest against the treatment meted out to her, she neither got any sympathy nor support from any women leaders.

who sticks to her issue-based agenda whether she is in or out of government. Even when she is a minister, she carries on with her campaigns, changing and bending rules or even brazenly breaking them if she finds that they stand in the way of what she thinks is right. Even though she gets a lot of negative press publicity because of her rough manner, it is significant that she has rarely left an issue half-way.

Most of her famed temper tantrums are over the corruption and inefficiency of her staff. She is well informed and zealous to a fault in whatever issues or tasks she takes up. She has never been involved in any corruption scandal when in office, despite being a minister four times. She makes sincere attempts to streamline the functioning of the ministries under her charge as well as to block or reduce major avenues of corruption. She is one of the few women politicians with an independent political base and has often won her elections with record-breaking margins without the support of any party. Not only that, her all-India appeal is such that in most parts of the country, her public meetings during election campaigns draw larger crowds than those of most senior politicians and ministers. She was the first woman in India to form a political party of her own. And yet, she has never been given full cabinet status as a minister.

During Maneka Gandhi's brief stint in the ministry of welfare, she introduced numerous innovative schemes. Within a few weeks, she sorted out the long pending task of creating a detailed listing of Backward Castes and Communities who qualify for welfare measures. During her period in office, more than 50,000 disabled people got artificial limbs, medical care and wheelchairs through special camps; she helped revive the factory for the manufacture of the famous Jaipur foot by giving them a grant to restart the closed factory; started six state-of-the-art disability hospitals—the first in Srinagar, where this service was sorely needed because of frequency of injuries due to violence by terrorists and security forces; drafted a new secular Adoption Act, which includes Muslims among those eligible to adopt children and also provides for foster parenting; gave a major push towards enhancing the number of adoptions in India and created a separate division to streamline the interface of non-governmental organizations (NGOs) with the ministry.

And yet, she was unceremoniously removed from that portfolio and shunted to the Ministry of Culture. And who replaced her? A man who topped the list of the 'ten worst ministers' in an opinion poll conducted by *India Today*. While she was still given only minister of state rank, he was given cabinet minister rank when he took over her former ministry. As though to rub in the insult, during her tenure as minister of social justice, the head of the Scheduled Caste/Tribe Commission was given cabinet rank, even though his office was actually an adjunct of Maneka Gandhi's ministry.

It is noteworthy that Maneka Gandhi did not ask for, nor was she keen to take charge of the Ministry of Culture. It was forced upon her as a demotion. After she agreed to this arrangement, that too was snatched away in a peremptory manner within weeks of her taking charge and she was dumped in the most peripheral office: minister of state for statistics. However, she insisted on and got a new office created for her–Ministry of Animal Welfare. She got it because there were hardly any takers for this job. Maneka managed to use the Ministry of Animal Welfare to stir several powerful establishments, including the medical research labs, just the way she had the entire industrial establishment up in arms when she was minister for environment.

Maneka remains the quintessential activist whether she is in or out of power. Her indefatigable activism has produced an incredibly long list of victories, which have led to enduring changes in the neglected field of animal rights. It is another matter that her headstrong commitment to these causes has won her many enemies and caused her political career serious setbacks.

Her dismissal from the Vajpayee cabinet was clearly in response to pressure from pharmaceutical companies and scientific establishments found guilty of gross malpractice in the name of medical research on animals. Also, now there are many more takers for the new Ministry of Animal Welfare she had created because she has introduced so many new legislations and checks against the abuse of animals that politicians now see it as a lucrative post. They can arm-twist various industries and traders dealing with animals and animal products because there is enough scope for extortion within this innocuous-sounding ministry as well. Therein lies the tragedy of governance in India as well as the inherent limitations of using stringent legislation as an instrument of reform in the absence of an accountable machinery of governance.

Every time Maneka is dropped, downgraded or shunted, the media tends to justify it on grounds of her sharp tongue and rough manners. But the corrupt and criminal among our ministers never get treated so shabbily. Neither has any male politician been given such short shrift, especially if they have an independent political base as well as a good performance record in office.

Need for Solidarity

While Maneka Gandhi herself has consistently refrained from projecting her case as one of gender discrimination, it is amply clear that the snubs administered to her are to a significant extent due to her being a woman. And yet, no woman politician from within the NDA coalition has said a word to protest her repeated ousts. Even more surprising is the fact that women's organizations have failed to register even a nominal protest in her defence.

One does not have to support or endorse the past or present actions of the women concerned in order to protest against the insulting behaviour meted out to them or systematic attempts to deny them the share of power and authority due to them. Reservations for women by themselves will not lead to their empowerment if they stay divided against each other within each party, and if there is no organized constituency of women ready to defend women politicians against gender-based slander and humiliation.

About the Author

Madhu Purnima Kishwar is Senior Fellow at the Centre for the Study of Developing Societies (CSDS), Delhi. The founder of Manushi Sangathan, an organization committed to strengthening democratic rights and women's rights in India, she is also the founder editor of *Manushi–A Journal about Women and Society*. Her research at CSDS, focused on the theme 'Laws, Liberty and Livelihoods,' is aimed at giving a pro-poor direction to economic reforms in India. She is also the Director of the Indic Studies Project and Convenor of International Conferences on Religions and Cultures in the Indic Civilization.

Kishwar has authored several books including *Deepening Democracy: Challenges of Governance and Globalization in India* (2005); *Off the Beaten Track: Rethinking Gender Justice for Indian Women* (1999) and *Religion at the Service of Nationalism* (1998), translated into Hindi as *Rashtriyata ki Chakri Mein Dharm* (2005). Much of her writing is based on her active interventions on various issues.

She has made several documentary films on varied themes including the culture of dowry; the disinheritance of women from family property; anti-liquor movements in India; state policies that have contributed to the improvement of traditional technologists in India; and License-Quota-Raid Raj affecting the livelihood of street vendors and rickshaw pullers.

She can be reached at editor@manushi-india.org.